A Creative Writing Handbook

Developing dramatic technique, individual style and voice

Edited by Emma Claire Sweeney, Heather Richardson, Derek Neale and Siobhán Campbell

BLOOMSBURY ACADEMIC
LONDON · NEW YORK · OXFORD · NEW DELHI · SYDNEY

This publication forms part of the Open University module A363 *Advanced creative writing*. Details of this and other Open University modules can be obtained from Student Recruitment, The Open University, PO Box 197, Milton Keynes MK7 6BJ, United Kingdom (tel. +44 (0)300 303 5303; email: general-enquiries@open.ac.uk).

Alternatively, you may visit the Open University website at www.open.ac.uk where you can learn more about the wide range of modules and packs offered at all levels by The Open University.

The Open University, Walton Hall, Milton Keynes MK7 6AA

First published 2009. Second edition 2025.

Unless otherwise stated, copyright © 2025, The Open University, all rights reserved.

In association with

BLOOMSBURY ACADEMIC

Bloomsbury Publishing Plc, 50 Bedford Square, London, WC1B 3DP, UK

Bloomsbury Publishing Inc, 1385 Broadway, New York, NY 10018, USA

Bloomsbury Publishing Ireland, 29 Earlsfort Terrace, Dublin 2, D02 AY28, Ireland

BLOOMSBURY, BLOOMSBURY ACADEMIC and the Diana logo are trademarks of Bloomsbury Publishing Plc

All rights reserved. No part of this publication may be: i) reproduced, stored in a retrieval system, transmitted or utilised in any form or by any means, electronic, mechanical, photocopying, recording or otherwise, without written permission from the publisher or a licence from The Copyright Licensing Agency Ltd. Details of such licences (for reprographic reproduction) may be obtained from: Copyright Licensing Agency Ltd (https://cla.co.uk); or ii) used or reproduced in any way for the training, development or operation of artificial intelligence (AI) technologies, including generative AI technologies. The rights holders expressly reserve this publication from the text and data mining exception as per Article 4(3) of the Digital Single Market Directive (EU) 2019/790.

Bloomsbury Publishing Plc does not have any control over, or responsibility for, any third-party websites referred to or in this book. All internet addresses given in this book were correct at the time of going to press. The authors and publisher regret any inconvenience caused if addresses have changed or sites have ceased to exist, but can accept no responsibility for any such changes.

Open University materials may also be made available in electronic formats for use by students of the University. All rights, including copyright and related rights and database rights, in electronic materials and their contents are owned by or licensed to The Open University, or otherwise used by The Open University as permitted by applicable law.

In using electronic materials and their contents you agree that your use will be solely for the purposes of following an Open University course of study or otherwise as licensed by The Open University or its assigns.

Except as permitted above you undertake not to copy, store in any medium (including electronic storage or use in a website), distribute, transmit or retransmit, broadcast, modify or show in public such electronic materials in whole or in part without the prior written consent of The Open University or in accordance with the Copyright, Designs and Patents Act 1988.

Edited and designed by The Open University.

Typeset by The Open University.

British Library Cataloguing-in-Publication Data: applied for

Library of Congress Cataloguing-in-Publication Data: applied for

Paperback: ISBN 978 1 3504 9779 5   eBook: ISBN 978 1 3504 9781 8   ePDF: ISBN 978 1 3504 9780 1

2.1

Printed sustainably in the UK by Pureprint, a CarbonNeutral® company with FSC® chain of custody and an ISO 14001 certified environmental management system, diverting 100% of dry waste from landfill.

The Open University has had Woodland Carbon Code Pending Issuance Units assigned from Doddington North forest creation project (IHS ID103/26819) that will, as the trees grow, compensate for the greenhouse gas emissions from the manufacture of the paper in this module.
More information can be found at https://www.woodlandcarboncode.org.uk/

Contents

Contributors		5
Introduction		7
Part 1: Ways of writing		11
1	Playing with genre	13
2	Worlds of fiction	31
3	Life writing: outer worlds	53
4	Writing narrative poems	71
Part 2: Dramatic writing		97
5	Dramatic stories	99
6	Story and image	121
7	Stories in sound	139
8	Dramatic journeys	161
9	Adaptation	181
Part 3: Developing style and structure		199
10	Splicing narrative strands	201
11	Life writing: inner worlds	221
12	Dramatic techniques in poetry	241
13	Persuasive techniques: using analogy and rhetoric	263
14	Voices and voicing	287
15	Time and timing	309
16	The long and short of it	331
17	Thematic connections	351
Part 4: Readings		373
1.1	'A Real Durwan'	375
2.1	Extract from the novel *The Water Dancer*	383
2.2	Extract from the novel *The Power*	384
2.3	Extract from the novel *Neverwhere*	384
2.4	Extract from the memoir *Russian Journal*	386
3.1	'Getting High in the Low Countries'	389
3.2	Extracts from the memoir *Once Upon A Time in the East: A Story of Growing up*	393
5.1	Extract from the screenplay of *Little Miss Sunshine*	399
5.2	Extract from the script of the stage play *Summer Rolls*	405
5.3	Extract from the script of the stage play *Sanctuary*	408
6.1	Extract from the screenplay of *The Power of the Dog*	413
6.2	Extract from the novel *Small Island*	423
6.3	Extract from the script of a stage play adaptation of *Small Island*	424

7.1	Extract from the script of the radio play *Breaking Up with Bradford*	433
7.2	Extract from the script of the audio monologue *The Dead Dad Show*	437
8.1	Extract from the script of the stage play *Talking in Tongues*	443
8.2	Extract from the script of the stage play *The Christ of Coldharbour Lane*	448
9.1	Extract from the novel *Small Island*	451
9.2	Extract from the script of a stage play adaptation of *Small Island*	453
10.1	Extract from the autobiography *An Angel at My Table*	457
10.2	Extract from the screenplay of *An Angel at My Table*	459
10.3	Extract from the novel *The Hours*	461
10.4	Extract from the novel *The Inheritance of Loss*	465
11.1	Extract from the memoir *Biting through the Skin*	467
11.2	Extract from an interview with Nina Mukerjee Furstenau	469
11.3	Extract from the essay 'Jesus Shaves'	470
13.1	Extract from the memoir *The Grassling*	473
13.2	Extract from the screenplay of *Small Axe: Mangrove*	474
13.3	'Walking for My Mother'	476
14.1	'The Real Deal'	481
14.2	Extract from the novel *Be Near Me*	485
14.3	'In truth: Andrew O'Hagan on the genesis of *Be Near Me*'	487
15.1	The memoir piece 'Bloodstream (1997)'	489
15.2	'Daylight Savings'	493
16.1	Extract from the novel *Reservoir 13*	499
17.1	Interview with Siobhán Campbell and Jane Yeh	507
17.2	Extracts from editors' introductions to themed anthologies	514

Glossary 519

Acknowledgements 529

Index 535

Contributors

Emily Bullock is a Senior Lecturer in Creative Writing and a Media Fellow at The Open University. Emily has an MA in Nineteenth-Century Literature from King's College London, and an MA in Creative Writing from the University of East Anglia; she completed her PhD at The Open University. Emily won the Bristol Short Story Prize for 'My Girl', which was broadcast on BBC Radio 4 in 2013. Her debut novel, *The Longest Fight*, was shortlisted for the Cross Sports Book Awards 2015. Her novel *Inside the Beautiful Inside* was published in 2020, and her collection of short stories, *Human Terrain*, was longlisted for the Edge Hill Prize 2022.

Siobhán Campbell holds degrees in literature and creative writing from Lancaster University and University College Dublin. She has been Visiting Professor at the University of North Carolina, Charlotte; and Associate Professor of English Literature and Creative Writing at Kingston University London. Her six poetry collections include *Heat Signature* and *Cross-Talk* (Seren Books). Awards include the Oxford Brookes International Poetry Prize, Irish Poem of the Year (2021) and prizes in The Troubadour, Michael Marks and the National Poetry Competition. She has been a mentor for emerging writers via Freedom to Write and is a Senior Lecturer in Creative Writing at The Open University.

Bill Greenwell is a poet, parodist and life writer. His collection *Impossible Objects*, published by Cinnamon in 2006, was shortlisted for the Forward Prize for Best First Collection; a second collection, *Ringers*, appeared in 2012. He won the *Mail on Sunday* Poetry Prize in 2004, and the *Magma* Editors' Award in 2017. He was *New Statesman*'s weekly satirical poet from 1994 to 2002. His poetry and parodies have appeared in more than 40 anthologies, and in many poetry magazines, as well as on BBC Radio 3 and Radio 4, and in *New Statesman*, *The Spectator* and *The Independent*. Before becoming a Lecturer in Creative Writing at The Open University, he taught poetry and fiction at the University of Exeter and University College Falmouth. He has also published four books of North-East local history.

Lania Knight holds a PhD in English and Creative Writing from the University of Missouri and is a Senior Lecturer in Creative Writing at The Open University. Her most recent book, *There is Fire Here*, is a collection of personal essays. Lania's novella, *Three Cubic Feet*, was shortlisted for the Lambda Literary Award in Debut Fiction, her poem 'Susurration' was shortlisted for the Rattle Poetry Prize and her essay 'The Allotment' was longlisted for the Nature Chronicles Prize. She has been awarded Arts Council England funding to bring poets to Cumbria, including Kim Moore, Gillian Allnutt and John Hegley.

Dónall Mac Cathmhaoill is a playwright and academic from Ireland. He has an MA in Feature Film, and wrote his PhD on modes of authorship in theatre for political advocacy. He has written numerous scripts for BBC Drama and independent producers. His radio play *Bull Epic* (BBC Drama, 2000) was nominated for the Imison Award; and the Classic Serial *Barry Lyndon*

(BBC Radio 4, 2003) was nominated for a Sony. Screenplays include *The Wayfarer*, winner of the BBC Northern Lights competition; and *Warning Signs*, for the BAFTA-nominated *Citizenship* series. In 2002, he won the Bill Miskelly Award. He was formerly Head of Education at Soho Theatre in London and is currently Lecturer in Creative Writing at The Open University.

Derek Neale is a fiction and script writer, and was the editor of *Writing in Practice: The Journal of Creative Writing Research* from 2017 to 2021. His publications include *Writing Talk: Interviews with Writers about the Creative Process* (Routledge, 2020), *The Book of Guardians* (Salt, 2012) and the first edition of *A Creative Writing Handbook* (2009), which he edited and co-wrote. He holds a PhD in Creative and Critical Writing from the University of East Anglia and is Emeritus Professor of Creative Writing at The Open University.

Joanne Reardon was born in Liverpool. Her publications include *The Weight of Bones* (Cinnamon, 2020), shortlisted for the Cinnamon Debut Novel Award. Her writing has been widely displayed in museums and art galleries within site-specific exhibitions, and her plays performed by BBC Radio Drama. She holds an MA from the University of East Anglia and a PhD from Lancaster University, both in Creative Writing. She was Literary Manager at the Bush Theatre and the National Theatre in London, and a producer in BBC Radio Drama. She is Senior Lecturer in Creative Writing at The Open University, having also taught at Lancaster and Edge Hill universities.

Heather Richardson writes fiction, creative non-fiction and poetry. She has published two historical novels, *Magdeburg* (Lagan Press, 2010) and *Doubting Thomas* (Vagabond Voices, 2017), and the creative non-fiction work *A Dress for Kathleen* (Story Machine, 2023). Her short fiction and poetry has won or has been shortlisted for several awards, including the Brian Moore Short Story Award and the Academi Cardiff International Poetry Competition. Until her retirement in 2024, she was Senior Lecturer in Creative Writing at The Open University. She holds an MA in Creative Writing from Lancaster University and a PhD in Creative Writing from The Open University.

Emma Claire Sweeney is a Senior Lecturer in Creative Writing at The Open University. She has been writer in residence at Mencap and she co-directs The Ruppin Agency Writers' Studio. Emma's novel, *Owl Song at Dawn*, won Nudge Book of the Year (literary category), and her group biography, *A Secret Sisterhood: The Hidden Friendships of Austen, Brontë, Eliot and Woolf*, co-written with Emily Midorikawa, was praised by Margaret Atwood for having 'done much service to literary history'. Emma has won Society of Authors, Arts Council and Royal Literary Fund awards, and has written for the likes of *The Paris Review*, *TIME* and *The Washington Post*.

Introduction

Emma Claire Sweeney, Heather Richardson, Derek Neale and Siobhán Campbell

'If there is no wind, row' goes the Latin proverb. This is handy advice for a writer. You are on the boat already – you have begun to write – and then the wind starts to drop. The dream you are attempting to put down in words still compels you; yet, in order to make something of that early inspiration, you need technical know-how. *A Creative Writing Handbook: developing dramatic technique, individual style and voice* is for writers who have already started; it is for those who want to go on to develop their style and approach. As you work through the activities in this book, you will observe how dramatic writing techniques can be used in other forms of writing. Developing a fuller understanding of this connection can revive the way in which you generate ideas, improve the drafting of your stories and poems, as well as extend the range of forms in which you write.

All writing benefits from the writer's decision to pause at vital moments, to follow the hunch that something could be improved, however slightly. When the writer waits, puts what they are working on away in a drawer, and then takes another look at it in a few days, this is not procrastination or avoidance. The habitual, assiduous rearranging of words, without promise of immediate reward, appears in most accounts of writing practice. Yet such drafting and redrafting is not done in a vacuum. Each consideration is an amalgam of a very personal inquiry – *what* do I want to say? – and an awareness of technique – *how* do I want to say it?

The novelist Joyce Carol Oates suggested that without craft, art is too private; and that without art, craft is just hackwork (Oates, 2003). Oates says that art comes from the personal, from the idiosyncrasy of a compelling idea. Yet it is nothing without the scaffolding of technique. This book will talk about many approaches to the craft of writing, some of them familiar and some of them new to you. It will suggest methods of generating ideas, but also explore new ways in which you can review your work. According to Oates, rewriting, revising and reimagining your work are the lifeblood of the creative process. It is this dedicated attentiveness to the original conception that can transform an idea, and it is this approach that can improve and develop your writing style.

A Creative Writing Handbook forms one of the core components of an Open University writing module (A363 *Advanced creative writing*). It is appropriate for use on other writing modules and courses, and can be used by writers' groups and by individuals working alone. It is suitable for writers who have not yet settled on a preferred form, through to more experienced writers who want to expand their range, to seek new directions and genres, or to hone the subtlety of their style. It may be worked through sequentially or used as a resource book for writers and writing tutors.

This book contains a series of reading, writing and editing activities which will prompt you to write both brief and more extensive pieces of work. These activities are designed to be worked through progressively but can also be used out of sequence. They can complement writing workshops by helping to generate new work and by prompting complex discussion about approaches and techniques. Each chapter will provide you with immediately relevant practice in an aspect of writing. Many of the writing tasks are challenging. You may also get hooked on activities, even on ones you initially find difficult. Such tussles can sometimes be productive. On occasion, you may find that an exercise grows into something unexpected: a character resists being confined to a page; a scene suggests a whole story; a personal memory evolves into a poem. Some tasks might generate substantial new work. These writing activities are also places to return to when you are seeking ideas. Many of them are designed to be repeated or to be tried in a variety of ways.

A writer can, and often will, discover different ways of writing in what they read. Each of the chapters in this book uses examples by established writers. You will read poems, extracts of fiction, life writing and scripts for screen, stage and audio performance, which suggest a range of possible approaches to the question of marrying form and content, craft and ideas. Reading can help your writing in a variety of ways. As the playwright Mark Ravenhill says:

> Feeling how a dramatist's words feel on your lips and your teeth, how it feels in your stomach, what it does to your chest, is really, really important … I think if people want to write, they should pick two or three dramatists whose work they really like and learn some of it and actually walk around the house, or if you feel very bold, at the bus stop, and speak that stuff aloud and see how it feels.
>
> (Ravenhill, 2007)

A Creative Writing Handbook has been written by nine published writers who are also experienced tutors. We have studied and taught writing in a wide range of institutions, including the universities of East Anglia, Lancaster, King's College London, Goldsmiths, Kingston, Cambridge, New York University, University College Dublin and the University of Missouri. Our approach covers four main forms: fiction, poetry, drama (performance scriptwriting for all media) and life writing. Many chapters in the later parts of this book feature more than one form and throughout we advocate an integrated approach to your writing. For instance, the relationship between forms – including comparing scriptwriting and fiction techniques, and the relationship between narrative and poetry – are discussed. You will encounter many different ways of writing and you should consider how your own writing might benefit from these various methods.

In Part 1 of this book, 'Ways of writing', you'll examine the influential roles of genre, world-building and setting in fiction and life writing, and explore the ways in which narrative can be utilised in poetry. It is important to be aware that all of these types of writing contain elements of drama and to consider its role in your own writing, whatever form you are working in.

Part 2, 'Dramatic writing', develops this awareness. You'll explore writing for a range of dramatic media, including the stage, audio performance and the screen, examining the ways in which drama uses images and sound to tell stories. You'll also explore and experiment with adaptation, which is an important skill for professional scriptwriters and an instructive practice for all writers. In addition, the chapters in this part include practical guidance on how to format your scripts according to the requirements of the media you are writing for.

In Part 3, 'Developing style and structure', you'll further explore fiction, life writing and poetry, and experiment with how the dramatic techniques you'll work with in Part 2 can open up new ways of approaching writing in these forms. By taking different approaches, you'll be able to generate new and exciting momentum, allowing you to be bold in your experiments and to be diligent and brave in your redrafting. For instance, you'll investigate how some of the methods used in writing scripts for performance can be used to revise and improve your writing in other forms. You'll go on to examine the use of rhetorical techniques to improve your writing style, and learn how variation in the use of analogy can improve your fiction, life writing and poetry. Finally, in Part 3, you'll look at how to uncover the thematic connections running through your writing, and how these can suggest new avenues to explore.

Part 4, 'Readings', includes examples of writing by a rich blend of established writers of all forms, working in a variety of styles. Collectively, they illustrate the many possible ways of writing for all media that are explored throughout this book. Each of these readings demonstrate certain techniques and what can be achieved with them, and are linked to an activity or activities that pose questions and include a discussion. Throughout the chapters of the book, these activities will enable you to reflect upon what a particular example of writing might mean to you and your own writing strategies.

Reading will always help you to carry on with your writing; you will want and need to read, and not just the extracts included in Part 4 of this book. These were chosen because they display possible methods; they represent solutions to the 'problems' of form and the personal responses of various writers to those problems. The writer will always be faced with such dilemmas. As Oates says:

> *I have to tell* is the writer's first thought; the second thought is *How do I tell it?* From our reading, we discover how various the solutions to these questions are; how stamped with an individual's personality. For it's at the juncture of private vision and the wish to create a communal, public vision that art and craft merge.
>
> (Oates, 2003, p. 126)

This book's aim is to refresh and sustain you as a writer, by showing, explaining and inviting you to try various ways of writing. By illuminating the potentially fruitful connection between different forms, and especially the influential connection of drama to other forms of writing, it aims to help you create work that is both crafted and artful.

Content and authorship

Creative writing teaching can sometimes engage with subject matter that some people might find challenging. The readings in this book explore a range of emotions and experiences, and include topics such as death, suicide, serious illness, rape, racism and trauma. Where this kind of content appears, it is indicated in the text preceding it, in the title of the reading or with a content note.

It is important to distinguish between the content of a reading and its intended effect. For example, a scene depicting race discrimination might be included in a piece of writing to highlight and explore such injustice, to anti-racist effect. This book looks at literature from the approach of 'reading as a writer', which is an active method of reading that focuses on the writing process. Taking this approach, you will explore strategies for differentiating between content and its effect. For example, you will learn to recognise and evaluate the techniques a writer has employed, as well as identifying how alternative writing choices might have created a different effect. In doing so, you will discover skills that you can employ in your own writing.

The readings and examples in this book have been carefully selected to demonstrate particular literary techniques and approaches. They have been authored by a wide variety of writers with an array of human strengths and weaknesses, and their inclusion does not necessarily imply endorsement of the behaviour or beliefs of their authors.

If you have any concerns about the content or authorship of any of the readings or examples included in this book, please consider carefully how you might want to engage with the texts and the activities that explore them, and seek support if needed.

References

Oates, J.C. (2003) *The faith of a writer: life, craft, art*. New York, NY: Ecco.

Ravenhill, M. (2007) Interviewed by I. McMillan for *Ian McMillan's Writing Lab*, BBC Radio 3, 18 January. Available at: https://www.open.edu/openlearn/history-the-arts/culture/literature-and-creative-writing/creative-writing/mark-ravenhill-on-play-writing (Accessed: 13 May 2024).

Part 1
Ways of writing

Chapter 1
Playing with genre

Derek Neale

1 Introduction

Figure 1 Different types of hats (photo: Pixabay/Pexels). Simple props in your writing, such as headwear, can offer clues about setting and genre.

In this chapter, you will explore what **genre** means. As well as investigating connotations of the term and considering what it might mean for the writer, you'll look at the way some genres are signposted for readers, and you'll come to play with such signposts as you try writing in a genre. You will also examine the strong links between fiction and drama (i.e. writing scripts for performance) in what you read and in your own writing. This and later chapters consider how writers of these two major **forms** use similar methods to create **scenes** (a scene is an episode of continuous action set in a particular time and place). You'll also discover ways of making the scenes in your own fiction more dramatic, exploring how varying pace and using different types of genres might improve your writing.

2 What is genre?

'Genre' is derived from the Latin word *genus*, meaning 'kind', and traditionally referred to the 'kind of writing' being read or written. Is it fiction? Is it poetry? Is it life writing? Is it drama? These are the overarching genres – now more usually called forms – that have evolved following Aristotle's discussions of genre over 2000 years ago, as recorded in his *Poetics* (2000). There is a whole constellation of other genres branching out from these main forms. For instance, **fantasy**, a type of fiction, is a genre, as are **historical fiction**, **romance fiction** and **science fiction**. This is what is more usually understood by the term 'genre' nowadays.

Throughout this book, the term 'form' will be used to refer to modes of artistic expression, such as fiction, poetry, life writing and drama (performance scriptwriting for all media), as well as types of text, such as short stories, novels, epic poems, memoir, biography, stage plays and screenplays for feature films. 'Genre' will be used when referring to types of stories that sit within fictional forms.

Readers bring expectations about form and genre to a piece of writing. These expectations are shaped by previous reading of similar works. On a simple level, if readers see a lot of space around the text on a page, they may assume that the text is a poem. This is a basic recognition of form and genre, but readers are capable of more subtle and sophisticated recognitions.

Activity 1 Reading: the effects of different titles

Read the following passage, considering what sort of writing it is:

> The church clock strikes eight, so those villagers who are awake know without checking that it is six. A cock crows. A body lies across the doorstep of the church, a line of crumb-carrying ants marches across the fedora covering its face. There is a serene, momentary quiet after the chimes cease. A figure glides past the church wall, before the silence is cracked by a baby crying.

Now read the passage again several times, each time applying a different title to it from the following list:

- *Murder in the Morning*
- *Woman in the Wind*
- *The Life History of Guillermo Brown*
- *The Betrayal*
- *My Problem with Peyote*.

After each reading of the passage, consider what kind of writing you think it is. Do elements of any particular genre suggest themselves in the voice and content of the **story**? Write these down.

Discussion

When reading the passage, you may have started constructing events in your mind beyond the evident details given, guessing at what sort of story this might be. A title can ignite readers' speculation about the type of story being read. You might be more familiar with some types of story than others, but unfamiliarity doesn't prevent you, or any reader, from trying to establish which type of narrative you are involved with.

The title *Murder in the Morning* alludes to a **thriller** or detective fiction because of the body on the church step, the prominence and confusion of time, and the possibility that the gliding figure might be the murderer.

Woman in the Wind suggests romance, a mystery or a ghost story, partly because of the alliteration which is reminiscent of nineteenth-century novel titles, such as Wilkie Collins' 1860 novel *The Woman in White* (2008). It refocuses the reader's attention towards the gliding figure, and the possibility that this is a spirit.

The Life History of Guillermo Brown implies that this is a fictional or real biography, in which the reader must try to decide whether the body with the fedora or the crying baby is the subject of the narrative.

The Betrayal redirects the reader to the symbolism of the cock crowing, which in many cultures is an emblem for coming out of the darkness, and in Christianity is often associated with Peter, one of the disciples, betraying Jesus (Matthew 26: 69–75 and Luke 22: 57–61). This title also raises questions such as: is the gliding figure an adulterer returning to the marital home?

The final title, *My Problem with Peyote*, suggests an autobiographical, confessional narrative – but one that might concentrate comically on hallucinations (peyote is a cactus containing the hallucinogenic substance mescaline), and which recasts the body as alive but intoxicated.

The passage in Activity 1 seems to offer no historical clues as to the era in which it is set. However, with a little research, you might find that the scenario probably takes place after 1882, when fedoras were first worn. But imagine how your perception of the story would change if that one item in the passage were different – if the hat were a Stetson, kufi, mantilla, beret, headscarf or coif instead? This simple prop in the narrative has the potential to connote a whole cultural, and sometimes historical, setting. Establishing this setting is a key part of signalling the genre of a piece of writing. Yet the assumptions different readers make are not always straightforward – for instance, if the hat in the passage was a bowler hat instead, it might suggest to some that the character lying on the church steps is a British man from the nineteenth or twentieth century. But to other readers, it might suggest a woman from South America: bowler hats have commonly been worn by women since the nineteenth century in countries such as Peru and Bolivia. This shows how important it is, in your own writing, to research and make yourself aware of all the connotations suggested by the props you include, and to be clear in the way you use them. You might want to play with the cultural references and ambiguities of such props and elements, too, but beware of confusing your readers.

2.1 Using genre

The literary critic Jonathan Culler says of genre:

> To write a poem or a novel is immediately to engage with a literary tradition ... The activity is made possible by the existence of the genre, which the author can write against, certainly, whose conventions he may attempt to subvert, but which is nonetheless the context within which his activity takes place, as surely as the failure to keep a promise is made possible by the institution of promising.

(Culler, 1975, p. 116)

By including certain elements that suggest a genre, the writer (whatever their gender!) is making a promise of sorts to readers. Yet promises are kept in degrees of fidelity. That is, in your writing, you might suggest a genre ambiguously and include elements that could be interpreted in several ways. This may lead different readers to think they are engaged in different sorts of promises, different genres. You can see such possibilities from the brief passage you read in Activity 1 and the subsequent discussion about hats.

Activity 2 Writing: with genre and research in mind

1. Choose one title from the list in Activity 1, or invent one yourself.

2. Using the passage of text in Activity 1 as your opening paragraph, write the next two or three paragraphs of the story (up to 500 additional words). You can alter the first given paragraph in any way you see fit, keeping in mind the genre (or genres) of your piece as you write.

3. Research the connotations of an object or prop in your writing that could lead readers to view that object in different ways.

Discussion

As you were developing the passage, you no doubt saw the potential for playing with your readers' expectations and developing the sort of 'promises' Culler (1975) suggests. Playing with genre in this fashion is a vibrant way to approach a writing project. Yet you should remain attentive; read over what you have written repeatedly. If you suggest too many different genres, your readers might become confused. It's important to retain control of the stylistic elements associated with each genre. Often it's better to suggest fewer genres – sometimes one will be enough.

In your development of the scenario in the first given paragraph, did you find that you were focusing on a particular character? Whatever decisions you make about genre, you also need to focus on character(s) and characterisation in your writing. Genre on its own won't lend enough life or detail to your story. Besides character, you should also attend to other fundamentals – the setting, the action and the vital, revealing details – in order to bring the story to life.

You may have found that the object or prop that you researched, and included in your writing, gave you more ideas and the confidence that you knew what you were writing about.

2.2 Genre as a descriptor

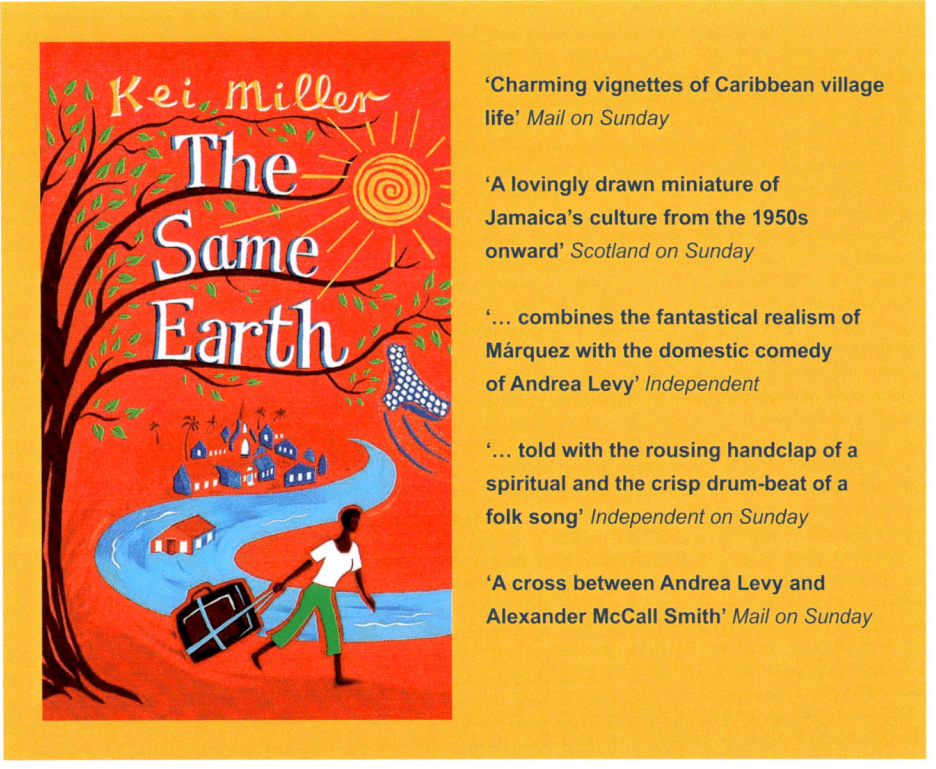

Figure 2 (a) Front cover of Kei Miller's novel *The Same Earth*, London, Weidenfeld & Nicolson, 2008. Illustration by Iain McIntosh. (b) Quotes from newspaper reviews about the *The Same Earth*.

Often a piece of literature can appear to be more than one genre. To illustrate, Figure 2 shows some review quotes written about *The Same Earth* (2008), a novel by the poet Kei Miller. These reviews reveal how the same book can suggest elements from different genres to different people. Readers of the work and the reviewers may be aware that Miller is a poet and that in itself may have affected their perception of the work – for instance, the *Independent on Sunday's* review comparing Miller's work to different kinds of song.

One of the reviews by the *Mail on Sunday* and the one by the *Scotland on Sunday* appear to describe *The Same Earth* as a type of life writing or social history. While the book certainly reveals aspects of cultural information (as novels often do), it is also driven by the usual motors of fiction – plot and character. Other reviews shown in Figure 2 mention Andrea Levy's novels and their genre of humorous **social realism**, and suggest that Miller's work also has similarities to both the **magic realism** of Gabriel Garcia Márquez's novels and the detective fiction of Alexander McCall Smith. Reviewers tend to use genre and existing authors in this way. They are looking for similarities, trying to describe the new work and to locate it in the existing literary landscape, but they aren't always concerned about how the work conforms wholeheartedly to just one genre. As these reviews indicate, Miller has somehow conjured all these different genre signposts in his writing, generating layers of interest. It wasn't his intention to write *just* a cultural or social history, or *just* a detective story, or a magic or social realist novel. Yet those genre labels all have traces in the novel.

2.3 Genre: going against the grain

One of the most effective ways in which a writer can use genre is to suggest one to the reader, but then play with that genre's conventions or, at some point, suggest a different genre. For example, a romantic story turns out to have a ghost, which implies a quite different set of possible story outcomes. The romantic narrative is often geared towards a denouement of marriage or similar 'happy' resolution, whereas ghosts often represent repressed memory and suppressed history – a past that refuses to be silenced and that is bound to disturb the story's trajectory.

Playing against the natural progressions of a genre by suggesting another can complicate readers' initial expectations of the story. By doing this, the writer might 'induce in [the] reader a series of intellectual reflections and emotional experiences very like those being enacted in and by the work itself' (Dubrow, 1982, p. 37). In this way, genre and content work in harmony to simultaneously trick and alert the reader to a larger meaning in the writing.

You can write with or against the grain of a genre. You might do the latter without realising it – for example, by dramatising the mundane, by writing comedic elements into a funeral scene, or by using a first-person 'I was there' testimony in your fiction. This latter tactic suggests a confessional or witness narrative, as if the fiction is really autobiographical. It is commonplace in fiction and has a long lineage – for an early example, see Daniel Defoe's novel *Robinson Crusoe*, first published in 1719: 'I was born in the Year 1632, in the City of *York*, of a good Family, tho' not of that Country, my Father being a Foreigner of *Bremen*, who settled first at *Hull*' (Defoe, 1983, p. 3). This opening works like a conventional autobiography, starting with a birth date and place names. Following this opening, the narrative goes on to give family names, details of the narrator's early career and rambling thoughts about going to sea.

Some **first-person** voices address the reader directly and more readily admit they are fictions, for example: 'Good morning! Let me introduce myself. My name is Dora Chance. Welcome to the wrong side of the tracks' (Carter, 1992, p. 1). This is the narrative voice of one of the Chance twins in Angela Carter's *Wise Children* (1992); the playfulness is immediately apparent in the direct address to the reader, and also in the character's eponymous name, as chance and fortune feature prominently in this non-realist fiction.

Some first-person narratives are more discursive than Defoe's early model. This can be seen in John Lanchester's *The Debt to Pleasure* (1997), where readers are five pages into the narrative before learning, in a subclause, that the main character is situated on a ferry crossing the English Channel. However, the reader is aware far earlier that various genres are at work in this novel. It is written as a series of seasonal food menus. The narrator, Tarquin Winot (another playful name), journeys from Portsmouth to Provence, so it is also a travel narrative. It is also a comedy, one in which the narrator's immodesty is often exposed: 'I myself have always disliked being called a "genius". It is fascinating to notice how quick people have been to intuit this aversion and avoid using the term' (Lanchester, 1997, p. 18). The reader is always being led to read between and behind what Tarquin says, to infer how he might really be perceived. The deluded character is set up as a snob and a bigot: 'There is … a deliriously vulgar "caviare bar" at Heathrow Terminal Four, just to the right of the miniature Harrods' (p. 18).

In *The Debt to Pleasure*, the narrative plays a mesmerising game with the aforementioned genres; the narrator speaks in increasingly comic boasts, while telling readers, as if this was a book of recipes, where to buy ingredients and listing methods for various dishes:

> Blinis. Sift 4 oz. buckwheat flour, mix with ½ oz. yeast (dissolved in warm water) and ¼ pint warm milk, leave for fifteen minutes. Mix 4 oz. flour with ½ pint milk, add 2 egg yolks, 1 tsp sugar, 1 tbs melted butter, and a pinch of salt, whisk the two blends together. Leave for an hour. Add 2 whisked egg whites. Right. Now heat a heavy cast-iron frying pan of the type known in both classical languages as a *placenta* – which is, as everybody knows, not at all the same thing as the caul or wrapping in which the foetus lives when it is inside the womb. To be born in the caul, as I was, is a traditional indication of good luck.

(Lanchester, 1997, p. 14)

You can see from this passage that the concrete information of the recipe leads into an odd, self-obsessed divulgence, typical of the narrator's digressions in the novel. Interestingly, though, the autobiographical part of the passage is presented as discursive – the food writing is the genre fronting the narrative. Yet even while Lanchester's novel may not conform to the usual sequencing of events and dramatic scenes, and while the possible genres accrue – travel, food, autobiography, family history, comedy – it is character that is still its most central and essential feature, just as with Defoe's more straightforward *Robinson Crusoe*.

Activity 3 Reading: for genre

Read the following passages of text (1–6) and identify the elements of style or content related to genre that are at work in each.

Passage 1

Through rotting kelp, sea cocoa-nuts & bamboo, the tracks led me to their maker, a white man, his trowzers & Pea-jacket rolled up, sporting a kempt beard & an outsized Beaver, shovelling & sifting the cindery sand with a tea-spoon so intently that he noticed me only after I had hailed him from ten yards away.

(Mitchell, 2004, p. 3)

Passage 2

Let's begin. Usually, I start by asking interviewees to recall their very earliest memories. You look uncertain.

I have no earliest memories, Archivist. Every day of my life in Papa Song's was as uniform as the fries we vended.

(Mitchell, 2004, p. 187)

Passage 3

Old Georgie's path an' mine crossed more times'n I'm comfy mem'ryin, an' after I'm died, no sayin' what that fangy devil won't try an' do to me … so gimme some mutton an' I'll tell you 'bout our first meetin'.

(Mitchell, 2004, p. 249)

Passage 4

    she thinks back to when she started out in theatre
    when she and her running mate, Dominique, developed a reputation for heckling shows that offended their political sensibilities
    their powerfully trained actors' voices projected from the back of the stalls before they made a quick getaway

(Evaristo, 2019, p. 2)

Passage 5

    as for Dad
    (you can call me Roland, no, you're my dad, *Dad*)
    he's sitting a couple of rows in front of her, wearing one of his Ozwald Boateng suits – brilliant blue on the outside, purple satin on the inside
    his head is shiny, thanks to cocoa butter first thing in the morning, last thing at night
    he's straight-backed, thanks to monthly Alexander Technique sessions to counteract what he calls academic hunchback syndrome
    every so often he casually glances around to see who's recognized him off the telly

    Dad's budget in clothes could pay her university fees for a year, the very fees he *says* he can't afford

(Evaristo, 2019, p. 45)

Passage 6

> Grace
> came into this world courtesy of a seaman from Abyssinia
> called Wolde, a young fireman
> who stoked coal into the boilers in the holds of merchant ships
> the hardest, filthiest, sweatiest job on board
> Wolde
> who sailed into South Shields in 1895 and left a few days later
> leaving behind the beginnings of Grace hidden inside her Ma
> who'd just turned sixteen
>
> *(Evaristo, 2019, p. 372)*

Discussion

Passages 1–3 are from different narrative strands of the same novel, David Mitchell's *Cloud Atlas* (2004). Altogether, there are six narrative strands in the novel, of different genres. The anachronistic clothing, word choice ('kelp' and 'Pea-jacket') and spelling suggest that the first passage is a historical narrative about the sea. Initially, the genre suggested in the second passage is 'interview'. But there is a strangeness about the voice, culminating in the use of the word 'vended'. Why not 'sold'? The oddness of the word choice suggests a futuristic genre. The third passage is set in a different type of future world. The dialect, with many apostrophes used to stylise the phonetics of the character's speech, seems brutal and uncivilised; it later transpires that the narrator is situated in a post-apocalyptic world.

Passages 4–6 are from Bernardine Evaristo's novel *Girl, Woman, Other* (2019). There are twelve narrative strands linked to different characters in the novel; these are three of them. Though the overall genre of the novel might be seen as literary fiction, each strand suggests subtly different genres. The fourth passage included in this activity, from a narrative strand about a playwright called Amma, can be read as a feminist story; the fifth passage, from a strand about a character called Yazz, could be seen as a teenage coming-of-age story; the sixth, about Grace, seems to be historical fiction. Yet there are unusual features common to all three: a lack of capitalisation and punctuation in the text, and all three passages have unconventional line-layouts, which look like lines of a poem or dialogue from a play. In this way, major forms other than the novel are suggested to readers throughout, allowing the narrative to function in less chronological and conventional ways.

2.4 Trying voices from different genres

In Activity 3, you read passages from three of the six juxtaposed sections of Mitchell's *Cloud Atlas* (2004). The genres of the three other sections in the novel are: a story set in the 1930s that is **epistolary** (fiction that is written in letters, emails or other forms of text communication); a farce set in the 1980s; and a thriller set in the 1970s, which is the only section in the novel that uses **third-person narration** by a voice from outside of the story. In all six sections, the **idiom** is crucial in establishing the narrative voice. Idiom is an expression or group of words that through established usage produces a meaning that is more than the literal definition of its individual component words; it can be a form of expression peculiar to a specific person or group of people. In first-person narrations, there is a vitally important link between character and narrative voice. But that vitality and sense of a consciousness can be injected into a third-person narrative, too, as seen with Evaristo's character, Yazz, in the fifth passage in Activity 3.

Activity 4 Writing: different genres

Invent two characters and a situation, and write the first page of a story (up to 500 words) containing elements of idiom and genre evident in one of the Mitchell or Evaristo narratives you explored in Activity 3. Consider:

- the ways in which you might be writing with or against the grain of a particular genre
- whether there is more than one genre suggested in your narrative.

Discussion

Thinking about genre in your writing can revitalise your approach. You may also find that the constraints of a particular kind of writing provoke you into writing against the grain of that genre. In the story you have written for this activity, you might have altered or elaborated upon the style of a genre, or forged a combination of genres (as seen with the combination of the interview and futuristic fiction in the second passage in Activity 3).

While offering excellent entertainment, the different genres in *Cloud Atlas* may prove difficult for some readers who struggle to locate an overall link between the narratives. This is a possible hazard of this sort of experiment with genre. Did you find this with your writing for Activity 4? If so, one solution is to refocus on the story's main character and ensure that character forms the connecting link.

Evaristo's *Girl, Woman, Other* is arguably less difficult to make sense of, even with so many narrative strands, because the overall story eventually comes to portray a community of disparate characters, bringing the twelve narrative strands together at the end of the novel. Did you find a way of unifying the elements of genre and different characters in the piece you wrote in response to Activity 4?

There is no denying that such energetic manipulation of genre can be vibrant and highly inventive, and a potent hook for readers. Yet it has its dangers. It's essential to have a strong enough unifying element or elements (such as character, plot or theme) to underpin the narrative.

3 Dramatised fiction

Along with poetry, life writing and fiction, drama – writing scripts for performance – is one of the major forms of writing (one of the 'overarching' genres introduced earlier in this chapter). Drama influences prose fiction in important ways. For example, as seen in the passages in Activity 3, Mitchell's *Cloud Atlas* and Evaristo's *Girl, Woman, Other* use the dramatic device of **impersonation** – that is, they use narrative voices that sound as if they are taken from a dramatic dialogue (you will learn more about impersonation in fiction in Chapter 14). You can use this form of stylised mimicry in your own writing, too, perhaps making the first-person narrative voice into more of a 'spoken' voice, as with Mitchell; or giving a third-person voice a teenage consciousness, as with Evaristo. This is a way of bringing storytelling alive and giving it dramatic energy. And there are other ways in which a story might be made more dramatic by using features typical in scriptwriting, such as dialogue, tight scene structuring, and omitting some narrative information (as drama performances tend to do), allowing greater audience engagement.

The short story writer Raymond Carver reissued his story 'The Bath' (1985) with a new title and more detail after it was first published. The story tells of a mother ordering a cake for her son's eighth birthday, but the boy gets knocked down by a car on the same day and falls into a coma. Meanwhile, the parents are hassled by phone calls from the baker who wants payment and the cake collecting. The story is bleak in that no communication seems possible between the distraught parents and the baker, and there is no resolution to the conflict or to the fate of the boy at the end of the narrative – at least not in the story's first published incarnation. In the reissued version of this story called 'A Small, Good Thing' (Carver, 2009a), published two years later, the characters are the same but are given names (in 'The Bath', they are simply 'the mother' and 'the father'), the story is twice the length and scenes are developed with more detail, and there are more aggravating phone calls from the aggrieved baker, which has the effect of ratcheting up the dramatic tension. The story now seems gripping, whereas the previously published version held a different kind of interest, being more concerned with the strange separateness of everyday lives. In 'A Small, Good Thing', the boy dies. Yet the clinching difference between it and 'The Bath' is that the mother and father have a confrontation and final scene with the baker, which, despite their son's death, offers the ritual sacraments of shared food and drink, and therefore some hope. Carver thought there was a truth in each version of the story and continued to publish both.

The longer, latter-published version of Carver's story, 'A Small, Good Thing', offers an example of the way in which the same story can be told differently and energised by including more points of dramatic tension and by offering a resolution scene. In Robert Altman's film, *Short Cuts* (1993) – an adaptation of a poem and nine stories by Carver – this version of the story is used because it has more of the ebb and flow of conflict, which is more suited to dramatic adaptation.

Carver often published different versions of the same story. 'A Small, Good Thing' was actually written *before* the first-published shorter version, 'The Bath' (Carver, 2009b, p. vii and p. 208), which was published when Carver was collaborating with the editor Gordon Lish. Instructive from Carver's writing process is how scrupulous and dedicated he was when editing, rewriting and publishing new versions of stories. He fully appreciated that editing could produce different types of story, the fiction often revealing the influence of drama and containing suggestions of different genres. In this instance, one version of the story contains more mystery and inexplicable conflict; the other version contains more episodes and well-developed conflict, and therefore more moments of dramatic tension.

When writing, editing and rewriting any genre, try to apply the same sort of diligence as Carver did in your own creative process. Pay attention to what type of story you might be writing and ensure that you attend to the pace of the storytelling to keep your reader interested. Editing for pace often involves tightening your scenes.

Box 1 Useful pointers for creating and editing well-paced scenes in your fiction

- Beware of preambles where characters enter scenes one by one.
- Beware of lengthy scene endings, waiting for the teacups to be drained and all the characters to depart.
- Think of the momentum you want to gain from a scene's ending.
- Remember, you can sometimes use the theatrical 'black-out', ending a scene suddenly, in order to cut to the next sequence of action.
- In orchestrating the action of your stories, you can vary the ways in which scenes start and end.

Activity 5 Revising: improving scenes, whatever the genre

Look back over one of the stories you have started in Activities 2 and 4 in this chapter, or a story you have previously written. Try to improve the dramatic shape and structure of your scenes and how they fit together by using the Carver example explored in this section and some of the suggested approaches shown in Box 1.

Discussion

Revising should be an essential part of your writing process. Writing is not a question of producing and submitting a first draft. Writers of all genres testify to the fact that the most important and productive part of the creative process – the part when the work finds its shape and becomes fully formed – is during the redrafting and editing stages.

When redrafting, it's important to identify the right climactic points in your narratives, where the tension rises and falls. It's also important to look for strong ways to end scenes. How to start and cut a scene at the appropriate moment is an essential storytelling skill. Economy in the way you write and link your scenes for all genres of fiction and life writing is something that can be gleaned from looking at dramatic scripts and performances. You will learn more about scenes in relation to writing for dramatic performance in Chapters 5–9 of this book.

3.1 Adaptation and genre

Although there are novelisations of film and TV dramas – *Star Wars*, *Doctor Who* and *The X Files*, for example – the most common transformation of stories from one form into another is from prose forms (fiction or life writing) into dramatic adaptations. Making plays or films from existing sources has an established pedigree for all media – audio, screen and stage. Shakespeare drew heavily on the 1587 edition of *Holinshed's Chronicles* (Holinshed and Harrison, 2014) for many of his plays. And films are often adaptations of short stories, novels or memoirs.

Activity 6 Reading: keeping adaptation in mind

Read 'A Real Durwan' (1999) by Jhumpa Lahiri (Reading 1.1 in Part 4).

1. Once you have read the story, note down any stylistic elements related to genre, as well as aspects of the way the story is told that interest you most.

2. Imagine you have been given the task of writing a dramatic adaptation of this story. Note down your answers to the following questions:

- What dramatic medium would best suit the story – stage, screen or audio (e.g. radio, podcast, etc.)? Why have you chosen this medium?
- What key elements would feature in such an adaptation – for example, images, dramatic exchanges, dialogue, descriptions?
- What would you discard from the original story in your adaptation?
- What would you like to keep from the original story but are unable to in such a dramatisation?
- Would you keep the same running order as Lahiri's version of events or would you alter it? Either way, why?
- Would you give Boori Ma more or less of a voice than in the original story?

Discussion

In Reading 1.1, the tenants of the flat-building do not know in which genre Boori Ma is telling her personal stories about the past. When she talks of her former life, is this a fantasy or is it a tragic tale? Is it a 'riches to rags' story or a realist story about social class?

This is an Indian story and a post-colonial story, but it also has a universal aspect. It includes some powerful images and similes: the hair knot 'no larger than a walnut', for instance. It is a story about the dispossessed; about someone who talks all the time but who has no voice. Boori Ma loses her bed to mites (real or imaginary), then to rain. This foreshadows what happens later in the story when the vulnerability of her living situation is fully exposed, just as it was when she lived in East Bengal.

The story establishes a strong habitual world with the inclusion of words and phrases such as 'every rainy season', 'lately' and 'twice a day'. But how would you transfer this into a dramatic script? Many of these can be handled by including just one repeat of a feature – the rain, for instance. The audience will understand what this means quickly.

Perhaps you chose film as your dramatic medium, so you could capture the image of the walnut-sized bun. Alternatively, you might have chosen audio because this could potentially retain something of the original's tone of narration. Boori Ma has more dialogue than any other character, but the story also implies that she talks much more voraciously than is illustrated. Therefore, in a dramatisation for the theatre, you might put Boori Ma at the front of the stage, with the flat-building behind her, delivering a **monologue** to the audience.

You will explore the techniques involved in dramatic adaptation more thoroughly in Part 2 of this book, especially in Chapter 9.

4 Conclusion

As you have seen in this chapter, readers' imaginations are informed by various forms and genres. Genre in its many guises is an exciting tool to use, to play with, but most of all to be aware of in your writing (and in your reading of other writers' work). There are subtle and intriguing ways in which you might alter the genre of your own stories as you revisit them to redraft and edit.

Drama is an influential form and its various media offer rich possibilities in terms of telling and retelling stories. In this chapter, you have looked briefly at some dramatic methods and how to use these when writing and revising your fiction. In later chapters, you will learn more about how dramatic methods can influence your writing style, starting in Chapter 2, which explores the importance of establishing imaginary worlds in your fiction.

References

Aristotle (2000) *Poetics*. Translated from the Greek by S.H. Butcher. South Bend, IN: Infomotions, Inc. Available at: https://ebookcentral.proquest.com/lib/open/detail.action?docID=3314345&pq-origsite=primo# (Accessed: 4 January 2024).

Carter, A. (1992) *Wise children*. London: Vintage.

Carver, R. (1985) 'The bath', in R. Carver, *Stories*. London: Picador, pp. 214–220.

Carver, R. (2009a) 'A small, good thing', in R. Carver, *Beginners*. London: Jonathan Cape, pp. 540–580.

Carver, R. (2009b) *Beginners*. London: Jonathan Cape.

Collins, W. (2008) *The woman in white*. Edited by J. Sutherland. Oxford: Oxford University Press. Available at: https://www.doi.org/10.1093/owc/9780199535637.001.0001 (Accessed: 5 December 2023).

Culler, J. (1975) *Structuralist poetics: structuralism, linguistics and the study of literature*. New York, NY: Cornell University Press.

Defoe, D. (1983) *Robinson Crusoe*. Oxford: Oxford University Press.

Dubrow, H. (1982) *Genre*. London: Methuen.

Evaristo, B. (2019) *Girl, woman, other*. London: Hamish Hamilton.

Holinshed, R. and Harrison, W. (2014) *Holinshed's chronicles: England, Scotland, and Ireland: Vol. 1, complete*. Project Gutenberg eBook edition. Edited by J. Hooker. Urbana, IL: Project Gutenberg. Available at: https://www.gutenberg.org/ebooks/44700 (Accessed: 19 January 2024).

Lahiri, J. (1999) 'A real durwan', in J. Lahiri, *Interpreter of maladies: stories*. London: Flamingo, pp. 70–82.

Lanchester, J. (1997) *The debt to pleasure*. London: Picador.

Miller, K. (2008) *The same earth*. London: Weidenfeld & Nicolson.

Mitchell, D. (2004) *Cloud atlas*. London: Sceptre.

Short cuts (1993) Directed by R. Altman. [Feature film]. Burbank, CA: Fine Line Features.

Chapter 2
Worlds of fiction

Joanne Reardon

1 Introduction

In this chapter, you will explore the importance of **world-building** in fiction, looking at examples from the genres of **fantasy** and **dystopian** fiction.

Fantasy fiction is defined in *The Oxford Dictionary of Literary Terms* as 'a general term for any kind of fictional work that is not primarily devoted to realistic representation of the known world' (Baldick, 2008a, p. 126). Dystopia is a term 'applied to any alarmingly unpleasant imaginary world, usually of the projected future' and dystopian writing is 'a significant form of science fiction' (Baldick, 2008b). In fantasy fiction, characters can move between different dimensions, perhaps using a knife to cut holes in time as in Philip Pullman's 1997 novel *The Subtle Knife* (2017), or stepping through shining mirrors into a wondrous castle as in Mizuki Tsujimura's *Lonely Castle in the Mirror* (2021). In dystopian fiction, the world as we know it is transformed – for example, in Philip K. Dick's 1968 work *Do Androids Dream of Electric Sheep?* (2012), an urban landscape becomes a post-apocalyptic wasteland and part-human androids inhabit the cityscape. In both fantasy and dystopian fiction, the importance of world-building is paramount, and that is the focus of this chapter.

2 A fantastic history

In terms of genre, fantasy and dystopian fiction are sometimes perceived as newcomers, but a look back to literature of the nineteenth century reveals that this is not the case. The **Gothic novel** shares many features with both genres. For example, Mary Shelley's *Frankenstein* (2020), published in 1818, explores themes of life and death in the story of a scientist who creates a monster that ultimately destroys him. In 1897, H.G. Wells introduced readers to alien invasions in *The War of the Worlds* (2017) and, in 1864, Jules Verne took readers on a *Journey to the Centre of the Earth* (2013). Twentieth-century writers followed in these footsteps, including John Wyndham who created *The Midwich Cuckoos* in 1957 (2008).

Readers around the globe have been reading about fantastic worlds for centuries. *Tales from the Thousand and One Nights (Arabian Nights)* (1973) is a collection of ancient folk tales written in the Islamic Golden Age of the eighth to thirteenth centuries. The poem *Beowulf* (Heaney, 1999), written *c.*700–1000 CE in Old English (Anglo–Saxon), tells the story of the hero Beowulf's battles with a monster called Grendel, Grendel's revengeful mother, and a dragon protecting a hoard of treasure.

A dragon guarding treasure appears again in J.R.R. Tolkien's 1937 novel *The Hobbit* (2013). Completed *c.*1469–70, Sir Thomas Malory's medieval **romance** *La Morte D'Arthur* (2004) recounts the legend of King Arthur and Queen Guinevere, the Knights of the Round Table and the quest for the mystical Holy Grail. These all bring the fantastic to readers in the form of magical lands and strange landscapes; of characters coming back from the dead or transforming into something else; or of monsters and long, arduous journeys through hostile, spellbound landscapes.

Some of these texts were written as **morality tales**. This is reflected strongly in contemporary fantasy and dystopian fiction, too, where social **allegory** is a key device used by writers. You will explore an example of this in Neil Gaiman's 1996 novel *Neverwhere* (2013) in this chapter, but there are many others. There are thematic echoes of Margaret Atwood's 1985 novel *The Handmaid's Tale* (1996) in Naomi Alderman's 2016 novel *The Power* (2017): both tackle issues of gender, power and corruption, yet were written more than thirty years apart. This shows how texts can 'speak' to each other, reaching back through time and forward into the future, influencing and adapting ideas and imagined worlds, and reinventing them for new readers.

Many of the works mentioned here have made their way into film and TV. For example, the director Robert Zemeckis adapted *Beowulf* (2007) using the pioneering animation technique of **motion capture** to introduce Beowulf and Grendel to a new audience; *The Midwich Cuckoos* has been adapted many times, most notably for the 1960 film *Village of the Damned*; and *Blade Runner* (1982) is a film adaptation of Dicks' novel *Do Androids Dream of Electric Sheep?* Fantasy and dystopian fiction lend themselves well to such visual media, not least because their imagined worlds are so rich and appealing, and so these tales are constantly being retold for successive generations.

3 Building a world

Figure 1 Rubin Eynon, *Gallos*, 2016 (photo: Gary Perkin/Shutterstock). A bronze sculpture at Tintagel, Cornwall, inspired by the legend of King Arthur.

Emphasising the importance of world-building in fiction, novelist and short story writer Lee Martin observes: 'Whether by birthright or adoption, fiction writers cozy up to particular landscapes and use them to give their writing authority, contribute to characterization, suggest plots, and influence tone and atmosphere' (Martin, 2007, p. 171). Characters must come from *somewhere*; they must belong to the world that forms the backbone to their story and to the events that happen within it. It is your job as a writer to make that *somewhere* believable for your readers.

3.1 Using what you know

It's easier to write about a place when you know it well, but what if you're writing about somewhere that doesn't exist, like the fantasy landscape of Middle-earth created by J.R.R. Tolkien for *The Hobbit* (2013) and *The Lord of the Rings* (2009) trilogy (first published in 1937 and 1954 respectively)? Or a dystopian world like the ice-bound planet of Winter in Ursula K. Le Guin's 1969 groundbreaking science fiction novel *The Left Hand of Darkness* (2017)? How do you create the world of your writing in such a way that the reader will believe that it is real?

You can use somewhere you already know as the inspiration for a new, invented world, or you can use your wider reading to imagine and inform your creation of this new world. This is something Tolkien did when building the world of *The Hobbit* and *The Lord of the Rings*. The landscape of these novels, Middle-earth, resembles the medieval world described in the fourteenth-century poem *Sir Gawain and the Green Knight* (Armitage, 2008), a text that Tolkien, as a scholar who specialised in texts written in Old and Middle English, knew extremely well. But the landscapes of these novels also resemble many of the places he knew, such as Maiden Castle in Dorset, which is believed to stand in for the Barrow-downs in *Lord of the Rings* (Garth, 2022). When these books came to be made into films, a very different landscape, New Zealand, became the place that stood in for Middle-earth. So, you can see that each reader interprets and imagines the invented landscapes in their own way from the writer's description of them; this is part of the joy of reading and creating these genres of fiction.

During a writing career of over six decades, Ursula K. Le Guin created some of the most memorable fantasy worlds for readers. In an interview in 2015, Le Guin said: 'As a writer I feel I'm taking the reader with me into this world that I see and discover, but of course I discovered that the readers make that world their own, and it's sometimes quite, quite different from what I imagine' (quoted in Plotz, 2015). By this she means that if you can create a vivid and realistic enough world for your reader, then they will feel confident enough to believe in it, to travel in it and to make it their own. Le Guin added that in an invented world, although it's important 'to describe more than a realist does … you have to leave out an enormous amount, too, and the leaving-out is half the art. There the reader is free to supply whatever they want to supply, to fill in all those white spaces that you leave' (quoted in Plotz, 2015).

In the introduction to his retelling of the Scandinavian Norse myths, *Norse Mythology* (2017), Neil Gaiman talks about place and landscape as being integral to the stories. The Norse myths date back to the Viking Age (*c.*790–1100 CE) and Gaiman explains how, as he worked on retelling and adapting the myths, he transported himself back to the time when they were first told: 'I tried to imagine myself a long time ago, in the lands where these stories were first told, during the long winter nights perhaps, under the glow of the Northern Lights, or sitting outside in the small hours, awake in the unending daylight of midsummer …' (Gaiman, 2017, p. xv). By putting himself in the landscape as he imagined it must once have been, he found he could place himself and the characters in the story. This is echoed by the short story writer and poet Graham Mort, who describes landscapes as 'the past and the future, as well as the eye through which each present moment slips' (Mort, 2001, p. 178). So, when you imagine yourself in a landscape where so many have walked before you (and this could be anywhere at all), you start to imagine what characters might have been there before you, or who might be there now or in future. In Activity 1, you are going to try to imagine that you are in one such fictional landscape.

Activity 1 Writing: creating fictional landscapes

1. Consider the two images shown in Figure 2 (written descriptions of both images are included after the figure caption). Then choose one and imagine that you are travelling through or towards the place it shows.

Figure 2 (a) J.M.W. Turner, *Old Welsh Bridge, Shrewsbury*, 1794, watercolour on paper. The University of Manchester, The Whitworth (photo: Whitworth Art Gallery/Bridgeman Images). (b) Antonio Sant'Elia, *La Città Nuova*, 1913, ink, pencil and watercolour on paper. Private collection (photo: Bridgeman Images).

Figure 2(a) shows a dilapidated medieval bridge over a river. There are buildings all the way along the bridge, leaning over and reflected in the water beneath. Above one of the arches stands a large decaying building. A wooden boat sails through this arch, and a glimpse can be caught of a new bridge in the early stages of construction. There are two men on the bridge with the town just visible in the distance behind them. Figure 2(b) shows a vast, desolate futuristic skyscraper with jagged edges and sharp angles, which jut out in every direction. It appears to be constructed of metal, glass and concrete, and each side of the building is very different to the other. Road and rail bridges run towards, across and beneath it as though it is the centre of things. No people can be seen in this image.

2. What are your first impressions of the place in the image you have chosen? List some details that you notice and imagine about it. For example, what can you 'hear' and 'smell' in the place? Also, think about where you have come from and why you are going to your chosen place.

3. Using your notes, write 200–300 words about the place and your journey to it.

Discussion

An image of a place, or someone's description of it, can help you to imagine that place in more detail. By putting yourself into the space of the image and describing what you see in it, or what you are told it shows, you will, almost without realising, start to move away from it and into your own imagination. Fantasy and dystopian fiction can be more visual than other forms of fiction, so using images in this way can really help to get you started. You can find images and image descriptions to inspire you in many places, from magazines and newspapers, to postcards, television travel programmes and online sources.

3.2 Turning real worlds into imaginary worlds

First published in 1996, *Neverwhere* (2013) by Neil Gaiman is set in the city of London. In Gaiman's text there are two Londons: London Above (the 'real' London) and London Below, an invented landscape that exists beneath the streets of the 'real' city. At first, London Below looks exactly like London Above, until small details reveal themselves and it quickly becomes apparent that it is a different city entirely. This is a device that fantasy and dystopian fiction writers often exploit, and you might have seen a screen example of this in the Netflix series *Stranger Things* (2016) where the world of the Upside Down, a nightmarish version of the actual world the characters inhabit, is situated directly beneath it. It is in this other world where danger lies and, just as folk and fairy tales tell us, the characters of the story must go on a journey to reach this place, negotiating the pathways between the worlds in order to retrieve something valuable or to bring someone, or something, back. This concept of the 'quest narrative' is central to fantasy fiction, a genre where so many stories are based around journeys. Built upon the idea of a character crossing a threshold from what the screenwriter Christopher Vogler calls 'the ordinary world' into a 'special world' (Vogler, 1999, p. 85) in order to complete a quest of some kind, it is important for building story and plot (so, you will encounter it again in the scriptwriting chapters of this book).

The main character in *Neverwhere*, Richard Mayhew, first encounters London Below when a door opens in the wall and a young woman collapses on the ground in front of him. The young woman, who is called Door, is injured. Richard rescues her, takes her back to his flat, and so starts his extraordinary encounter with this strange version of London beneath the ground. Door has opened an actual door to London Above while fleeing villains who have killed her family in London Below, and who want to kill her too. She sends Richard on a quest to London Below to find her a bodyguard.

Figure 3 'He looked to see where she had come from, but the wall was blank and brick and unbroken' (Gaiman, 2013, p. 25). (Photo: Robert Linale/Alamy).

Richard crosses the threshold from London Above (the 'ordinary world') by going down a manhole into the sewers to gain his first glimpse of London Below (the 'special world'):

> It was daylight *(how was it daylight? a tiny voice asked, in the back of his head. It had been almost night when he entered the alley, what, an hour ago?)*, and he was holding on to a metal ladder that ran up the outside of a very high building *(but a few seconds ago he was climbing up the same ladder, and he had been inside, hadn't he?)*, and below him, he could see …
> London.
> Tiny cars, Tiny buses and taxis. Tiny buildings. Trees. Miniature lorries. Tiny, tiny people. They swam in and out of focus beneath him.
>
> *(Gaiman, 2013, p. 49)*

You'll notice from this passage from *Neverwhere* that not only is the city Richard encounters different (yet also strangely the same), but time also seems to be as unreliable as the new landscape. This notion of unreliable time is something you'll return to later in this chapter. In London Below, Richard discovers a city populated by monsters, angels and knights in armour. This is also where the desperate people live, the homeless, forgotten and dispossessed – not unlike contemporary London, where homelessness and poverty exist side by side with the affluence and wealth that one expects from a capital city in the twenty-first century. Gaiman uses the device of the morality tale (which you were introduced to in Section 2) to powerful effect in *Neverwhere*. He has often spoken about the social allegories of the book:

> *Neverwhere* began with the idea of people who fall through the cracks … I wanted to try and talk about homelessness, I wanted to talk about [the] mentally ill, I wanted to talk just about the people who fall through the cracks in society. But I wanted to try and do it in a way that wasn't literal. It seemed to me that if I started talking about homelessness, the only people who were going to read the book about homelessness were people who were interested in homelessness, and what I wanted to write was a book that people who weren't interested in homelessness were going to read and start to identify and learn from. The idea was very much trying to take everything and push it over into metaphor, and just say, 'OK, there is a London beneath. There is a London where the people who fall through the cracks go.'
>
> *(Gaiman speaking in a BBC interview,* Neil Gaiman – Neverwhere*, 2013)*

Using fantasy or dystopian fiction to explore difficult subjects in this way can bring bigger social and cultural issues into sharper focus. If a reader encounters these subjects through the lens of the fantastic, they are, in a sense, once removed, and it is this 'safe' distance that allows them to engage, debate and question the issues in the story. For example, we might recognise echoes of 'Big Brother' – the ever-watchful eye on the population in the dystopian world of George Orwell's 1949 novel *Nineteen Eighty-Four* (2000) – in the constant vigilance of CCTV in our cities, towns and villages today. In *Nineteen Eighty-Four*, Orwell uses a story to deliver a message to the future; this is not so different to the approach of the writers of ancient morality tales, which conveyed warnings of 'be careful', 'be watchful', 'be on your guard'. The way in which landscape and setting are used in the writing plays a key role in this because if a reader does not believe in the setting and the characters that inhabit it, they won't believe in the book as a whole or the message it is trying to convey.

> ### Activity 2 Reading: comparing worlds in fiction
>
> Read the passages of text from the novels *The Water Dancer* (2020) by Ta-Nehisi Coates (Reading 2.1 in Part 4) and *The Power* (2017) by Naomi Alderman (Reading 2.2).
>
> 1. Read through both passages once, noting how each writer introduces the world of their novel.
>
> 2. Read the passages again, slowly this time, making note of specific details in each.
>
> - Do these feel like real or imagined worlds to you? What techniques have the authors used to show this – for example, how is the setting in each revealed through character?
> - What are the small details that stand out for you in terms of the setting in these two passages?
>
> ### Discussion
>
> On first reading, you might have noticed that *The Water Dancer* uses a first-person narrative viewpoint and the past tense, so the narrator's impression of his world is revealed through its direct effect on him. *The Power* instead brings some distance by using the third person, but the use of present tense lends more immediacy to the events.
>
> Small clues reveal that these are both imaginary worlds even though, like in *Neverwhere*, they are recognisable. *The Water Dancer* uses unexpected terms such as 'Tasked' and 'Lockless', and a reference to a 'gift', which the reader doesn't yet fully understand from this short passage. *The Power* uses strong sensory imagery to reveal unusual events: sights, smells and sounds to evoke the scene of a girl using her 'power' to conjure electricity in the sea.
>
> The details I picked out about the setting of each of these passages (the details you noticed might be different) include the way the narrator in *The Water Dancer* focuses on colours and senses to bring a strong awareness of himself in this place. In *The Power*, I was struck by the way sounds and smells seem to leap from the page. And I wondered why the girl was wading into the sea in her jeans. Both passages feel unsettling because of these unusual details.

3.3 Unsettling your reader

From the examples in this chapter, hopefully you can see how the worlds of fantasy and dystopian fiction can unsettle readers, while at the same time delivering a compelling story to transport them. There are many devices that writers can use to unsettle readers and one of the most common is the distortion of time. Let's consider two examples of this, the first from George

Orwell's *Nineteen Eighty-Four* (2000), first published in 1949, and the second from Gaiman's *Neverwhere* (2013), published much later in 1996:

> It was a bright cold day in April, and the clocks were striking thirteen. Winston Smith, his chin nuzzled into his breast in an effort to escape the vile wind, slipped quickly through the glass doors of Victory Mansions, though not quickly enough to prevent a swirl of gritty dust from entering along with him.
>
> *(Orwell, 2000, p. 3)*

> Richard looked back. The sign on the station said: *Knightsbridge*; he didn't know whether to smile or to mourn. It felt like the small hours of the morning. Richard looked down at his watch, and was not surprised to notice that the digital face was now completely blank. Perhaps the batteries had died, or, he thought, more likely, time in London Below had only a passing acquaintance with the kind of time he was used to. He did not care, he unstrapped the watch and dropped it into the nearest bin.
>
> *(Gaiman, 2013, p. 108)*

Both writers use the device of time to alert the reader that they are entering a different world. The first line in Orwell's text states 'the clocks were striking thirteen', so the reader immediately knows this is not the world as they know it because clocks do not strike thirteen. The fact that the character, Winston, sees nothing odd in this shows that he's familiar with his world; it is we, the readers, who are the outsiders. In contrast, Gaiman's character, Richard, has no sense of time at all – even though he thinks it might be the small hours of the morning, the face of his watch is blank. As soon as the characters in a story place themselves outside of time as they (and we, the readers) know it, the world they inhabit becomes unfamiliar. You might have felt this yourself when waking from a deep sleep, not knowing what time it is, or emerging from a strange dream that leaves you feeling disorientated.

It's this appearance of familiar things, such as a clock striking, followed by the sudden upending of what a reader knows to be correct about these things in their 'ordinary' world that creates the strangeness, making it clear that a story is taking place in an 'other' world . That is, everything on the surface *looks* the same, but it's *not* the same, and the trick for a writer is to explore the gaps between the two. To do this, as a writer you have to make the unlikely seem normal and everyday in the context of the world you have created, which will, in turn, make the world of your fiction believable for your readers. Using devices like the distortion of time is just one way to do this; the example of dystopian fiction in Activity 3 shows another – using the distortion of climate and weather to unsettle readers.

Activity 3 Reading, writing and editing: distorting the ordinary world

First, read this opening paragraph from Liz Jensen's novel *The Rapture* (2009):

> That summer, the summer all the rules began to change, June seemed to last for a thousand years. The temperatures were merciless: thirty-eight, thirty-nine, then forty in the shade. It was heat to die in, to go nuts in, or to spawn. Old folk collapsed, dogs were cooked alive in cars, lovers couldn't keep their hands off each other. The sky pressed down like a furnace lid, shrinking the subsoil, cracking concrete, killing shrubs from the roots up. In the parched suburbs, ice-cream vans plinked their baby tunes into streets that sweated tar. Down at the harbour, the sea reflected the sun in tiny, barbaric mirrors. Asphyxiated, you longed for rain. It didn't come.
>
> *(Jensen, 2009, p. 3)*

Next, think about some form of extreme weather – for example, unusually heavy rain or snowfall, violent storms, or endless, unbearable heat (as in the example from *The Rapture* you just read). Then, write two paragraphs:

1. Begin the first paragraph with 'Nothing worked any more …', and write about what no longer works in your imagined world because of this extreme weather. Try to write about five things.

2. Begin the second paragraph with 'What worked instead was …', and write about what has replaced everything that has been lost as a result of the extreme weather. Again, try to write about five things.

3. Once you have written your two paragraphs, edit them into a new, single paragraph of around 300–400 words.

Discussion

I tried this for myself and wrote about extreme high winds in springtime in England (when we would least expect them). I thought about what damage they might cause, including to power and transport infrastructures, and how this would affect the months ahead. I struggled to think about what would work instead as a result of this extreme weather (as, perhaps, you did). But then I imagined that people might come together to help each other repair the damage, so I was able to find five positive outcomes of the extreme weather, and this also helped me to develop some characters.

At the time of writing, Europe has just experienced a summer of unprecedented temperatures, and some things that might have seemed impossible a few years ago became very real as a result – some resembled the details in the opening paragraph of *The Rapture*. It is the familiar details in Jensen's text that make the difference here. There's no sign that the novel is set at any time other than in the present, but it's the distortion of what is familiar into something else that alerts us, as readers, that we are not in the 'real' world as we know it. The use of the second-person narrative further enhances the idea that 'you', the reader, are as much a part of this story as the narrator; it's not that common a device in fiction, but it can be a very compelling way of enticing a reader.

This novel, which is also a psychological thriller, addresses issues of climate change and mankind on the brink of disaster, all set within a very personal story. It is an example of dystopian fiction as social allegory, which is being used to make the reader think.

3.4 Using research to build worlds

Writing fantasy and dystopian fiction requires as much research as any other genre of fiction. It's tempting to think that because the worlds are imaginary, you can just 'make it all up'. You can't. The worlds that you build in your fiction might be pieced together from imaginary or researched worlds. They can be futuristic or fantastical, but if the worlds you describe are not rich in detail, they won't convince you and they certainly won't convince your readers. It is useful to think of research material as something that has the potential to be adapted into something more dramatic; this is often where writers find their inspiration. For example, *The Rapture* was influenced by Jensen's research around global warming and climate change (Jensen, 2009, pp. 343–344). In Activity 4, you will think about research a little more and consider how you can use it for building your fictional worlds.

Activity 4 Reading: researching imagined worlds

Read a longer passage of text from Gaiman's *Neverwhere* (Reading 2.3). The setting is a shifting, floating market that can appear at any time, in any place, in London Below. This passage describes Richard's first encounter with the market when it appears in a version of Harrods, the London department store.

1. What research might Gaiman have undertaken to write this passage?
2. How has he used research to create a richly detailed scene?

Discussion

On the surface, the scene depicted in Reading 2.3 seems like any busy marketplace anywhere in the world. Gaiman, like many of us, has probably visited markets just like this, so some of his research will be first-hand experience. The market has a medieval feel to it, so maybe he also looked at old paintings of markets in the distant past. Some details are very specific, however, such as 'Send 'em up the wooden hill to Bedfordshire' (Gaiman, 2013, p. 110), which refers to the nursery rhyme 'Up the wooden hill to Blanket Fair' (1996), so might have required some closer research. Or maybe Gaiman simply remembered the rhyme from childhood. Tiny details in this scene remind the reader of the novel's key theme: the plight of the dispossessed in a society where anything and everything is for sale.

Some details in Reading 2.3 suggest the deeper research Gaiman might have done in order to make the world of London Below feel real. Let's look more closely at the detail 'a man thrust what appeared to be a child's severed hand clutching a candle towards him, as he passed, muttering "Hand of Glory, sir? Send 'em up the wooden hill to Bedfordshire. Guaranteed to work"' (Gaiman, 2013, pp. 110–111). A 'Hand of Glory' refers to a mythical, magical artefact said to be the dried and pickled hand of a hanged man, which was made into a candle and used by thieves to render the occupants of a house insensible through sleep, and to make the person carrying it invisible. Pairing this gruesome, dark item with a childhood bedtime nursery rhyme (going 'up the wooden hill to Bedfordshire' refers to the nursery rhyme 'Up the Wooden Hill to Blanket Fair') creates a sinister scenario.

There is no evidence that the 'Hand of Glory' existed but it is an artefact that appears a lot in fantasy fiction – for example, in *Harry Potter and the Chamber of Secrets* (Rowling, 1999, p. 42) and *Harry Potter and the Half-Blood Prince* (Rowling, 2010, p. 576), where it belongs to Draco Malfoy. I only know what a 'Hand of Glory' is because I researched the details myself from secondary sources. While it's possible that Gaiman would have already known what one was (since we all absorb so many strange and unusual facts during the course of our lives), to build it into such a meaningful and dramatic detail, which adds resonance and depth to the whole scene, might have required a little more digging.

Activity 5 Writing: using research to add detail

1. Choose one subject from this list:

- the work of a rat catcher
- ley lines
- cloud formations
- fossil collecting
- ghost walks.

2. Compile a list of possible sources and then undertake some research about your chosen subject. You might start by looking online: if you enter any of these subjects into an internet search engine, a variety of results and research options will come up, including official websites, videos, podcasts, images, the titles of books, and more. You can also find information offline, in magazines, books and other sources in libraries. There is a lot of information out there and you have to select what you use carefully.

3. Make notes about a piece of information from your research findings that feels most promising as the basis for a story.

4. Write up to 400 words of fiction using that piece of information.

5. Go back to your original research findings. What, from those, have you used in your 400 words, and what have you rejected?

Discussion

It's always helpful to allow yourself time to conduct this kind of research as a springboard for your writing. If you find yourself being attracted by another idea in the process, follow your instinct and discard the original. Be flexible. You might find that you reject all, or almost all, the research you do and head off in a new direction entirely. A word of caution, though: you will almost certainly find that research gives you far too much material to work with, and the hardest thing will be deciding what to use. There is a strong temptation to include everything that you've researched in a piece of writing, but you need to suppress any instinct you have to do this. Think back to the way Gaiman uses the 'Hand of Glory' in Reading 2.3 – less is always more.

4 Building your world

This chapter has introduced you to various devices that writers use to build meaningful worlds for their readers. It has also looked at how you can use research to add depth and colour to your fictional worlds. In Activity 6, you will create a piece of writing that you can carry forward and develop in any way you choose, using a combination of these devices.

Activity 6 Reading and writing: imagined worlds from real foundations

Read the extract from Andrea Lee's (1993) memoir *Russian Journal* (Reading 2.4), first published in 1981. The setting of this extract is a market but, unlike the one depicted in *Neverwhere*, this is a real market, one in Moscow at Easter time in the 1970s (so, some of the details might seem a little old-fashioned).

1. Note down any details in Reading 2.4 that stand out to you.

2. Put the extract to one side and concentrate on the details you've noted. Use these to write 300–400 words of continuous prose describing your version of this market.

You can change the details you've noted into something unexpected. You could create your own versions of the vegetables on display or bring a sense of the weather into the description (you might use some of the writing you did for Activity 3 here). You could bring other characters into the scene, too. What would they be selling or buying? And where is your market? Is it somewhere you already know or somewhere you've invented?

3. Leave what you have written for a day or two, then return to it and go over it again. Do you need to do more research to improve your piece? If so, this is the time to do it. Rewrite and edit as needed, and try to introduce a distinctive rhythm to the prose. Include fresh and unusual words and phrases.

Discussion

When you build a world for your fantasy or dystopian fiction, it's better to create something unique, but it can help to use real landscapes and settings as a basis – such as those in diaries, newspapers or your own memory – and change them into something unusual. Or use images (as you did in Activity 1 in this chapter) to help you change a familiar world into an unfamiliar one.

You can probably see the rewards of the alterations and adaptations you undertook as a result of stepping away from your writing for a day or two and then returning to it to redraft.

At every step, there will have been choices to make. When you go back to edit something you have written previously, you will make changes to the shape, the rhythm, the tone, and the density of the language, transforming it into a more effective piece of writing for your reader.

5 Conclusion

This chapter has introduced you to world-building through the genres of fantasy fiction and dystopian fiction. You have explored and learned how to build believable worlds for your reader, and through studying the work of some of the most influential fantasy writers, including contemporary writers of these genres, you've seen how important it is to read as a writer – and to read widely.

This chapter has also illustrated how research can provide you with the necessary detail you need to give your fiction – and the worlds you create within it – an air of authenticity. Finally, through considering research and revision, you have seen that you can transform the words you set down. This process of transformation is at the heart of drama (performance scriptwriting for all media), which is the form of writing you will explore in Part 2 of this book.

References

Alderman, N. (2017) *The power*. London: Penguin.

Armitage, S. (2008) *Sir Gawain and the green knight*. London: Faber and Faber.

Atwood, M. (1996) *The handmaid's tale*. London: Vintage.

Baldick, C. (2008a) 'Fantasy', in *The Oxford dictionary of literary terms*. 3rd edn. Oxford: Oxford University Press, pp. 126–127.

Baldick, C. (2008b) 'Dystopia', in *The Oxford dictionary of literary terms*. 3rd edn. Oxford: Oxford University Press, p. 100.

Beowulf (2007) Directed by R. Zemeckis. [Feature film]. United Kingdom: Warner Bros.

Blade runner (1982) Directed by R. Scott. [Feature film]. United Kingdom: Columbia–EMI–Warner.

Coates, T.-N. (2020) *The water dancer*. London: Penguin.

Dick, P.K. (2012) *Do androids dream of electric sheep?* London: Weidenfeld and Nicholson.

Gaiman, N. (2013) *Neverwhere*. London: Headline Publishing Group.

Gaiman, N. (2017) *Norse mythology*. London: Bloomsbury.

Garth, J. (2022) *The worlds of J.R.R. Tolkien: the places that inspired Middle-earth*. London: Frances Lincoln.

Heaney, S. (1999) *Beowulf: A New Translation*. London: Faber and Faber.

Jensen, L. (2009) *The rapture*. London: Bloomsbury.

Lee, A. (1993) 'Russian journal', in M. Morris and L. O'Connor (eds) *The Virago book of women travellers*. London: Virago, pp. 456–457.

Le Guin, U.K. (2017) *The left hand of darkness*. London: Gollancz.

Malory, T. (2004) *Le morte d'Arthur* (2 vols). London: Penguin Classics.

Martin, L. (2007) 'Writing the landscape', in J. Steele (ed.) *Wordsmithery: the writer's craft and practice*. London: Palgrave, pp. 171–179.

Mort, G. (2001) 'Landscapes and language', in J. Bell and P. Magrs (eds) *The creative writing coursebook*. London: Pan Macmillan, pp. 177–185.

Neil Gaiman – Neverwhere (2013) BBC Radio 4 Extra, 4 March. Available at: https://www.bbc.co.uk/programmes/p015s82k (Accessed: 29 January 2024).

Orwell, G. (2000) *Nineteen eighty-four*. London: Penguin Modern Classics.

Plotz, J. (2015) 'The story's where I go: an interview with Ursula K. Le Guin', *Public Books*, 15 June. Available at: https://www.publicbooks.org/thestorys-where-i-go-an-interview-with-ursula-k-le-guin/ (Accessed: 22 January 2024).

Pullman, P. (2017) *The subtle knife*. London: Scholastic.

Rowling, J.K. (1999) *Harry Potter and the chamber of secrets*. London: Bloomsbury.

Rowling, J.K. (2010) *Harry Potter and the half-blood prince*. London: Bloomsbury.

Shelley, M.W. (2020) *Frankenstein, or, the modern Prometheus: the 1818 text*. Edited by N. Groom. Oxford: Oxford University Press.

Stranger things (2016) Netflix. Available at: Netflix (Accessed: 22 January 2024).

Tales from the thousand and one nights (Arabian nights) (1973). Introduced and translated by N.J. Dawood and illustrated by W. Harvey. London: Penguin Classics.

Tolkien, J.R.R. (2009) *The lord of the rings*. London: HarperCollins.

Tolkien, J.R.R. (2013) *The hobbit*. London: HarperCollins Children's Books.

Tsujimura, M. (2021) *Lonely castle in the mirror*. Translated from the Japanese by P. Gabriel. London: Doubleday.

'Up the wooden hill to Blanket Fair' (1996), in I. Opie (ed.) *My very first Mother Goose*. Somerville, MA: Candlewick Press, p. 60.

Verne, J. (2013) *Journey to the centre of the Earth*. London: Everyman Library Classics.

Village of the damned (1960) Directed by W. Rilla. [Feature film]. United Kingdom: Metro-Goldwyn-Mayer (MGM).

Vogler, C. (1999) *The writer's journey: mythic structure for storytellers and screenwriters*. London: Pan Macmillan.

Wells, H.G. (2017) *The war of the worlds*. London: Vintage Classics.

Wyndham, J. (2008) *The Midwich cuckoos*. London: Penguin.

Chapter 3
Life writing: outer worlds

Lania Knight

1 Introduction

Figure 1 A man with a backpack looking out at a vista (photo: arrowsmith2/Shutterstock).

Life writing includes writing based on your own life, such as **memoir** and **autobiography**, as well as writing based on the lives of others, such as **biography**. In this chapter, you'll look at approaches to choosing, writing and integrating the 'outer world' (or worlds) into **life writing**. Outer worlds and setting encompass the physical, geographical location of a piece of writing – that is, they are where the story you are telling takes place. A setting in life writing may be a place you've been to or a place you're currently observing, or it may be a place you need to imagine based on what you've read or what others have told you.

Remember that life writing is constructed. As the writer, you choose the frame for your work, just as a photographer does for their photography; and you choose the sequence your story or account unfolds in, as a choreographer does for a dance. You also choose how much to emphasise the outer world in your writing. Some writers foreground setting – the story is so rooted in the place where it is happening that the description of its outer world is placed front and centre. Other writers sprinkle in description of the outer world here and there, instead focusing on character, plot or reflection.

As you work through this chapter, you'll learn and practise techniques for observing, remembering and imagining outer worlds, enabling you to use these techniques to great effect in your life writing.

2 Proximity, distance and sensory detail

When writing about the world that your story or account takes place in, for life writing (and indeed fiction) it's helpful to remember to use all five senses: sight, hearing, smell, taste and touch. It's easy to rely on visual details to describe a place, but you can give your readers a more fulsome understanding of setting by using all the senses to enrich your description.

Dara McAnulty is a neurodiverse naturalist, conservationist and activist living in Northern Ireland. In his book *Diary of a Young Naturalist* (2020), he describes the natural world utilising his senses, sometimes in a heightened way. This helps to focus the reader's attention on sensory input, enabling them to imagine the sights, sounds, smells and textures of the place, and so taking them there. Even when it rains – perhaps especially when it rains – there are opportunities for McAnulty to notice and describe the natural world: 'The wind chops at our exposed faces, our eyes and mouths fill with salt and freshness. Even in shades of grey and black, the sky here holds such light and space and colour. It doesn't have the heaviness of a suburban sky, perhaps because there's just so much expanse' (McAnulty, 2020, p. 29). Notice that McAnulty includes sensory details of feeling and tasting in this passage, which are 'up-close' experiences, while other details, such as what he sees, signal distance. Descriptions involving touch and taste will always be intimate, for example, in this passage, 'our eyes and mouths fill with salt and freshness', whereas far-off descriptions of things seen can give a sense of expansiveness, such as 'the sky here holds such light and space and colour' (McAnulty, 2020, p. 29). Notice, too, that McAnulty sometimes blends intimate sensations like 'heaviness' with more distant phenomena like that of a 'suburban sky'.

Activity 1 Reading and writing: sensory details that evoke proximity and distance

1. Read the following passage from 'Getting the Hang of the Wind' (2021) by Chris Powici, a Scottish poet and essayist. In this passage, he draws on multiple sensory descriptions to try to capture something strange about an upland moor north of Stirling, a place where he often goes walking. As you read, consider:

- what sensory details Powici mentions, and which of these are intimate and which are distant

- how the use of proximity and distance contributes to Powici's thoughts on whether this place is 'wild'.

> After the knee-buckling slog of pedalling uphill for the best part of two hours I decide it's time to work my legs another way. I walk along the wind farm track towards the moorland ridge. Behind me, to the southeast, a pale half-moon is showing through the blue deeps of the early evening sky. Ahead of me the bright, unclouded sun hangs low over the peak of Uamh Bheag. Apart

from the wind, the only sound is the soft crunch of my shoes on the loose stones of the track. The only movement is the quiver of grass and the relentless shadows of turbine blades sweeping across the moor. Up here, things feel peaceful *and* weird.

Then something stirs in the heather. A red deer hind is watching me walk towards her. I pause. For a few seconds we stand, utterly still, gazing at one another. I forget all about the vastness of the turbines and the noise of the blades.

The hind turns and bounds silently across the moor until she is lost in a haze of evening sunlight. The noise returns. The question remains: can I still call this a wild place?

(Powici, 2021, p. 5)

2. Write a brief passage of 200–300 words about an experience that you have had recently or in the past that includes up-close sensory details as well as descriptions of something more distant. Try to incorporate details from all your senses, and be as particular as you like about what 'up-close' and 'distant' mean to you.

Discussion

This passage from Powici's 'Getting the Hang of the Wind' is set in a rural part of Scotland and focuses on setting, describing a sense of something 'weird'. For Powici, it is the sound of wind turbines in what was once considered a 'wild' place that he finds strange. He is familiar with the landscape he describes and his observations are part of an ongoing relationship with this place. Powici utilises the perceptions of several senses including sight and sound, as well as physical feelings (bodily sensations), to move back and forth between what is up-close and what is farther away. His question about whether it is a 'wild' place seems, in this excerpt, to find an answer in whether it *sounds* wild.

In your own life writing, you can ask challenging questions like, 'Is this a wild place?' And to answer such questions, you can utilise sensory details in your writing of setting, which alternate between intimacy and distance. In doing so, you may find answers, or perhaps you will uncover more questions that lend further depth to your writing.

Writing in a way that draws upon multiple techniques can bring richness to anything you're describing. In this case, it is attention to sensory detail, proximity and distance that will enrich your writing, whether that be about a face, a room or a mountain.

3 Journeys

Writing about a journey can be useful for structuring life writing of all kinds, including memoir, biography or autobiography. Writing about an actual, physical journey draws on elements of travelling: there is preparation beforehand (e.g. buying kit, checking routes, arranging transportation), the journey itself, and then the return home. Similarly, these stages can provide a natural shape and way of writing about more metaphorical journeys of learning, development or changes in life. The very nature of a journey also means that it provides different settings along the way.

3.1 A challenge

Sometimes we undertake a journey as a challenge, and sometimes the journeys life takes us on are challenging. Climber Helen Mort combined two challenges – motherhood and climbing mountains – in her memoir *A Line Above the Sky: A Story of Mountains and Motherhood* (2022). In this passage, Mort connects the two, moving back and forth in subtle ways between her experience of labour in a birthing pool and her memory of climbing with a partner:

> The midwife was animated, energetic. I was given a transparent plastic nozzle attached to a long tube and I clutched it in my right hand. Outside, the sky was heavy, a premonition of snow. … I took a tentative breath. *Deeper*, Claire said. I took a long shuddering gulp. Soon, it felt like second nature to me. My limbs tingled and my head spun. I was a climber at altitude, sucking on supplementary oxygen through a mask.
>
> …
>
> It made me drunk, giddy, warm and distant. I began to hover somewhere above my own swollen body. I was following Andrew up Ama Dablam, steady and sure-footed, knowing the rope was between us. And as my body began to push of its own accord, convulsing beneath the surface of the water, I tried to take myself away to the other side of the world, to put myself in a place of ice and weather.
>
> *(Mort, 2022, pp. 5–7)*

This passage is tense and vivid. Mort uses several senses to describe her experience of labour, and she also evokes an outside world that is familiar and comforting to her – that of ice-covered mountains. One setting is intimate and the other is expansive.

In 'Getting High in the Low Countries' (2016), David Webster, a cyclist and climber, writes about the daunting challenge he set himself to climb the Excalibur climbing wall in the Netherlands (Figure 2) to raise money for charity. He'd previously had a stroke and had undergone years of physical rehabilitation before he decided that he was ready to take on this challenge.

Figure 2 Excalibur climbing wall, height 37 m, 2004, Bjoeks Climb Centre, Groningen, Netherlands (photo: © Anna Richterova/Dreamstime).

Activity 2 Reading: description of a challenge

Read 'Getting High in the Low Countries' (2016), David Webster's short piece about climbing the Excalibur climbing wall (Reading 3.1 in Part 4). Note his back-and-forth structure between his past and the immediate task of climbing Excalibur.

Discussion

Decisions about structure can sometimes be difficult when undertaking life writing. Using a journey as a scaffold can help with deciding where to begin, how to get there and where to end. In his written piece, Webster (2016) moves from the climbing wall in the Netherlands to his home life, to his rehabilitation centre in the UK, and back again. This back-and-forth structure is made clear in different ways in Webster's writing. Sometimes there are larger than normal areas of white space between paragraphs in the piece that visually indicate a shift from one setting to another. At other times, Webster tells the reader that a big event might be just ahead, such as the opening line, 'Middle-age, it seems, is full of surprises', and two-thirds of the way through, 'what happened to me in later June 2012 felt like a derailment'. He also indicates to the reader where the action is taking place in terms of geography – that is, the setting of a particular section of his writing – with lines like: 'I fiddle with my harness at the base of the "Excalibur" climbing tower in Groningen, Holland'; and, later, 'One evening I was bouldering outdoors with my friend. By the next, I was in the Stroke ward of my local hospital'.

Webster also clearly indicates the shift from describing climbing Excalibur to thoughts in his head by changing his use of language. When he is climbing, he uses present tense and vivid details, such as, 'By now, I can detect a slight quiver in my hands'. However, when he is thinking or remembering, he uses past tense and reflection in his writing: 'The journey to this tower began years before. In my 30s, my path seemed marked out'.

3.2 A pilgrimage

A 'pilgrimage' is traditionally a journey undertaken for religious reasons, but in more modern times it has also taken on other meanings. It can refer to a journey that someone goes on to allow them time to contemplate an idea or intention, or to process an event.

In her 2012 memoir, *Wild: A Journey from Lost to Found* (2013), American writer Cheryl Strayed wrote about walking 1100 miles of the Pacific Crest Trail in the United States, alone. The walk was a way for her to process the grief she was suffering as a result of her mother's early death from cancer, as well as to confront her own addiction to heroin. This short passage from the prologue comes just after Strayed has taken off her boots to rest and one of them has slid over the cliff edge:

> I was alone. I was barefoot. I was twenty-six years old and an orphan too. … My father left my life when I was six. My mother died when I was twenty-two. … My two siblings scattered in their grief, in spite of my efforts to hold us together, until I gave up and scattered as well.
>
> *(Strayed, 2013, p. i–ii)*

As this passage shows, on the first pages of her memoir, Strayed lets the reader know about some of the events that have led to her journey and the reasons she is undertaking her pilgrimage. This is emphasised in her writing by the use of **metaphor**, as she draws a vivid parallel between herself and her orphaned boot; she is walking the Pacific Crest Trail to process her grief as an orphan.

I Belong Here: A Journey Along the Backbone of Britain (2021) is a memoir by English writer Anita Sethi, who decided to walk the Pennine Way after she was racially attacked on a train in England. Like Strayed, events in Sethi's life were a catalyst for her embarking on this journey. The person who verbally attacked her was convicted but Sethi continued to suffer episodes of panic afterwards. When a close friend died, Sethi found that she needed something to pull her out of her tailspin, so she decided to embark on the walk. She was inspired by many sources, including Chaucer's fourteenth-century work *The Canterbury Tales* and Strayed's *Wild: A Journey from Lost to Found* (2013). As she walked, Sethi (2020) contemplated what it means to be 'a brown woman' in the UK, and her memoir *I Belong Here* conveys her journey as 'one of reclamation'. Like other pilgrimages, Sethi uses the template of walking to give structure to the questions she poses for herself about her life and her country.

3.3 A return

Figure 3 Netherley, Liverpool, 2008 (photo: courtesy of Paul Farley). 'The kind of wall that invites a ball to be kicked against it' (Farley, 2008).

When you return to a place you've been away from for a while, it seems possible to see it through new eyes. Memory, nostalgia and the passage of time are key aspects of life writing, and are important to notice and to explore. By returning to a place that was once familiar, you can describe the effects of time on the outer world. English poet Paul Farley and novelist Niall Griffiths both grew up on the Woodlands Estate, a housing estate in Netherley on the edge of Liverpool. Many years later, they returned together as adults to see what had become of the houses they'd once lived in. They wrote about it together, in the form of a dialogue, in 'Netherley' (2008). In the opening lines, Griffiths recalls their first conversation:

Which part of Liverpool are you from, Paul? I asked. *Estate on the outskirts. You wouldn't know it,* he said. *I might do. Try me.* And a couple of hours passed in reminiscence. *Remember the chippy? The white bridge?* Paul mentioned my brother's name, closer to himself in age. So we had to go back. I hadn't been there for thirty years.

(Farley and Griffiths, 2008, p. 153)

Outer worlds that inspire life writing can, on the surface, be seemingly uninspiring to look at, such as Farley's photograph of a huge brick wall that he encountered when he returned to what remained of the Woodlands Estate in 2008 (Figure 3). However, it is the memories of the world that an image like this represents that are important. Something as simple as a brick wall can connect a writer to other times in their life, evoking thoughts and feelings from the past that come across in their writing in the present.

In his essay 'Little Boxes' (2019), Stuart Maconie wrote about revisiting Worsley Mesnes, the housing estate in Wigan where he grew up. In this passage, Maconie describes feeling both familiar with a place after being away for a long time, as well as the changes he notices now that he's returned:

> Even after all these decades, I still know where to turn, guided by old desire-lines grooved into the heart.
>
> …
>
> I move into the heart of the estate, headed for my old house. My surroundings look smart and fresh and not at all dilapidated. The grass has just been cut, perhaps by the council, although it occurs to me that many of these houses now will be owner occupied …

(Maconie, 2019, pp. 50, 52)

After his mother died, journalist Gary Younge also returned to the housing estate where he grew up, thirty miles north of London. In the final paragraph of his essay 'Stevenage' (2012), he writes:

> My secondary school, vamped up as a specialist engineering college, recently had its last intake and will close this year. In between the two schools is Shephalbury Park, where we used to spend summers at the play scheme. Portakabins now stand to one side as changing rooms for the footballers and cricketers who use the park.

(Younge, 2012)

In this passage, Younge's memories of his school and the park are overlaid with what he sees when he returns years later, including a much-changed secondary school now being used for different purposes and due to close.

In contrast to these three examples, there are sometimes places you return to again and again. When you visit a place many times over the course of your life, you are likely to gain a unique perspective and deep insight into that setting. English writer Robert Macfarlane lives in Cambridge, England, but as a child he hiked the Cairngorms in Scotland with his grandparents, returning there every summer. This had a tremendous influence on his life and led to his writing of *Mountains of the Mind* (2003), which won the *Guardian* First Book Award in 2003. Similarly, Nan Shepherd was a writer who lived in Scotland and hiked the Cairngorm mountains her entire life. She wrote about her deep connection to the place in her memoir *The Living Mountain* (2011), originally published in 1977.

Activity 3 Writing: a personal journey

For this writing activity, you have two options to choose from. Either:

1. Write a brief passage (200–300 words) about yourself or someone else who has travelled from one place to another with some sort of intention. For example, think about the work of Sethi and Strayed (Section 3.2): both writers were clear on *why* they were making their journeys *before* they set out. Some possibilities for your own piece might include writing about yourself or someone you know who has walked, run or swum for a charity event. You could write about a short local journey, like visiting a memorial bench in a park, or a longer journey across land or sea. The focus here is intention. Try to write about the planned aim of the journey, as well as the journey itself.

Or:

2. Write a brief passage (200–300 words) about yourself or someone else who has *returned* somewhere that you/they were once familiar with. The account might be about a single return to a place, like Farley and Griffiths'. Alternatively, it could be about a return journey to a place that you or someone else have been back to many times over a lifetime, like Macfarlane's multiple returns to the Cairngorms.

Discussion

Return journeys and travelling with intention can yield interesting life writing, helping to add layers to a piece. There is the physical journey to describe and there is also the 'inner' journey, which can include thinking about an intention beforehand, preparation, the journey itself and remembering it afterwards.

4 Using language to access memories, observations and imagination

Elements of different 'languages' can help us to connect to outer worlds and describe setting. By languages, here, I mean anything from familiar and unfamiliar phrases, to **idiom**, to remembered or forgotten tongues (that is, languages we may have heard or spoken as a child but no longer use or encounter).

Examples from my own life include the words '*pirogue*' and '*bayou*' and the phrase '*sacré bleu*'. My paternal grandmother, 'Grandma Gracie', was Cajun, which means that her ancestors (and mine) were part of a group of French emigrants who left France in the seventeenth century and sailed to Acadia, Canada, and then eventually landed in Louisiana in the United States. Grandma Gracie grew up in a small town in Southwest Louisiana and didn't speak English until she went to primary school. My father used to tell stories about her, saying that she lived on a *bayou*, an American French word for a swampy, marshy area, and that she went to school in a *pirogue*, a French word for a small boat. He remembered her saying *sacré bleu*, an exclamation of exasperation, to him as a child when she was upset with him. Recalling these words and phrases helps me to remember my grandmother's house in New Orleans, where my father lived as a child, and the town in Southwest Louisiana where my grandmother grew up.

In the introduction to her memoir *Lowborn: Growing Up, Getting Away and Returning to Britain's Poorest Towns* (2019), Kerry Hudson writes about words she remembers from the first twenty years of her life – 'chav, scav, lowlife, NED, underclass, lowborn' (p. 10) – and she uses these words as a platform to ask herself if she has 'escaped'. They are the impetus for her return to all the towns and cities she's ever lived in, beginning with Aberdeen in Scotland. Although these words are remembered from her childhood, they led Hudson on a journey that allowed her to observe and write about the present state of places she had lived in years and decades before.

Activity 4 Writing: language that connects us to people and places

Start a list of words or phrases that you remember from your childhood or that someone you know recalls from their own past. Keep adding to this list as you work through this section of the chapter.

Discussion

A great deal of life writing comes from memory. This includes your own (or someone else's) memories of settings. Remembering through elements of language, like words and phrases, can help connect you to your past, and to that of others, and is one way to arrive at compelling detail to include in your writing. Sometimes, as in my example at the start of this section, in helping us to remember the past, language can also serve as a way into *imagining* the lives and experiences of previous generations, too.

Sometimes, a writer may have never been to the place they are describing, so they have no memories of it. Robin Wall Kimmerer is a scientist, mother and member of the Citizen Potawatomi Nation. The history of her family and her tribe is one of displacement and forced migration. In her essay 'The Council of Pecans', Kimmerer uses the origin of a single word, 'pecan', to find her way into her account, which traces the movement of her extended family and imagines places she has never been, describing settings and events she's never experienced. This passage from 'The Council of Pecans' is from Kimmerer's book, *Braiding Sweetgrass: Indigenous Wisdom, Scientific Knowledge, and the Teachings of Plants* (2013):

> The word *pecan*—the fruit of the tree known as the pecan hickory (*Carya illinoensis*)—comes to English from indigenous languages. *Pigan* is a nut, any nut. The hickories, black walnuts, and butternuts of our northern homelands have their own specific names. But those trees, like the homelands, were lost to my people. Our lands around Lake Michigan were wanted by settlers, so in long lines, surrounded by soldiers, we were marched at gunpoint along what became known as the Trail of Death. They took us to a new place, far from our lakes and forests. ... In the span of a single generation my ancestors were 'removed' three times—Wisconsin to Kansas, points in between, and then to Oklahoma. I wonder if they looked back for a last glimpse of the lakes, glimmering like a mirage. Did they touch the trees in remembrance as they became fewer and fewer, until there was only grass?
>
> ...
>
> When they got to Kansas, they must have been relieved to find groves of nut trees along the rivers—a type unknown to them, but delicious and plentiful. Without a name for this new food they just called them nuts—*pigan*—which became *pecan* in English.
>
> *(Kimmerer, 2013, pp. 12–13)*

Kimmerer uses elements of language to write about the details she knows, and to help her imagine and write about the details of things she doesn't know. When life writing includes scenes that other people have experienced but which you haven't, or settings you've never visited, it can feel daunting to 'get it right'. There are ways to signal to the reader that you are using your imagination – for example, Kimmerer states 'I wonder if ...', and asks questions like, 'Did they touch the trees ...?' (Kimmerer, 2013, p. 13).

Activity 5 Writing: using language, observation, memory and imagination

Find a word or phrase from the list you started in Activity 4 that is connected to a setting in some way. Write a brief passage (200–300 words) about what that place means for you or for someone you know. Use this as an opportunity to investigate your past or that of someone else.

Discussion

For Activity 4, I wrote a list of some words and phrases that my paternal grandmother used to say, including '*boudin*' (a type of French sausage), 'tinned chocolate syrup' and 'cayenne pepper'. As I was writing about them for this activity, I began recalling more details about my grandmother's kitchen. I could see the two ceramic bowls painted with tulips that she used for serving red beans and rice. From there, I began to remember mornings spent eating leftover cornbread soaked in 'coffee-milk' for breakfast. She'd sprinkle sugar on top that would dissolve granule by granule into a crunchy, sweet crust.

Where did your investigation lead you? Did any sensory details come to mind? Did you recall things that perhaps you'd forgotten? Sometimes, investigating memories from the past can lead us in unexpected directions. For now, just enjoy the exploration: it may bring about some surprising results!

5 Writing in the moment

Another way to write an effective and detailed description of the outer world is to write in the moment. For example, I once challenged myself to write a story set in a town in China where I would be living for five weeks. When I arrived, I went for walks each day and wrote down my observations in a notebook. It was the first time I'd ever tried to write a story incorporating description based on direct observations of a place, while they were fresh in my mind. The piece was published in a UK magazine and the editor said that he loved how vivid and descriptive it was. The time that I spent in China is such a strong memory for me now, I think in part because I'd set my intention to notice my surroundings and write down my observations. I also learned from this experience: the practice of observing and writing in the moment is an excellent way to strengthen your ability to evoke outer worlds and setting in your writing.

For writers, as for visual artists, it can be invigorating to observe your surroundings and draw on them immediately, while they can be easily remembered. Hudson's writing in *Lowborn: Growing Up, Getting Away and Returning to Britain's Poorest Towns* (2019) demonstrates the power of such observation; of going somewhere to get a fuller sensory experience of what it's like in the 'here and now'. And in her 1977 book *The Living Mountain*, Shepherd shows how walking repeatedly through the same landscape over a lifetime can yield powerful imagery. In your own work, find ways to write about how you or someone else senses the world in the here and now, whether that's in your bedroom, a writing space, a back garden, a city street, or an entire mountain range.

6 Bringing it all together

British writer Xiaolu Guo was born in China. When she was newborn, her parents gave her to a farming couple. Then, as an infant, she was given to her grandparents who lived in a small fishing village at the edge of the East China Sea. At the age of seven, Guo met her birth mother, and then later emigrated to the UK. She writes about all of this in her memoir *Once Upon a Time in the East: A Story of Growing up* (2017). After the birth of her own daughter, Guo returned to China, to her grandparents' fishing village, for the first time in decades. Because she had been away for so long, she saw the village of her childhood in a different way – through the eyes of an adult. Her perception of the place was in contrast to what she had remembered it being like as a child. This gave her plenty of inspiration for writing about the setting.

Activity 6 Reading: *Once Upon a Time in the East*

Read the two extracts ('Village of Shitang' and 'The Return') from *Once Upon a Time in the East: A Story of Growing up* (2017) by Xiaolu Guo (Reading 3.2). Take note of the different techniques used by Guo to write about the setting and describe the fishing village where she grew up – both how it was in the past and how it was on her return after many years.

Discussion

Guo writes both extracts (Reading 3.2) as an adult returning to a place. Many years have passed since she last saw the fishing village where she lived with her grandparents and her life has changed entirely, as has her perspective. She captures something of her child-like perceptions of the setting in 'Village of Shitang' and 'The Return' reveals her adult insights.

This chapter has explored many of the techniques used by Guo in these two extracts, including the use of sensory detail, proximity and distance, writing about a journey that involves a challenge or an intention, return journeys and using language to access memories, observations and detail.

Guo's use of the senses to describe each scene creates a vivid experience for the reader, and her observations about language in 'The Return' provide a link between the fishing village of her childhood and the same place, years later, when she sees it again as an adult.

7 Conclusion

This chapter has considered the role and inclusion of setting and outer worlds in life writing, looking at many kinds of life writers and their stories, set in all sorts of locations – from housing estates to remote mountains to distant villages. You've read about the stories that people tell about themselves and those that they tell about others.

In your own life writing, the outer world you capture in a piece may be comprised of several places, such as various towns or cities where you have lived, or it may be just one village – or even one room.

References

Farley, P. (2008) 'Netherley: image 3 of 16', *Granta*, 102, 15 July. Available at: https://granta.com/netherley-photographs/ (Accessed: 25 April 2023).

Farley, P. and Griffiths, N. (2008) 'Netherley', *Granta*, 102, 7 July. Available at: https://granta.com/netherley/ (Accessed: 25 April 2023).

Guo, X. (2017) *Once upon a time in the east: a story of growing up*. London: Vintage.

Hudson, K. (2019) *Lowborn: growing up, getting away and returning to Britain's poorest towns*. London: Chatto & Windus.

Kimmerer, R.W. (2013) 'The council of pecans', in R.W. Kimmerer, *Braiding sweetgrass: Indigenous wisdom, scientific knowledge, and the teachings of plants*. Minneapolis, MN: Milkweed Editions, pp. 11–21.

McAnulty, D. (2020) *Diary of a young naturalist*. Beaminster: Little Toller Books.

Macfarlane, R. (2003) *Mountains of the mind: a history of a fascination*. London: Granta Books.

Maconie, S. (2019) 'Little boxes', in K. de Waal (ed.) *Common people: an anthology of working-class writers*. London: Unbound, pp. 42–54.

Mort, H. (2022) *A line above the sky: a story of mountains and motherhood*. London: Ebury Press.

Powici, C. (2021) 'Getting the hang of the wind', in K. Jamie (ed.) *Antlers of water: writing on the nature and environment of Scotland*. Edinburgh: Canongate Books, pp. 1–12.

Sethi, A. (2020) 'I belong here', *Anita Sethi: writing*, 1 January. Available at: https://anitasethi.com/2020/01/01/i-belong-here/ (Accessed: 20 February 2024).

Sethi, A. (2021) *I belong here: a journey along the backbone of Britain*. London: Bloomsbury Wildlife.

Shepherd, N. (2011) *The living mountain*. Edinburgh: Canongate Books.

Strayed, C. (2013) *Wild: a journey from lost to found*. New York, NY: Atlantic Books.

Webster, D. (2016) 'Getting high in the Low Countries', *Dispirited: how contemporary spirituality makes us stupid, selfish and unhappy*, 25 November. Available at: https://dispirited.org/2016/11/25/getting-high-in-the-low-countries/ (Accessed: 12 February 2024).

Younge, G. (2012) 'Stevenage', *Granta*, 119, 10 May. Available at: https://granta.com/stevenage/ (Accessed: 25 April 2023).

Chapter 4
Writing narrative poems

Siobhán Campbell

1 Introduction

Figure 1 John Henry Dearle, 'Orchard' wallpaper, 1899, colour woodblock or machine, print on paper. Published by Morris and Co., London (photo: The Stapleton Collection/Bridgeman Images). Dearle's orchard image brings the cycle of flower, seed and fruit to mind, which is reminiscent of how a story can grow organically within a poem.

In this chapter, you'll learn how poets shape the stories they tell in narrative poems, using characters, specific settings and different poetic techniques.

A narrative poem tells some kind of story or part of a story. Some have a narrative arc, with a beginning, middle and end, but many contemporary narrative poems reveal only part of a larger story and imply the rest. Like other kinds of poetry, narrative poems may contain some of the elements of fiction writing, including characters, plot, setting, conflict and resolution. They often have one narrator, the 'speaker' of the poem, and are written using **figurative language**. They may use **internal rhyme** or half rhyme, as well as stanzas and line lengths to help create meaning, though many contemporary narrative poems are written in free verse (without a fixed pattern of rhythm or rhyme).

2 The origins of narrative poetry

Narrative poetry grew out of our natural impulse to tell stories. The early poems of this sort were passed on orally, and poets employed rhyme and repetition so that stories could be memorised and performed more easily. Ancient Greek **epic** poems such as the *Odyssey* (2014) and the *Iliad* (2015), written around the late eighth to early seventh century BCE and attributed to Homer, are part of this spoken tradition of narrative poems. The *Mabinogion* (Davies, 2007) is a Welsh text that uses some of the **episodic** techniques of narrative poetry, despite being written in prose; the stories in it were compiled in the twelfth to thirteenth centuries CE from earlier oral traditions. Another type of poem that suits narrative is the **ballad**, which is traditionally written in quatrains (four-line **stanzas**), often telling the full story of a person's life and deeds:

> In Scarlet town, where I was born,
>   There was a fair maid dwellin',
> Made every youth cry *Well-a-way!*
>   Her name was Barbara Allen.
>
>   ('Barbara Allen', no date)

This first quatrain of the seventeenth-century (or earlier) folk ballad 'Barbara Allen' has a traditional ABCB rhyme scheme, where the last words of the second and fourth lines rhyme – though, here, they arguably end on a **half rhyme** ('dwellin'' and 'Allen'). Like other ballads, 'Barbara Allen' is frequently set to music. As is often the case with older works, the author is unknown because the lyrics have been passed down through oral tradition.

Ballads tell a story in episodes, sometimes using each stanza to move the story along, while longer narrative poems can include many stories. But most narrative poems, regardless of length or the number of stories within them, are made memorable by a strong plot or by evoking vivid images – or, most likely, both. **Imagery** – which is figurative language that draws on the senses of taste, smell, touch, hearing and sight – is arguably the most important device used in any poem, as it is how a poet affects a reader's emotions.

Works from the tradition of narrative poetry that are worth seeking out for their striking stories include 'The Raven' by Edgar Allen Poe (2012), published in 1845, where the raven stands in metaphorically for the speaker's grief; and Christina Rossetti's 'Goblin Market' (2010) published in 1862, which tells the story of sisters Lizzie and Laura and their encounter with magic. Story-led poems like these usually have a distinct setting that acts as the backdrop for the story in the same way that a physical backdrop does in the theatre. The more specific and exact a setting, the more real it will feel to a reader. In your own poetry writing, try to develop the habit of using exact details to help the reader feel what you want them to feel.

Activity 1 Reading and writing: a narrative poem

In this activity, you will first 'read as a writer', and then draft a poem of your own.

1. Read the narrative poem 'When I Am Asked' (1996) by Lisel Mueller.

> **Lisel Mueller** was a German-born American poet, translator and teacher. Mueller arrived in the United States in 1939 after her family fled Nazi Germany. She worked as a literary critic and academic, and she began writing poetry in the 1950s, publishing her first collection in 1965.

Content note: Please be aware that this poem briefly mentions the death of a parent.

When I Am Asked

When I am asked
how I began writing poems,
I talk about the indifference of nature.

It was soon after my mother died,
a brilliant June day,
everything blooming.

I sat on a gray stone bench
in a lovingly planted garden,
but the day lilies were as deaf
as the ears of drunken sleepers
and the roses curved inward.
Nothing was black or broken
and not a leaf fell
and the sun blared endless commercials
for summer holidays.

I sat on a gray stone bench
ringed with the ingenue faces
of pink and white impatiens
and placed my grief
in the mouth of language,
the only thing that would grieve with me.

(Mueller, 1996)

2. Use the structure of 'When I Am Asked' to draft your own narrative poem. Begin with a sentence starting with 'When …' (you can use or adapt one of the openings listed in this activity, or write your own). Then use that first line to generate the next few lines until you have your first stanza.

When I found out that …

When I first went to …

When I learned how to …

When I had my first …

When I heard the bass drum …

When I felt the red velvet …

When I tasted honeydew melon … .

Start your second stanza with a marker of time. Again, you can come up with your own first line for this stanza, or use or adapt one of these:

It was after the …

On the last day at …

Before I discovered my …

That summer holiday …

After the thaw … .

Begin your third and fourth stanzas with active verbs that have the protagonist – the speaker – doing something in a particular place (the 'setting'). At this stage of writing your poem, you will have a feel for what the speaker might do, especially if you can imagine them in a particular place and time. Examples of active verbs are:

I ran …

I sang …

I wrote …

I avoided …

I tore …

I asked …

I stood … .

Discussion

'When I Am Asked' has some of the characteristics that you will learn to recognise in narrative poems. It tells a story, there is a 'speaker' (the person who appears to be 'telling' it), and there's an incident or scene, which here is the June day when the protagonist sat on a bench and felt the weight of her grief. It also includes markers of time which, as you'll learn, help to orientate readers in a story. In this poem, they include 'when' and 'soon after my mother died'.

This activity, and the narrative poem you have drafted in response to it, shows how the structure of one poem you have read can feed into a new poem. Quite often, as you revise your work, your version will move very far away from the original. But even so, if you were ever to publish a poem that has been inspired by another, the convention is to write: *after [author] and '[title]'* under your own title in italics. For example:

My poem
after Lisel Mueller's 'When I Am Asked'

2.1 Robert Frost: using speech rhythms and dialogue

As with most other contemporary poems, contemporary narrative poems are usually written in **free verse** – a mode of poetry that does not use fixed or repeated **metre** or rhyme, but instead tends to follow the rhythm of how people normally speak. The American poet Robert Frost (1874–1963) has had a lot of influence on the contemporary narrative poem. Although he tended to write in **blank verse**, often using metrical lines of ten syllables, Frost's influence comes from how he made poems memorable by using the rhythms of natural speech and by giving characters dialogue. He often used a close-up focus on a scene where several people are present to tell the story of an incident. His poem '"Out, Out—"' (2016), which is about a boy's fatal encounter with a saw, was first published in 1916, just as young American men were called up to fight in the First World War. These two short extracts show how a narrative poem can incorporate characters and dialogue into a particular scene:

…

Doing a man's work, though a child at heart—
He saw all spoiled. "Don't let him cut my hand off—
The doctor, when he comes. Don't let him, sister!"
So. But the hand was gone already.

…

… They listened at his heart.
Little—less—nothing!—and that ended it.
No more to build on there. And they, since they
Were not the one dead, turned to their affairs.

(Frost, 2016, pp. 168–169)

At the end of '"Out, Out—"' (the last four lines shown here), the reaction of those present is quite matter-of-fact, which is in contrast to most readers' shocked reaction to the content. This poem is typical of Frost's work: it tells an apparently simple story and incorporates the reactions of other characters, while raising wider questions, which in this case may refer to how young boys are sent to slaughter by war.

3 Narrative encounters

A simple story, one that we all know, is where someone tells you about a meeting with another person. Often, these include an account of an incident, and the best have an engaging 'did you hear?' quality, which draws the reader or listener in. This idea, of an incident retold, is one way to begin thinking about how to write a narrative poem. In this kind of retelling, it is clear to a reader or audience that both the speaker and anyone else in the poem are characters, just as they are in fiction.

A short narrative poem that rests on an interaction or conversation between two people, and the **tension** this creates in the depicted scene, can manage to imply a larger story or even a whole history. Dialogue and the use of questions can help to move the action along within the poem. Choices about where to include stanza breaks or how to use white space on the printed page can add to the effects a poet wants to achieve.

Activity 2 Reading: conflict and tension in poems

Read the two poems 'In My Country' (1993) by Jackie Kay and 'Divorce' (2009) by Carrie Etter, which both tell a story.

- Where do you find conflict or tension between the characters in each poem?
- What do you notice about the use of questions in both poems?

> **Jackie Kay** is a fiction writer, poet and playwright. Born to a Scottish mother and Nigerian father, she was raised in Glasgow by adopted parents. Her work often explores questions of identity, and she is known for her lyrical storytelling.

Content note: Please be aware that this poem explores racist attitudes towards the speaker.

In My Country

> walking by the waters,
> down where an honest river
> shakes hands with the sea,
> a woman passed round me
> in a slow, watchful circle,
> as if I were a superstition;
>
> or the worst dregs of her imagination,
> so when she finally spoke
> her words spliced into bars
> of an old wheel. A segment of air.

> *Where do you come from?*
> 'Here,' I said, 'Here. These parts.'
>
> *(Kay, 1993)*

> **Carrie Etter** is a UK-based American poet and writer, essayist, editor and creative writing tutor whose first collection of poetry *The Tethers* was published in 2009. Her work often articulates trauma through linguistic innovation.

Divorce

> Forced to apologise
> for the dirty sheets, he looks
>
> proud in his shame.
> I left that bed years ago
>
> and have returned to collect
> a forgotten book, a favourite blanket.
>
> He knew the names of trees better
> than makes of cars, but neither well.
>
> He remembers which sister
> I like least and asks
>
> how she is doing.
>
> *(Etter, 2009)*

Discussion

In her poem 'In My Country', Kay uses the title as the first line of the story she is telling. So, the first line of the first stanza, 'walking by the waters', carries on from 'In my country', as part of the same sentence. This draws attention to the title being related to both the specific place being described (which may be near Glasgow, Kay's home city) and the wider context: that of the experience of a Black Scottish person who is wrongly assumed to not be from that place. The use of two stanzas also helps to add tension to this poem, as the white space between them tends to slow the reader down – it makes us really notice what comes after the space. The impact and harshness of 'the worst dregs of her imagination' in the first line of the second stanza is even more striking because of its placement.

In this poem, Kay seems to be contrasting the simplicity of the natural friendly encounter, where the river 'shakes hands with the sea', to the uneasy 'superstition' and racism of the woman the speaker encounters. The speaker's retort to the woman's question ('Where do you come from?') could not be simpler: 'These parts'. These final words of the poem bring the reader back to the possible meanings of the title. Who is allowed to say where they are from when that might be challenged? There's a sense that this question, 'Where do you come from?', has been asked of this speaker several times before, implying the wider societal problem of endemic racism.

Like 'In My Country', in Etter's poem, 'Divorce', there's immediately something out of kilter between the two characters: in the first two stanzas the 'he' feels 'forced to apologise' but manages to still look 'proud'. It's clear that the speaker is revisiting a place and feeling positive about having 'left that bed years ago', with the 'bed' also standing in, metaphorically, for the life. 'Divorce' captures two people in one moment but implies their whole life story. The tension between the characters leads the reader to wonder what will happen next. Because it is written in couplets of two lines until the final single line, the white space between the couplets has the effect of slowing down the reader, making us more likely to grasp the full significance of the poem.

'Divorce' includes the question that 'he' asks the speaker about the sister he knows is least liked, pretending (the reader assumes) to care how 'she is doing'. Etter may be having fun here, showing the questioner as rude, but also implying that the speaker has the upper hand in the end.

The poems you've considered in Activity 2 show how a tension-filled encounter can generate a poem; and also how a brief encounter can imply a larger context, whether that be a relationship, a life or a broader social situation. In the next activity, you will try out this approach for yourself.

Activity 3 Writing: a narrative encounter

1. Decide upon two characters for a poem. You could use the speaker of your Activity 1 poem as one of them or reuse two characters that you have created for activities in previous chapters of this book. Jot down some thoughts about the tensions between your characters. A quick way to focus in on this is to ask yourself what each character wants in life, and what they regret.

2. Now decide on a setting where the encounter between your two characters takes place. Thinking about an exact location means that you can visualise images of that setting. Write some notes for each character related to this setting, thinking about what they can see, hear, smell, taste or touch. This will help to generate concrete details about the poem's setting that make it feel real to a reader.

3. With your characters and setting in mind, begin **freewriting** around what you think the incident or encounter might be. Freewriting is a way of allowing your 'writing mind' to free-associate thoughts, feelings, words and phrases without, at this stage, pausing to revise. Feeling free to write anything can be satisfying and can generate surprising turns of phrase, which may end up in your poem – or in another poem you write in the future!

Think about what your characters would say about the incident. Do they wish it had happened differently? How would they retell it to a friend over coffee?

4. Draft a short poem, about 12 to 20 lines long, selecting ideas, words or phrases from the notes you have made for steps 1–3 of this activity.

Discussion

Once you have this (or any) poem in draft form, you may find that you have further thoughts about it as you carry on with your day. Keep a notebook handy to capture these thoughts. When you go back to revise your poem, consider whether using questions or stanzas, as in the work of Kay and Etter, might add to the reader's enjoyment of it. You might also think about whether your poem implies any larger story or context.

4 Time in narrative poems

Figure 2 Idoma Janus type dance headdress, *c.*1900, wood, Africa (present-day Nigeria). Tishman Collection, New York (photo: Werner Forman/akg-images). Janus, a god in ancient Roman beliefs, is often depicted with two heads, one looking towards the past and the other to the future. The way in which time is used in poems can give something of the same effect.

As discussed in Section 2, the ballads of the past often have a very clear shape of 'beginning, middle and end'. Many begin with the birth of the person, then they recount their deeds, and, finally, they give the story of their death. Contemporary narrative poems may still have this 'beginning, middle and end' shape, but the **narrative arc** they follow might not be as obvious. They often focus on a specific incident or sequence of happenings that is fixed in a particular timeframe. Or they may retell a memory from the past almost as if it's recurring in the present.

Activity 4 Reading: managing time and memory

Read 'Mid-Term Break' (1998) by Seamus Heaney, first published in 1966, and Sebastian Matthews' 2004 poem 'Buying Wine' (2007). As you read, consider how the poets deal with the stories they are telling. How is the passing of time shown in the poems: what words and phrases are used?

On your second reading, mark the verbs that use 'I' in the poems. What do you notice about the tense of these verbs?

> **Seamus Heaney** was a Northern Irish poet and playwright known for his poetry about rural life, Irish history and mythology, and the complexities of politics and conflict in Northern Ireland. His work often explores themes of identity and memory.

Content note: Please be aware that this poem mentions the death of a young sibling.

Mid-Term Break

I sat all morning in the college sick bay
Counting bells knelling classes to a close.
At two o'clock our neighbours drove me home.

In the porch I met my father crying—
He had always taken funerals in his stride—
And Big Jim Evans saying it was a hard blow.

The baby cooed and laughed and rocked the pram
When I came in, and I was embarrassed
By old men standing up to shake my hand

And tell me they were 'sorry for my trouble'.
Whispers informed strangers I was the eldest,
Away at school, as my mother held my hand

In hers and coughed out angry tearless sighs.
At ten o'clock the ambulance arrived
With the corpse, stanched and bandaged by the nurses.

Next morning I went up into the room. Snowdrops
And candles soothed the bedside; I saw him
For the first time in six weeks. Paler now,

Wearing a poppy bruise on his left temple,
He lay in the four-foot box as in his cot.
No gaudy scars, the bumper knocked him clear.

A four-foot box, a foot for every year.

(Heaney, 1998)

Sebastian Matthews is an American poet and memoirist, whose writing explores themes of family, identity and mental health.

Buying Wine

When we were boys, we had a choice: stay in the car or else
follow him into Wine Mart, that cavernous retail barn,

down aisle after aisle—California reds to Australian blends
to French dessert wines—past bins loaded like bat racks

with bottles, each with its own heraldic tag, its licked coat
of arms, trailing after our father as he pushed the ever-filling cart,

bent forward in concentration, one hand in mouth stroking
his unkempt mustache, the other lofting up bottles like fruit

then setting them down, weighing the store of data in his brain
against the cost, the year, the cut of meat he'd select at the butcher's:

a lamb chop, say, if this Umbrian red had enough body to marry,
to dance on its legs in the bell of the night; or some scallops maybe,

those languid hearts of the sea, a poet's dozen in a baggy,
and a pinot grigio light enough not to disturb their salty murmur.

Often, we'd stay in the car until we'd used up the radio
and our dwindling capacity to believe our father

might actually "Just be back," then break free, releasing
our seatbelts, drifting to the edges of the parking lot like horses

loosed in a field following the sun's endgame of shade; sometimes
I'd peer into the front window, breath fogging the sale signs,

catching snippets of my father's profile appearing and disappearing
behind the tall cardboard stacks. Once I slipped back into the store,

wandering the aisles, master of my own cart, loading it to bursting
for the dream party I was going to throw. But mostly, like now,

as I search for the perfect $12 bottle, I'd shuffle along, dancing bear
behind circus master, and wait for my father to pronounce, tall

in his basketball body, wine bottles like babies in his hands, "Aha!"

(Matthews, 2007)

Discussion

In 'Mid-Term Break', you probably noticed how, by mentioning time from one morning to the next, this poem reveals specific moments from when the news breaks, to when the brother's body is laid out. It begins with the idea of counting in the first stanza and ends, in the final stanza, with another measurement – that of the four-foot-long coffin for the boy who was four years of age. In between these, Heaney uses other exact notations of time: 'two o'clock', 'ten o'clock', 'six weeks'. When reading this poem as a writer, you might ask what these markers of time express or how they add meaning to the poem. One answer might be that the speaker is trying to hold on to some of the more innocent, normal ways in which he might have counted time until now (e.g. the inclusion of the image of the school bell), and that this contrasts with the trauma, disruption, and upending of time that he experiences on the death of a sibling.

On first reading, you might think (as I did) that the poem 'Buying Wine' is a story with a beginning, middle and end. It does have this shape but there may be more going on. Some words that relate to time in this poem include 'when', 'then', 'often', 'sometimes' and 'once'. These provide a scaffold for the incidents described. Matthews also brings this memory from the past up to date by using another marker of time: 'mostly, like now' (at the end of the twelfth stanza), which both implies that the son is still following the 'circus master' and, because of this metaphor, it also manages to convey that there may have been a change: that the father may, by now, be dead. Could Matthews be implying that the power of the incident described is that it remains in the memory and that it can viscerally 'feel' as if it is taking place again and again, every time someone reads the poem? Once you've had that thought, it's easy to see how the idea that the father 'might actually "Just be back"' (stanza 9) is metaphorically significant when paired alongside the notion of the 'sun's endgame of shade' (stanza 10) and the appearance and disappearance of the father's profile (stanza 11). All these examples add up to show how the poem relates to loss. Its use of memories, and the power of poetry to keep these memories alive, may be what we, as readers and writers, take away from it.

In 'Mid-Term Break', verbs that are related to the speaker are mainly used in the simple past tense: 'I sat', 'I met', 'I came in', 'I was embarrassed', 'I went up', 'I saw him'. The very simplicity, even starkness, of these statements draws attention to the quiet horror that the speaker feels. Heaney makes a clear choice to use simple, direct language and the result is more dramatic than if he had chosen overdone descriptions. Action verbs are our friends when writing poetry and you'll notice how they are used in different ways in the poems in this chapter.

Because most stories have a timeline to help the reader understand the sequence of events, you will often find time-related words in narrative poems. Contemporary poets have mostly moved away from using the format of older ballads, which tended to tell of someone's major deeds from birth to death, and instead embed issues related to time in more intriguing ways. As you have seen in this chapter, narrative poems can capture ongoing memory and the passing of time in many ways. For example, initially you might have thought that Matthews' 'Buying Wine' was a simple poem, but having worked through Activity 4, perhaps you now see it as an **elegy** of sorts? The following technical decisions taken by Matthews in the writing of the poem augment his use of time and memory:

- **Setting**: Matthews uses a very specific setting, the Wine Mart, which allows for exact and concrete details.
- **Character**: the poem is a deft character sketch of the father with some of his quirks underlined.
- **Tense**: it begins in the past tense, 'we had a choice', then uses several 'ing' endings to imply things that happened several times (e.g. 'trailing').
- **Structure and shape**: the poem is written mainly in couplets (many including lines of 14 syllables or more, making roughly similar line lengths). There's a stanza break after every couplet, so the white spaces slow down the reading, helping to emphasise the meditative quality of the poem. The final line stands out, as it is on its own as a single-line stanza.

In Activity 5, you will experiment with using words and phrases related to time to help scaffold your own poems.

Activity 5 Writing: using markers of time

1. Make some notes about specific incidents and the exact settings they took place in. These could relate to memories of a character you've created (perhaps one of the characters from Activity 3 in this chapter). Or you could adapt one of your own memories, but change the detail to suit the speaker or a character you will include in a poem. Then allow yourself to do some freewriting (inspired by the most interesting words you have noted down) to create lists of more words and phrases. Pick out one or two that seem most promising and add more phrases or single words to them that more fully describe the setting or why it might be important.

2. Draft a poem of between 12 and 20 lines that includes one of the memories you made notes about in step 1 of this activity. Use two or three of the following markers of time to help you initially structure your poem:

> When …
>
> Then …
>
> Always …
>
> Sometimes …
>
> Often …
>
> Never …
>
> Before …
>
> Now … .

As you draft your poem, think about whether you could use different tenses as Matthews does in 'Buying Wine' (which you read in Activity 4). Would using other markers of time, such as seasons, the time of day, or words like 'morning', 'afternoon' and 'evening', help to root the poem more in the physical reality – that is, the setting you are imagining or reimagining?

Discussion

Not all writing activities will suit every writer. You may have found the prescriptive directions of this one too 'mechanical' or, conversely, it might have sparked a poem that will warrant redrafting and revision into a finished state. Either way, when you have a workable draft in place, you can consider eliminating some of the markers of time you inserted at the start as your scaffolding. These kinds of words do draw attention to themselves, so you should always check whether they are working in your poem: for example, are they expressive (as in Heaney's 'Mid-Term Break') or do they help to keep the narrative moving along (as in Matthews' 'Buying Wine')?

In this section, you have read two narrative poems that demonstrate interesting ways of dealing with time, and you've drafted a poem that shows an awareness of this aspect of poetry. As you read and write more poetry, you will become more adept at noticing how other poets move the action along in their work. Whenever you read a poem, make it a habit to look for the technical decisions the poet has made and think about the effects they are trying to achieve. In the next section, you will take a look at the varying pronouns used in narrative poems and what the different options offer you as a writer.

5 Pronouns and point of view

When reading certain poems, it can feel as though you, the reader, are being addressed by the speaker of the poem – as if you are being invited in and spoken to directly. This feeling does not diminish even when you know that the speaker is not the poet themselves, but instead a 'character' made up by them (as is often the case). So, it seems that our shared humanity and our capacity for understanding, and even caring, extends to the experiences of characters in poetry, as long as those characters appear to us in their own, fully-imagined lives. In the same way, some of us are fascinated by and become sympathetic to the stories of characters in soap operas, TV dramas or films.

In terms of poetry written in the first person, while the speaker may in fact be the poet or a persona close to theirs, it's best (as you have seen in this chapter) to use the convention of calling them 'the speaker'. This acknowledges that a poem is a creative work, which is constructed by the poet, and it can also avoid the danger of the reader making assumptions about the poet from the text.

Activity 6 Reading: implying the 'I' and addressing the 'you'

Read the extract of the poem 'What I Do' (2006) by Roxane Beth Johnson, and Amy Gerstler's poem 'What I Did With Your Ashes' (2015). As you read, notice how the titles of these poems, 'What I Do' and 'What I Did With Your Ashes', set up a powerful narrative expectation.

- What do you notice about Johnson's use of verbs at the start of lines in this extract?
- What do you notice about Gerstler's use of 'you'?
- What **similes** and images are striking in these poems?
- How are line lengths or stanzas being used by these poets?

> **Roxane Beth Johnson** is a writer and poet born in Louisiana. Her writing explores themes of identity, family, and creative expression in contemporary America. Of African American and Italian heritage, Johnson has said that her literary influences include the poets Anne Sexton, Wallace Stevens and Rainer Maria Rilke.

Content note: Please be aware that this poem explores racist attitudes towards the speaker.

What I Do

Eat cereal. Read the back of the box over and over. Put on my red velvet jumper with white heart shaped buttons. Walk to the bus, pick up discarded cigarette butts and pretend to smoke.

Get on the bus. Girls yell, *Wire head, ugly black skin*. Take a window seat, under the radio speaker. Look for cats hunting in the fields.

Go to class. Stay in at recess. Steal chewing gum, plastic green monkeys and cookies from desks. Eat in bathroom stalls. Pure white light pours in.

Try to get a bloody nose by punching myself in the same bathroom after lunch.

The teacher passes around pictures of herself pregnant. *You were fat!* I yell. Everyone laughs. I lap it like licking honey from a spoon. *I was pregnant, what's your excuse?* Everyone laughs. I swallow stones.
…

(Johnson, 2006)

Amy Gerstler is an American poet and writer who has published numerous collections of poetry, non-fiction and fiction. She also writes art criticism and journalism, and collaborates with visual artists and musicians. Her work often employs wit to explore themes of love, loss and survival.

What I Did With Your Ashes

Shook the box like a maraca.

Stood around like a dope in my punch-colored dress, clutching your box to my chest.

Opened your plastic receptacle, the size of a jack-in-the-box. But instead of gaudy stripes, your box is sober-suit blue, hymnal blue.

Tasted them. You've gained a statue's flavor, like licking the pyramids, or kissing sandstone shoulders. I mean *boulders*.

Remarked to your box: "REINCARNATION comes from roots meaning 'to be made flesh again.'"

Stowed your box under my bed for a week to seed dreams in which you advise me. (This didn't work.)

Opened the Babylonian Talmud at random. Read aloud to your gritty, gray-white powder: "There are three keys which the Holy One, blessed be He, has not entrusted into the hands of any messenger. These are: the key of rain, the key of birth, and the key of the resurrection of the dead." Worked myself up to watery eyes. Any intensity evaporated the instant I stopped reading.

Tried to intuit your format, sift it from tides of void. Does shape play a role? My watch ticked in an exaggerated way. Closed my eyes, sent forth mental tendrils seeking the nothing of you. They curled back on themselves, weaving around the wing chair, a dog's leg, a lamp stand, eventually heading back toward the nothing of me.

(Gerstler, 2015)

Discussion

In Heaney's 'Mid-Term Break', which you read in Activity 4, verbs are used with the pronoun 'I' and the past tense. But in 'What I Do', Johnson drops the first-person pronoun, using 'Eat', 'Get', 'Go', and so on, at the start of new lines without 'I' before them. This has the effect of increasing the pace of the poem, as well as employing the present tense to cleverly imply habitual and repeated action, almost like a continuous present. This works subliminally on the reader, as it dawns on us that 'what I do' is more like 'what I do *daily*', or a litany of the kinds of happenings and experiences that the speaker has to repeatedly face. While Gerstler also leaves out the pronoun 'I' in the body of the poem, the speaker of 'What I Did With Your Ashes' is addressing someone deceased. This use of the implied 'you' is powerful as it can also be addressing the reader.

In 'What I Do', long lines are **enjambed** to bring the sense over to the next line, which increases the pace. This extract of the poem uses short stanzas, so there are plenty of reading pauses and these help the reader to keep up with the meaning. In 'What I Did With Your Ashes', a similar approach is used until the final two stanzas move into something that appears more prose-like, though the author chooses carefully where to break the lines. For instance, the 'be/He' break in the seventh stanza is memorable because of the rhyme and the capital letter 'H' in 'He'.

Beginning 'What I Did With Your Ashes' with short one- and two-line stanzas and then switching to longer 'poetic paragraphs' for the final two mirrors the speaker's increasing feelings of disintegration, which also moves the narrative along. In the final stanza, Gerstler hints that, here, structure mirrors content, saying: 'Does shape play a role?'

Similes (comparisons using the words 'like' or 'as') can have the same effect on a reader's emotions as imagery. They can help to bring a particular mood or tone to your writing. In 'What I Do', the simile 'like licking honey from a spoon' (stanza 5) feels positive to a reader but the retort from the teacher undermines that mood immediately. For a poet, writing a poem is not just about having a story to tell, it's also about deciding on how to shape that story to match your intent as a writer. Gerstler does this in 'What I Did With Your Ashes'. The images and similes she uses increase in power as they go: the maraca (stanza 1) is an image based on sound, while the 'punch-colored dress' (stanza 2) suggests the idea of being punch-drunk on grief as well as feeling punched by loss. But my favourite is 'like licking the pyramids' (stanza 4), as it speaks to the traumatic oddity of tasting someone's ashes.

In this chapter, you have seen how stories with conflict or tension, where there's a distinct setting and a clear timeline, can make compelling narrative poems. You have considered how using different lengths and patterns of stanzas to shape a poem can help the reader, and how writing devices, such as imagery, similes and varying pronouns, can all add to the overall effect of a poem. In Activity 7, you will write a narrative poem that puts what you have learned in this chapter into practice.

Activity 7 Writing: bringing it all together

You have two options to choose from for this writing activity. Either:

1. Draft a poem with the working title 'What I do in [add a place of your choice here]'. The place you choose can be a workplace, a leisure setting, a specific building or wherever you feel there are exact and physical details that can become important for your speaker.

Or:

2. Draft a poem with the working title 'When you [add a verb and a consequence]', for example: 'When you started to cook …' or 'When you threw away my ring …'.

Whichever option you choose for this activity, decide what mood you want to create in your narrative poem and try to get that across to the reader in your writing. In addition, include at least two similes (using 'like' or 'as') in your poem.

Once you have the bones of a draft, even if it's messy with notes all over it, begin to think about structure and line length, and consider whether you will try it in stanzas or not.

Discussion

When you are drafting a poem, it's important to read it to yourself, many times. This continual revisiting of the poem is a vital part of the process. It allows you to get to know your own work on a deeper level, and to discover which words and phrases really work, and which parts are more problematic. There are many ways of becoming familiar with your own poems. Poets often read their work-in-progress aloud, or perform it in some other way. If you prefer more tactile and visual methods, you might print your poem and highlight the areas which feel most true to your intent. You could also copy out more challenging lines onto a separate page, in order to work on them in isolation. Any and all of these activities will help you to move your draft poem on to its next, more finished revision.

Box 1 A note on drafting and revising poems

Revision literally means 'seeing again' (re-vision) and poets often revise ideas or a full draft after taking a break from it. That's why it's important to keep notes when you are working on a poem (whether in a notebook or somewhere else, like your phone). It's the half-ideas and random words and phrases in my notebook that, when revisited, can suddenly begin to shape up into more fully formed thoughts.

Trying out a line that you have noted down, in first one way, and then another, can sometimes spark a new idea that really clinches the piece you are working on. Conversely, sometimes you will return to a previous draft you have left alone for a while and, on re-engaging with it, realise that it did indeed work, and it *doesn't* need revision. This is why it's important to keep all your drafts!

Don't be alarmed if it takes weeks or even months of revising and redrafting for some poems to reach their final version. Many poets work on several poems at the same time, each at different stages of completion. It's during the redrafting process that you may begin to notice a relationship between the poems you are working on – perhaps you have the beginnings of a sequence of poems on your hands?

6 Conclusion

In this chapter, you have been introduced to different approaches to writing narrative poetry. You've learned about managing pace and time, and you've considered the effects of variations in pronouns and stanzas. You've read several contemporary examples of narrative poetry and drafted new work of your own that can feed into the next writing that you do.

Writers are always inventing, even if basing our work on real experience. But whether you decide to write your poems always in earnest, using 'I' to indicate you, the poet, or whether you invent a persona – a character – as the speaker of your poem, for whom you use 'I', readers may still assume that it is you, the poet, speaking. You can decide how you feel about that, but I have always taken it as something of a compliment as it implies that the world of the poem you've created has felt 'real' to a reader. You will read more about voices and voicing in writing in Chapter 14 of this book, which will complement your learning from this chapter.

The narrative poem is often considered a cousin of, and sometimes a direct sibling to, the **lyric poem**. In other chapters of this book, you will read poems that have a narrative but which are driven even more by rhythmic power or musicality. It's always worth remembering, though, that it is exact detail and well-chosen images that make a poem memorable – as you've seen in this chapter, narrative poems use the dynamic of story to help sustain that memorability.

Part 2 of this book (Chapters 5–9) focuses on dramatic writing. You will find that much of your learning from this chapter concerning character, tension and management of time will be valuable as you explore the possibilities of drama for your own writing.

References

'Barbara Allen' (no date). Available at: https://www.poetryfoundation.org/poems/50273/barbara-allen (Accessed: 27 February 2024).

Etter, C. (2009) 'Divorce', in C. Etter, *The tethers*. Bridgend: Seren Books, p. 12.

Frost, R. (2016) '"Out, out—"', in R. Frost, *The collected poems of Robert Frost*. New York: Quarto Publishing, pp. 168–169.

Gerstler, A. (2015) 'What I did with your ashes', in A. Gerstler, *Scattered at sea*. New York: Penguin Books, p. 53.

Heaney, S. (1998) 'Mid-term break', in S. Heaney, *Opened ground: poems 1966–1996*. London: Faber and Faber, p. 12.

Homer (2014) *The Odyssey*. Translated from the Greek by B.P. Powell. Oxford: Oxford University Press.

Homer (2015) *The Iliad*. Translated from the Greek by P. Green. Oakland: University of California Press.

Johnson, R.B. (2006) 'What I do', in R.B. Johnson, *Jubilee*. Tallahassee, FL: Anhinga Press, pp. 41–42.

Kay, J. (1993) 'In my country', in J. Kay, *Other lovers*. Hexham: Bloodaxe Books, p. 24.

Davies, S. (ed.) (2007) *Mabinogion: translated with an introduction and notes*. Oxford: Oxford University Press.

Matthews, S. (2007) 'Buying wine', in S. Matthews, *We generous: poems*. Pasadena, CA: Red Hen Press, pp. 98–99.

Mueller, L. (1996) 'When I am asked', in L. Mueller, *Alive together: new and selected poems*. Louisiana: Louisiana State University Press, p. 198.

Poe, E.A. (2012) 'The raven', in E.A. Poe, *The raven and other favourite poems*. New York: Dover Thrift Editions, p. 28.

Rossetti, C. (2010) 'Goblin market', in C. Rossetti, *Goblin market*. Illustrated by A. Rackham. Mineola, NY: Dover Publications.

Part 2
Dramatic writing

Chapter 5
Dramatic stories

Dónall Mac Cathmhaoill

1 Introduction

Good storytelling provides the reader, listener or spectator with a series of incidents where characters experience conflicts, unexpected developments and surprises. These are the characteristics of all dramatic writing and are essential when writing scripts for stage, screen and audio drama (including radio plays and podcasts). This chapter introduces the fundamental concepts used in writing for such dramatic media. These concepts can be put to good use in whatever writing you do, including that for other forms, such as fiction, life writing and narrative poetry.

In 1968, the director Peter Brook wrote of the possibilities of drama: 'I can take any empty space and call it a bare stage. A man walks across this empty space whilst someone else is watching him, and this is all that is needed for an act of theatre to be engaged' (Brook, 1996, p. 7). This quotation gives rise to the central principle of dramatic writing: anything *can* happen, and something *must* happen. For an audience to be engaged, you need only have characters, action, and interaction, which normally takes the form of dialogue between characters.

In this chapter, you will learn how to create credible and engaging characters, and look at ways to construct an engaging narrative using the basic dramatic elements of dramatic action and dialogue. You will also learn how to format scripts for the stage. In Chapters 7 and 8, you will see how other drama scripts, those for audio dramas and screen dramas (**screenplays**), are formatted.

2 Character

As humans, we revel in watching other humans perform. And while some dramas have very little action and some have little or no dialogue, all have characters. Strong, engaging characters are essential for drama, and character is perhaps the most important single aspect of any dramatic writing, whether for a stage play, film, TV series, podcast or any other media. An audience might enjoy a script where not much happens as long as it has strong characterisations, with lots of contrasts and complexities, but they will certainly lose interest in a work where characterisation is weak or not credible, or lacking depth and complexity.

Characters are one of the principal ways through which audiences experience and identify with the events of a drama. This will depend, to a large extent, on the attributes of the characters – are they kind, lazy, thoughtful, selfish, ambitious, curious, weak-willed or self-deluding? The range of possible character attributes is enormous. Audiences will respond in a powerful, personal way to well-written characters: depending on the attributes of characters, audience members may empathise with them, experience a sense of recognition, or feel affection, repulsion or amusement towards them. These provoked responses make the audience engage with and feel invested in the drama, so they want to see it through to its conclusion.

Activity 1 Writing: character attributes

1. Imagine a character: someone in a doctor's waiting room or on a train. Write a couple of simple biographical details for your character, such as their age and where they are from.

2. Now write a list of five to ten character traits for them, noting two or three words for each. Focus on personal attributes, such as temperament or sociability, rather than physical details such as appearance. Be sure to include positive and negative attributes, as all people possess a mix of both.

3. Write four lines of description for your character, giving them a name and describing some biographical details (age, job, relationship status, and so on) that fit with the personal attributes you have noted.

Discussion

This identification of a few character traits and biographical details is a starting point for creating dramatic characters. The realistic mixture of strengths and flaws is important in terms of making characters identifiable for audiences. Importantly, your characters will change and develop, and other aspects of them may be revealed through the writing of your script.

In most fictional writing, including scripts for plays, there is a central character (or characters) whose story we follow. As readers or as members of an audience, we get to know the characters' personal qualities as the drama unfolds, through their actions, words and interactions with other characters. Sometimes we see aspects of ourselves, or of people we know, in them. As the story develops, we find that we care about them and, therefore, about what happens in the drama. It is this audience engagement that a writer seeks when creating fictional characters.

2.1 Creating characters

Figure 1 A selection of characters.

Strong characters are also essential for creating an engaging narrative: it is the differences between characters and their respective wants and objectives that lead to **conflict**. Dramatic conflict can be defined as what happens when characters' wants are thwarted or opposed by others. If a drama has strong characters, and the characters have contrasting wants and needs, conflict will arise naturally and the drama will be interesting to watch.

Some dramas centre on an intriguing, sympathetic or singular individual in a situation where they are likely to encounter enormous challenges. This is the case with films derived from comic book characters, such as those produced by Marvel Studios. However, many dramas do not depend on the presence of uncommonly gifted, brave or heroic protagonists. They are instead written about 'ordinary' people. The characters have flaws, quirks and idiosyncrasies, and when dealing with obstacles and conflicts, they make the types of choices (and mistakes) that real people make. They are like you and me, and we can relate to their difficulties and dilemmas as they encounter and deal with conflicts. That is what makes these dramas successful. In the best dramas, the characters are also complex and unique, full of individual qualities. So, engaging characters are both easy to identify with *and* uniquely of interest. Activity 2 considers some unique and relatable characters.

Activity 2 Reading and writing: relatable and unique characters

1. Read the extract from the screenplay of the 2006 film *Little Miss Sunshine* (Reading 5.1 in Part 4), which was written by Michael Arndt (2007) and directed by Jonathan Dayton and Valerie Faris.

The **scene** shows the Hoovers, an ordinary American family, having dinner. There can be few more everyday situations. The scene introduces us to all the lead characters in the drama – family dinner scenes are excellent for this. Once you have read the script extract, consider what you have found out from the scene about each of the family members.

- What makes each character 'ordinary'?
- What makes them distinctive?

2. Write these features and observations about each character in a list with two columns titled 'Ordinary' and 'Distinctive'.

Discussion

You may have noticed that the scene you read in Reading 5.1 is effective because all the family members are credible and 'real', as well as uniquely different. They have enough about them that is typical of their age and social background, making it easy for audience members to identify with them – they will know someone like that, or perhaps even think a character is like them in certain ways. But these characters also have qualities that are unique to themselves and it is these individual attributes that make them intriguing. This means that an audience is able to experience their problems and conflicts with a mix of identification of the 'ordinary' *and* curiosity about the 'distinctive' (see Table 1).

Table 1 Some attributes of the characters in *Little Miss Sunshine* (Arndt, 2007, pp. 12–16) that make them 'ordinary' or 'distinctive'

Character	'Ordinary'	'Distinctive'
Sheryl	Sheryl is a suburban housewife and mother.	Sheryl holds down a job, runs the family home, looks after her ill brother and supports her husband's career, all with grit and good humour. While the others are concerned with their own issues, Sheryl is concerned with everyone's problems.
Frank	Frank, Sheryl's brother, is staying with the family. He is a literature academic.	Frank is staying with the family because he has recently attempted to take his own life after a disastrous and ill-advised affair with a student.
Richard	Sheryl's husband, Richard, is a devoted father and loving husband.	Richard is attempting to build a career as a life coach, which is making him self-righteous, opinionated and hard to tolerate in family situations.
Grandpa	Richard's dad, Edwin, is a retired widower who lives with the family.	Edwin is living with the family because he has been kicked out of his care home for taking heroin.
Dwayne	Dwayne, the elder of the Hoover children, is a teenage goth.	Dwayne is reading Nietzsche, which has made him nihilistic, and he has taken a vow of silence. He communicates in written notes, if at all.
Olive	Olive, the endearing youngest in the family, is chirpy, innocent and good-natured.	Olive is a competitor in beauty queen contests for young children.

This scene (Reading 5.1) shows the audience brief glimpses of the attributes of each of the principal characters, and sketches in important **backstory**. It sets up the stories that will be played out in the remainder of the script. It also establishes the wants and needs of the characters – the things that will inform their stories across the entire narrative. How these character wants and needs evolve, and the success of the characters in attaining their goals will form the heart of this family story. These character stories are explored further in Chapter 8.

Good characterisation is an important first step in creating a script for any medium. And it is important to remember that inspirations for characters are all around: as a writer, you can create or 'build' them from aspects of people you know, or those you have read about or imagined.

You will want to design your characters so that their attributes serve the story you are writing. This might mean giving them attributes that will bring them into conflict with other characters, or that will require them to change as the story develops. For example, a controlled and serious character might find themselves in conflict with a free-spirited character. As the writer, you are in control of these decisions and can craft your characters to suit the needs of the writing. Inevitably, many important decisions about characters will be made as they evolve during the writing of the drama. The process of writing is what brings them to life. One of the great pleasures of writing drama is having the beginnings of a character – a few qualities or attributes that serve your script – and then imagining the rest, and seeing how that character grows and changes, as the story progresses.

Activity 3 Writing: creating characters from observation

Sit in a park or a public space, a café or a canteen and observe the scene in front of you until an individual catches your eye. Alternatively, choose one of the fictional characters shown in Figure 1 at the start of this section. Once you have identified a character who interests you, use your imagination to answer the simple questions shown in Box 1 (making up the details about them). You may want to consider some of the personal attributes you identified for a character in Activity 1 of this chapter.

Discussion

In all forms of writing – whether for dramatic performance, narrative forms such as the novel, or non-fiction including life writing – creating an engaging character can provoke the interest and investment of the reader or audience. They will identify with characters who are relatable, and characters who have unique qualities will provide intriguing possibilities in terms of plot. Your characters' wants and needs will profoundly affect how the story develops: determining what characters want will put them on track to conflicts with other characters who have opposing or contrasting wants. Identifying a character's deeper needs will point the way towards the resolution of the drama.

It is always useful to conduct exercises to interrogate these aspects of character (Box 1). Doing so will provide you with character information that is useful for developing the dramatic storyline of your work. However, much of the character material you develop in this way won't become explicit in the script: many of the inner attributes of a character – such as their strengths and weaknesses, dreams and fears – won't be described or discussed, but will be revealed in their actions. However, it is important that, as the writer, you know these details, to be able to weave them into the dramatic material (rather than making them obvious).

> **Box 1 Creating characters using observation and imagination**
>
> **Biographical details**
>
> What is the character's approximate age? Are they married, single, partnered or widowed? And, if they are single, were they always single? Do they have close family? Who are their family relationships with?
>
> **Background**
>
> What is their social background? What is their educational background? (i.e. Have they finished school? If so, did they go to college or university? Or did they go through vocational training?) What is their income level and how do they earn their income? What are their hobbies and interests?
>
> **Dreams**
>
> What is their ultimate life goal – their dream? What do they most want? What do they most need? What is in conflict with this? What qualities can they rely on to achieve their goals?
>
> **Strengths**
>
> What are their special skills and strengths? What inner strength and abilities can they draw on in times of need? What support do they have within their circle of friends and family members?
>
> **Weaknesses**
>
> What are their main fears and doubts? In which areas do they lack confidence? What prevents them from achieving their ultimate life goal or dream? What is their greatest nightmare or fear?

2.2 Character differences and conflict

As you read in Section 2.1, character and conflict are intertwined in drama. Characters generate conflict, which is the source of action, and action creates a dramatic story or narrative. Therefore, thinking about possible differences that may lead to conflict with others is important for writing credible, well-rounded characters. As you've seen, such differences can be characters' opposing wants and goals, but differences in things like their social backgrounds, class, status, values and beliefs can lead to additional types of conflict and add complexity and credibility to characterisations. For example, in the scene you read from *Little Miss Sunshine* (Arndt, 2007) for Activity 2, all the characters have different wants. Frank wants to find out why Dwayne is staying silent, but of course Dwayne refuses to speak. At the same time, Olive wants to know why Frank has bandaged hands. Frank wants to tell her, but Richard doesn't want him to. In fact, Richard tries to control everyone's behaviour in some way. And Sheryl wants Richard to be less controlling.

Figure 2 Toni Collette as Sheryl in *Little Miss Sunshine*, directed by Jonathan Dayton and Valerie Faris, Big Beach Films, 2006 (photo: 20th Century Fox/Fox Searchlight/Kobal/Shutterstock).

Activity 4 Writing: developing character difference

Look back over the character you created in Activity 3.

1. What attributes do they have that might make them come into conflict with others? Make notes about these. This will enable you to develop an outline of the kind of person (your second character) who might have different wants and characteristics to your first character.

2. How might your first character's attributes, including their strengths, flaws and other characteristics – such as social class and status, values and beliefs – lead them into conflict, specifically with your second character? List three or four areas that are likely to cause conflict between them.

You now have additional ideas for the development of a second character. Make notes about this second character, using the same process you used in Activity 1.

Discussion

Creating characters who have different wants, needs, values and beliefs naturally establishes the conditions for conflict. This is also true when characters feel positively about one another. In the play *Blink* (2012), the writer Phil Porter creates two characters, Jonah and Sophie, who have much in common, including the recent loss of a parent. However, they come from very different social backgrounds. Jonah has escaped from a religious cult on a remote farm after the death of his mother, while Sophie has been brought up in genteel, middle-class comfort in a London suburb and has been left the family home by her father. Ultimately, the differences between them lead to conflict in their relationship. This mixture of similarities and differences, leading to identification and to conflict, is common in relationship dramas.

3 Action and dialogue

The conflicts that emerge from character differences form the foundations of the narrative of a script. Dramatic writing for any medium offers an exciting way to tell stories by letting an audience witness these conflicts, allowing them to directly experience the incidents, choices and outcomes – the events – that make up the story. It allows the reader, listener or spectator to experience the events of the story as they happen to the characters. Together, these incidents are known as **dramatic action**.

Character also lies at the heart of the **dialogue** used in a script. Each character should have their own way of speaking: it is the job of the writer to give them unique and distinctive voices that reflect their personalities. Dialogue also moves the dramatic action forward and shows us how characters respond to the action. Together, action and dialogue make up almost the entirety of any script for dramatic performance, and getting the balance right between these elements lies at the heart of writing a successful script.

3.1 Dramatic action

Drama theorist Manfred Pfister describes dramatic action as 'the existing situation, the attempt to change it and the new situation' (Pfister, 1988, p. 199). This formulation describes the 'arc' of dramatic action: the way the events of the story are arranged to provide the audience member with the greatest possible interest, engagement and intrigue from one situation to the next. In this section, you will learn about the essential elements of action in drama, and how this encompasses description, physical action and dramatic action.

Activity 5 Reading and writing: directions and descriptions

1. Read the script extract from *Summer Rolls* (2019) by Tuyền Đỗ (Reading 5.2).

The opening scenes of this stage play set up the story of a family that flees Vietnam at the end of the Vietnam War to come to England. You will notice that the script has a mixture of descriptions of the scene, directions for actions undertaken by the actors, and words to be spoken by them as dialogue.

2. Now write your own opening description for a scene in which a parent gives instruction to a child. Write a few lines to describe the scene briefly. Include the setting, time of day, the weather, and any other details that are essential to the atmosphere of the scene. You should also include details of the characters who are in the scene. This should be no more than five lines in total and should not include any character dialogue.

Discussion

Most of the information required to stage a scene is set out at the start, in the opening lines that describe the setting of the action. These descriptions are known as 'directions' in screenplays and audio dramas, and 'stage directions' in stage plays. They encompass both descriptions of the scene and directions for action.

These directions or stage directions should describe location, time of day, and anything that is important to the action and atmosphere of the setting. You should, however, avoid excessive detail. In general, only include details that are essential for setting up the scene. Remember that you are the writer and so are responsible for creating the action and dialogue. It is a up to the director, along with the designers, to decide many of the details concerning how the drama looks and sounds to an audience.

Writing directions to describe scene settings and action is a skill that requires practice – and rewriting. Everything that is essential to understanding the action of the story must be included. Directions must set the scene, tell us who is present, describe the physical actions of the characters and create atmosphere. But all of this must be achieved with economy: directions and descriptions must not be overlong. They should create a space for the actors, the director and designers to interpret and create their vision of the scene, and for the audience to use their imagination when viewing or listening to it.

All the events that take place in a scene – the physical actions and incidents, lighting and sound effects, character interactions, and the dialogue – together make up the dramatic action of the script, which will drive the story forward. These are all important elements that you can use in your writing to develop a dramatic narrative. In the majority of plays, a large part of the work of developing the narrative is done by the dialogue.

3.2 Dialogue

Almost all scripts include dialogue and it serves many important purposes. Firstly, it gives the audience a sense of the characters interacting. It is from these interactions that conflicts, alliances, loyalties and betrayals arise. Dialogue makes these interactions happen before our eyes and makes them feel real. However, good dialogue does much more than this. It also develops the story, and it tells the audience key information about characters, giving insights into their opinions and feelings. Importantly, this insight is often revealed through a contrast with the dramatic action: characters seldom say how they really feel. They conceal their thoughts, they tell lies, they make light of serious things and deflect attention. In this way, dialogue exposes thoughts and feelings that are in contrast with the things we see in the actions of the characters.

There are so many ways that dialogue can be revealing for the audience, and every line of dialogue in a script should be doing something, whether that's progressing story, giving character detail, revealing social and personal background – or often doing all of these things at once. Every line should earn its place. If your characters are talking but the audience is not learning something new, they will quickly become bored!

Idiom

As a writer, it is important that you think about *how* your characters speak, as well as *what* they say. Just as our own accents, choice of language and ways of phrasing reveal something about our characters and backgrounds, the elements of dialogue in a script can give an audience important information about the characters in the story, including their:

- social class
- age
- background
- education level
- nationality.

Some writers create characters who speak in a certain idiom or **dialect** – a variety of language usage which is peculiar to a limited district, ethnic group, class of people or section of society. The dialect of such characters is stylised in a script by focusing on certain aspects of the language those characters might use. British playwright Tanika Gupta often writes with an alert ear for the ways in which different groups in society use language. You will explore this further in Activity 6.

Activity 6 Reading and writing: how characters speak

1. Read the extract from the 2002 play *Sanctuary* by Tanika Gupta (Reading 5.3).

Try to identify the elements in the dialogue in Reading 5.3 that typify the way that the various characters speak.

2. Now write a few lines for the character you created for Activity 3, in which they describe another character (perhaps their sibling or a parent). What are the ways of speaking that are specific to them?

Discussion

In *Sanctuary* (2002), Gupta includes a range of different voices and idioms:

- Caribbean English for the character of Sebastian
- middle-class English in the case of the vicar, Jenny
- Asian English as spoken by Kabir
- African English for the character of Michael.

Sometimes it is necessary to instruct an actor that a character should speak with a certain accent – a London or an American accent, for example. You can see in Reading 5.3 that Gupta does this, including an instruction in the script for the actor playing Michael (at the start of the first line of his dialogue) to say his lines using an 'African accent'. Such voices are useful to the dramatist because they help create instantly recognisable characters. Yet the danger here is that you can inadvertently perpetuate negative stereotypes based on class or ethnic background. As a writer you must always be alert to how you present characters from all backgrounds, to ensure that you do not resort to stereotype.

Individual voice

Of more importance than idiom is a character's idiosyncratic speech patterns, the form of expression and use of language peculiar to an individual. This is sometimes referred to as a character's **idiolect**. The way a character speaks is often what makes them distinctive, as their use of language allows individual qualities to be portrayed, such as their social background, personality, values, and ways of thinking. Therefore, a specific character's dialogue should always be consistent (even if that means it is not always grammatically correct), reflecting their individuality. In your writing, remember to check whether:

- the lines of dialogue can be spoken (or whether they are too 'written')
- the lines of dialogue are too grammatically correct, or whether they follow the grammar of the character as they should
- there is a clear enough difference between the voices in the dialogue
- the idiom or dialect for each character is clearly established in the lines of dialogue and in bracketed instructions
- the voices of your main characters are those of individuals.

As with everything in dramatic writing, the use of idiom, accent, and identifiers of class, gender, ethnicity and other characteristics, should be in the service of the script and help to develop the dramatic action.

4 Conflict

As you have seen in this chapter, the opening pages of a script such as *Summer Rolls* (Đỗ, 2019) will usually establish the location of the drama, and introduce the characters. Often the characters will be in a situation that naturally generates conflict. For example:

- a person might be in an unhappy marriage with a partner who takes them for granted
- a country might be suffering under a cruel and despotic government
- a mother might be desperate to protect her child from the horrors of a war.

This will cause characters to take action of some sort – they will desire something that challenges the prevailing situation. For example:

- an unhappily married person may decide to start an extramarital affair
- a citizen may decide to join a group opposed to a despotic government
- the parent of a struggling family might decide to send their child overseas alone, to a safer country, as in *Summer Rolls* (see Activity 5 and Reading 5.2).

These decisions to take action and make a change invariably bring the characters into conflict with forces that are opposed to their desires, and it is from these developing conflicts that the story progresses and the drama emerges.

4.1 Initiating conflict

The moment when your characters face the prospect of change, or they decide to initiate change, is when the first conflicts begin. This often takes place in the first few pages of a script. It moves us from the opening situation to the heart of the drama and is often called the **inciting incident**. Something will happen to your central character or characters that 'incites' the dramatic action. It will cause them to make choices, which will generate further obstacles and conflicts, and this sets the story in train.

The cycle of obstacles, conflicts, choices and actions constitutes the basic internal structure of dramatic action. You will find it helpful to apply this in your writing: a situation presents a difficulty or obstacle; this creates conflict; a character must then make a choice, which results in an outcome; the outcome creates further conflict, and so on until the end of the drama. This basic structure of dramatic action is repeated many times in a script, as represented in Figure 3.

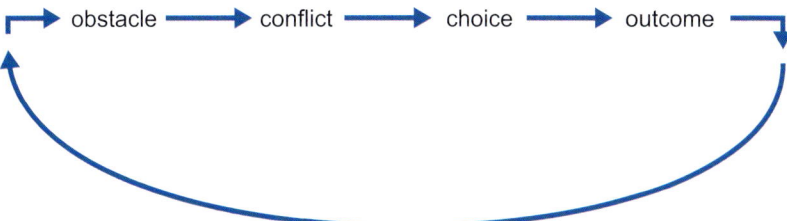

Figure 3 The cycle of obstacles, conflicts and choices.

Each character in a story will pursue their own wants and needs, and make the choices that they think will best suit them. Thus, in every scene of a script, characters will be confronted with (often difficult) choices. They will make decisions that result in either good or bad outcomes. They may even choose not to act, which is also a decision with outcomes. It is up to you, as a writer, to decide how the conflict develops and how the cycles of conflict come to an end.

4.2 Interpersonal and inner conflicts

It is important to note that conflict can come from many sources, including a character's interactions with those in their inner circle – those who are close to them – or even from aspects of the character's own nature, creating internal conflicts. For example, in the TV drama series *The Sopranos* (1999–2007) which is about the family of gang boss Tony Soprano, Tony's mother Livia is clearly part of the family, but she is an oppressive figure whose influence is entirely antagonistic. She undermines Tony at every opportunity, continually causing conflict. Similarly, in Shakespeare's *Hamlet* (2002), written around the end of the sixteenth century, the titular character spends much of the play debating with himself the best way to exact revenge on his uncle, Claudius, who poisoned his father, the king. Hamlet's internal conflicts about whether, and how, to enact his revenge show his struggles with self-doubt. And in the scene from *Summer Rolls* (Đỗ, 2019) that you read earlier in this chapter (Reading 5.2), the mother clearly wants her son to escape on the boat, fearing for his life. However, the son does not want to leave. This sets them against one another – their goals are in conflict.

So, conflict can exist on many levels. Characters can find that they are battling an external enemy (a villain or antagonist), opposition within their own immediate circle, or even aspects of their own inner nature (fear, indecisiveness, self-doubt). Often, a character will face opposition on more than one of these levels! The drama in a script flows from the challenges that these inner and outer conflicts create for the main characters. Conflict on multiple levels makes for dramas that are layered and complex.

5 Layout: formatting a stage script

Different dramatic media have different conventions regarding the layout of a script on the page. In Chapters 7 and 8, you will examine layouts for audio drama scripts and screenplays for films, respectively. In this chapter, Figure 4 shows some of the features of the standard layout for a stage script. This standard stage play format is a good model to use when writing your own scripts; you should refer back to it as a guide for layout and formatting. However, you may encounter plays with slight differences in formatting. This is particularly the case with published scripts where the requirements of a book's design might necessitate changes to the standard layout. Note also that some theatre companies and producers may have specific requirements for script presentation; always be sure to check what these are before writing and submitting any script for consideration.

Looking at Figure 4, you can see at once that there is a clear differentiation between the spoken and the unspoken elements, indicated by generous spacing between sections of the script. This is because the actors need to be able to see their lines immediately, and to be able to identify any relevant stage directions at a glance. There is a clean, continuing margin between the names of the speakers and their dialogue.

It is important to use an appropriate layout when submitting a script you have written for consideration. The appearance of the script is the first impression that agents, directors and producers will have of the work. If a script is not laid out appropriately for its given medium, it is liable to remain unread.

Timing a script is notoriously difficult, so using the correct script layout will also enable you to assess the play's running time. The best way to do this is to read the script through in real time so that you have an accurate assessment of the time it takes to read all the lines of the dialogue at the intended pace, including all the scripted actions and pauses. Set a timer and read the script out loud, pausing where there are actions, replicating the pacing of the scene as best you can. Make a note of the timings. If you want a more accurate timing, repeat the process more than once and then note the average running time.

5 Layout: formatting a stage script

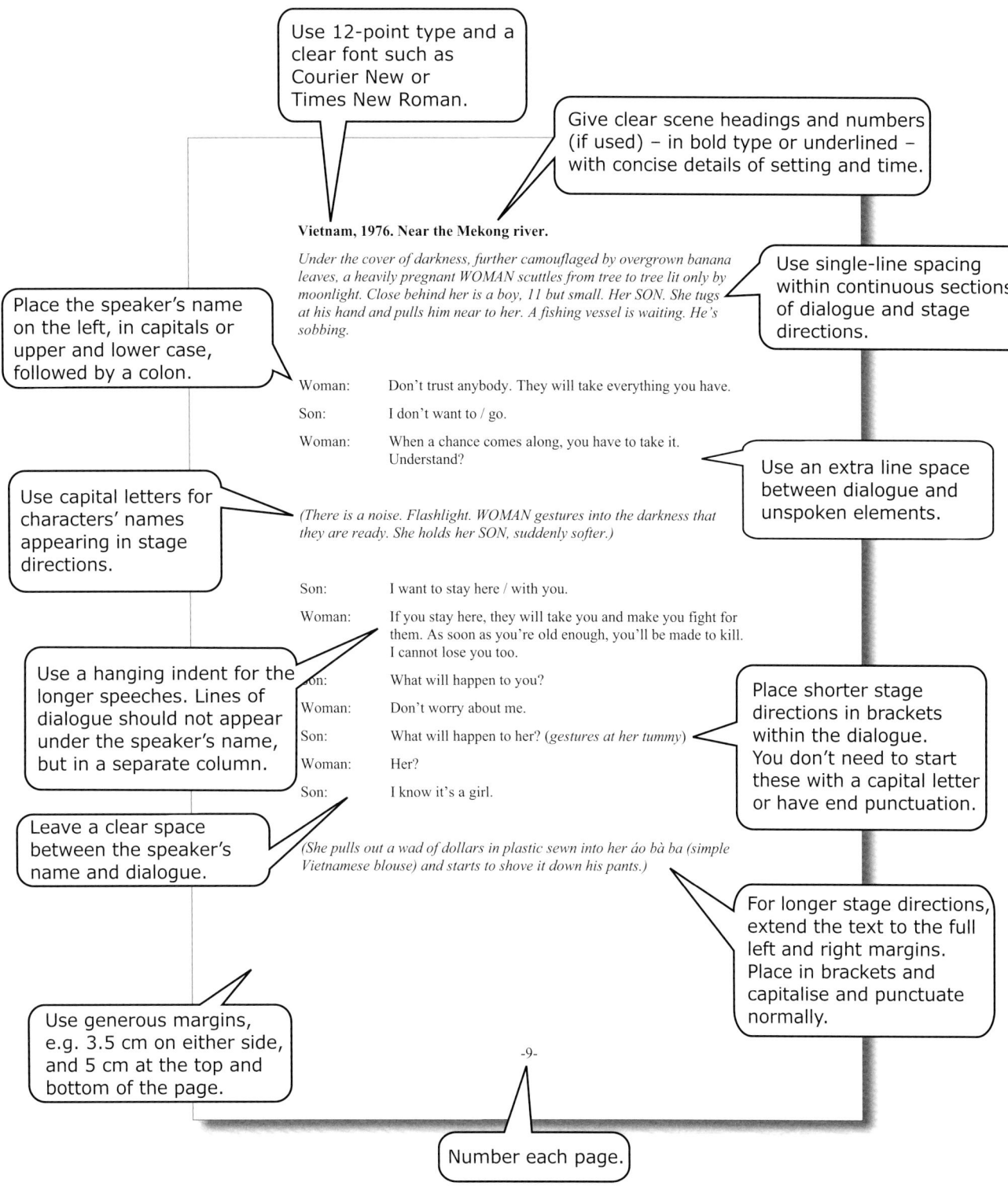

Figure 4 Page 9 of *Summer Rolls* (Đỗ, 2019) with annotations highlighting features of a stage script.

6 Conclusion

By developing characters who are relatable and unique, writers can create a world where conflict emerges and action develops organically, making for compelling stories that will engage audiences, lead them to identify with the characters, and become emotionally involved in their conflicts.

Script specialist Martha Alderson writes: 'The establishment of the first goal at the beginning of the story launches the dramatic action plot. … Dramatic action causes the protagonist to react, which, in turn, forms her first stated or overt goal' (Alderson, 2011, p. 77).

Without strong characters, scripts will lack drama and their stories are unlikely to engage audiences. A well-crafted character faced with a situation that requires a response will take action that other characters will oppose, provoking conflict, and dramatic stories will result. As Peter Brook points out in the quotation at the start of this chapter, all that is needed to make dramatic writing is a location, some characters in that location, and (inter)action. Once your characters make decisions, they will likely come into conflict with other characters and then the drama begins.

References

Alderson, M. (2011) *The plot whisperer: secrets of story structure any writer can master*. Avon, MA: Adams Media.

Arndt, M. (2007) *Little Miss Sunshine: the shooting script*. [Screenplay and notes]. New York, NY: Newmarket Press.

Brook, P. (1996) *The empty space: a book about the theatre: deadly, holy, rough, immediate*. New York, NY: Simon and Schuster.

Đỗ, T. (2019) *Summer rolls*. London: Bloomsbury Publishing.

Gupta, T. (2002) *Sanctuary*. London: Bloomsbury Publishing.

Little Miss Sunshine (2006) Directed by J. Dayton and V. Faris. [Feature film]. Los Angeles, CA: Fox Searchlight Pictures.

Pfister, M. (1988) *The theory and analysis of drama*. Cambridge: Cambridge University Press.

Porter, P. (2012) *Blink*. London: Oberon Books.

Shakespeare, W. (2002) *Hamlet*. London: Penguin Classics.

The Sopranos (1999–2007) [DVD]. Burbank, CA: Warner Home Video.

Chapter 6
Story and image

Dónall Mac Cathmhaoill

1 Introduction

Figure 1 Gary Oldman as George Smiley in *Tinker Tailor Soldier Spy*, directed by Tomas Alfredson, Working Title Films, 2011 (photo: Moviestore/Shutterstock).

Writing drama – and indeed writing in any form, for any medium – is in large measure about writing strong visual images. Novelists, poets, life writers, playwrights, screenwriters and writers of audio content all use words to create images in the mind of the reader, spectator or listener, allowing them to conjure up imaginary worlds.

This chapter is concerned with how stories are told through such images in stage and screen drama (which includes film, TV and streamed online content), and how they can be used to enrich the experience of the spectator. When you write a script for a stage play, these visual images are created live and in front of the audience. With screen drama, the images are usually created in advance and then projected, streamed or broadcast. In both cases, strong images that engage the spectator are vitally important. (Creating images in audio drama writing is somewhat different; this is considered in Chapter 7 of this book).

2 Telling stories with pictures

Imagery and 'word-pictures' form an important part of any creative writing, but for writers of stage or screen drama learning how to use imagery effectively in order to conjure these pictures in the minds of audiences is a key skill, which is essential for success. Drama writers use images to serve two main functions: to advance the story (visual storytelling) and to convey **genre**, mood, tone and theme (visual imagery). Therefore, specifying the images that the audience members will see is an integral part of any script.

Section 2.1 looks at how images are used to advance the story of a script for dramatic performance. Later in this chapter, Section 3 explores the ways in which design can be used to establish the imagery of a drama.

2.1 Action and image

A screen drama in which all the characters sit around and talk, and the camera does not move or reveal anything of visual interest, will be a very boring experience for the spectator. Screenwriters have almost unlimited opportunities to create worlds using pictures. They can specify any setting in the known world, and indeed any setting in unknown or non-existent worlds: downtown Mumbai in the 1988 film *Salaam Bombay!*; the planet Sirius 6B in the science fiction film *Screamers* (1995); a secondary school in east London in *To Sir, With Love* (1967); or a fantasy world of fauns and monsters in post-Civil War Spain, the setting for the 2006 film *Pan's Labyrinth*. The possibilities are limited only by the writer's imagination and (if the script gets commissioned) the budget available for its production.

It is also true that a stage play where the characters just sit and talk will likewise miss out on opportunities to engage the audience, and may provide them with a very static and uneventful experience. In all dramatic genres, for all media, the key is **showing** as much of the dramatic action as possible through images, rather than **telling** audience members what has happened or what to think. Showing action involves the audience as participants in the imaginative process and asks them to actively interpret what is happening.

Chapter 5 established that dramatic action is a vital component in writing dramatic stories. How this dramatic action is presented depends, of course, on the particular medium that the script is intended for. In audio drama, the images are created entirely through sound – both dialogue and sound effects. Writers for the theatre and screenwriters, however, can tell their stories visually using physical action – that is, the activities of the actors that take place in front of the audience or camera – as well as dialogue.

The following example helps to illustrate how these different media approach the challenges of telling stories using action. Imagine the classic crime drama or action-adventure scene of the safe break:

> Two burglars break into the home of a billionaire financier to steal vital papers that will enable them to prove the massive fraud that has been committed by the finance company. They uncover the safe, concealed behind the Dutch Old Master painting, and set to work. But something is wrong: the combination they have been told will open the safe is not working. Suddenly there's a sound outside. Lights in the vestibule. Someone is coming! They replace the painting and scurry to hide behind the Queen Anne chaise.

- **In a stage play script**, it is likely that much of the action described in this scene would be shown, with minimal dialogue. But the failure of the safe combination might need a few lines of dialogue to explain what is happening, as the audience might not be able to interpret this through the actions of the performers alone.
- **In a screenplay**, the entire scene can play out without dialogue, solely showing the on-screen action, with camera angles focusing on the hands of the burglars as they work, and close-up shots of the actors' faces showing their frustration when the combination doesn't work and their panic as they hear the sounds outside.

It's also important to note that if the writer of the script for this scene were to include inessential dialogue, the audience might find it jarring. A safe-break scene, after all, is one where you would expect the action to take place as silently as is humanly possible: that is, with minimal dialogue on stage, and entirely without dialogue, using only physical action, in a screenplay. The use of unnecessary dialogue in this instance would be **exposition**: it would be telling the spectator or audience what is happening, rather than letting them witness it, and giving them plot information without bothering to make it dramatic. This is exactly the kind of thing that makes an audience lose interest in a story. Good dramatic writing strives, for the most part, to be economical, and one reason for this is because audiences do not like to be *told* what to think, what to look at or how to feel. Unnecessary dialogue or scenes that do not move the story forward, and are therefore surplus to requirements, will turn them off quickly.

Activity 1 Reading: screenplay choices that reflect character

Read Reading 6.1 in Part 4, which is an extract from the screenplay for the film *The Power of the Dog* (2021), a western written and directed by Jane Campion, based on the 1967 novel by Thomas Savage. The dining-room scene in this extract (Scene 17) brings together the main characters and sets the tone of their interactions for the rest of the film. As it is an adaptation, Campion has opted to make significant changes to the same scene in Savage's novel. In the original version, there is no mention of Phil lighting his cigarette the way he does in the screenplay.

- Why do you think Campion has rewritten this scene as she has?
- What do the choices she has made for the screenplay tell us about the characters of Phil Burbank and Peter Gordon? List a few qualities for each character that you discern from reading the scene.

Discussion

In this scene, Phil and Peter come face to face for the first time. This pairing will form the central antagonistic relationship of the drama. Phil's simple act of destroying one of the paper flowers made by Peter as table decorations sets the two characters in opposition from the first moment of their acquaintance. But as a piece of visual storytelling, it does much more than any dialogue exchange could do. The flowers (and the fate of one of them) are expressive both of Peter's supposed effeminacy and of Phil's brutality and determination to suppress the feminine. The destruction of the flower sets up the story, and the two main characters' conflicted relationship, in one small, simple physical action. It also tells us a great deal about the types of people they are: Peter is naturally creative, while Phil has a powerful destructive streak.

From the example of the dining-room scene in *The Power of the Dog*, you can see how action and imagery overlap. The burning of the paper flower by Phil Burbank is an example of action telling the story. It is also an example of powerful imagery at work, enhancing the scene and providing further layers of meaning. This interaction of imagery and action points the spectator towards all the main themes of the film: toxic masculinity, homosexual desire, and the suppression of the feminine.

As the writer and director of this film, Jane Campion uses many other strategies to show the difference between these two central characters, including how they speak, their appearance, their attitude to the other people in the dining room, and how they interact with the other characters. These differences – or contrasts – are important in writing drama. Visual contrasts are explored in greater detail in Section 3.4 of this chapter.

This scene is also a strong example of a golden rule of scriptwriting mentioned earlier: engage your audience by allowing them to witness the action of the story, so they are actively involved in the developing drama. This principle is generally known as 'show, don't tell', but it could just as easily be called 'let the audience be involved in the drama'. Doing so will greatly improve every moment of your script and the responses to it. Indeed, many successful films tell their stories largely without dialogue, being almost entirely made up of physical action, imagery and acting. Notable examples include the Oscar winners *The Artist* (2011) and *Life of Pi* (2012). These films tell complex stories with almost no dialogue. This is possible because the editing techniques used in filmmaking allow for details to be built up and for camera shots to be related to one another. This process is known as **montage**.

2.2 Editing pictures and montage

Montage is a process, which happens partly in the editing suite and partly in the spectator's mind, whereby the placing of images or camera shots beside one another results in a perceived meaning. This method was called 'montage' by the Russian filmmaker Sergei Eisenstein (1988) in the early part of the twentieth century.

Sometimes the use of montage can induce wider meanings to do with theme and poetic parallels. For instance, in Eisenstein's film *Strike* (1925), there is a camera shot of attacks on striking workers juxtaposed with a shot of a bull being slaughtered. This suggests a comparison: the workers are being treated like cattle. In general, though, the purpose of montage is quite straightforward, to facilitate the move from one narrative point to the next and create meaning by showing the dramatic action, moment by moment. Together, these moments create **story beats** (often just referred to as 'beats'), which follow from one to the next. Story beats are the incidents that, when put in succession, result in scenes. Especially in film, scenes can often be dialogue-free, composed entirely of images that show dramatic action. How this action is presented (the number and length of scenes and how much dramatic action there is in them) is the main tool available to the writer to control the pace and rhythm of the script.

2.3 Beats, scenes and sequences

Montage also allows the writer and the filmmaker to compress the action of the script into a manageable timeframe. The placing of shots one after another creates a sense of one thing following another, in linear fashion. This implies the passage of time. Of course, some dramas do not go forward in time – films like *Titanic* (1997), *Stand By Me* (1986) and *The Shawshank Redemption* (1994) tell their stories in flashback. Others move backwards and forwards in time. However, the overwhelming majority of scripts show events evolving in a linear progression.

For a scriptwriter, the process of building a pattern of evolving narrative – moment by moment, story beat by story beat, scene by scene – is the same no matter what dramatic medium you are writing for. How you show this progression of the dramatic action of the story – constructed using beats, scenes, and sequences of scenes – will determine the tone, mood, pacing, look and feel of your script.

Scenes change when the location changes or time moves forward. So, scenes can take the audience from one place to another; or they can carry the action in one place forward in time by 'cutting away' from a scene and coming back to a new scene in the same place, but later in time, when there has been a change or a development. (Scene changes are also occasionally used to go backwards in time.) On stage, a scene can run for a considerable length of time. Scenes in films usually only run for a few minutes at most; just the amount of time it takes to move the plot forward.

In general, scenes are about showing essential action using story beats, which cause developments that change the nature of the story or fundamentally alter its progress. It could be a change in the material situation of a character, the development of a new character relationship (or a change in an existing one), or an external event that causes a situation to change, such as the arrival of a stranger or an extreme weather event. Most scenes have at least one major story beat and it is possible that multiple story beats can take place in a single scene. However, a scene which does not have any story beats at all is almost certainly unnecessary and probably needs to be cut from the script!

The dining-room scene in *The Power of the Dog* screenplay (Campion, no date) that you read earlier in this chapter (as part of Reading 6.1) includes several beats essential to the story:

- All the main characters meet for the first time.
- Rose works hard and is clearly a capable businesswoman.
- Phil behaves in a way that is rude, uncouth and aggressive.
- Peter is shown to be sensitive and creative.
- Phil mocks Peter's sensitivities, culminating in his burning of the paper flower Peter has made.

Activity 2 Reading and writing: story beats and character

Look again at Reading 6.1. This excerpt from *The Power of the Dog* screenplay (Campion, no date) includes a number of scenes leading up to the dining-room scene. Each includes an event or series of incidents that develop the story. These story beats also provide essential character information.

Write a list of three story beats for each of the three central characters in the sequence: Rose Gordon, Peter Gordon and Phil Burbank. Note down what you think each of these story beats tells you about these characters.

Discussion

Scenes, made up of story beats, move a story forward by bringing characters into contact with one another, and revealing how their wants and needs are in conflict. As discussed in Chapter 5, character and conflict are integrally connected. As a story moves forward, characters make choices that add complexity to their relationships with other characters. Over the course of a script, a writer will elaborate the story beats to develop these relationships and often resolve conflicts between characters.

As the script extract from *The Power of the Dog* (Reading 6.1) shows, the forward movement of a narrative is created by building scenes one on top of the other. These groups of scenes are called **sequences**. By using scenes and sequences, the writer has a great deal of control over how the audience will experience emotions while watching a drama: controlling the length of scenes and the way they work in sequence is an important tool. Longer scenes are useful for setting up the world of the story and characters. By contrast, very short scenes in quick succession can be used to build excitement. For example, if a character (let's call her Ali) is late for an important meeting, the sequence showing this might involve lots of short scenes with single story beats, as Ali rushes to the rendezvous:

- Ali grabs her coat and bag from the table by the front door.
- She runs down the stairs of her apartment block.
- Ali tries to hail a taxi. No luck.
- She jumps on to a bus.
- She jumps off the bus.
- She runs down the street to the café where the meeting will take place.
- Sweaty and hot, she swings through the café doors.

Each of these short scenes might only be a few seconds long, and all together they might only be a minute of screen time. However, this short sequence covers a lot of action and gives the spectator a sense of Ali's rushed pace.

Most drama scripts will use a mixture of long and short scenes to vary the pace of the action. It is important to think about the length of scenes in your own writing and how the rhythm of the drama is affected by your choices in putting scenes into sequences. Keeping control of the pace and rhythm of the drama (using the length of scenes) and how the story moves from one scene to the next are key skills for all writers.

Activity 3 Writing: a visual sequence

Write a sequence containing four to eight scenes where a character prepares for a meeting and travels across town to get to it. The meeting could be a business appointment, a date, or a coffee with friends. Write in the present tense, do not use any dialogue, and only include descriptions of the action in each scene. Each scene should be one to three lines long. You may wish to use the character you developed in Activity 3 in Chapter 5 for this exercise. When read together, the sequence of scenes should give hints about what type of meeting the character is going to.

Discussion

In writing this sequence, you will have made many decisions about the dramatic action you have chosen to depict. If you examine your scenes, you will see that you can tell a great deal about the type of drama it is just from these choices, and the way the scenes work together in sequence to develop mood, tone and, especially, pacing. From the visual information contained in the scenes, it should also be clear what type of meeting your character is preparing for and travelling to.

3 Visual qualities and design

As you have learned, dramatic action is often purely visual – scripts benefit from showing physical actions rather than describing them. In this way, images are a vital tool in dramatic storytelling. But as noted in Section 2 of this chapter, images serve a second important function in a script: their aesthetic qualities establish genre, convey mood and emotion, set up key locations and characters, and hint at major themes. As a writer, you must consider how the images you conjure in your script will influence the audience.

3.1 Genre and the visual

In Chapters 1 and 2, you looked at genre and the ways in which writers establish the world of a piece of writing. When setting out to write a drama, it is important to think about where your script will sit in terms of genre. Audiences often choose what they want to watch (whether film, TV or live theatre) on the basis of their genre expectations, and a writer can use these expectations to subtly signal the genre to the audience. For example, if the opening image of a film shows a spaceship zipping past a small, purple planet, and then it cuts to a scene of children playing in a suburban garden, the audience will understand that, though the action has moved to a garden, the film is a science fiction film.

Modern genre designations come from theatre and literature, and film genres were originally seen as versions of popular fictional forms such as comedy, detective fiction, adventure stories and supernatural stories. Over time, genres have blended to make hybrids: the 'romcom' blends romantic drama and comedy, and the 'comedy horror' does the same with comedy and horror, and so on. The genres mentioned here are not an exhaustive list: genres are continually being reinvented and elaborated.

It is also worth pointing out that there are scripts that do not easily fit into any single genre, and some that deliberately avoid genre identification. This is a perfectly valid decision for a writer to make if it serves the drama. The writer can choose to work within the expectations of a genre, or to innovate and make decisions that confound expectations.

Choices about genre and the design of visual elements of a drama are important for a number of reasons. They:

- allow writers to establish the tone and mood of their scripts
- help writers to pitch their drama scripts to producers
- position the work in the market and enable marketing decisions
- help potential audiences to identify the type of drama and decide if it is of interest to them.

Having a clear idea of the type and genre of script you intend to write, and how it will look, can only be helpful to you as a writer.

3.2 Character and design

Writers of drama for visual performance need to make many decisions related to genre, styling and setting, which establish the visual language of the script. As discussed, such design decisions can be used to signal genre, tone, mood and theme, and they are also important in establishing character. For example, a spy who drives an Aston Martin (such as James Bond in many of the films in that franchise) is a very different character to a spy who takes public transport, like George Smiley (see Figure 1 at the start of this chapter) in the film *Tinker Tailor Soldier Spy* (2011).

Every choice about the settings of scenes in a script reflects on the characters who are located in those settings. So, interior locations associated with a principal character, especially rooms in their home and personal spaces such as their office or car, tell the audience a good deal about that character. Likewise, clothing is a way of expressing the individuality of characters – what they wear is a very personal choice, as it is for all of us. George Smiley (Figure 1) wears rumpled suits and a mackintosh raincoat; James Bond prefers a sharp tuxedo.

Importantly, it is not the writer's job to give detailed direction in the script relating to the choice of sets, costumes and props. But often a scriptwriter will specify one or two design details that give an indication of character. For example, in Sofia Coppola's film *Marie Antoinette* (2006), the eighteenth-century French queen is presented as a playful teenager (she became queen at the age of eighteen, after all). Coppola, who wrote the script, gives Marie scenes of shopping, gorging on pastries and champagne, and trying on clothes to a punkish soundtrack; she even gives her a pair of twenty-first century Converse trainers.

Remember, though, that if you add design ideas to your script, these details are only suggestions to the director and the designers. They should be added sparingly and only when they are essential to the storytelling. If you include too much design detail in a script you are writing, it can deter producers from reading on.

3.3 Settings and mood

Choices about settings and locations are also an important aspect of visuals for the writer. They can set up the world of the drama and indicate where it sits in relation to genre conventions. While the visuals of interior locations principally reveal things about character (often these are details about the psychology of the lead characters), exterior locations do a lot to tell a spectator or audience about the tone and mood of a scene.

There are many examples of films where the locations or settings of the story function to emphasise the mood of the drama or characters. In the action film *Zero Dark Thirty* (2012), directed by Kathryn Bigelow, the dusty chaos of post-invasion Iraq adds to the dramatic tension; the wide-open emptiness of the arid landscapes outside Tehran in *Taste of Cherry (Ta'm e guilass)* (1997), directed by Abbas Kiarostami, produces a wistful and lonely feeling; the damp, chilly landscapes in *Black '47* (2018), directed by Lance Daly, give a sense of the desperation in Ireland during the Great Famine; and the contrasting pinks, reds and yellows in every scene of *In the Mood For Love* (2000), directed by Wong Kar-Wai, give the film a warm, romantic glow. In every case, the director and cinematographer of these films, in conjunction with their crews, chose the locations and decided how they should be dressed, lit, photographed and edited. But also, in every case, the writer of the script will have specified interesting places for scenes to take place.

In your own dramatic writing, for any medium, always think carefully about the location of scenes. For example, when two characters have a confrontation ask yourself questions such as: 'Is it better for this scene to take place in the kitchen, or on the seafront promenade in the midst of a raging storm?' Whichever option you choose will change the mood and tone of your story dramatically.

Activity 4 Writing: adaptation – genre and mood

Choose a piece of writing you have written in response to an activity in Part 1 of this book (Chapters 1–4). Pick an element of it that can be adapted as a dramatic scene. This might be a setting from a poem you have written, something you've observed in a piece of life writing, or a narrative strand in a story.

1. Write the introduction to the scene, using description and directions to set up the world of the story, the location and the characters in the scene. What genre is your adapted scene? What is the prevailing mood: is it upbeat, languid, energetic, reflective or grim?

2. Now change your scene description and directions so that the story is in a different genre. Referring back to the Chapter 1 discussion of genre will help you with this. How do the changes you have made affect the mood of the scene? Is it very different from your first adaptation of this scene or largely the same?

Discussion

The small details you have added at the start of your adapted scene will give a sense of genre, style, tone and mood. You may have found that the location you chose implied a sense of mystery or that your opening directions suggested a historical setting.

A great deal of the signals in a script that convey genre to an audience are contained within scene descriptions and directions, which also tell readers and those involved in producing the script what type of story it is. These openings to scenes are excellent places to experiment with different options in your writing; you can try setting them in different locations or changing a central character or relationship.

Creating the world of your drama through the use of scene directions is a skill that you need to practise. As you write and rewrite a script, you will find that often a scene will come alive when you make a small change to the setting, giving your writing a different mood or tone. As you will learn from the sections that follow, these changes can also create tensions between characters who may have contrasting responses to the settings of the drama and the world around them.

3.4 Visual contrasts

Contrasts in the visual qualities of a drama serve several purposes. They allow the writer to show character differences, build obstacles and conflicts, and to develop the story. Visual contrasts can be used to comic or ironic effect and they can also give relief to an audience by providing variety, thereby sustaining their interest.

By using contrasts, a writer can point out differences between characters or their lives, which can be used to give texture and meaning to a script. In *Monsoon Wedding* (2001), the story of the complex arrangements for a Punjabi wedding allows writer Sabrina Dhawan to draw together characters that represent the contrasts between the traditional (Figure 2(a)) and the modern. Many of the wedding guests are from the United States and their western dress (Figure 2(b)), ostentatious spending and mobile phones signify some of the differences between the traditional values inherent in an Indian family wedding and the values of the modern world.

(a)

(b)

Figure 2 (a) Cast members on the set of *Monsoon Wedding*, directed by Mira Nair, Mirabai Films, 2001. Photographed by Nan Goldin (photo: Nan Goldin/Mirabai/Delhi Dot Com/Kobal/Shutterstock). (b) Parvin Dabas (left) and Naseeruddin Shah (right) as characters Hemant Rai and Lalit Verma wearing western dress in *Monsoon Wedding* (photo: Moviestore/Shutterstock).

Visual contrasts in dramatic writing can also be a source of drama and of comedy. They can encourage audience members to engage with themes, evoke their sympathy or provoke their ridicule, and so are another important way in which the writer can tell the story using images.

4 Researching the visual

Writers need to undertake careful research when setting a story (including a script for dramatic performance) in a particular time and place. Most of the action in Andrea Levy's novel *Small Island* (2004) is set in the period just after the Second World War, when fate throws the characters of the book together in London. This time period and setting for the book mean that Levy, and also Helen Edmundson (the playwright who adapted the novel for the stage in 2019) and the screenwriters of the BBC TV adaptation (2009), would have needed to do extensive research on the visual aspects of the story.

Figure 3 Front cover of Andrea Levy's novel *Small Island*, Tinder Press, 2004 (photo: © Richard Haughton/Hulton Getty Archive. Cover design: Headline. Reproduced with permission of the Licensor through PLSclear).

Activity 5 Reading: researching the visual

1. Read the extract from Andrea Levy's 2004 novel *Small Island* (Reading 6.2), which tells the story of a group of Jamaican émigrés in London during and after the Second World War. In this scene, we witness the moment when, having travelled from Jamaica, Hortense joins her husband, Gilbert, in London.

- What kind of things do you think Levy would have researched to write this extract? Make a few notes of details you find interesting.

2. Now read the same scene presented as drama in the stage play by Helen Edmundson (2019), which was staged at the National Theatre in London (Reading 6.3).

- What methods does Edmundson use to show us the details of the room Gilbert lives in?
- What can you tell about Gilbert from the way he presents the room to Hortense?
- How does Hortense's response to the living space help you to understand her character?

Discussion

In the novel extract (Reading 6.2), the description of Hortense's impressions of the room when she first enters it are detailed and precise. This would have required Andrea Levy to research these domestic details thoroughly.

However, this kind of description, if merely spoken by Hortense, would not be dramatic for an audience watching a stage play. Instead, in the play script (Reading 6.3), Edmundson has given Gilbert lines of dialogue where he shows these details to Hortense over the course of the scene. This dialogue focuses the audience's attention on the precise details of the room, which tell us a lot about the situation in post-war England. Additionally, Gilbert's manner of showing these details to Hortense, and her horrified responses, are effective in revealing the two characters. Hortense comes across as fussy and somewhat superior; Gilbert, by contrast, has an unpretentious attitude. Edmundson has used the visual details of the room in this scene to advance the story, reveal character, and give the audience information about the world in which the drama is set.

In order to write this scene, Edmundson most likely had to do extensive research into design aspects of post-war London homes, including finding out what room interiors looked like, what everyday objects were in use, and what the living conditions were like for people of the Windrush Generation who arrived in England in the late 1940s.

5 Conclusion

Images serve a range of purposes in dramatic writing and can be grouped into two categories: visual storytelling and visual imagery. Often images – or word pictures – are used to advance the story in a very economical and effective way using visual storytelling. The interactions between characters, physical actions showing incidents in the plot, and visual revelations can provide audiences with a very direct and immediate way of understanding what is happening. Visuals and imagery in dramatic writing can also be used to convey less tangible but equally important ideas and qualities. They can give audiences a sense of the genre of a work and the tone and mood of a story, as well as providing insight into characters and expressing important differences between them and the worlds they inhabit.

Almost all the key decisions relating to design in a dramatic production will be taken by the director and the designer(s) supporting them: they will create or select the lighting styles, sets, props, costumes and much else besides. It is therefore not the writer's job to specify what these decisions should be. However, by adding a few carefully chosen visual details in their script, the writer can convey the style, tone, genre and many other important elements of the story.

References

The artist (2011) Directed by M. Hazanavicius. [Feature film]. Paris: Warner Bros France.

Black '47 (2018) Directed by L. Daly. [Feature film]. Dublin: Element Pictures.

Campion, J. (no date) *The power of the dog*. [Screenplay]. Available at: https://deadline.com/wp-content/uploads/2022/01/The-Power-Of-The-Dog-Read-The-Screenplay.pdf (Accessed: 5 May 2024).

Edmundson, H. (2019) *Small island*. London: Nick Hern Books.

Eisenstein, S. (1988) *Selected works. Volume 1: writings 1922–34*. Edited and translated from the Russian by R. Taylor. London: British Film Institute.

In the mood for love (2000) Directed by Wong Kar-Wai. [Feature film]. Hong Kong: Block 2 Pictures.

Levy, A. (2004) *Small island*. London: Headline Publishing.

Life of Pi (2012) Directed by A. Lee. [Feature film]. Los Angeles, CA: 20th Century Fox.

Marie Antoinette (2006) Directed by S. Coppola. [Feature film]. Los Angeles, CA: Sony Pictures Releasing.

Monsoon wedding (2001) Directed by M. Nair. [Feature film]. Mumbai: USA Films.

Pan's labyrinth (El laberinto del fauno) (2006) Directed by G. del Toro. [Feature film]. Madrid: Warner Bros. Pictures.

The power of the dog (2021) Directed by J. Campion. [Feature film]. London: BBC Film/See-Saw Films.

Salaam Bombay! (1988) Directed by M. Nair. [Feature film]. Mumbai: Alliance/Cinecom Pictures.

Screamers (1995) Directed by C. Duguay. [Feature film]. Culver City, CA: Triumph Films.

The Shawshank redemption (1994) Directed by F. Darabont. [Feature film]. Los Angeles, CA: Columbia Pictures.

Small island (2009) BBC One, 6 and 13 December, 21:00. Available at: https://www.bbc.co.uk/programmes/b00pdyg0 (Accessed: 12 September 2024).

Stand by me (1986) Directed by R. Reiner. [Feature film]. Los Angeles, CA: Columbia Pictures.

Strike (Stachka) (1925) Directed by S. Eisenstein. [Feature film]. Moscow: Goskino.

Taste of cherry (Ta'm e guilass) (1997) Directed by A. Kiarostami. [Feature film]. Tehran: Artificial Eye.

Tinker tailor soldier spy (2011) Directed by T. Alfredson. [Feature film]. London: StudioCanal.

Titanic (1997) Directed by J. Cameron. [Feature film]. Los Angeles, CA: Paramount Pictures.

To Sir, with love (1967) Directed by J. Clavell. [Feature film]. Los Angeles, CA: Columbia Pictures.

Zero dark thirty (2012) Directed by K. Bigelow. [Feature film]. Los Angeles, CA: Sony Pictures Releasing.

Chapter 7
Stories in sound

Joanne Reardon with Derek Neale

1 Introduction

In this chapter, you will learn how to write audio drama, which is any drama that is received by the listener through an **aural** medium: mainly radio plays and podcasts. The terms 'audio drama' and 'radio drama' are used throughout this chapter.

In an audio drama, elements of the storytelling must be identified by sound alone, which can be both a constraint and a strength. Listeners of audio drama are deprived of visual stimuli: instead, the writer must prompt them to become integrally involved in constructing the setting and events of the story, as well as the characters and their costumes, by using a variety of dramatic techniques, from dialogue to music and sound effects. What a listener 'sees' in their imagination, provoked by what they hear, creates the drama. This is also how a writer of audio drama makes an emotional connection with their audience, and creating this connection is key to ensuring that each listener wants to stay with the performance to the end. A theatre audience usually can't leave a play until the interval, but with radio or podcasts, especially if accessed via a smartphone, listeners can leave the performance more easily, at any moment, by the click of a button. Unless listeners are engaged with the imaginative world of a drama within the first few minutes, this is a very real possibility. Therefore, the emotional connection you, as a writer, set up with an audience at the start of an audio drama is most important. You should think of the opening as a trailer for the whole drama.

The intimacy of audio drama can be one of its greatest strengths. Listening to a play or a podcast is usually a solitary experience, so when writing audio drama it helps to imagine that you are writing it for just one listener who may be sitting at home, driving or commuting, or listening as they walk. This is a very powerful place to be for a writer: it makes it easier to imagine how *you* would feel if you were the listener. It creates a strong, one-to-one intimacy for the dramatic performance. An example of this is one of the earliest radio plays, *Danger* written by Richard Hughes (1966), which was first broadcast in 1924. It is set in a coal mine after an explosion which places all the characters in complete darkness. Such a device – effectively taking away the sight of the characters – forces this kind of intimacy between listeners and the characters in the play because they all want to know the same range of information. The audience of listeners, like the characters, can't see (with their eyes) what's going on: this is a very effective setting for a radio play.

2 Creating pictures with sound

Writing for audio drama allows you to be inventive with settings, which can be as small and intimate as a kitchen in a bedsit or as wide and empty as a desert. You can also be ambitious with a cast of thirty or you can tell the story of just one character. You can present a vast world to an audience, which can take them anywhere.

Audio dramas don't need a physical set: the story can take place anywhere because on radio or in podcasts the setting is all in the listener's imagination. As a writer, you can transport your listening audience in time: into the past – perhaps to ancient Rome as in Ben Power's *Emperor and Galilean* (2023), an adaptation of Henrik Ibsen's 1873 play – or into the future. For example, the podcast drama *Forest 404* by Timothy X Atack (2019) is an environmental thriller set in a futuristic natural landscape where, as a listener, you are immersed in the sounds of a strange, deep forest.

It's not only setting that offers writers of audio drama more freedom; within the setting, the size of the cast is also more adaptable. Actors can (and often do) play several different parts, using different voices each time. Because of this, you can write a cast of many more characters in an audio drama than you could ever have in a new stage play (because theatres are always more constrained by their funding than, for example, streaming services for film or TV).

Dramatist Paul Sirett writes both stage and audio drama. *Bartholomew Abominations* (2020), one of his 'big' plays, was broadcast on Radio 4 in 2020 in collaboration with Naked Productions and Graeae Theatre (a theatre company that places Deaf and disabled artists centre stage). The play is a reworking of Ben Jonson's 1614 play *Bartholomew Fair*, which, in its original state, has 30 named parts. Sirett's version has 22 named parts and is set in the near future. It is a political commentary about modern British identity, reflecting on narrow-minded disability discrimination and the rise of English nationalism in the early twenty-first century. In his book on playwriting, *The Playwright's Manifesto: How You Can Be the Future of Playwriting* (2022), Sirett makes the important point that for anyone who wants to write a play with a large cast, '*Thinking big* isn't just about cast size, it is also about ambition' (Sirett, 2022, p. 141). In *Bartholomew Abominations*, the ambition was about adapting a seventeenth-century play into one that speaks to the twenty-first century. Sirett goes on to say that 'As a concept, the idea of the big must, therefore, be approached from two perspectives: large-scale plays with a big cast and small-scale plays with BIG ambition' (Sirett, 2022, p. 141). So, ambition in writing drama isn't just about cast size, it's about what you do with that cast.

In audio drama, you have choices. You can write more intimate plays with just a few characters or broader plays with larger casts – both equally allow you to tackle challenging political subjects or to write smaller domestic dramas, thrillers and romances. Whatever you decide, you will still have to bring the characters and the world of your story to life. Activity 1 encourages you to think about how to do this.

Activity 1 Reading: keeping a listener engaged

Read the extract from the start of the radio play *Breaking Up with Bradford* (2017a) by Kamal Kaan (Reading 7.1 in Part 4).

- How are the characters established in this extract? For example, how does the dialogue reveal the characters and their relationship to one another?
- How is the setting established? Think about the way the tone changes within a short time and what effect this has. Also consider how the listener, on hearing this extract, can tell where they are: is this hinted at by the way the characters speak and the idiom of their accents (indicated in the way the dialogue is written in the script)?
- What is the overall effect of the extract? How does Kaan use this opening of the play as a trailer for the whole drama?

Discussion

Characters: signposts to character (and setting) in Reading 7.1 are given through the dialogue, what the characters do and how they react to each other when they meet again after some time apart. Sid notices immediate changes in Kasim (his soft jumper, the way he speaks), as does Kasim with Sid (he's been working out in the gym). Kasim is slightly awkward with Sid, for example when he's vague about where he got the jumper from when Sid teases him about it.

Setting: the play begins in Cambridge, where (we learn later) Kasim is at university. He is writing what sounds like a love letter to the city. Notice how the language is different in this opening to the later scenes: it is poetic and sad. When Kasim reaches Bradford, the setting changes immediately, which has an effect on the tone. The writer wants the listener to hear the contrast between Cambridge (Figure 1(a)) and a station in a busy industrial city like Bradford (Figure 1 (b)), so sound effects (SFX) include the noise of trains, a busy station, ticket barriers, Kasim folding his bicycle, him pulling a suitcase along, and Bradford being announced as the train's destination. These sound effects – and the accents of the station staff member and Sid – are in stark contrast to the wistful opening of the play.

Overall: as an opening to a play, this extract is intriguing and raises questions for the listener. Why has Kasim returned to Bradford when he doesn't seem to want to? What is waiting for him there?

Notice, too, that this script includes subtle directions that a listener won't necessarily hear, but which give the actors direction for how they should relate to each other. You would hardly ever (or never) use directions for physical action like this in an audio script because these are hard to translate into audio performance. But although the audience won't see, for example, Kasim feeling Sid's biceps or the two characters embracing, the action is already implicit in the dialogue at this point – listeners can 'see' it in their imaginations.

(a) (b)

Figure 1 (a) Punting on the River Cam in Cambridge, 2010 (photo: Alistair Laming/Alamy) and (b) Bradford city centre buildings, including the City Hall, 2013 (photo: Andrew Paterson/Alamy).

3 Developing character through dialogue

You've learned from earlier chapters in this book that characters, in all forms of writing, can be revealed through what they say (to themselves and each other). This is especially important in audio drama because listeners can't see the characters who are speaking. Dialogue in dramatic writing is not simply conversation; dialogue drives the events of the story forward, and one element of this is that characters must sound distinct from one another. This doesn't mean including lots of different accents in your writing – although you can use this technique to distinguish one character from another, such as in *Breaking Up with Bradford*, where Sid has a strong Bradford accent and Kasim has lost his, and this distinction reveals something about their characters. In the scenes you read (Reading 7.1), it's suggested that Kasim has tried to leave his Bradford past behind (it's even hinted at in the title of the drama) and the way he speaks reflects this. But as well as having different accents, Kasim and Sid are also distinct from one another in *the way* they say things. For example, Kasim becomes hesitant, almost reluctant, to answer Sid's question about where his jumper came from, but soon slips into the familiar **vernacular** of his hometown, which represents his attempt to blend back in. It's clear that this could cause issues further on because Kasim is behaving in a way that is against how he really feels. This will create the dramatic conflict that will drive events in the play.

In order to develop your ear for dialogue, to help you write it, listen to the way people speak in reality. If you ever eavesdrop on a conversation in a café or at a party, for example, you'll notice the way people rarely finish what they're saying; they go off at tangents or forget what they're saying halfway through, and they interrupt each other. If people know each other well, they might predict what the other is going to say and so finish sentences for them. But in all cases, what you're listening for is *how* they speak and how much this can vary. Make a note of it in your writer's notebook next time you're out and about and use what you hear to help you write the dialogue in your work. Another thing you might notice is the way people seem to be saying something important without actually saying it. In drama, this is called **subtext**; you can see this very clearly in the scenes from *Breaking Up with Bradford* you have read, where there is a lot that Kasim is *not* saying. This subtext will also contribute to the dramatic conflict in the play.

Reading 7.1 also shows that audio drama scripts don't need to include 'set-ups' or background history. Characters should hit the ground running, as Sid and Kasim do, because the listener needs to be engaged immediately and not have the inclination to switch off – the play should hook them from the start. In Activity 2, you're going to try writing the opening of an audio drama for yourself.

Activity 2 Writing: using dialogue to create a scene

Write a brief scene for an audio drama where two characters meet after a long time apart. You can create new characters or use two you've already written for a previous activity in this book. Decide on a location (e.g. a train or bus station, a café, or the scene of an accident on the street). Try to write about two A4 pages of a script.

Think about how to use dialogue and sound to create character and setting in your script. Make sure that the information you include is prompted by characters and events in the scene, and not just by the need to deliver information to the listener.

Avoid exposition – that is, don't write dialogue for your characters that explains every detail of what is happening in a scene. You should only include what characters need to know, and avoid them telling each other (and the audience) what they already know or what the audience would prefer to imagine for themselves.

Discussion

When writing audio drama, you need to provide the listener with some emotional engagement. This is often achieved by suggesting your characters' emotions, including fear, anger, yearning, annoyance, sadness and joy. Kasim's letter to Cambridge at the start of *Breaking Up with Bradford* (Reading 7.1) shows his mixed emotions at his experience of Cambridge. Returning to his home city is difficult, but he doesn't explicitly tell us why. Hopefully, you were also able to write actions within your scene that demonstrated emotion without the characters having to say how they actually feel. Another example of this would be when Kasim hesitates before admitting his jumper is cashmere because he's embarrassed at owning such an expensive, luxury item. Look again at the piece you've just written to check whether you have created emotion in your scene without having to state it explicitly.

4 Point of view in audio drama

Intimate **monologue** (a voice directed to the ear of the listener) is often used in audio drama to establish point of view. Kasim's 'letter' to Cambridge at the start of *Breaking Up with Bradford* (Reading 7.1), for example, creates the effect of an inner voice, inside a character's head. Such monologues can emulate the subtleties and variations of the first-person narrative, meaning audio drama, more than stage or screen drama, has the potential to capture the original texture and tone of a novel, short story, biography or memoir.

When writing prose fiction, you should always be aware and in control of **point of view**. Similarly, in audio drama you should keep a tight rein on the number of people who can reveal their thoughts directly in monologues. This will often be only one character, as you've seen in *Breaking Up with Bradford*. But however many of your characters you allow to speak directly to the audience, establish your method early on and be consistent. You can't have a character revealing their thoughts for the first time in the final minutes of a play if they haven't been doing this throughout.

Interior monologues can be useful for creating a balance between the exterior world (the setting) and the interior world of the play (what is going on inside a character's head). The interior world of *Breaking Up with Bradford* is in Kasim's head as he addresses the two settings (which represent the exterior world of the play) of Cambridge (Reading 7.1) and Bradford:

<u>SFX: KASIM BRINGING THINGS INTO THE GARDEN, CHILDREN PLAYING, OVER WHICH KASIM SPEAKS:</u>

KASIM: (V/O) Bradford, you beauty!

From our house on the hill,
you can see the glistening moors spread out like an emerald carpet.
Nearby reclines the handsome Lister's Mill and beside it,
the hermit crab shaped Valley Parade stadium.

How I've longed to be wrapped in your terraced streets again, knitted with multi-lingual threads of races and faces – Bradfordian lasses and the posh middle classes.
Home is where the heart is; the heart is where you are.

Let me rest my check against the beating under your shirt?

(Kaan, 2017b, p. 8)

The short, intimate monologue you have just read from Scene 4 of *Breaking Up with Bradford* is written in the script as voice-over (V/O), which means that in the audio performance, the listener will hear Kasim clearly. His voice will be louder and feel closer, as though he is talking to the listener directly. There will still be residual noise heard behind the speech from the sound effects of the garden, which represent the exterior world in this scene.

4.1 Audio monologues

An audio monologue can be adept at revealing the inner thoughts of a character, but the voice speaking to the audience still has to be dramatic to engage a listener. You can make a monologue dramatic by making it **dialogic** – that is, by writing it so that your character is speaking directly to the listener, having a conversation with their own thoughts (their internal dialogue), or addressing another character that the listener cannot hear.

> **Box 1 Some tips for writing dramatic and engaging monologues in audio drama**
>
> - Include other voices within the monologue (e.g. 'He said to me, "What have you been up to?", and I said to him, "What do you think I've been up to?"'). This will make it feel more interactive and dramatic.
> - Have an addressee implied in the speech (e.g. 'you see'; 'Do you understand?'). The listener is the 'addressee' and this brings them into the drama, making them feel as though they are part of it.
> - Listen to the rhythm created by repetitions and variations in speech – vary the pace and use punctuation to change the rhythm. You can do this by writing long, drawn-out lines followed by quick, short-clause lines.
> - Reveal a 'see-saw' equivocation in the speaker, such as an internal debate.

Figure 2 Train racing towards Edinburgh, 2016 (photo: John Stephens/Alamy).

Activity 3 Reading: using radio monologues

Read the extract from the audio monologue *The Dead Dad Show* (2019) by Annalisa Dinnella (Reading 7.2), which was inspired by *Six Marimbas*, a piece of music written by Steve Reich in 1986.

As you read the extract, pay particular attention to what the character, James, says and *how* he says it. Refer to Box 1 and think about these questions:

- How is the listener implied in the speech? What difference does this make to the way the listener is engaged?
- How are other characters brought into the monologue?
- How does the writer vary the pace and rhythm of the speech?
- Is there an internal debate going on in this monologue? What does this achieve?

Discussion

The listener is implied in this extract of *The Dead Dad Show* because they feel part of the story, rather than being outside of it, through the use of the present tense. The character, James, hits the ground running – everything happens in real time and events never stop. He addresses the listener at the very start by introducing himself in the dream (where he imagines he's on stage) and then throughout using the first-person viewpoint 'I'.

Other characters are brought into the monologue through sound effects and through James talking directly to them – for example, he addresses a character who doesn't answer: 'Hey buddy'. And the listener is implied in James's speech: 'And, no, I haven't wet myself. But thanks for asking'.

The pace and rhythm of the writing reflect the way James's thoughts jump about. He speaks in short sentences, sometimes containing just one word, but uses longer sentences, broken up, when his thoughts are jumping about. The **non-linear** storytelling, which switches from a comedy club, back to the train as the brakes hiss and James wakes up from his dream, has the effect of varying the rhythm of the monologue, too, through changing locations. From this moment on, everything happens at breakneck speed as the listener is party to James's thoughts running from one thing to another, forming free associations, until something happens (his hand hits a foot and he realises someone else is in his 'private' cabin with him). The listener feels part of all of this through the internal debate James has with himself throughout.

If you create a dramatic monologue for audio drama, think carefully about *why* you're using it. You will have to create a strong voice and have a good reason for wanting to write in that voice. You should also ask yourself if this is the only way your story can be told. *The Dead Dad Show* is a good example of effective use of monologue because it's about a character who is using comedy as a way of dealing with grief, and so a one-man stand-up show lends itself to one voice. As Dinnella says:

> In [the] relentless repetition [of Steve Reich's musical piece *Six Marimbas*], I heard the chugging and rattling of a train. I was also reminded of that cyclical 'spiral-of-doom' my brain sometimes goes into at about 4 o'clock in the morning when I can't sleep. Using these two images, I decided that the obvious place to start was with an insomniac on a sleeper train. And, because I automatically associate sleeper trains with the Edinburgh Festival (long story) I decided my insomniac character should also be a comedian. The rest of the monologue took shape from there.
>
> *(Dinnella, quoted in El-Nemr, 2019)*

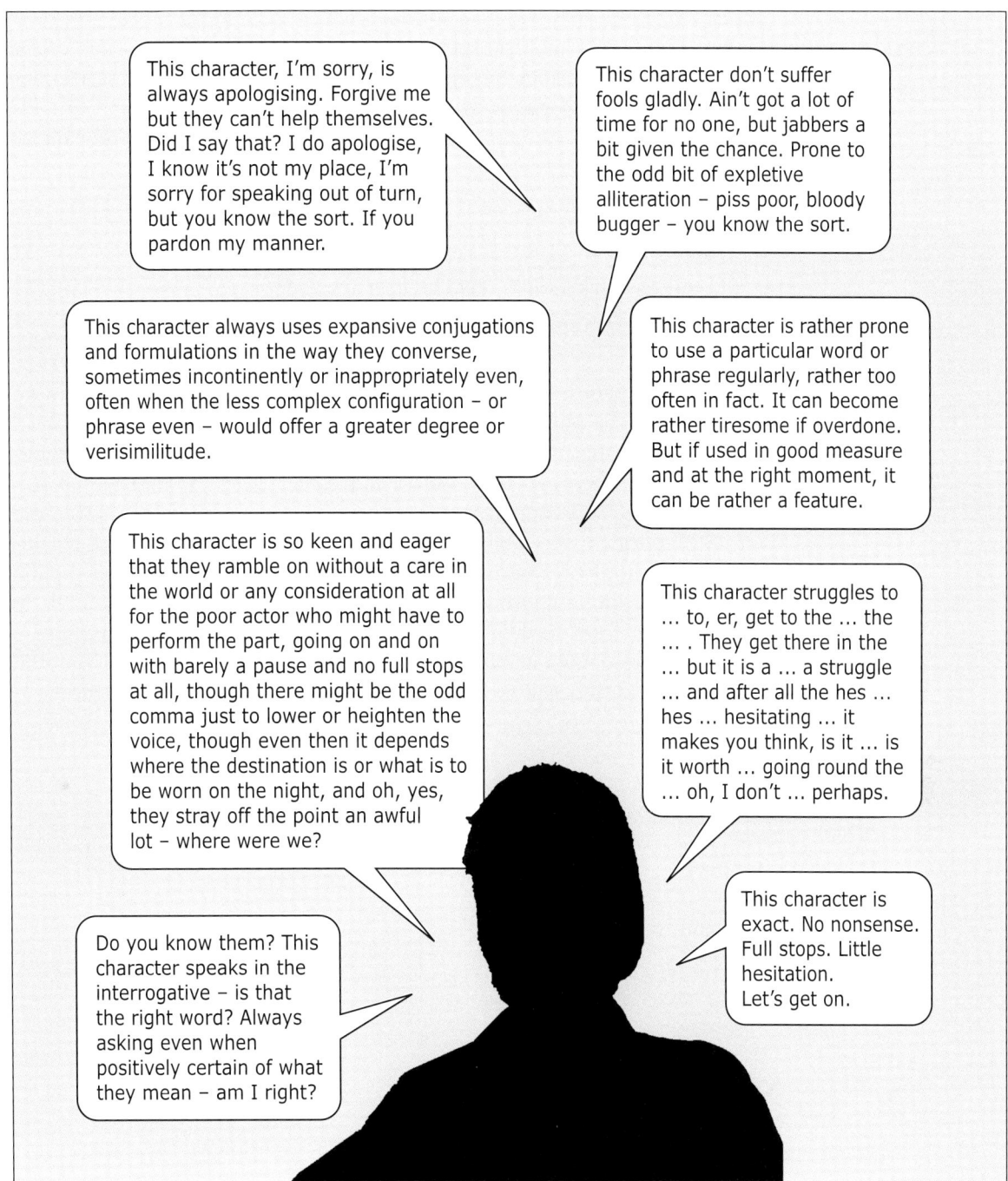

Figure 3 Writing distinct and consistent voices is key for audio drama.

Activity 4 Writing: creating a character through monologue

Look at Figure 3, which shows examples of character voices (each of the speech bubbles describes the character traits). Using one of these character voices, write two A4 pages of monologue for radio on the theme of lost love. Establish your character in a specific place – if you need a prompt for a place, choose from:

- a bookshop or library
- a queue
- the toilets at a cinema, restaurant or theatre
- a bus stop or train station platform.

Discussion

At first, you might have found that by repeating one speech pattern in your writing, you were not able to create a character. But at some point, you probably found that the given pattern you followed from Figure 3 developed into something less regular and more individual. The important thing is to 'hear' the voice; the more you listen to its rhythms and cadences, the more you will be drawn into a character. Whatever patterns of speech a character uses, there will always be modulations and variations in pace and rhythm according to content and mood. You will, of course, gain more knowledge of your character from further research and imaginative investigation, by inventing more details about their life, appearance and relations. You may have found that you had to do this in order to write this monologue.

5 Adapting for audio

Quite often in audio adaptations of long narratives, such as novels, there is a narrowing down of the timeline of the story and, most probably, of the cast list, too. As Linda Hutcheon says of Lindsay Bell's 2001 radio adaptation of Virginia Woolf's 1927 novel *To the Lighthouse*:

> The characters who remain double as storytellers, but many are eliminated to keep the focus on the Ramsay family and Lily Briscoe. The words we hear come from the novel, but they are moved around, recontextualized, and read by different voices. These changes allow the aural version to give a sense of the novel's linguistic texture, its associative range, and its narrative rhythm.
>
> *(Hutcheon, 2006, p. 41)*

In this way, the adapter edits the original but can give a distinct flavour of that text and its various voices. As you have learned in this chapter, audio drama can make listeners feel as though they are inside the head of a character. It also has the flexibility to shift the focus of a story quickly from, for example, a scene in the Himalayas to a scene in the Antarctic, then to a house in Bermondsey, without the need for expensive costumes, stage lighting or extravagant special effects. Compared with film, there are practically no production costs in making such shifts in audio drama; and compared with stage dramas, the shifts can be achieved quite naturalistically, without the need for scene changes or creating effects through lighting design. Another strength of audio drama is that surreal situations in the writing can be realised more easily than in other kinds of dramatic performance.

At the start of this chapter, you were introduced to the idea that everything is possible in audio drama and to think about being ambitious when writing for audio performance. The adaptation of science fiction writer Ray Bradbury's short story 'The Veldt' (1962) for radio by Mike Walker in 2007 offers a good example of this and the flexibility of audio drama. The original story, written in the early 1950s, is set in 'the future' and comments on the technological revolution happening in 1950s homes, with the advent of vacuum cleaners and televisions. In the story's world, every conceivable domestic task is performed by 'the house' rather than the occupants of the house: children are scrubbed in the bath automatically; tables serve meals that have been prepared by a fully-automated stove. The biggest innovation is a children's playroom in which the walls transform into virtual 'play worlds'. During the story, this room turns into the African veldt, complete with vultures and lions. In one scene, the family leave the dinner table and walk to the playroom, and suddenly, on entering the room, they are in Africa. This is achieved instantly in the radio adaptation with the sound of a lion's roar. In future scenes, when the listeners hear the lion, they know where they (and the characters) are. So, in terms of setting, the establishment of a futuristic world in an audio drama presents no greater technical challenge than creating a contemporary world.

Activity 5 Writing: adapting prose to a script for audio drama

Write **two** scenes (about five A4 pages in total) as the opening of an audio drama, adapting the start of **one** of these pieces of fiction writing:

- Reading 1.1: Jhumpa Lahiri's short story 'A Real Durwan' (1999).
- Reading 2.2: an extract from Naomi Alderman's *The Power* (2017).
- Reading 2.3: the market scene from Neil Gaiman's *Neverwhere* (2013).

It's up to you how to do this: your adaptation could include features such as a monologue for one of the scenes, scene links, a narrator, and characters with contrasting voice patterns.

This might be the start of a bigger piece of audio drama, but for this activity concentrate on trying to create a cohesive structure, where your two scenes are connected.

Discussion

Think about Hutcheon's comments at the start of this section, where she considers how a certain economy of casting and storytelling means that you need to cut some elements of the original story right back. An adaptation in whatever form is always going to be slightly different to the original. This means that sometimes you will need to invent elements that are not present in the original to make the dramatic logic of the storytelling more plausible. For instance, you might have found it necessary to invent some part of a character's past that isn't in the original story (such as how they came to be in this setting at this point in the story), which helps to explain why the character behaves the way they do.

6 Creating scenes in audio drama

Scene, derived from the ancient Greek word *skene*, meaning 'tent' or 'stage', appears something of a misnomer when used in the context of audio drama, where there is no tangible performance space. Audio drama uses the 'theatre of the mind' but, nonetheless, is still made up of scenes, which are the primary dramatic units of any script. As on the stage or on screen, a scene's duration is ruled by shifts in location and time, and by the culmination of a specific episode of dramatic action. Switching time periods and adopting a non-linear approach to plotting can be more easily achieved in an audio play than on stage because, for example, there is no stage furniture to move or lighting issues to address. Even so, events still have to be well signposted – you have to make sure that your listener knows 'where' they are in time. But often the different scenes in an audio script do not have headings and the division between them is not marked (whether or not you mark the scene divisions in your script is often decided by the type of story you are trying to tell).

Audio drama is a continuous form, so whether the scenes are numbered and headed in the script or not, the writer, and subsequently the producer of the performance, have to decide how to achieve the transitions between them. This can be done through a range of tactics, such as using music or sound effects to denote scene changes. In *Breaking Up with Bradford* (Reading 7.1), music is used to shift the setting from Cambridge to the train Kasim is travelling on, heading for Bradford; the music provides the link between the two scenes, playing across the end of Scene 1 and moving straight into Scene 2. The Steve Reich music and the sound effects have the same role in *The Dead Dad Show* (Reading 7.2). Without these clearly delineating the scenes and differentiating the passing of time, the drama would just move from one point in James's thoughts to the next.

7 Layout: formatting a script for audio drama

Figure 4 is a sample page from a radio script with notes highlighting particular features of the formatting. What do you notice about the way in which the script is laid out?

This example (Figure 4) is broadly similar to the BBC's guidance on layout for radio plays (Carless, 2004), and is a good model to use when writing your own scripts. Note, though, that other broadcasters may have specific requirements on presentation. Be sure to check what these are before submitting any audio script you write for consideration.

Here are some further tips:

- Use punctuation, pauses and silences to control the speech rhythms of monologues and in dialogue.
- As with stage dialogue, remember that a dash (–) at the end of a line designates that a line has been interrupted.
- Remember, too, that an ellipsis (…) at the end of a line designates that the line trails off.
- A pause within a line of dialogue is differentiated from the speech. It is usually bracketed and in capitals: (PAUSE); use these cautiously.
- Notice in Figure 4 how the man is described as (NARRATING) when he is talking as if the listener is hearing his thoughts. There are other possible conventions for showing this, such as putting (VO), short for 'voice-over', or (INTERNAL) before such speeches.

Using the appropriate script layout indicates to producers and script editors that your submitted script has been written specifically for audio. The layout of the script in Figure 4 is unambiguous; spoken and unspoken elements are clearly separated by typographic conventions. It is important to use these conventions and not invent your own.

As an approximate measure of running time, if you use the layout advice given here, each A4 page will average out at one minute of audio. Be aware, though, that this is an average and not an accurate gauge for individual pages or for all scripts. The only way to gauge the running time of a script exactly is to read through it in real time, so that all the sound effects and the different pace of lines are assessed accurately.

7 Layout: formatting a script for audio drama

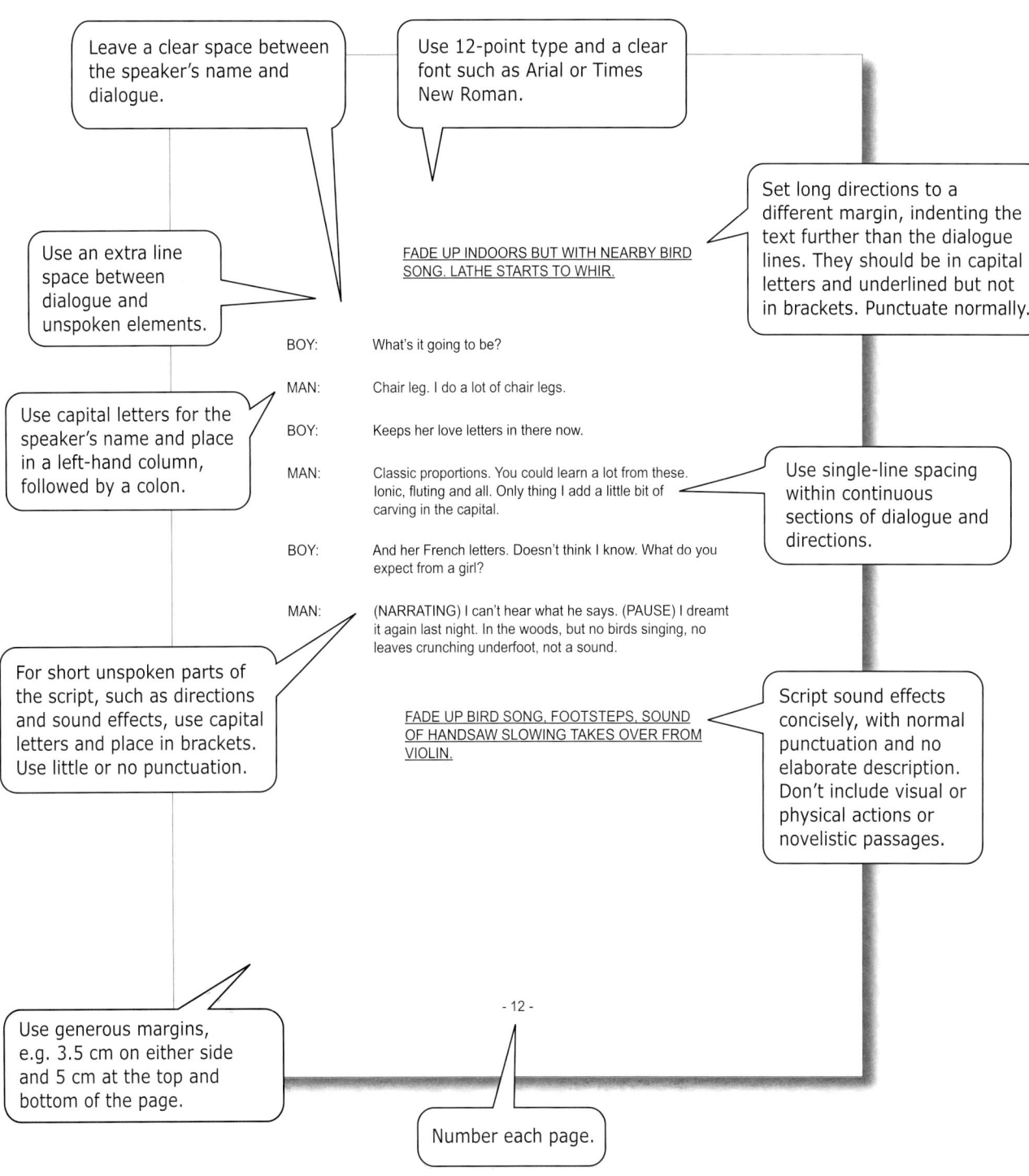

Figure 4 Layout for a radio script.

8 Conclusion

This chapter has introduced you to audio drama and ways to develop your own writing for this medium. You have learned how to format an audio script, and considered the various ways you can engage your listener in the world of your play, right from the start. You've explored how to use sound to tell stories and how to create different voices and viewpoints to do this.

Creating believable worlds for your audience is just as important in audio drama as it is in any dramatic medium, and you've looked at and tried ways of doing this throughout the chapter. The most important thing to remember though, and it bears repeating, is that what your listener 'sees' in their imagination is always stimulated by what they hear. This is how you will connect with your listener, and how you can make sure they stay with your drama right to the end.

As you progress through this book, you're learning the importance of reading as a writer. Writing audio drama is no different: listen to as many radio dramas or audio podcasts as you can, to help you find the inspiration and confidence to create your own dramas.

References

Alderman, N. (2017) *The power*. London: Penguin.

Atack, T.X. (2019) *Forest 404* [Podcast]. 5–31 March. Available at: https://www.bbc.co.uk/programmes/p06tqsg3/episodes/downloads (Accessed: 29 April 2024).

Bradbury, R. (1962) 'The veldt', in R. Bradbury, *The illustrated man*. London: Hart-Davis.

Carless, M. (2004) 'BBC radio format: scene style', *BBC Writers*. Available at: https://www.bbc.co.uk/writers/documents/bbcradioscene.pdf (Accessed: 29 April 2024).

Dinnella, A. (2019) *The dead dad show*. (Directed by M. Beeby. BBC Radio 3, 11 June, 22:45) [Script], pp. 1–4. Available at: https://www.bbc.co.uk/writersroom/documents/music-monologues-the-dead-dad-show-annalisa-dinnella.pdf (Accessed: 18 March 2024).

El-Nemr, A. (ed.) (2019) '5 writers commissioned for BBC Radio 3 music monologues', *BBC Writers*, 10 June. Available at: https://www.bbc.co.uk/blogs/writersroom/entries/b6cbb1ff-7146-4298-9461-bbe933f7917f (Accessed: 20 March 2024).

Gaiman, N. (2013) *Neverwhere*. London: Headline Publishing Group.

Hughes, R. (1966) 'Danger', in R. Hughes, *Plays*. London: Chatto and Windus.

Hutcheon, L. (2006) *A theory of adaptation*. Abingdon: Routledge.

Kaan, K. (2017a) *Breaking up with Bradford*, BBC Radio 4, 17 August, 14:15. Available at: https://www.bbc.co.uk/programmes/b0910ndm (Accessed: 26 April 2024).

Kaan, K. (2017b) *Breaking up with Bradford*. (Produced and directed by C. Riches. BBC Radio 4, 17 August, 14:15) [Script]. Available at: https://www.bbc.co.uk/writers/documents/breaking-up-with-bradford-kamal-kaan.pdf (Accessed: 18 March 2024).

Lahiri, J. (1999) 'A real durwan', in J. Lahiri, *Interpreter of maladies: stories*. London: Flamingo, pp. 70–82.

Power, B. (2023) *Emperor and Galilean*. Directed by C. Prekopp. [Radio play]. BBC Radio 3, 2 July, 19:30 (Part 1) and 9 July, 19.30 (Part 2). Available at: https://www.bbc.co.uk/programmes/m001n80y (Accessed: 8 March 2024).

Sirett, P. (2020) *Bartholomew abominations*. Directed by J. Sealey and P. Thomas. [Radio play]. BBC Radio 4, 7 November, 15:00. Available at: https://www.bbc.co.uk/programmes/m000p603 (Accessed: 29 April 2024).

Sirett, P. (2022) *The playwright's manifesto: how you can be the future of playwriting*. London: Methuen Drama.

Walker, M. (2007) *The veldt*. (Produced and directed by J. Kampfner. BBC Radio 4, 22 May).

Chapter 8
Dramatic journeys

Dónall Mac Cathmhaoill

1 Introduction

Figure 1 A scene from Lynn Nottage's *Clyde's*, directed by Lynette Linton, Donmar Warehouse, London, 2023. From left to right: Patrick Gibson, Ronkẹ Adékọluéjọ́, Sebastian Orozco and Giles Terera (photo: Marc Brenner).

This chapter explores how dramatic structure, genre and audience expectations overlap, and examines how consideration of these three elements informs the choices made by the writer.

Drama is produced for a wide range of media, and writers of drama have a great deal of choice about what stories they wish to tell and how they wish to present them. Ultimately, these choices will depend on the intended audience – and audiences for dramatic works are as numerous and diverse as the media, genres and styles of dramatic writing.

As you read this chapter, you will consider questions of dramatic structure in greater detail, exploring some of the more common models used to structure scripts and how dramatic conventions relate to audience expectations.

2 Dramatic structure: action and emotion

As you saw in Chapter 5, dramatic action is any story development, such as a plot point or change in character relationships, typically caused when a situation or incident necessitates a choice and results in an outcome. This arc of dramatic action – an incitement, a development and a final outcome – conforms to the 'three-act structure' described by Aristotle over 2000 years ago in his *Poetics* (2000) and it underpins many dramas. It is often characterised as a journey undertaken by the characters. The journey can be a physical one, but more often it is a journey of emotional discovery. In some cases it is both, as with many road trip films.

In the film *Little Miss Sunshine* (2006), the family of characters take a physical journey across several American states, in a camper van, to get their youngest member, Olive, to a beauty pageant in Redondo Beach, California. However, this physical journey is really secondary to the emotional journey the characters make, which is concerned with resolving their personal and familial conflicts. This points to the two progressive plot lines in a dramatic script: the action in the story, which forms the principal focus of the audience at the outset; and the emotional developments – in characters and character relationships – located *within* the action of the script.

2.1 Outer and inner journeys

As characters travel through a dramatic story, these two areas of the story (the 'outer' and 'inner' journeys) develop in tandem. They are often called the **action line** and the **emotion line**.

- The action line, or outer journey, charts what happens in the plot, through the obstacles, dilemmas, choices and outcomes that the characters deal with, within the drama. It is concerned with conflicts external to the **protagonist**.
- The emotion line, or inner journey, plots the emotional changes the characters go through: the issues and challenges they face, the choices they make in response to these, and the outcomes of these choices. It is concerned with conflicts that are located in the characters' emotional lives.

During the course of the physical road trip journey in *Little Miss Sunshine* (2006), all the characters experience major twists in the action line, suffering tragedy and humiliation. They make terrible choices, behave badly and their dreams and ambitions are thwarted. This culminates in Olive's humiliation in the beauty pageant: her dance routine (choreographed by Edwin, her grandfather) is horrendously off-tone for the competition. In the emotion line of the film, however, something wonderful happens. Having lost out on their hopes and aspirations, the characters become closer and, in the end, they are thrown together in solidarity through their support of Olive. Rather than accept her humiliation, the family members rally and treat her as if she has won a tremendous victory. The action line in the film leads to failure but the emotion line leads to success.

Often the characters in a dramatic script will be frustrated in their main goals but will succeed in resolving an inner problem. This is what happens in the stage play *Clyde's* (2023) by Lynn Nottage. The characters (Figure 1) are former prisoners trying to earn a living on the breadline. At the end of the play, they have the same problems as they had at the beginning but they have won a great victory in reclaiming their self-respect.

2.2 The heroic journey

The three-act structure of an incitement, a development and a final outcome aligns perfectly with the conceptual framework of a heroic journey. Such a journey has three obvious stages: the setting off (the beginning), the encounters and challenges on the road (the dramatic middle) and the arrival at the destination (the end). It is important to remember that such conceptual frameworks are just tools for enabling us to talk about dramatic structure. However, these ideas have been present throughout the history of dramatic writing in the West.

The heroic journey framework essentially describes any dramatic narrative in which the lead character deals with a challenge. The journey can be a physical challenge, an emotional challenge or both (as in the 2006 film *Little Miss Sunshine*). Starting out from a place of safety at the beginning of the story, the hero or heroine takes on the challenges and conflicts of the drama. They also confront their own shortcomings and the inner needs that make up their deeper character. For this reason, the concept of a heroic journey is also often referred to as a 'quest narrative'.

Both of these concepts reference the sources of these ideas – European myths and legends, and folk tales – and build on the work of several influential writers of the Western tradition of storytelling, notably the American literature academic, Joseph Campbell. Campbell's thesis is that myths and folk tales all express a core narrative, the 'monomyth', which tells the story that underpins all the myths and folk tales of history: one of an archetypal hero on a quest, which also entails a journey from non-awareness to awareness. Campbell's book *The Hero With a Thousand Faces* (1949) brought these ideas to a wide audience. His ideas, which had a direct influence on writers and directors in Hollywood, were later developed and simplified by screenwriter Christopher Vogler in his book, *The Writer's Journey: Mythic Structure for Writers* (2007). Vogler structured the heroic journey in 12 steps entitled 'The Hero's Journey' (see Figure 2). In his book, Vogler is clear that he uses the term 'hero' in a non-gender-specific sense.

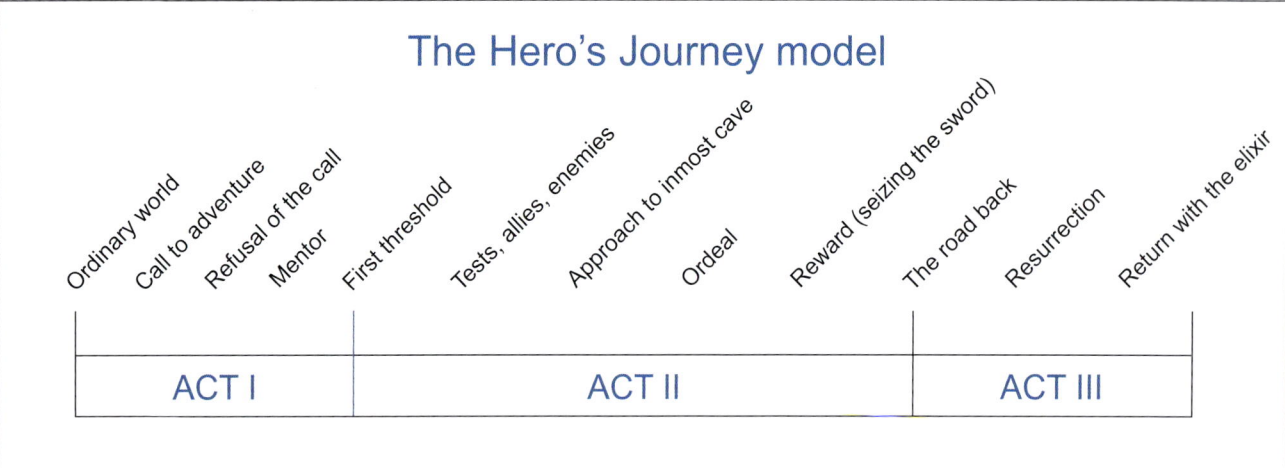

Figure 2 The Hero's Journey model, adapted from 'The Hero's Journey model' in C. Vogler, *The Writer's Journey: Mythic Structure for Writers*, CA, Michael Wiese Productions, 2007, p. 8 (reproduced with the permission of Christopher Vogler).

Limitations of the model described by Campbell and developed by Vogler (Figure 2) have been pointed out, especially with regard to its framing of a mythic quest in masculine terms of battles, monsters and mastery. Alternative models that foreground the feminine have come to prominence to challenge this. Notable is the feminine hero's journey developed by Victoria Lynn Schmidt in her book, *45 Master Characters: Mythic Models for Creating Original Characters* (2001). The stages of this feminine journey have been summarised as:

1. **Illusion of the perfect world**
   The heroine lives in a false state of security, naivety or denial.

2. **Betrayal/disillusionment**
   The heroine's delusional view of the world is ruptured, precipitating a crisis.

3. **The awakening**
   The heroine realises that the world is not as she had idealised it and decides to act. However, she has not arrived at full realisation and retains some belief in the idealised world view.

4. **The descent: passing through the gates of judgement**
   The heroine faces her new situation with doubts and insecurities, as she still clings to elements of the idealised world.

5. **Eye of the storm**
   The heroine has some successes in her early challenges, which provokes a sense of security that proves false.

6. **All is lost/death**
   The heroine realises that her success is fleeting and that her coping strategies have masked the reality. She is close to giving up.

7. **Support**
   A person emerges who offers support to the heroine, most often a friend, a goddess or another female ally. She accepts help.

8. **Rebirth/moment of truth**
   With the new support comes renewed hope and an acceptance of her own weaknesses.

9. **Return to a new world**
   The new situation allows the heroine to face the world anew, and to see it as it is. She carries on in her spiritual journey towards self-realisation.

(Source: adapted from The Heroine Journeys Project, no date)

While there are clear differences between Schmidt's conceptual framework and Vogler's, they also have important points in common. Both:

- describe the narrative structure as a journey
- consider the narrative as comprised of a departure, an adventure and a return
- operate on a form of the three-act structure, with a beginning, a rising action and then a falling action, and a conclusion.

They are useful tools for structuring the major events of a narrative and shaping the overall journeys your characters take.

Activity 1 Writing: the character journey

Write three paragraphs (half an A4 page) describing the journey of a character in a piece of writing that you like – this can be a story, a play or a film, an audio drama or a narrative poem. Your first paragraph should describe the world at the beginning of your chosen piece of writing; the second should cover the developments that form the core of the character's journey; and then, in your final paragraph, describe how the story ends.

Discussion

You can see from this activity that almost any story, whatever the form or genre, can be described as a journey. Often this need not be a physical journey. Instead, it can be a process of development where the lead character undergoes some type of change, responds to a difficult choice or reaches a resolution for a set of problems. The three-act structure which you have created in your three paragraphs is just a means of structuring the unfolding events of a story in a way that is easily understood, and that helps you, the writer, to make decisions about the progression of the narrative.

The structuring principles you used in Activity 1 are a means for writers to look at and make sense of structure, and to organise their narrative material to create a script that, in turn, makes sense to the reader, spectator or listener. They can also be applied to the arc of a single scene (as you will read in Section 3). Doing so helps to ensure that each scene in a script is dramatic, holds the audience's attention and impels the story forward.

3 The dramatic arc

The structure of a whole drama, the dramatic arc, tends to be shaped in such a way, so that it is coherent for audience members. However, the same principles operate in each scene of the script and well-written dramatic scenes will display the three-act structure in miniature.

One way a writer can start to structure a dramatic narrative in a scene is to pose a question in the opening moments that will intrigue an audience. There are an almost infinite number of questions that will hold an audience's attention: who is this character? What do they want? How will they achieve it? How will they persuade their friend to support them? Where will they find the money? These questions set up the dramatic situation and create the conditions whereby a character, or characters, will encounter an obstacle or conflict. In a scene, this is known as 'the complication'. The scene will end with a situation that either resolves the initial question, creates an ongoing dramatic issue, or magnifies the problems of the protagonist. This moves the drama forward into the next scene.

3.1 Set-up and payoff: the arc of a scene

The chain of events within a scene is often described as: set-up/complication/payoff. It is made up of individual story beats (as discussed in Chapter 6) that carry the audience through the scene. The shape that the story beats create exactly maps on to Aristotle's structure of a beginning, a development in the middle, and an ending where something has changed.

Table 1 Dramatic arc: scene set-up, complication and payoff

Act 1	Act 2	Act 3
Beginning	*Middle*	*End*
Creating the world of the story	A challenge, followed by conflicts	Bringing the conflicts to an end and reaching resolution
Lack of awareness	Dealing with the internal conflicts	Reaching awareness
Start of scene	**Middle of scene**	**End of scene**
Set-up	*Complication*	*Payoff*
A situation	A choice	A decision and a new situation
A problem or question	Wrestling with the problem; finding answers	New problems, new questions, new knowledge

When a writer develops the idea for a story, they often start with a simple idea, a few lines of story and a character or characters. From these starting points, they must proceed to develop a narrative. Building the dramatic narrative is one of the most exciting and challenging parts of writing a good drama. One way to approach this is to set down the basic elements of the story and then write out the storyline for each character as a sequence of scenes. You can then check that each sequence (a set of connected scenes) – and indeed each individual scene – contains a set-up, a complication and a payoff, to ensure all the sequences and scenes are serving your dramatic purpose and keeping the audience engrossed.

3.2 The outline

When you reach the point in writing a drama where you know what the purpose of each scene in the script is, it becomes possible to create an outline of the whole work. There are many ways (each with a different name) to write and present plot summaries. These are often referred to collectively as the **short documents**. As well as being immensely helpful for the writer, they are used at every stage of producing a drama, by directors, producers, agents and other industry professionals. The more common short documents are the **step outline** or **beat sheet**, **storyboard**, short outline, **synopsis** and **treatment**. They all do essentially the same thing: they lay the beats of a story out in a way that reveals the entire story arc. This enables you, as the writer, to examine each beat in its place in the story and to consider its positioning within, and value to, the drama.

Perhaps the most useful short documents are the step outline and the beat sheet, which show each step of a story in order and enable a quick assessment of dramatic structure. These documents often go through many iterations and drafts. Some writers like to write scenes or story beats on index cards that they can lay out in an order and then change that order, or move blocks of story around to arrive at the best sequence. Others might use sticky notes, writing a story beat on each note and arranging (and rearranging) them on a wall or board. Using these methods, writers might colour code the story events, using different colours for the main characters, certain themes and settings. It is important that you, as a writer, use a system for structuring your scripts that works for you and that you enjoy. If you are new to writing drama, you may find that examining the way other writers structure their scripts is a good way to develop your own ability to organise story beats into outlines. Identifying the beats in an existing script will help you to understand how professional writers structure their story material.

Activity 2 Reading and writing: beats in a scene

1. Read 'Scene Three' from the script of the 1991 play *Talking in Tongues* (2013) by Winsome Pinnock (Reading 8.1 in Part 4).

As the scene unfolds, the situation changes dramatically for the characters and for the audience. This change is the inciting incident of the play, driving much of the action that follows.

What are the key moments that form the beginning of the scene, the inciting incident (that is, a key turning point), the middle and the end?

2. Write an outline for the scene as a list of bullet points, with each bullet point highlighting each major story beat.

Discussion

Dramatic scenes often create questions in the minds of the audience members, and many of the questions that emerge in one scene are 'carried' into the next one by the audience. In the case of the scene you have read from *Talking in Tongues*, the arrival of Fran and Bentley changes things for the other characters in the scene, raising questions for the audience (and us, as readers of the script) about how they will respond. Creating questions for an audience keeps them interested in what might happen next, drawing them from the present scene into the scene that follows, and ensuring that they remain emotionally involved in the drama.

All outlines of dramas serve one purpose for writers: to help them identify and record the important story developments in the order they appear in the script. A very simple outline will have three steps covering the three main moments in the story: the beginning, middle and end. The outline shown in Table 2, however, has 11 steps, organised into three acts.

Table 2 Example of a step outline or beat sheet

Act	Scene	Story beats
Act 1	1	Amra and Elena find a stray dog wandering in the park. They decide to try to find its owner. Elena names the dog Scruff.
	2	Amra puts an advert about Scruff on the community noticeboard.
Act 2	3	Elena cares for Scruff. She walks and bathes him, and tries to comb his coat. Scruff remains looking scruffy.
	4	Amra gets a response to her advert on the community noticeboard. It is from someone called Alex who says they lost a dog fitting Scruff's description late last week.
	5	Amra tells Elena about the response from Alex. Elena has grown attached to Scruff; she doesn't want to give him up.
	6	Amra meets Alex and explains the situation. She says she will try to persuade Elena to give Scruff back. It is clear that Alex finds Amra attractive.
	7	Elena is persuaded to return Scruff to Alex. Alex thanks Amra and asks if she would like to go out for dinner sometime.
Act 3	8	Elena is distraught. She accuses Amra of pursuing her own interest by going out with Alex.
	9	Alex and Amra go on a date. When they return to Alex's, Scruff is gone.
	10	Amra goes round to Elena's. Scruff is there. He has escaped from Alex's and gone to Elena's.

| *Ending* | 11 | Alex agrees that if Scruff now prefers to be with Elena, that she should keep him. Amra and Elena make up. Amra tells her that she is going on another date with Alex. |

Some forms of outline provide much more detail than the example in Table 2. For instance, a treatment is usually a document that shows all the plot developments in order, but also adds lots of information on the mood and style of the piece. Conversely, a synopsis often presents the entire plot of the drama in a prose summary that describes only the main developments. Synopses can be as short as half a page or as long as several pages.

These kinds of outlines are useful as structuring frameworks to help writers to plan their scripts, to explore possible plot developments, and to bring the drama into focus. They also allow writers to exercise control over the story elements and reveal ways that their script can be improved. Ultimately, they help to interest producers and others in the script, too.

While the three-act structure, as shown in the example in Table 2, has been pervasive since it was outlined over 2000 years ago by Aristotle in his *Poetics* (2000), it is not the only way of looking at script structure. Classic tragedies, such as those by Shakespeare, often have five acts; though these, too, can be described as adhering to Aristotle's principles (as they have a beginning, middle and end). In his book, *Into the Woods: How Stories Work and Why We Tell Them* (2013), the writer and producer, John Yorke, outlines how the five-act structure can be used by drama writers. The five-act structure he describes generally has the steps shown in Figure 3.

Activity 3 Writing: a short script outline

1. Select a piece of writing that you have worked on in Part 1 of this book (Chapters 1–4). This could be a poem, story or piece of life writing. Write a series of bullet points describing the journey of the central character(s). Remember, this doesn't need to be a physical journey; it can be an emotional journey – a passage from ignorance to knowledge, for example. To help you write your bullet points, consider:

- where your character(s) start out from
- where they get to at the end
- what places they pass through on the way.

2. Now arrange your bullet points to make an outline for a short stage play or audio drama of approximately 15 minutes in length. You can roughly estimate the timing for your outline by setting a timer and then reading it through, visualising each scene in full. You should allow time for all the actions as well as the dialogue, imagining the movements of the actors and the quiet moments where there is no speech; for an audio drama, allow time for all sound effects. This will be a 'guesstimate', but don't worry too much about length at this stage, or about how many steps you have.

Discussion

When you review the outline you have written, you should find that you can clearly divide the steps into three categories: the opening scenes or sequence, the end scenes or sequence, and everything in-between (the middle). However, you may find that you can divide your outline up further. For example, after the opening scenes have established the dramatic situation, you might have a moment of transition that leads into the middle section. And there may well be a crisis that takes place in the middle of the script – often the middle section rises to a climax before the end sequence begins. No matter how many steps your script outline has, it is important to think about how these elements are arranged. The structure of the script will determine, to a great extent, the emotional effect it has on audiences.

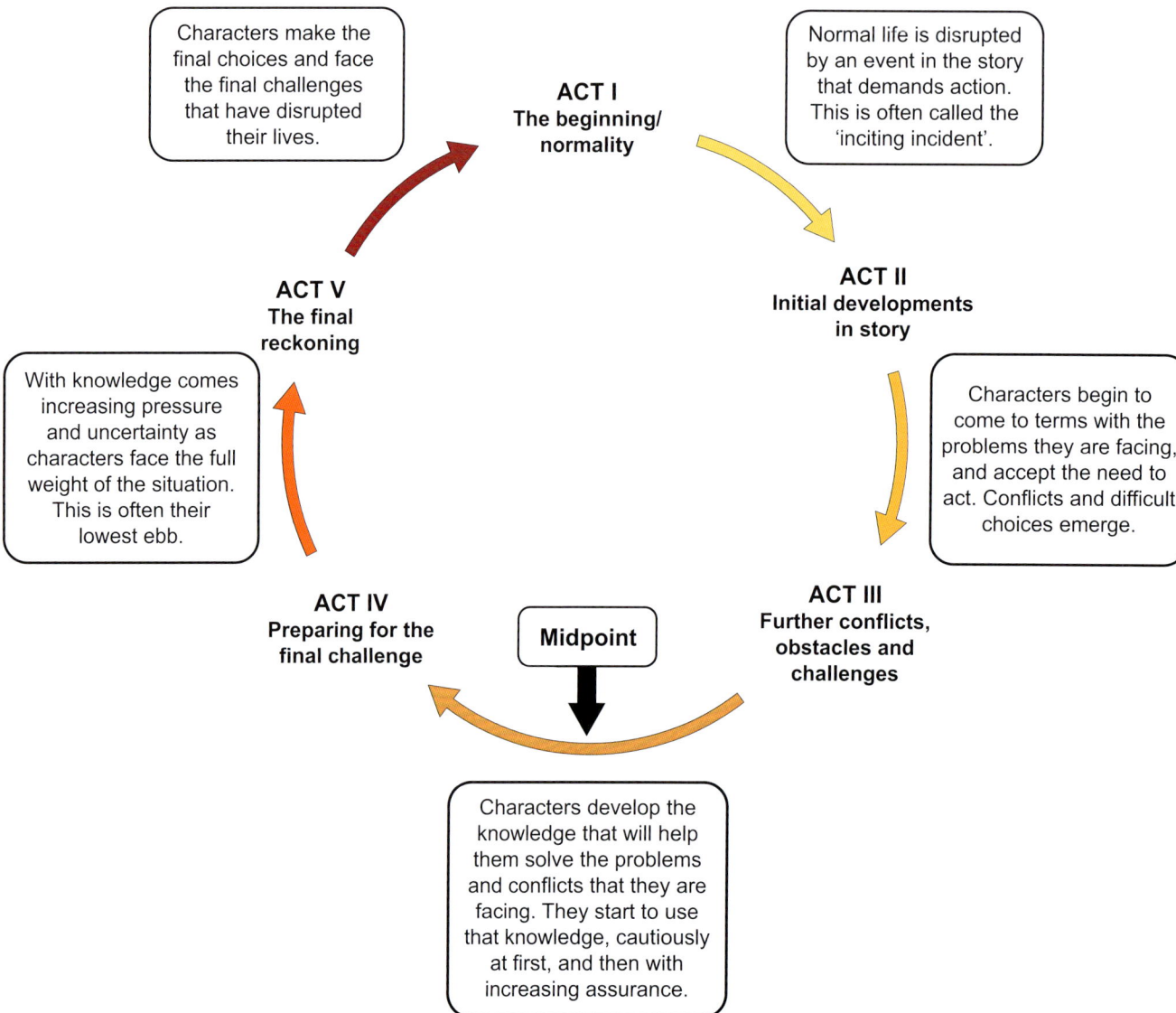

Figure 3 The five-act structure, adapted from 'The 3-D Roadmap of Change' in J. Yorke, *Into the Woods: How Stories Work and Why We Tell Them*, London, Penguin, 2013, p. 106.

4 Creating the world of the drama

As you read in Chapter 2, really effective writing brings the reader or audience member on a journey into a unique world; so, creating that world convincingly is a key skill for a writer to master. This is especially important in dramatic writing, where the journey into an unknown world or an exceptional situation is often at the heart of the script.

Moreover, for writers of drama, decisions about the world of their script are often directly related to the media they are writing for, whether that's film, TV, theatre or audio drama, and to the conventions that exist for different genres within that dramatic medium. As you saw in Chapter 1, the choice of genre in writing sets up audience or reader expectations and sets the tone and mood of the writing. In drama, it is equally important for determining the form the drama takes.

4.1 Dramatic conventions and realism

Many writers seek to recreate the real world, writing scripts that show a version of life that is as close as possible to reality. This is the dramatic equivalent of literary **realism**. Film is a particularly good medium for this and many films are written in a realist style. Films such as *Ratcatcher* (1999), written and directed by Lynne Ramsay, and *The Selfish Giant* (2013), directed by Clio Barnard, aim to show their subjects and worlds with an uncompromising eye for the 'real' and the everyday. Such films tend to be exact in their presentation of the social circumstances and living environments of their characters.

Stage drama, by contrast, places constraints on the writer, who has to think of ways to convey the world of the play, often by inference: for example, the offstage world is suggested through dialogue, sound and visual effects. Things happen in the space that is just beyond the action space (the stage in a conventional theatre) and the audience accepts this **offstage action**.

One of the most obvious conventions of stage drama is the placing of the action in front of an audience, yet characters interact without acknowledging the presence of that audience. This invisible 'screen' dividing the fictional world of the drama and the audience is known as the 'fourth wall'. Some writers choose to breach this boundary, though, writing dialogue that the actors deliver to the audience directly. This happens in many Shakespeare plays – such as *A Midsummer Night's Dream* (1992) and *As You Like It* (1993) – and in films like *Persuasion* (2022), directed by Carrie Cracknell, and *Amélie* (2001), directed by Jean-Pierre Jeunet.

Another dramatic convention involves the changes between scenes: in many live dramatic performances, one scene will end and the next one will begin, often in a different location in the story but without the need to physically change the stage set (if there is one). Audiences will accept these changes so long as they understand the action. If the scenes are well-written and the action is clear, there is no need to have fussy set changes.

Writers use these non-naturalistic conventions and techniques in all dramatic media to create dramatic worlds. In writing a script, even one that is set in the 'real' world, a writer is creating fiction. This is true even when the characters in the drama are representations of real people, whether contemporary or historical figures. The writer must cut out the uninteresting episodes and mundane details that might bore an audience. What they create is a fictionalised world where the story is shaped and crafted with skill and artifice. To achieve this, many scripts take liberties in creating the world of the drama. They will use dramatic conventions to present a story development that seems unlikely or impossible and make it credible. Sometimes they will bend the conventions to produce a dramatic effect.

An interesting and unusual example of the use of dramatic conventions can be seen in the original theatre production of the play *Pastoral* (Figure 4), written by Thomas Eccleshare (2013). The play describes a series of environmental calamities that lead to populations abandoning a city. But a small group of characters remain and, as they sit holed up in a small flat, trees and plants grow through the building, erupting through floors and into their living space.

Figure 4 A scene from Thomas Eccleshare's *Pastoral*, directed by Steve Marmion, Soho Theatre, London, 2013. From left to right: Richard Riddell as Hardy, Polly Frame as Arthur, Anna Calder-Marshall as Moll (seated) and Hugh Skinner as Manz (photo: Elliott Franks).

This unique and original dramatic premise is used to describe the consequences of environmental destruction by humans in a powerful, visual and action-filled way. During the performance of the play, tree trunks and foliage explode through the stage sets. This is clearly not what would happen in real life – but the non-realist style of the writing means that the audience will accept these eruptions of nature into the play.

Of course, it is not the job of the writer to decide how these effects are achieved in the performance of a drama. The scriptwriter should specify *what* happens but the director, designers and production team will decide *how* it happens. Nonetheless, it is important that, as a dramatist, you are not limited to writing in a realistic or naturalistic style. If you use the conventions of the medium, you can enable audiences to believe your premise. Knowing this, the writer can free their imagination to create worlds that are like ours, but different in subtle ways.

Activity 4 Reading and writing: setting up a scene

1. Read the scene from the play *The Christ of Coldharbour Lane* by Oladipo Agboluaje (2016), which was first performed in 2007 (Reading 8.2). This scene uses a combination of sounds, props and set items to create a London Underground railway carriage. Note down some of these techniques as you read, along with the effects they create.

2. Referring to the notes you have made, write the opening directions for the first scene of the script you outlined in Activity 3. Make use of techniques similar to those used by Agboluaje in Reading 8.2. A judicious use of props, staging or lighting effects will help you establish your scene if you are writing a stage play, but be careful to add these sparingly. If you have opted for an audio drama, try using sound effects to convey as much as possible in these opening directions.

Discussion

The stage directions and design in the scene you have read from *The Christ of Coldharbour Lane* involve a few very simple elements to recreate the London Underground carriage. The use of a pole and a few seats give the actors a basic set. This is augmented by the prop newspapers that the actors use to avoid eye contact. Importantly, sound effects made by the actors speaking rhythmic words recreate the sound of the train. Equally important, though, is how Agboluaje captures the mood of a busy commuter train by specifying simple things like the lack of eye contact, and the physical positions and movements of the actors' bodies to recreate those that might be adopted by commuters on the Tube in London (or any busy, metropolitan transport system).

5 Layout: formatting a screenplay

Figure 5 is a sample page from a screenplay for a film. This layout is broadly similar to the BBC's guidance on layout for film and television screenplays (BBC, 2024). There are many differences between this layout and that of stage and radio scripts – not least the positioning of the names of speakers. In screenplays, these sit above the dialogue, whereas in both stage and radio scripts they sit on the left.

Screenplays are formatted so that the reader can easily visualise the story, acknowledging the centrality of images in screen drama. Descriptions of actions are written across the page, so they read like prose, whereas other elements (character names, dialogue and **parentheticals**) are placed in a central column. Figure 5 shows the standard screenplay format and is a good model to use when writing your own. However, you may encounter screenplays with slight differences in formatting. This is particularly the case with published scripts where the requirements of a book's design might necessitate changes to the standard layout. Note also that some producers and broadcasters may have specific requirements for script presentation; always check what these are before writing and submitting any script for consideration.

Activity 5 Writing and editing: formatting a script

1. Return to the scene you began to write in Activity 4 of this chapter. Add the first lines of dialogue (between one and four lines in total) to the stage directions you have already written. Ensure that you also include the names of the speakers and any short directions that are required.

2. Check your script against the layout diagram for the appropriate dramatic medium shown in this book. If you have written a stage play, you should check your script layout against Figure 4 in Chapter 5; if it is an audio drama or radio play, check your script against Figure 4 in Chapter 7; and if you've written a screenplay, check it against Figure 5 in this chapter. Then make any necessary adjustments to the formatting of your work.

Discussion

It is vitally important to always check the formatting of your writing, to ensure that the layout conforms to the required format for the medium you are writing for. You can do this at the same time as proofreading your work for any errors in punctuation, spelling, and so on.

You must present your script in a way that shows it off to best effect. Using the industry standard format for screenplays (Figure 5), as with other types of script, ensures that those who read it will not be put off by your work before they've had a chance to engage with it in any detail.

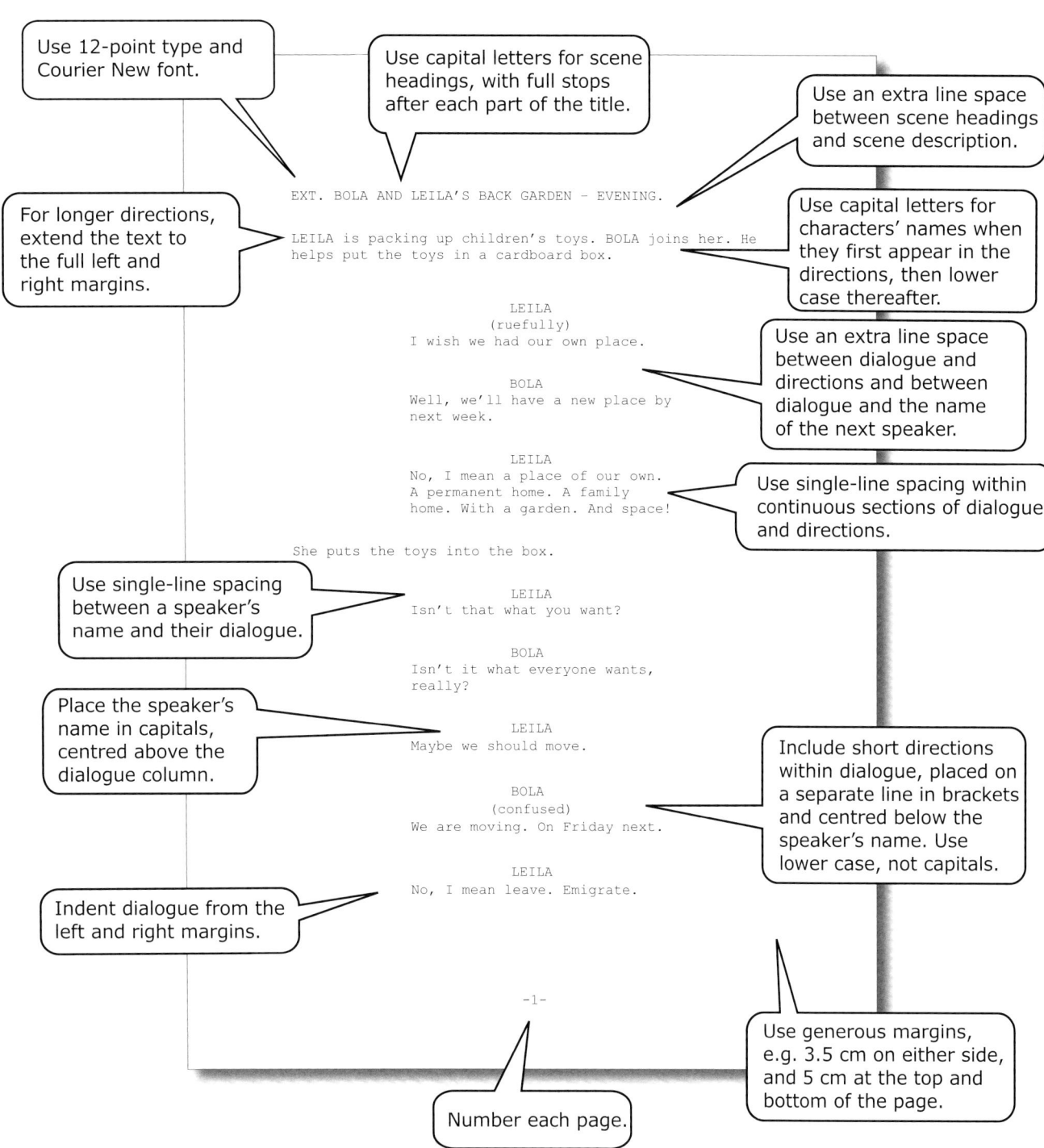

Figure 5 Layout of a screenplay.

6 Conclusion

When writing any drama, it is important that you develop a sense of what type of story you want to tell, how that story should be structured, and how the audience will experience the world of the drama. You will need to make choices about the structure, style and genre of your script. By having a clear idea of these central elements, you will be able to create a script that suits the story you are telling.

Ultimately, the drama must work for the audience: it must have a form that is right for the people who will watch it or listen to it. Giving serious thought to dramatic form and making choices that work for the audience, and the medium, will go a long way towards ensuring the success of the drama.

References

Agboluaje, O. (2016) *The Christ of Coldharbour Lane*. London: Oberon Books.

Amélie (Le fabuleux destin d'Amélie Poulain) (2001) Directed by J.-P. Jeunet. [Feature film]. Paris: UGC Fox Distribution.

Aristotle (2000) *Poetics*. Translated from the Greek by S.H. Butcher. South Bend, IN: Infomotions, Inc. Available at: https://ebookcentral.proquest.com/lib/open/detail.action?docID=3314345&pq-origsite=primo# (Accessed: 4 January 2024).

BBC (2024) 'Medium and format', *BBC Writers*. Available at: https://www.bbc.co.uk/writers/resources/medium-and-format/ (Accessed: 29 April 2024).

Campbell, J. (1949) *The hero with a thousand faces*. New York, NY: Pantheon Books.

Eccleshare, T. (2013) *Pastoral*. London: Oberon Books.

The Heroine Journeys Project (no date) *Victoria Lynn Schmidt's heroine's journey arc*. Available at: https://heroinejourneys.com/heroine-journey-ii/ (Accessed: 17 May 2024).

Little Miss Sunshine (2006) Directed by J. Dayton and V. Faris. [Feature film]. Los Angeles, CA: Fox Searchlight Pictures.

Nottage, L. (2023) *Clyde's*. London: Nick Hern Books.

Persuasion (2022) Directed by C. Cracknell. [Feature film]. Beverly Hills, CA: Netflix.

Pinnock, W. (2013) 'Talking in tongues', in L. Goddard (ed.) *The Methuen Drama book of plays by Black British writers*. London: Methuen Drama, pp. 119–200.

Ratcatcher (1999) Directed by L. Ramsay. [Feature film]. Glasgow: Pathé Distribution.

Schmidt, V.L. (2001) *45 master characters: mythic models for creating original characters*. Cincinnati, OH: Writer's Digest Books.

The selfish giant (2013) Directed by C. Barnard. [Feature film]. London: Artificial Eye.

Shakespeare, W. (1992) *A midsummer night's dream*. Stansted, Essex: Wordsworth Editions.

Shakespeare, W. (1993) *As you like it*. Stansted, Essex: Wordsworth Editions.

Vogler, C. (2007) *The writer's journey: mythic structure for writers*. 3rd edn. Los Angeles, CA: Michael Wiese Productions.

Yorke, J. (2013) *Into the woods: how stories work and why we tell them*. London: Penguin.

Chapter 9
Adaptation

Dónall Mac Cathmhaoill

1 Introduction

Writers of drama find source materials and ideas in many places. You may have read a travelogue that offers a promising setting. That story that was reported in your local newspaper may provide an exciting plot twist. The biography of a well-known sports person who overcame hardship might suggest characters. Or, as often as not, there will be people in your wider circle – friends, family members, acquaintances or friends of friends – who have had unusual or inspiring experiences that are just crying out to be turned into a piece of writing.

In many ways, writers are always adapting material: from family history, overheard conversations or personal stories. Often, though, a writer will want to adapt from a short story, book, magazine article or other source. These are known as third-party sources and the copyright of these works will almost always belong to someone else.

This chapter explores the challenges and opportunities offered by the adaptation of written works from various media, and provides knowledge and skills to enable you to work with pre-existing material. It explains some of the processes involved in adapting from a literary medium to a dramatic one, looking at how different media, such as the stage, radio and screen, demand different choices of the writer – perhaps some existing material may need to be omitted, or new material developed and added. This chapter also touches on questions of ownership and rights, and looks at the demands of the different forms of dramatic writing: screenplays, audio drama scripts and plays for live performance.

2 Adaptability

Figure 1 *The Phantom of the Opera* adaptations (clockwise from left): Lon Chaney and Mary Philbin in the film *The Phantom of the Opera*, directed by Rupert Julian, Universal Pictures, 1925 (photo: Granger/Shutterstock); Peter Davison as the Doctor, Nicola Bryant as Peri and Christopher Gable as Sharaz Jek in the TV episode *Doctor Who: The Caves of Androzani*, BBC, 1984 (photo: © BBC Archive); and Dave Murray and Paul Di'Anno of Iron Maiden on stage at the Hammersmith Odeon, London, 14 March 1980 (photo: Pete Still/Redferns/Getty Images).

Perhaps the overriding consideration in choosing a piece of work to adapt must always be its suitability to the medium for which you intend to adapt it.

'Brokeback Mountain' (2006), a short story first written by Annie Proulx in 1997 and published in the collection *Close Range*, was adapted for the screen by Larry McMurtry and Diana Ossana. It made an excellent film directed by Ang Lee (2005), but it would not necessarily have made a good stage play. The vast outdoor settings, contrasting with the intimacy of the central relationship of the two main characters, would have been much more difficult to present on a small stage than on film (interestingly, though, it was adapted for a stage opera in 2014).

Nightmare Alley (2021) is a film adaptation by Guillermo del Toro and Kim Morgan of the novel by William Lindsay Gresham (1946). This work would not have made a successful audio drama: much of the action focuses on the stage trickery of mentalist Stanton Carlisle, and these purely visual scenes would be impossible to present as audio. It would rely on a character describing Carlisle's tricks and ruses as they happen, which in turn would torpedo the central idea of those scenes: that he was utterly convincing and audiences did not realise he was cheating.

By contrast, some stories have such flexibility and universality that they can be adapted for any media. This tends to be true of mythological stories that have universal messages. The folk tales collected by the Brothers Grimm are a good example. The story of *Cinderella / The Glass Slipper* was well known in many versions before the Grimms included it in their book of folk stories in 1812. It has been adapted into many versions since, including stage plays, ballets, operas, prose stories, TV dramas, animations, feature films, video games and audio dramas. Likewise, the 1910 Gaston Leroux novel *The Phantom of the Opera* (2018) has been adapted into numerous works in many media, including a stage musical, TV dramas, films and even a heavy metal song by the English band, Iron Maiden (Figure 1).

2.1 Adapting your own work

One of the most common types of adaptation is when a writer adapts their own work. They might find, for example, that one of their short stories would make a good stage play; or that their material for a stage play depends heavily on sound effects and so it could make a good audio drama script. You will have given some thought to these issues as you read Chapter 8, which asked you to develop a short script outline based on your own writing.

When you are adapting your own original work for another medium:

- you know the original text better than anyone and you will most likely have clear ideas on how to adapt the work
- you can make decisions about what is working and what to keep and what to change, without the duty of being 'faithful' to the original
- you do not have to concern yourself with the legal considerations of adapting the work of another writer (discussed in Section 2.2).

Most importantly, if you have written a piece of work and you have a gut feeling that it will work well in another medium, this is a powerful motivator to rewrite it. And of course, you will have already done the hard work of developing the narrative, characters, themes and other elements. In this sense, a writer who adapts their own work starts with an advantage.

Whatever the source text, even if it is a work of your own, the primary challenge of adaptation remains: finding an approach that offers the possibility of making something unique and original. A screenplay or script adapted from another work, such as a short story or novel, must have the same qualities as any good piece of original dramatic writing. It should:

- have a strong narrative arc
- have relatable and intriguing characters, who will engage the sympathy – or antipathy – of the audience
- present the characters with situations of conflict
- show the progress of a situation that results in difficult choices and profound change for the characters.

If you decide to adapt a piece of your own writing for a new medium, these considerations should be central to your thinking and choice of text.

2.2 Adapting the works of others

While many authors are very open to the idea of their work being adapted, not all are. It is, as a rule, much easier to adapt pre-existing works of any kind when you already own the rights or where the works are out of copyright. In either of these cases, you will be able to adapt with freedom and without regard for the response of a third-party author or their estate. If a work is out of copyright, the adapter does not need to seek consent to adapt the work and does not need to share any income gained from their adaptation with the author of the original work or their estate. As with adapting your own work, this allows you, as a writer, the freedom to do what you think will work best for the material and the audience. However, it is important to be sure that a work is out of copyright before commencing an adaptation.

Box 1 Rights and adaptation

If you plan to adapt the work of another person, you should first find out whether the rights to adapt that work are likely to be available to you. Copyright for most works of literature expires 70–100 years after the author of the work has died (though there are exceptions). Obtaining the rights to adapt the works of others that are still in copyright can be difficult and expensive. For these reasons, many writers opt to adapt their own work rather than that of others.

If a work is still in copyright, you must gain the consent of whoever owns the rights to adapt it: this is almost always the original writer of the work or their heirs. Often this is done through the writer's agent or a legal representative. The writer (or their heirs) may impose conditions on the use of their work and they often expect a share of the profits made from any adaptation. A deal must be struck that compensates the original writer for the reuse of their creation.

Ultimately, whether you adapt material that is out of copyright or texts where you have the consent of the original author, the *adapted* work will be *your* script, with your name on it. It is therefore important that you feel you can take the third-party material and make something from it that is uniquely yours.

When planning an adaptation of your own work or that of another writer, it is good practice to first list the attractive aspects of the project – that is, what it is that draws you to the material and why you think it would make a good adaptation. This list can be used along with a **beat sheet** and other **short documents** when you are trying to sell your script to producers or interest directors in your work.

3 Editing the text

Having chosen a suitable work to adapt, whether a short story, a narrative poem, a piece of life writing or something else; and having established the copyright status of that work, ensuring that you have (or can secure) the rights so you can adapt it, next, you must set about making that material work for the medium you have chosen and the audience. If it is to become a work for the theatre, can the scenes be staged live successfully? Must some of the action take place offstage? Will this become reported action, described in dialogue by one character to another? Or can that awkward-to-stage scene be cut entirely? This part of the adaptation process is all about discussions of inclusion and exclusion: what to keep and what to get rid of.

Activity 1 Writing: making selection decisions

Reread the short story 'A Real Durwan' (1999) by Jhumpa Lahiri (Reading 1.1 in Part 4), with a view to adapting it as a script. You will need to decide the dramatic medium for the planned adaptation: will it be a script for the stage, screen or an audio drama?

1. As you read 'A Real Durwan', note down the main beats that you think are important to the story.

2. Next, look through your list of story beats and mark those that you will not use for your script. Write a word or two beside each one to explain why you have discarded it.

3. Finally, write a beat sheet for your script. What are the story beats you will include in the script? Note whether you intend to present these story beats:

- as actions or action sequences
- as dialogue
- using a technique such as sound effects, camera shots or montage.

Discussion

You will find that some material in the story is repetitive, such as Boori Ma's many descriptions of the luxury of her former life. But in a script, this only needs to be represented once. You will also have encountered things that, depending on the dramatic medium for which you have chosen to adapt the story, cannot be represented as they appear in the original short story. For example, Boori Ma's sweeping and cleaning cannot be 'shown' in an audio drama and may have to be the subject of a dialogue exchange – perhaps between Boori Ma and Mrs Dalal. In making these choices, you are engaging in the main activity of adaptation: the selection of material that is suited to the medium you intend to use.

As a general rule, when adapting from another source, you must keep all the narrative material that is essential to telling the story – that is, your *new* story, not the original one. You should always remain focused on the work you want to create through the process of adaptation.

3.1 Faithful and unfaithful adaptations

When critics and reviewers discuss adapted works, they often make much of the extent to which the adaptation is 'faithful to the original'. Ultimately, this is a discussion for fans of the original work and has little bearing on the success of the adaptation. It serves no one if you adapt a work with great fidelity to the original, which then fails as a stand-alone script because you have not edited, shaped, restructured and rewritten the original to enable it to work effectively for the dramatic medium you have chosen. In fact, no adaptation can truly be called 'faithful': all make changes to the original work. This is a challenge for writers who are adapting their own work, as they must be prepared to cut and dispense with material from the original that does not work for the new dramatic medium.

William Makepeace Thackeray's 1844 novel *The Luck of Barry Lyndon* (2008) follows the fortunes of the hero, Barry, as he joins an English regiment fighting in the Seven Years War. In his 1975 film adaptation, *Barry Lyndon*, Stanley Kubrick creates visually powerful cinematic action from the battles described in the novel. However, in the adaptation of the same novel that I wrote for BBC Radio 4 (Mac Cathmhaoill, 2003), the war is quickly passed over in a few lines. It cannot be omitted because it is an important beat in the story, but it holds no real interest for a writer of audio drama as it offers little for radio audiences. As a writer, your choices during adaptation should be governed by what is best for the medium and what will therefore work best for the audience.

3.2 Acts of creation in adaptation

As well as retaining key narrative material and cutting out things from the original work that will not serve the adaptation, another tool available to writers, which is vitally important for creating effective dramatic adaptations, is invention.

Sometimes, in order to make a story work for a given medium, it is necessary to add new material. This could mean creating entirely new scenes, an additional character, or even changing the ending. Doing so might feel presumptuous, particularly if you are very fond of the original work you hope to adapt (and you should be). However, it is necessary to be brave sometimes in order to make the material really work for the new medium. That said, invention is a tool that should be used with caution when adapting a work and only where necessary. Ultimately, if you add too much new material, it begs the question, 'why have you opted to adapt this story at all?' So, if you find that a third-party text requires radical revision, including the invention of many new scenes, characters or plot points, then you should seriously consider whether it is an appropriate text to adapt for the dramatic medium you have chosen.

However, if the work of rewriting is well done – through choosing what to keep, cutting that which is not needed, and adding new material judiciously – the result can be fresh and original, stand as a coherent dramatic work in its own right, and still manage to stay faithful to the original text. The drama adaptations of Andrea Levy's 2004 novel, *Small Island*, are examples of how this can be successfully achieved (you were introduced to these in Chapter 6).

Levy's novel was adapted for the stage in 2019 by Helen Edmundson and performed that year at the National Theatre. In this stage version, the action focuses on the overlapping stories of three main characters: Hortense, Gilbert and Queenie. The BBC TV dramatisation of the novel (2009) focuses on Hortense, Gilbert and Queenie, too, but it also gives more screen time to the character of Michael. Hortense is the principal character and our way into the story in this TV adaptation, which uses a similar structure to that of the original novel, switching back and forth in time between Jamaica in 1940 and London in 1948. In contrast, Edmundson's stage play has a more conventional linear structure.

Both of these adaptations of *Small Island* are successful because each does what is necessary to make the 500+ page novel work in a new form. They retain the core narrative and the main characters, but make changes to the structure and foreground certain characters. In the case of the stage play, this means condensing the action and using a linear structure. The changes made in both adaptations are essential to make the material of the novel work for the dramatic media for which they are intended. They succeed because they take account of audience expectations, as well as the limitations and demands of different dramatic forms (explored in previous chapters).

Activity 2 Reading and writing: adapting into sound

1. Read Reading 9.1, an extract from Andrea Levy's novel, *Small Island* (2004), and Reading 9.2, an extract from the script of the 2019 stage play adaptation of *Small Island* by Helen Edmundson. Both readings cover the same moment in the story: Hortense's interview for a job. But if you compare them you'll discover something quite interesting. The interview scene takes up almost four pages in the novel, but in the stage version it is not played out at all: instead, it is delivered as reported action by Hortense when she emerges from the interview.

2. Write no more than four lines of description for an audio version of the same scene from the original novel (Reading 9.1), detailing how you would present this material in sound. How much of the dialogue from the novel would you use in your audio adaptation of this scene? Would you include sound effects? Bear in mind that you might only have a couple of minutes in the audio drama for this entire scene.

Discussion

As you have seen in previous chapters of this book, different dramatic media have different strengths and present dramatic action in different ways. The writer of a screenplay must outline the action in fewer words, using only essential dialogue, knowing that the director will show much of the detail in camera shots. Stage plays must present dramatic action in a relatively small space, in front of a live audience. Inevitably, some incidents that are difficult to stage will happen offstage. In audio drama, the scene directions, descriptions and action must be conveyed to the audience through sound. All three media require different approaches by the writer to give the audience the most engaging experience.

3.3 A note on voice-over

There are many ways a writer can represent narrative material when adapting from one medium to another. For instance, if you are adapting a film with dynamic action sequences into an audio drama, you may well be tempted to write a narration describing the action, delivered as a voice-over. Similarly, if you are trying to represent the innermost thoughts of a character in a high-action scene in a screenplay, you might write this as an inner monologue, where the character's thoughts are presented in voice-over.

However, it is important to exercise great caution when using voice-over, narration or internal monologues. Often these devices can slow down the pace of the script, distracting the audience by taking their attention away from what is happening and causing them to lose focus on the story. But perhaps one of the most important reasons to use these techniques with caution is because producers and directors often regard them as lazy ways to convey information. At worst, they are considered expositional and undramatic: they convey story information in a way that is not particularly interesting for an audience. They should be used sparingly, if at all, and only where they add real value to the script. In every case, writers of drama should always ask themselves: 'Can this story information be written as a dramatic scene?' If the answer is yes, then that is usually the best way forward.

4 Forms, audiences and markets

Figure 2 Leah Harvey as Hortense in a play adaptation of Andrea Levy's *Small Island*, directed by Rufus Norris, performed on the National Theatre's Olivier stage, London, 2019 (photo: Brinkhoff/Mögenburg).

Edmundson's stage adaptation of *Small Island*, discussed in Section 3.2, had to work for the main stage of the Olivier Theatre at the National Theatre in London. It had to be ambitious in the scale of its production, with sound, set, costume, lighting, special effects and movement design all essential in creating an epic production that would fill the vast stage (Figure 2) and reach more than 1100 people sitting in its auditorium. While this is a challenge of huge scale that most writers are unlikely to encounter, the same issues of writing for the size and scope of the intended performance, venue and audience exist for all writers of drama, whether they are adapting material for a small fringe theatre or for a production by a touring company, where everything needed for the performance has to fit inside a van.

The Olivier Theatre draws a wide spectrum of theatregoers, from committed theatre aficionados to tourists visiting London. The plays staged there are mass-marketed and audiences attend hoping for a unique and memorable experience. They expect to see a play with the highest production values, often featuring well-known actors.

By contrast, smaller venues such as fringe and studio theatres will attract smaller audiences, often from the local area, with far fewer tourists than might be at the Olivier Theatre. In general, the work in these venues will be produced with less money and fewer resources, and the cast often won't include famous actors. The performance space will also impose limitations on what can be produced if it is smaller or has limited technical provision. The scale of production possible means that most smaller venues have a very clear sense of the types of plays that will work for their audiences.

These differences between potential producers and venues, and the expectations of audiences in different settings, are vitally important: they can help a writer to make important choices. In particular, a writer of drama must always have an eye on the audience. Knowing who your drama is for is a major signpost for the type of work it must become. It can help you to decide on the scale of the work, including the size of the cast, and so anticipate the likely cost of producing the work and the possible venues or producers who will be interested in taking it on.

If you start the work of adaptation knowing what kind of work you will most likely create, who the audience is for that work, and which venues and production companies like to produce works of that type, the process of writing and getting it produced will be much easier.

4.1 Adapting for the screen

Adapting an existing work for the screen is dependent on the same principles as writing original material for any visual dramatic medium (as discussed in Chapter 6). Filmed drama – whether for the big screen, television, online or streamed services – is essentially about creating memorable images and telling a story through visual action. Therefore, if you are choosing a text to adapt that will be presented on screen, your choice must take account of the visual possibilities of the work. If the original does not have much visual action, is it a good choice for a screen adaptation? Alternatively, can additional screen action be created? You should think about how the visual qualities of the story can be augmented by other storytelling elements, such as the introduction of new characters, incidents, settings and even narrative strands.

Figure 3 Still from *Sita Sings the Blues*, directed by Nina Paley, 2008 (photo: Photo 12/Alamy).

When the American artist, animator and director Nina Paley decided to adapt the classical Indian poem the *Ramayana*, written over 1000 years ago by Valmiki, she first made a short film called *Dandaka Dharma* (2005) based on a portion of the poem. Subsequently, Paley expanded this short film to include the main plot details of the *Ramayana*, along with a parallel narrative about her own marriage, to create the animated film *Sita Sings the Blues* (2008). The result is a rich and playful mix of adapted work and autobiographical narrative (Figure 3).

Throughout the adaptation process, it is vital to remember the essential qualities of screen drama:

- It is visual.
- It is composed of action.
- It has dialogue scenes as well as action sequences.

The first task of any screenwriter adapting a work for the screen is to look at the visual possibilities of the material. Often it can help to initially write down all the important scenes and story beats in the original that could be conveyed to a spectator without dialogue. By doing so, the visual qualities of the material become more apparent: the screenwriter can begin to 'see' the story as a film and can then rewrite some of the key beats as sequences of visual action. After this, decisions can be made about what dialogue should be reused from the original material (this is the process you followed in Activity 1 of this chapter). The writer can then start to expand the script, inventing new material if it is needed – developing additional essential dialogue and adding any new beats or scenes needed for the adaptation.

Activity 3 Writing: identifying story beats

Review the step outline and directions for the opening scene that you wrote in Activities 3 and 4 of Chapter 8.

1. Write a beat sheet for an adaptation of this work as a screenplay. Create at least five beats that capture the essential scenes that tell the story. Do not write any dialogue for your screenplay at this stage: see how much you can achieve with visual action only.

2. Now write at least two scenes of your screenplay. In doing so, think of how to convey the beats of the story using visual action only. Be sure to correctly format the scenes you write, following the guidance for formatting screenplays in Chapter 8. Refer to Figure 5 in Chapter 8 to check whether you have done this correctly.

Discussion

You may have realised that in writing visual scenes, you have created gaps in your narrative where the uninteresting details between dramatic story beats have been omitted. Events cannot always be shown continuously – in fact, they rarely are. When these gaps appear in the narrative, the writer may decide to keep the audience guessing. Used carefully, this tactic of leaving some parts of the story open and withholding information from the audience can encourage them to stay engaged with the story in order to find their own answers to their questions.

4.2 Adapting for audio drama

The essential elements for writing audio drama, as discussed in Chapter 7, are also the key considerations for a writer wanting to adapt existing material into a script for audio performance.

It is often simpler to choose a work to adapt for audio drama than choosing one for the screen or the theatre. It must be a work that is effective as audio: if it has a great deal of purely visual material, it might be difficult to represent that in sound. Alan Bennett's stage play *The Lady in the Van* (1999) is about an elderly lady who, as the title suggests, lives in a van. The action is therefore confined to a small space and is largely dialogue-based. These features meant that it worked well as a radio play when it was adapted in 2009 (House, 2009).

There are limited storytelling means and techniques available to writers adapting material for audio. For any text one proposes to adapt, it must be possible to tell the story using only:

- dialogue
- sound effects
- music
- voice-over narration.

Activity 4 Writing: adapting for audio drama

Adapt one of the scenes you wrote for Activity 3 in this chapter into a scene for an audio drama. Remember to lay the text out in the proper format for an audio script, separating the sound effects and any music from the lines of dialogue. Refer to Figure 4 in Chapter 7 to check whether you have done this correctly.

Discussion

Inevitably, to complete this activity you will have to add dialogue to your audio scene in order for unseen action to be comprehensible to the listener. When adapting material from any medium into audio drama, parts of a story that have previously been seen must now be rendered in sound. What was previously visual action must either be described in dialogue or indicated by sound effects in the audio production. More likely, a writer will include a mix of both suggestive lines of dialogue and clear, indicative sound effects. Dialogue from the original material is, of course, easier to adapt for audio drama, but remember that the listener cannot see the different speakers, so the distinctiveness of the voices of all the characters in audio drama is vital.

4.3 Adapting for the stage

Adapting for the stage presents a more complex set of challenges than adapting for audio drama or for the screen. Choosing a text that works for the medium is not so much about scale or space in the first instance – though those things need to be considered when thinking about the performance space the adaptation will best suit. It's more about the work's potential for live performance: can the scenes and episodes of the story be presented live on a stage in front of an audience.

Sometimes live performance might involve multimedia presentation. For example, adapting the short story 'Brokeback Mountain' (2006) into a stage play for a small venue would present significant challenges (as previously discussed in Section 2). But projecting a video or still images of the landscape from the original story on to the background for the performance could give a live audience a sense of that scenic grandeur. The stage also offers the possibility of actors using words to convey story, so some things that cannot be shown onstage can be presented in speech. And there is the possibility of using offstage action, as discussed in Chapter 8 and earlier in this chapter: characters can tell one another (and the audience) about things that happen in other locations, offstage, which the audience cannot see.

As already noted, it's important that a writer's decision about what work to adapt for the stage is also informed by whether the adaptation will fit its proposed venue (if it is known). Theatres vary enormously in size, shape and audience configuration, as well as in the resources they have available: financial, human and technical. It is important that the choice of text takes account of this.

Live dramatic performance offers writers of stage adaptations innumerable resources and technologies to work with, including the various techniques that are available to writers of screen and audio drama, which can be embedded in live performances through the use of recorded audio and video. These resources and technologies can be classified into four general categories:

- live techniques involving people (actors, choruses, the audience, extras – or 'supers' as they are often called)
- live techniques involving design (sound, lighting, smoke, water, sets, costume, etc.)
- recorded techniques involving video or film
- recorded techniques involving audio.

Activity 5 Writing: adapting for live performance

1. Look again at the step outline you wrote for Activity 3 in Chapter 8. From your outline, select two or three story beats that are not consecutive in the storyline but which could each be scenes in a stage play.

2. Write these scenes (no more than four A4 pages or five minutes' performance time in total). Make sure that your scenes all have a set-up and a payoff, and that they propel the drama forward. Be sure to correctly format

the scenes you write, following the guidance for formatting stage scripts in Chapter 5. Refer to Figure 4 in Chapter 5 to check whether you have done this correctly.

3. What stage resources and technologies might be useful in adapting the scenes you have picked?

Discussion

The process of selecting story beats to adapt will inevitably cause you to think of the technical demands of staging these parts of the story. Drama performed in the theatre has a unique quality: it must happen live, in front of a physical audience. This means that writers must work to a compact framework when writing or adapting for the stage, to ensure that every part of the story can be presented within a defined space and timeframe. This implies a reliance on economical storytelling and the judicious use of staging technologies, including lighting design and sound effects, and theatre conventions, such as offstage action.

5 Conclusion

Adaptation offers writers of drama the opportunity to use pre-existing material to develop new dramatic works. This has advantages: often the characters are already well-developed, many story beats are in place, and the themes have been worked out before work starts on the adaptation. Because material by other writers usually has underlying rights and is subject to copyright laws, an adapter will have to negotiate to secure the rights to adapt the work; so, instead many writers opt to adapt older works that are out of copyright or their own writing. This means that they can work on the adaptation without any legal obligation to the original writer or their estate.

Whatever the source material, a writer must ensure that their adaptation results in a good match between the original text being adapted, and the medium for which it is intended. From there, as with all writing, the primary concern is that the adaptation works for the intended audience.

Part 3 of this book (Chapters 10–17) will further develop the ideas you have explored in this part (Chapters 5–9). It will enable you to apply the techniques for writing drama that you have learned and practised so far to your writing for other forms, including fiction, poetry and life writing.

References

Barry Lyndon (1975) Directed by S. Kubrick. [Feature film]. London: Columbia-Warner Distributors.

Bennett, A. (1999) *The lady in the van*. London: Faber & Faber.

Brokeback Mountain (2005) Directed by A. Lee. [Feature film]. Los Angeles, CA: Focus Features.

Dandaka Dharma (2005) Directed by N. Paley. [Short film]. New York: Nina Paley.

Edmundson, H. (2019) *Small island*. London: Nick Hern Books.

Gresham, W.L. (1946) *Nightmare alley*. New York: Rinehart & Company.

House, G. (2009) *The lady in the van* Directed by G. House [Radio play]. BBC Radio 4, 21 February, 14:30.

Lahiri, J. (1999) 'A real durwan', in J. Lahiri, *Interpreter of maladies: stories*. London: Flamingo, pp. 70–82.

Leroux, G. (2018) *The phantom of the opera*. Translated from the French by A.T. de Mattos. London: Canterbury Classics.

Levy, A. (2004) *Small island.* London: Headline Publishing.

Mac Cathmhaoill, D. (under the name 'Don McCamphill') (2003) *Barry Lyndon* Directed by L. Jackson. [Radio play]. BBC Radio 4, 12 January, 15:00. Available at: https://www.bbc.co.uk/sounds/series/b00t2wq4 (Accessed: 10 December 2024).

Nightmare alley (2021) Directed by G. del Toro. [Feature film]. Los Angeles, CA: Searchlight Pictures.

Proulx, A. (2006) 'Brokeback Mountain', in A. Proulx, *Close range: Brokeback Mountain and other stories*. New York, NY: Harper Perennial, pp. 281–318.

Sita sings the blues (2008) Directed by N. Paley. [Feature film]. New York: GKIDS Inc.

Small island (2009) BBC One, 6 and 13 December, 21:00. Available at: https://www.bbc.co.uk/programmes/b00pdyg0 (Accessed: 12 September 2024).

Thackeray, W.M. (2008) *The luck of Barry Lyndon*. Oxford: Oxford University Press.

Part 3
Developing style and structure

Chapter 10
Splicing narrative strands

Derek Neale

1 Introduction

Figure 1 Janet Frame standing behind the three actresses (from left to right: Karen Fergusson, Alexia Keogh and Kerry Fox) who played her in the film adaptation of her autobiography, *An Angel at My Table*, directed by Jane Campion, Hibiscus Films, 1990 (photo: Hibiscus; Sharmill/Kobal/Shutterstock).

Chapters 5–9 explore how storytelling works in screenwriting. In particular, Chapter 6 shows how the juxtaposition of film shots – often called **montage** – works to reveal the **narrative**: that is, two dissimilar images put side by side create a new meaning and move the story along. Such methods can also usefully influence the way in which you write your fiction or life writing. In this chapter, you'll look at such **intercutting** between different elements of the narrative and how this might be done on a small scale, at the level of juxtaposed images and scenes; and on a larger scale, with spliced (interwoven) storylines or **narrative strands** about different characters or episodes within the overall story. On both the smaller and larger scales, you will come to see how these techniques can create tension and pace, helping to make prose narratives more economical and enabling readers to become more actively involved in co-creating the narrative with the writer.

2 Cutting quickly

In your prose writing, the pace and ease of movement through the narrative can often be improved by using montage. In Activity 1, you will read and compare a passage of life writing and an excerpt from a script, both portraying the same sequence of events. The purpose of this activity isn't to suggest that one approach is better than the other, but to investigate if any of the script methods might be useful for your fiction or life writing.

Activity 1 Reading: comparing script and prose narratives

Read a passage from Janet Frame's autobiography, *An Angel at My Table* (2008), first published in 1984 (Reading 10.1 in Part 4), and an excerpt from the published screenplay (Jones, 1990) of the film version of the book (Reading 10.2).

- Compare how the narrative is written and progresses in the two approaches. What are the differences?
- Do you notice any montage in the film script – is there any juxtaposition of images or cutting between scenes?
- Are there any methods used to tell the story in the script version that you might use in your fiction or life writing?

Discussion

Scriptwriting, as seen in Reading 10.2, shows economy and concision in its storytelling. An increased pace is achieved by cutting from one element of the narrative to another with no linking explanation. The sequence of events in the screenplay of *An Angel at My Table* is similar to that in the prose version, but some aspects have been cut or compressed, including the complication of the Egyptian coins; the interrogation of Janet's brother and sister by Miss Botting; and Janet's punishment by her father. By omitting this last disturbing episode, and also a series of thought processes that appear in Frame's original version, the film script maintains a focus on Janet's immediate predicament.

Another major difference in the script is that the scene in the shop, where Janet buys the chewing gum, has been cut. Instead, the image of the money being stolen is juxtaposed with the scene where Janet distributes the gum. The audience is asked to deduce that Janet has bought chewing gum with the stolen money. Some will even suppose that she is sharing her spoils to buy friendship. Awareness of a prevailing poverty is implied by Miss Botting's certainty that the money had been ill-gotten. These elements aren't spelled out in the script; the audience is required to participate and to imagine the context.

A defining aspect of life writing is its potential to portray the interior life of its narrator or characters, as Frame does (you will learn about the 'inner world' in life writing in Chapter 11 of this book). Storytelling in film more commonly allows the audience to interpret what a character is thinking from their actions and appearance; by focusing more on what characters do or say in a scene. Also, the audience is often able to interpret what a character is thinking because of the use of techniques such as the **close-up**, when the camera focuses on a character's face, magnifying it to many times its natural size. This technique isn't apparent in Jones' script but the final film version of *An Angel at my Table* includes several close-ups of the young Janet Frame.

2.1 Story beats

In the script version of *An Angel at My Table*, another aspect that works to move the story forward at pace is the clarity of the **story beats** – the crucial points in the story's progression (as discussed in Chapters 6 and 8). In the excerpt you have read (Reading 10.2), these run as follows:

- Beat 1: Janet stealing the money
- Beat 2: Janet distributing chewing gum
- Beat 3: Miss Botting investigating and confronting Janet
- Beat 4: Janet facing the blackboard in an empty classroom at lunchtime
- Beat 5: Janet in the afternoon, finally confessing
- Beat 6: Janet in the playground, hearing voices saying 'thief'.

This sequence has precision and clarity. In Activity 2, you will see if you can achieve this in your own writing.

Activity 2 Reading and writing: montage and story beats

Choose a passage (300–750 words) from a story or piece of life writing that you've been working on. Review it and think about rewriting it, still as prose, using some of the scriptwriting techniques discussed so far (e.g. montage, cutting between images or scenes, and tightening the story beats).

1. Look for opportunities to juxtapose images or scenes in your chosen passage, to create a similar montage effect to that in Jones' script.

2. Analyse the story's progression in the passage, identifying the story beats you might utilise in any redraft.

3. Note how your passage would benefit from your proposed edits (that you identified in steps 1 and 2 of this activity). For example, will the narrative be tighter? Will there be richer visual contrasts? Will there be improvements to the pace of the action, with fewer explanatory or linking passages? How would your passage be different compared to your original piece of writing? Would you cut any elements or add anything new?

Discussion

Your revised piece might have fewer scenes or images, with unnecessary descriptions cut, and the movement through the action may gather pace. Your readers might need to engage with the spaces you've created between images and scenes to reveal the story. However, you need to gauge any omissions carefully. There could be explicit thought processes in your passage that are more difficult to tighten – recall in Reading 10.1 Frame's distinctive longing for places she loved and her distrust of her siblings. These thought processes are essential to the life writing, bringing surprise, complexity and poignancy to the story, but all are omitted in the film. In these sorts of rewrites – and when editing generally – always refer back to your primary focus and check that the story still makes sense.

3 Converging characters

Figure 2 Frames from the film *Life of an American Fireman*, directed by Edwin S. Porter, 1903 (photo: GRANGER – Historical Picture Archive/Alamy).

One of the first films to use juxtaposed shots, Edwin S. Porter's 1903 docudrama *Life of an American Fireman*, cuts between different scenes of incomplete action: from the firemen racing towards a fire, to the scene of the mother and child trapped inside the building, then back to the firemen arriving at the fire, and so forth. These form two different, parallel narrative strands – two storylines about separate characters. When the two sets of characters meet (the firemen rescue the mother and child), the two narrative strands converge as one. This outcome is relatively obvious for the audience to pick up on long before the firemen arrive at the scene.

This storytelling method, splicing representations from each narrative strand until they converge, seems natural to us now when watching a film. The point at which longer spliced narrative strands might converge in a novel or memoir can sometimes seem less obvious to a reader, though. This uncertainty is something that you can use in your prose storytelling; it is a good source of tension because readers are always speculating about how the strands might meet. One of the most commonly used methods in film and fiction is to cut between strands involving two major characters. Peter Carey's novel *Oscar and Lucinda* (1988), announcing two narrative strands in the title, offers an example of this. Oscar Hopkins' narrative strand begins when he is young:

> Oscar was fifteen, an age when boys are secretive and sullen. Yet he did not question his father's views. He knew his own soul was vouched safe and when he read the Bible, aloud, by the fire, he placed no different interpretation upon it than the man who poked the little grate and fussed continually with the arrangement of the coal. They both read the Bible as if it were a report compiled by a conscientious naturalist. If the Bible said a beast had four faces, or a man the teeth of a lion, then this is what they believed.
>
> *(Carey, 1988, p. 8)*

The setting of this strand is Devon, England, in 1856. Oscar's naturalist father ('the man who poked the little grate') is a member of the Plymouth Brethren, a Nonconformist Christian movement.

Lucinda Leplastrier's narrative strand begins in the mid-nineteenth century as well, but in New South Wales, Australia:

> The doll was her ninth birthday present. It had come in a ship across the world, just as her mama and papa had. She was very pretty with bright blue eyes and corn-yellow hair. Her cheeks were as smooth as china, and cool against your neck on a hot day. The doll had been purchased by Marian Evans who had gone in a coach to a great exhibition, especially to buy it. At that time Lucinda – much impressed by what she called the 'expedition' – did not know what an exhibition really was, but it later occurred to her that the doll must have come from the building she was to so admire in her adult life – the Crystal Palace.
>
> *(p. 78)*

When realising that there are two separate strands, readers weigh up contrary and similar facts about each of the characters – so, in this case: Australia, England; male, female; their ages of 15 and 9; their depiction as solitary children with no siblings. Readers also naturally look for how two characters might one day converge. The explicit mention of 'the Crystal Palace' (which was built in London in 1851 to house the Great Exhibition) in the second extract suggests the historical setting. From the contrast in locations, readers may also expect an antipodean journey, and we get one: Lucinda and Oscar first meet on a voyage from England to Australia. Carey also plays on readers' other probable expectation that the characters might converge romantically. This is also implied by the nameless narrator's suggestions of their link to both Oscar and Lucinda: for instance, in the first paragraph of the book, we learn that Oscar's father is the narrator's great-grandfather (Carey, 1988, p. 1). In the novel, romantic expectations are partially fulfilled, but the more substantial point of convergence for these characters is that both are gamblers.

3.1 Meetings

Finding the way in which the narrative strands of two characters converge can define the proportions of your story. Sometimes the meeting can be a relatively low-key event, but much depends on where you position such events in the narrative.

In Tobias Wolff's short story 'Bullet in the Brain' (1996), a tale of only 2500 words, two characters converge: a book critic and a bank robber. The story is told in a **third-person** narrative, which is closely aligned with the main character, the critic Anders, 'known for the weary, elegant savagery with which he dispatched almost everything he reviewed' (Wolff, 1996, p. 200). Wolff gives only a few lines of dialogue to the bank robber, who is more a catalyst for the story. However, from the title onwards, the reader is aware that there will be a collision between the characters.

In the story, Anders is in a queue at a bank, noticing and, crucially, critically reviewing the type of language being spoken by those around him. The bank robbers enter the scene using the clichéd language of 'the street' from movies ('dead meat', 'bright boy' '*capiche*'). Anders laughs at this, which gets him into trouble. After a very brief interaction, he is shot in the head – but Wolff makes this happen in the centre of the narrative, so the bullet heralded by the title doesn't end the story. Although Anders dies, paradoxically he lives on for a few more pages, with the rest of the story dealing with an incident from his past. This memory, sparked by the bullet entering his head, illuminates Anders' personality for the reader. Noticeably, it's just one event, not a more clichéd 'life passing before his eyes', though the narrator informs the reader of some events Anders does not remember (a clever way of sneaking in some **backstory**). By positioning the shooting in the middle of the story, Wolff gives emotional depth to Anders' characterisation. Readers come to better understand his sense of humour, cynicism, and the tragedy and comedy of his life through his last thoughts.

Activity 3 Writing: a day in the life of two characters

1. Write up to 150 words in the third-person about a single day in the life of a character who lives in a village or on a particular street in a city or town. This can be fiction or life writing, and either historical or contemporary.

2. Write another third-person account of the same day (up to 150 words) concerning the activities of a different character in the same village or street.

3. Decide when, in the timeframe of the day, your characters will meet. Also think about why the characters are converging – for example, one may be looking for the other; they could be in the same shop; or both might be involved in an accident. Write up to 100 words about this meeting.

Discussion

There is an excitement in creating two characters in this way. You have a given timeframe (in this case, a day) and a natural structure and tension in the convergence. Characters can converge in a number of ways: it might be very dramatic, as in Wolff's 'Bullet in the Brain', or they might just pass in the street. Characters meeting at the end of your timeframe can work but is often problematic, as this can compromise the type of story you are trying to write. 'Bullet in the Brain' would be a completely different story if the fatal meeting was at the end of the narrative.

4 Time and length

Carey's *Oscar and Lucinda* (1988) is a novel in which there is plenty of room to include intercutting narrative strands, where each strand belongs to a separate character and the telling of the story alternates between these strands. There is less scope for this technique in briefer narratives – though it can prove a useful approach in short stories, it is often problematic because there isn't enough space. For instance, in Wolff's story, there is no room for any detail about the robber.

When writing and editing your stories, you should always ask: whose story is it? This is very good advice for short fiction where the story invariably belongs to one character. Yet, in longer stories, where the narrative belongs to two (or more) characters, you might want to structure the narrative using an intercutting approach. An intercutting approach can help to enliven and fully engage readers in longer, more complex narratives. When structuring a story in this way, it is better to launch all strands as soon as possible. Beware of leaving it too long to establish other strands after the first, because late-coming narrative strands might seem subordinate and frustrate readers who want to stay with the character with whom they started the story. If you intercut in a more balanced way, you will hopefully create tension and intrigue.

Using a tight timeframe, such as a single day, is a handy constraint for writers as it assists in structuring the action of a story, keeping it focused and well-paced. Numerous novels have action happening in a single day, including: Virginia Woolf's 1925 novel *Mrs Dalloway* (1996); Hanif Kureishi's *Intimacy* (1998); Adam Silvera's *They Both Die at the End* (2017) and Jon McGregor's *If Nobody Speaks of Remarkable Things* (2002), which portrays a day in the life of a single street. Other novels and stories have similarly defined, if longer or shorter, timeframes – for instance, the action of Caleb Azumah Nelson's 2021 novel *Open Water* (2022) takes place over the course of a year, and Wolff's story 'Bullet in the Brain' happens over the space of just a few minutes. Whether your narrative is a novel or a short story, establishing the timeframe – the start and end point – is all-important.

4.1 Gathering strands, controlling tension

What you might discover when first trying this method of splicing narrative strands is that by cutting between two strands, you interrupt the linear progression of the action. This is useful because it can prevent some parts of your story from appearing too straightforward – that is, the narrative might otherwise become too processional or unrelenting, too full of major events to be plausible. Also, by stopping the action at crucial points, you might be able to leave your readers on a precipice, wanting to know what happens next. So, switching between narrative strands at points of finely wrought tension is comparable to when the curtain falls at the end of an act in a stage play. It leaves readers, like theatre audiences, tense and eager to continue after the interval.

You'll be familiar with the importance of ending a scene promptly from your reading of Chapter 1. It's equally important to find the opportune moment when cutting from one narrative strand to another. The new, interloping strand can offer a contrasting – faster or calming – effect on pace, and so splicing the different strands can sustain interest and tension. However, it's important to be balanced when using this method. You don't always need to leave every scene on a cliffhanger. Doing so could make the narrative too predictable; it's better to vary your method to keep your readers fully engaged.

It's equally important to offer some small promises (often implicit) that any new strand you introduce will eventually link back to the previous narrative strand. The incoming strand should also have an immediately apparent interest and momentum of its own – you can't afford to include a meaningless strand that doesn't help to push the whole story along. Beware of strands that cause readers to desert you.

A crucial element to be gauged in how you arrange your stories is how much narrative space you give to each strand. For instance, in Carey's *Oscar and Lucinda*, the first seventy pages introduce Oscar, and the next thirty introduce Lucinda. The film adaptation (Jones, 1998), however, splices the two strands almost immediately, starting Lucinda's story before Oscar's. There is less time to establish major characters on screen, so it's important to launch them early. This is also often the case with short stories.

You should reassess the balance between narrative strands in your own work as you write and during editing, checking to see that each narrative is in the right proportion. Having different proportions for each strand can fundamentally alter the nature of your story. Carey's *Oscar and Lucinda*, for instance, gives more narrative space to Oscar because the novel is more his story. But if the textual proportions were altered, and Lucinda was given more of the narrative, she would become the main character instead.

5 Using a linking narrative or trusting your readers

Oscar and Lucinda deploys the framing device of a contemporary relative retelling family history. This might be termed a 'linking narrative' because it pulls all the narrative strands together. John Berger's novel *To the Wedding* (1996) links the narratives of several characters spread across Western and Eastern Europe, travelling to a wedding by train, car and motorbike. Yet they are all 'heard' by a male character, Tsobanakos, who resembles Tiresias from Greek myth – a figure who is blind but all-seeing. His first-person voice is the linking narrative in *To the Wedding*.

Other methods of linking narrative strands might involve a third-person voice, that of a character closely involved with the story's action. Or the strands might be linked in unexpected ways, such as in Ruth Ozeki's *The Book of Form and Emptiness* (2021), in which they are linked by a dialogue between the voice of a book and the subject of that book – a character called Benny.

A common option for writers is to not use a linking narrative, but to instead trust readers to make the connections between the different narrative strands. In spliced passages that don't use a linking narrative, the various sections are simply juxtaposed; the writer trusts readers to make the connection. For example, in Chapter 1, you encountered excerpts from Bernardine Evaristo's *Girl, Woman, Other* (2019), which has twelve different character narratives intercutting throughout the novel, with no linking narrative.

Michael Cunningham's novel *The Hours* (1999) cross-cuts between three different story strands in three different eras (1923, 1949 and the late 1990s), though these strands have no overarching narrator or linking narrative pulling the parts together. The 1923 strand is a biographical narrative about the novelist and essayist Virginia Woolf, which covers her suicide in 1941. This immediate context of her death features in the novel's prologue (Cunningham, 1999, pp. 3–8), acting as a hook for readers. It offers a glimpse of what happens in the future, a moment towards which all three narratives then travel. It sets up the expectation of convergence.

Some narrative strands have a literal culmination, as is the case with the Woolf strand and her suicide in *The Hours*. It works in a more thematic way for the other narrative strands in the novel. For instance, the Los Angeles 1949 strand portrays a woman, Laura Brown, in the grip of mental turmoil, struggling desperately with the conventions of motherhood and married life. The possibility of suicide gathers menacingly throughout her narrative. In the 1990s New York strand, the theme of suicide appears via the character of Richard, a writer and the best friend of Clarissa Vaughan (whose name is a nod to the titular Clarissa Dalloway from Woolf's own novel *Mrs Dalloway* (1996), first published in 1925). Richard is suffering from the effects of AIDS and he has written a novel in which his heroine commits suicide. The theme of suicide is also paralleled in *Mrs Dalloway*, where the character of

Septimus Warren Smith, suffering from the traumas of the First World War, kills himself. You will learn more about thematic connections in Chapter 17.

Of special interest in *The Hours* (which was also Woolf's working title for *Mrs Dalloway*) is the way that Cunningham, within each of the three narrative strands, imitates but also creates a variation on Woolf's use of **stream of consciousness** in *Mrs Dalloway*, a style of narration that emulates the way in which the mind of a character flits from one thing to the next. This seems entirely fitting given *The Hours'* focus on Woolf's life and *Mrs Dalloway*. It causes readers to reflect upon and update their thinking about Woolf and the earlier novel, by splicing the past with the present, and the biographical with the fictional in an **intertextual** fashion.

6 Poetic cutting between strands

Like *Oscar and Lucinda*, Kiran Desai's novel *The Inheritance of Loss* (2006) contains the alternate narratives of two characters. The first is Sai, an orphan and the granddaughter of a retired judge who lives in Kalimpong, north-east India, during an uprising in the Himalayan territory. The other character, Biju, is the son of the judge's cook. Having not yet attained legal status in the United States, Biju works in various New York restaurants. His many chores include stirring vats of bolognese sauce at Pinocchio's restaurant and delivering Szechuan wings with French fries using a bicycle when working for Freddy's Wok. The novel cuts between Indian and US narratives, but cutting is also an integral method within each strand. The narratives often don't contain consecutive action but jump between moments and places. This section from Biju's narrative gives a flavour of his fragmentary life:

> *Biju at the Baby Bistro.*
>   Above, the restaurant was French, but below in the kitchen it was Mexican and Indian. …
>
> ———
>
> Biju at Le Colonial for the authentic colonial experience.
>   On top, rich colonial, and down below, poor native. Colombian, Tunisian, Ecuadorian, Gambian.
>
> ———
>
> On to the Stars and Stripes Diner. All American flag on top, all Guatemalan flag below.
>   Plus one Indian flag when Biju arrived.
>
> ———
>
> *(Desai, 2006, p. 21)*

From this fast-moving catalogue of kitchens in which Biju has worked, the reader sees how much he has learned about politics and population distribution. The significant thing about Desai's narrative is that she uses such brief sections and deploys this device so freely. This is not a cutting between strands or distinct characters but between brief episodes in time and action – and sometimes just between images.

Sai's narrative is generally more consecutive than this example but nonetheless often cuts back and forth in time, and splices the present with strands about the cook's and the judge's respective pasts, as well as Sai's initial journey to Kalimpong.

Activity 4 Reading: novels without linking narratives

Read an extract from Cunningham's 1998 novel *The Hours* (Reading 10.3) and an extract from Desai's *The Inheritance of Loss* (Reading 10.4).

Reading 10.3 is a passage from the 'Mrs Brown' strand of *The Hours*, set in 1949, including sections from Woolf's *Mrs Dalloway*, which Laura Brown is reading. Reading 10.4 is a passage from *The Inheritance of Loss* set at a time not long after the death of Sai's parents, when she has just come to live in the house of her grandfather, the judge. In this passage, the cook has presented the judge and Sai with bowls of peppery tomato soup.

1. What specific aspects do you notice about the narrative strands written by Cunningham and Desai?

2. What is the effect of the section breaks within the narrative strand in Desai's novel?

Discussion

Cunningham's novel is a tribute to Woolf's *Mrs Dalloway*. Not only does he use parts of Woolf's novel as core elements in his own novel's content and thematic concerns, but he also, daringly, attempts a stream-of-consciousness narrative in each of his three strands. The voices he creates are relatively similar and all use the present tense, giving his characters quicker access to their flights of uncertain and associative thought. All three strands can be seen to be grappling with the past, asking questions of it, in much the same way as Woolf's stream-of-consciousness narrative voice in *Mrs Dalloway*.

The breaks in the storytelling in the Desai excerpt (Reading 10.4) are poetic. That is, the structuring resembles the arrangement of stanzas within a poem, and the level of story development between parts of the narrative is prompted for readers, it seems, by the sort of memory association evoked by a poem, more than the chronology of events in a narrative. Similarly, it gives a primacy to images as a poem might. For example, the unreliable electricity supply is a mundane and tedious fact of life for the inhabitants of Kalimpong, but the image of the bulb fading is paradoxically magnified and made distinct by being in its own section, between two breaks. It symbolises the faded grandeur and rottenness of the world of Kalimpong, as do the worn sheets, replaced by equally rotten, toe-pierced tablecloths, and the 'microscopic jaws' reducing 'the house to sawdust' (Desai, 2006, p. 34).

(a) (b)

Figure 3 (a) Author Kiran Desai holding a copy of her 2006 novel, *The Inheritance of Loss* (photo: PA Images/Alamy) and (b) a poster for *The Hours*, a 2002 film adaptation (directed by Stephen Daldry) of Michael Cunningham's novel of the same name, featuring the three main characters (from left to right): Clarissa Vaughan played by Meryl Streep; Laura Brown played by Julianne Moore; and Virginia Woolf played by Nicole Kidman (photo: Paramount/Miramax/Kobal/Shutterstock).

Novels such as Desai's *The Inheritance of Loss* offer a hybrid method of storytelling. The novel's overall narrative is preoccupied with personal and cultural memory, yet the strands of past and present entwine without any conspicuous or intrusive blocks of backstory. The imagery in Reading 10.4, highlighted in the discussion of Activity 4 (worn sheets, toe-pierced tablecloths, microscopic jaws), is part of the poetic effect, one that is amplified by the formatting – the space around the words lends an emphasis (such as with the light bulb) and helps to form the meaning of the piece. While the spliced strands in this method are often about different characters in different locations, they can also be about the past and the present, or different facets of just one character. Similarly, the intercutting of strands in *The Hours* interweaves 1990s New York with various pasts, other locations and separate character journeys.

7 Different streams of consciousness

The excerpt from *The Hours* (Reading 10.3) is focused on the consciousness of Laura Brown as she reads *Mrs Dalloway*. Similarly, in *Mrs Dalloway*, Woolf's narrative is centred on the consciousness of Clarissa Dalloway. Yet Woolf's use of stream of consciousness flows a little wider on occasions, straying to the consciousness of other characters, even if focused primarily on Clarissa's thoughts. This is exemplified in Reading 10.3 at the point where the narrative gains access to the thoughts of another character, Scrope Purvis, as Clarissa waits for Durtnall's van to pass.

Cunningham fleetingly uses some of this more wide-ranging stream of consciousness later in *The Hours*, but not to the same extent that's found in Woolf's novel. Cunningham's narrative – as seen in Reading 10.3 – is generally much more controlled and each narrative strand is focused on individual points of view. This is a far safer approach for writers when trying the stream-of-consciousness method for the first time, otherwise you risk blurring the focus of your story and confusing your readers.

Activity 5 Writing and editing: honing character narratives

Write a story (750–1000 words) by adding to or editing the narratives and meeting of your two characters from Activity 3. Include juxtaposed strands, alternating between the two characters, and put their meeting where you think it works best in your story (it doesn't need to be at the end of the timeframe). As you work on your story, consider:

- whether you want to include a linking narrative, either using an anonymous third-person voice or a witness account by a character in the story (first-person voice)
- using a method like Desai's (Reading 10.4), concentrating on certain images and using section breaks freely
- using interlocking thematic or literal elements, as Cunningham does
- whose story you are writing and how that affects the proportions of each strand. Is there an equal balance or is one strand more dominant?

Discussion

Splicing narrative strands is difficult to achieve satisfactorily in a brief narrative, but attempting it may give you the incentive to use such methods for longer writing projects, including novels. There is no right way of going about drafting your story. Writing an individual character's narrative in its entirety, from beginning to end, doing the same for your second character, and then cutting up the two strands to rearrange them; or writing the whole narrative, from beginning to end, section by section, are both viable approaches. But ensure that your reader is able to follow the story and isn't baffled by your method.

8 Challenges of story structure

Each story you write will create its own demands and will usually suggest the structural methods best suited to the type of story it is. There is more opportunity to splice narrative strands in a novel, for example, because there is more space to do so, and this can offer a stimulating bonus to both you as the writer and to your readers, relieving the possible tedium of always 'being with' just one character. However, not all stories are suited to being told in this way: don't try to force the spliced strands method if a story would be better told in a single narrative strand, by a single character.

Intercutting experiments can create structural challenges. For example, how do you launch each narrative strand? How should you unify the separate parts by the end? At what point should you make the switches between strands? If you want to include a linking narrative for the strands, you might first think of an anonymous third-person voice – an **omniscient narrator** who is all-knowing, with access to your characters' thoughts and knowledge of all events, past, present and future. But this is not necessarily always the best or easiest option. The focus for readers (and you, the writer) can become confusing with such an all-knowing narrative voice, which can also consume a considerable amount of narrative space. Point-of-view constraints can be useful to avoid a loss of focus – perhaps your narrator has knowledge of only one character, for instance. You also have to decide whether to make the narrator present as a character. The challenge in choosing to use a first-person, witness narrative is where to position that narrator. This can be a stimulating problem, and often, as with the narrator in *Oscar and Lucinda*, it can add another layer of intrigue and speculation for readers.

Desai's use of lines to mark the division between subsections of the prose within strands (see Section 6 of this chapter) is unusual. Other writers might denote a break or the difference between sections with an asterisk or an extra line space. Whatever typographic device you choose, the danger of structuring your story with both spliced strands and subsections is that the narrative can become confusing, fragmentary or static. A story written in this style still has to carry readers forward and make clear where they are and which characters they are with. Working on a basic level, a key editorial aid in checking such a narrative during writing is to ask a trusted reader – a fellow writer, friend or family member – to specifically pinpoint any places in your story where they get lost.

Key to splicing narrative strands effectively is giving your readers adequate signposts, enabling them to distinguish between characters and strands. Also, ensure that you establish the method of narration early in your story, whether you're sticking with one character strand or more, and be consistent in this method. Remember the benefits of scrutinising small details in your storytelling: gauge forward progression and story beats to hone pace and tension. Splicing strands can be a very concise way of telling a story, one that fully engages readers' imaginations.

9 Conclusion

In this chapter, you've seen how the use of montage-type techniques, quick cutting between images or scenes, can increase the pace of your storytelling. You have also explored splicing together the narrative strands of major characters and how this can poetically empower images to work on a symbolic as well as a literal level.

By trying the methods of cutting between narrative strands, you've played with the positioning of events, so creating contrasting scenes and imagery, varying the pace of your storytelling and creating the possibility of delayed narrative fulfilment. Your readers' expectations about narrative strands eventually converging can create tension and genuine reading pleasure – they are seeking the gratification of an end after all. The more intriguing the route to that end, the more your readers will enjoy the journey.

References

Azumah Nelson, C. (2022) *Open water*. London: Penguin.

Berger, J. (1996) *To the wedding*. London: Bloomsbury.

Carey, P. (1988) *Oscar and Lucinda*. London: Faber and Faber.

Cunningham, M. (1999) *The hours*. New York: Farrar, Straus and Giroux.

Desai, K. (2006) *The inheritance of loss*. London: Hamish Hamilton.

Evaristo, B. (2019) *Girl, woman, other*. London: Hamish Hamilton.

Frame, J. (2008) *An angel at my table*. London: Virago Press.

Jones, L. (1990) *An angel at my table: the screenplay, from the three volume autobiography of Janet Frame*. [Screenplay]. London: Pandora.

Jones, L. (1998) *Oscar and Lucinda*. [Screenplay]. London: Faber.

Kureishi, H. (1998) *Intimacy*. London: Faber and Faber.

Life of an American fireman (1903) Directed by E.S. Porter. [Short film]. New York: Edison Manufacturing Company.

McGregor, J. (2002) *If nobody speaks of remarkable things*. London: Bloomsbury.

Ozeki, R. (2021) *The book of form and emptiness*. Edinburgh: Canongate.

Silvera, A. (2017) *They both die at the end*. London: Simon and Schuster.

Wolff, T. (1996) 'Bullet in the brain', in T. Wolff, *The night in question*. London: Bloomsbury, pp. 200–205.

Woolf, V. (1996) *Mrs Dalloway*. London: Penguin.

Chapter 11
Life writing: inner worlds

Lania Knight

1 Introduction

This chapter will look at 'inner worlds' – yours and those of others whom you may be writing about, with the aim of understanding how they contribute to creating a piece of life writing. By 'inner worlds', I am referring to thoughts, reflection, and the sifting through of ideas that happens in a piece of life writing, whether it has you as a main character – as in **memoir**, **autobiography** or **personal essay** – or whether it has someone else as a main character – as in **biography**.

As a form, life writing tends to make a contract with the reader who expects a degree of authenticity, even as they also accept that the author may be using speculation or imagination alongside writing from fact. In the next section, you will learn some techniques for life writing that include utilising speculation and imagination. In later sections of this chapter, you will look at challenging questions, startling moments from childhood, metaphors for the process of life writing, adapting the concepts of 'showing' and 'telling' to life writing, as well as some thoughts on what 'insight' means in life writing.

2 Using 'I wonder if …'

Sometimes, despite all our best efforts, we do not have all the facts, whether about our own past or someone else's. An excellent way to explore and expand on moments where there is a gap is to ask 'I wonder if …'

Recall the passage from Robin Wall Kimmerer's essay 'The Council of Pecans' (2013) that you read in Chapter 3. In the first section of the essay, Kimmerer recreates moments from the past. She uses historical facts, as well as references to language, geography and botany to bring the reader into the scene where she is beginning to describe the forced removal of her ancestors from Wisconsin. Kimmerer was not alive during the forced migrations; however, she uses techniques that convey accuracy so that the reader trusts her story, and she utilises collective personal pronouns – 'we' and 'us' – to connect herself to her ancestral heritage. Once the setting and her connection are established, she asks questions:

> I wonder if they looked back for a last glimpse of the lakes, glimmering like a mirage. Did they touch the trees in remembrance as they became fewer and fewer, until there was only grass?
>
> *(Kimmerer, 2013, p. 13)*

A paragraph or two later, she speculates,

> When they got to Kansas they must have been relieved to find groves of nut trees along the rivers.
>
> *(Kimmerer, 2013, p. 13)*

Kimmerer examines this scene by utilising three different phrases: 'I wonder if …', 'Did they …' and 'They must have …' Questions and speculation of this sort allow you to explore what you don't know, or what you may not have experienced directly, regarding your subject. Kimmerer knows many facts about her ancestral past, but she was not there to experience it herself. When you start to think of life writing as an art form rather than just a retelling of events, you notice devices like this. Kimmerer is able to nudge the essay in the direction she wants by asking questions about loss and about addressing that loss.

In the next activity, practise using questions and speculation to write around or towards a scene where gaps are present.

Activity 1 Reading and writing: 'I wonder if ...'

Read the passage below which is reproduced from Chapter 3, which I also authored. Assume that what I have shared in the passage encompasses everything factual that I know about the events and the persons being described.

Rewrite this passage by adding in questions and speculation. Feel free to use the three phrases discussed above – 'I wonder if …', 'Did they …' and 'They must have …' – or come up with your own.

> My paternal grandmother, 'Grandma Gracie', was Cajun, which means that her ancestors (and mine) were part of a group of French emigrants who left France in the seventeenth century and sailed to Acadia, Canada and then eventually landed in Louisiana in the United States. Grandma Gracie grew up in a small town in Southwest Louisiana and didn't speak English until she went to primary school. My father used to tell stories about her, saying that she lived on a *bayou*, an American French word for a swampy, marshy area, and that she went to school in a *pirogue*, a French word for a small boat. He remembered her saying *sacré bleu*, an exclamation of exasperation, to him as a child when she was upset with him.
>
> *(Chapter 3, Section 4)*

Discussion

I didn't get to ask my grandmother why she said '*sacré bleu*' when my dad was a child because she died when I was young. This not-knowing is an opening for speculation. Was she exasperated with him? Did she have a difficult time as a mother? From the facts I have given you, it might be possible to read more about Cajuns in Louisiana, or about travelling to school in a *pirogue* on the *bayou*, or what it is like to grow up speaking one language and then learning to speak another at school.

As you begin to work on your own life writing, see these openings or gaps in information as opportunities for doing more research, asking questions of family members or others who might have been present, and engaging in creative speculation.

3 Challenging questions

When you ask challenging questions in a piece of life writing, this opens up opportunities for exploring why something might have happened and what your role – or that of the person you are writing about – was. Challenging questions might include: 'Why did this event happen?', 'Why was this choice made?', 'Why is this event so difficult to stop remembering?' or 'Did it happen the way I or the person I'm writing about think(s) it did?' When you ask challenging questions like these, you invite the reader to begin to wonder about the answers.

Imagine that you travel somewhere as an adult and, on your travels, you see things that surprise you, or maybe even startle you. Maybe you want to ask awkward questions that are difficult or impossible to answer. A British friend of mine frequently travels in Asia and South America, teaching English as a second language. He says that when people travel and encounter things that are unfamiliar, they often describe them as 'strange' or 'weird'. There were many things my friend found odd when he first encountered them: eating live eels; letting someone put hot glass jars on your back; sharing a mug of tea with ten other people, all sipping through the same metal straw. But he came to understand that these activities were commonplace to those engaging in them.

Encounters like these can provide a wealth of writing opportunities when examined further. If your own experiences, or those of someone you are writing about, leave you wondering, these can be useful prompts for life writing. Ask questions about these encounters and you could gain new ways of seeing them.

Figure 1 Librairie Delamain bookshop in Paris, 1988 (photo: Gala Images Archive/Alamy).

In her book *The Secret Life of France* (2013), Lucy Wadham writes about her life in France as an English woman. As a teenager, she visited her older sister in Paris and, later, married her sister's flatmate, Laurent. In the opening chapter, she puts forward the question that drives the entire book:

> When I moved to Paris to be with Laurent we made a pact that I would make an effort to adapt to life in Paris but if, after five years, I was still homesick we would move the family to London. That was more than twenty years ago, and although Laurent and I are no longer together, I am still here. What follows is an attempt, by reliving my perplexed discovery, rejection and ultimate acceptance of this country, to understand why that is.
>
> *(Wadham, 2013, p. 8)*

Wadham asks herself why she has stayed in France all these years even though it has been immensely challenging. The answer is not easy or straightforward, and it comes in the form of a memoir describing her experiences. It is the not-knowing, and the questions that the not-knowing provokes, that provide the opportunity for creative writing.

Kyo Maclear, a Canadian writer and artist, spent a winter in the city of Toronto, watching birds. Maclear's father had fallen ill, and her caregiving duties had fragmented time in a way that made it impossible to continue creating her art. In the prologue to her book *Birds Art Life Death* (2018), she asks questions which the chapters that follow attempt to answer. This is like Wadham's question-and-answer structure in *The Secret Life of France*. The difference, though, is that where Wadham's memoir moves backwards in time to find answers, Maclear's moves forwards:

> I had a growing feeling that my life, with its new shape and needs, required a different, less militant arrangement of time. What if I stopped fighting for the trance of long-form days, where I would be uninterrupted and ambitiously absorbed in a big project? … Could I find a graceful way to work and be in the world that might still pull me up and forward?
>
> *(Maclear, 2018, p. 16)*

Here, the writer is signalling to the reader that the rest of the book will be an exploration of these questions. Unlike in *The Secret Life of France*, where it is spelled out to the reader that they are going back in time, in *Birds Art Life Death* it is a movement forward. Maclear is using 'What if …' and 'Could I …' to indicate that, at the start, she does not know the answers and that, in order to find them, she must proceed with a kind of life experiment – urban birdwatching. Maclear's book is a (forward-looking) unfolding of her experiment, whereas Wadham's is a (backward-looking) unpicking of 'How did we get here?'.

Figure 2 A woman writing at a desk, early twentieth century (photo: colaimages/Alamy).

In 1928, English novelist Virginia Woolf gave two public lectures which she later adapted into her 1929 book *A Room of One's Own* (2004). Her work provides an excellent example of how a surprising encounter followed by questions – or, as in the excerpt below, musings and wonderings without actual question marks in the text – can open up a wealth of opportunities for life writing.

In the text that precedes the excerpt below, Woolf describes a (possibly fictional) scene where she is denied entry to a library on a university campus she is visiting and then how she is sitting by a river, pondering, waiting for a luncheon to begin. By night-time, she has had plenty of time to think about the library, about the conversations at the luncheon and the disappointing dinner that followed in the evening. On her solitary walk to her sleeping quarters, she is mulling over the day and begins musing:

I thought of the organ booming in the chapel and of the shut doors of the library; and I thought how unpleasant it is to be locked out; and I thought how it is worse perhaps to be locked in; and, thinking of the safety and prosperity of the one sex and of the poverty and insecurity of the other and of the effect of tradition and of the lack of tradition upon the mind of a writer, I thought at last that it was time to roll up the crumpled skin of the day, with its arguments and impressions and its anger and laughter, and cast it into the hedge.

(Woolf, 2004, pp. 27–28)

Then she arrives at a striking insight: 'a woman must have money and a room of her own if she is to write fiction' (Woolf, 2004, p. 4). Her original task was to give a set of lectures about 'women and fiction'. In contemplating how to interpret the topic 'women and fiction', she began musing and wondering, reflecting on her observations. She then used these musings to structure her lecture and deliver her insight about what women need to write fiction.

In the next activity, it is your turn to muse, wonder and ask questions. Roll up your sleeves and get started.

Activity 2 Writing: ask questions

First, think of something that was surprising to you or to the person you're writing about, such as an unexpected encounter or receiving a gift out of the blue.

Take a few moments to describe this event in a vivid way. Woolf had situated the reader firmly in October with descriptions of leaves and the sky and wind. What time of year are you writing about? What time of day? Do you recall what you (or the character you are writing about) ate, or to whom you (or they) spoke?

Second, give yourself several minutes to write a list of questions about the surprising event. It is fine if you do not know the answers and, in fact, it is probably more interesting if you don't. If you get stuck, start with small, specific questions, such as about who was there and what they were saying, and then move outwards from there, asking bigger, more abstract questions, such as why this moment mattered and what sorts of conclusions you, or the person you're writing about, came to.

Discussion

Writing a vivid description of an unexpected event and then following that with questions, especially questions that might be difficult to answer, is an excellent way to begin working on a piece of life writing. Do not worry if it is rough or clunky, or if you don't know all the answers yet: this is an opportunity to explore.

4 Startling moments in childhood

In the previous section, you read about startling moments that people encountered as adults, and how questions about those moments can lead to new ways of understanding them, even if those questions are unanswerable. In this section, you will look at a similar situation, but with a different focus – that of childhood.

Recall, from Chapter 3, Anita Sethi, who walked the Pennine Way and wrote about it in her memoir *I Belong Here*. In a separate essay, 'A Trip to the Countryside', she describes a visit to the Lake District that she made as a child with her mother. Until this trip, Sethi's memories of being in nature were based in local parks in Manchester, where they lived, and a school outing to Chester Zoo. Her mother was a single parent for whom time and money for trips was limited, but they were able to travel to the Lake District when her mother received a subsidised weekend, staying in a bungalow in Cumbria. On arrival, Sethi says, 'I breathed more deeply than I ever had done before and for the first time I could remember, it was a joy to breathe … I walked through the grass, which tickled my bare brown legs' (2022, p. 245). The transition from city to countryside is handled in a delicate way, highlighting the difference between the fear of violence in the city and the open, safe comfort of the Lake District.

Then, just as we are enjoying this moment with Sethi, she tells us about something startling that happened:

> I played outside, picking flowers, and watching an elderly couple who pruned vegetables in the garden next door. They were not saying much but appeared to be watching and listening to us.
>
> 'You don't see many brown folks out here in the countryside', mumbled the man as he paused from pruning to gaze towards me, squinting, his face contorted in a frown, then going back to his gardening.
>
> *(Sethi, 2022, p. 245)*

When a startling moment like this happens, it can be unsettling, especially to a child. It is something that can be remembered long after the event, as for Sethi. Although startling moments like this are difficult for children to experience, they also hold great opportunity for life writing. The surprise of the interaction and the years that have passed since it occurred combine to provide two important elements of life writing: event and impact. In this extract, I have only presented the lead-in and the surprising event itself. It is clear from the rest of the essay and from Sethi's life choices – for example, walking the Pennine Way as a brown woman after a racial attack – that this event not only had an impact on her as a child but also led to a deeper, though troubling, understanding as an adult of how she is perceived by others.

4 Startling moments in childhood

Figure 3 Passengers on a bus in Agra, 2009 (photo: mauritius images GmbH/Alamy).

Activity 3 Reading: event + time = impact

Read the extract from Nina Mukerjee Furstenau's prologue to *Biting through the Skin* (Reading 11.1 in Part 4). Furstenau was born in Thailand to Indian parents and her family moved to Kansas when she was a child. This extract describes a trip to India with her parents, and a startling moment that occurred on a bus which, as an adult, she credits with changing the trajectory of her life.

Take note of the description of the event and any questions, wonderings or musings about it, as well as the impact it had on her life.

Discussion

Furstenau's approach to writing about this childhood moment is different from that of Sethi: we are immediately on the bus with her in India, experiencing the sights and sounds with her as a child. After the detailed scene ends, we are with Furstenau as an adult: 'I realise now how paralyzed I was seeing a child beg for food' (Furstenau, 2013, p. xvii). Next, she contrasts this moment with her life back in Kansas, and what it was like sitting around a dinner table with her family. The final move of the extract is to connect the moment on the bus in India to those evenings spent eating dinner with the news playing on the television in the background, and then to her decision as an adult to work in the Peace Corps, a government-funded charity in the United States that places community workers in developing countries abroad.

In this example, first you have the event: Furstenau as a child on a bus, watching a boy eat a banana without peeling it. Next, there are the years that follow, which allow time for reflection and mulling over what happened.

Finally, there is the impact: a deeper awareness of poverty and hunger, and a personal decision to dedicate two years to work as a volunteer in the Peace Corps.

Startling moments in childhood – like those that Sethi and Furstenau experienced – can be unsettling and take years to understand, but they offer a great opportunity for life writing. Questions about startling events often take time to develop and to be answered: they are childhood questions that require adult consciousness to be resolved.

5 Those golden nuggets

> Sometimes what happens is that you poke your pick into a piece of respectable earth and silver shows up in an iron-ore vein and God knows where you're heading. You follow it and you have to revise everything in light of the silver.
>
> *(Gardner, quoted in Tomlinson, 1986, p. 64)*

'Mining' is a useful metaphor for the process of life writing. Linguist Barbara Tomlinson listened to scores of interviews with writers and found four activities that they used most often for comparison to writing: cooking, mining, gardening and hunting (Tomlinson, 1986). In the quotation above, from 1978, fiction writer and literary critic John Gardner is describing the process of writing fiction in terms of mining. It is also valuable to think of composing life writing in this way. So far in this chapter, you have read about some of the ways that asking questions or reflecting on the past can look on the page. Sometimes, like mining, it can seem like a lot of hard work for a tiny nugget of wisdom.

There are other useful metaphors for life writing as well – for the process of figuring out what you want to say about your topic, how you want to structure the piece and how the reader might experience your work. These might be devising, or solving, a puzzle or a game, and tying, or untangling, a knot. If the puzzle is too difficult or the knot tied too tight, then you and possibly your reader will give up. If it is too easy, you and your reader may get bored and move on to something else.

Activity 4 Reading: solving a childhood mystery

Read the transcript of an excerpt from my 2023 interview with Nina Mukerjee Furstenau (Reading 11.2) in which she talks about how, for many years, she was unsure about whether she had imagined the moment when she saw a boy eating a banana, peel and all, or if it was real.

Examine her process of enquiry regarding that moment and note where it is like the 'solving a mystery' metaphor, discussed earlier in this section.

Discussion

In this excerpt, Nina explains that she had thought for years that the boy and the banana were a dream. When she begins to realise, as an adult, that she has made many life decisions based on this 'dream', she decides to investigate. As a girl, she did not want her mother to know that she had given her food to a person who was begging for sustenance. As an adult, she can ask her mother questions and not worry about her mother's reaction. Through this conversation with her mother, Nina solves the mystery of whether this event was a dream.

Spending time with an 'important and weighted' moment and then writing about it, as Furstenau describes it, has since become her 'superpower' as a writer.

You may wish to reflect on whether there are any mysteries about your life, or that of someone you're writing about, that could be solved by spending time with a weighted and important moment and then writing about it.

6 Scene-building refresh: showing and telling

One of the advantages of learning how to write in multiple forms is the fertile crossover that is possible when applying techniques from one form to another. I started as a fiction writer, but I soon began studying dramatic writing. The opportunity to create a story entirely in dialogue and write stage directions, with three-dimensional, living people acting it out in front of an audience enhanced my fiction writing: my 'ear' for dialogue and my 'eye' for staging and movement developed exponentially within the space of a few months.

In this book, you have been studying multiple modes of writing practice, and all of these will spill over onto each other. Before you move on to learning more about writing poetry in Chapter 12, there is something about scene-building that I want to share with you. In Chapter 6, you learned about visual storytelling in film; this has parallels with showing 'outer worlds' in life writing, as we discussed in Chapter 3. In Chapter 7, you learned about audio drama, a form that often invites the listener inside the speaker's mind; this has parallels with telling readers about the 'inner worlds' in life writing, which you are exploring in this chapter. Next, you will look at a passage of life writing, paying particular attention to both **showing** and **telling**.

In the following passage from Vanessa Onwuemezi's essay 'Brother' (2022), she focuses on her little brother. She begins with showing the 'outer world', a description of the scene and some dialogue. Next, she shifts to a 'telling' mode and conveys his 'inner world', what she imagines him to be thinking. Then she goes back to 'showing' us she was laughing; and the last part is a mix of both, explaining that most of the time the scene looks slightly different than it does this time.

> One quiet morning I heard him shout 'Yes?' in his sleep, ripping through the still air, down the corridor, his eyes closed. He was hearing his name called from the outer edges of his psyche. A voice knitted into the slow-running stream where he floated between waking life and that of his dreams. Even there he couldn't be left alone. And I was laughing from my room, most of the time I wouldn't let him cross the threshold [into my room] and would watch him wait patiently outside.
>
> *(Onwuemezi, 2022, pp. 57–58)*

This is an excellent tool for considering style and voice. When you read line by line and categorise a writer's approach, a different picture of their writing emerges, and you begin to see how showing and telling interact with and balance each other.

> ### Activity 5 Reading: scene mark-up
>
> Read a passage from the end of 'Jesus Shaves' (2001), an essay by American humorist David Sedaris about learning to speak French (Reading 11.3).
>
> Identify where he is showing the 'outer world' and where he is telling the 'inner world.' You can use different-coloured markers or pens. Use whatever works for you to help you see the different components for building a scene.
>
> ### Discussion
>
> Much of the opening of the passage focuses on showing, with lots of dialogue and description. You can almost see and hear the class struggling with telling a French-language version of a holiday they know well. However, with the line 'It was a decent point', the writing shifts more into telling. Sedaris begins to ask himself questions about the event and tries to find answers. The passage draws the reader in with showing and then encourages a new way of seeing an event with 'telling,' including asking questions that are not easily answered.

How did you find that exercise? This form of close reading takes time and intense concentration, but it can also help you, in your own writing, to become adept at noticing the details of how other writers shape their work.

7 So, what is insight?

Insight is understanding the significance of why your story, or your subject's story, matters. Asking 'I wonder …' or 'What if …' is reflection, but the process of reflecting on those questions leads you to insight.

For example, in Furstenau's prologue, she shows us the story of giving the banana to the boy and watching him eat it, skin and all. And then she tells us why that matters: it was a living, breathing example of the effects of poverty, and it changed forever the way she saw herself and her family, as well as her family's privilege and financial status.

In Sedaris's essay, he wonders if he and his classmates could make more sense of Christianity without the language barrier. This is reflection. It is in the final paragraph of the extract, when he answers this question and considers the idea of faith, that the insight comes: 'In communicating any religious belief, the operative word is *faith*, a concept illustrated by our very presence in that classroom' (Sedaris, 2001, p. 179).

8 Conclusion

In this chapter you have looked at exploring inner worlds through the use of scene-building elements and asking questions.

You can apply what you have learned in this chapter to other forms of creative writing, and even critical writing. Asking questions, giving yourself time for reflection and then offering your insights is a process that is integral to critical thinking. In life writing, the form is flexible enough to accommodate an outright declaration of your insights. In other creative forms, it can be wise to be more subtle.

References

Furstenau, N.M. (2013) *Biting through the skin: an Indian kitchen in America's heartland*. Iowa City: University of Iowa Press.

Furstenau, N.M. (2023) Interviewed by L. Knight for The Open University, 27 June.

Kimmerer, R.W. (2013) 'The council of pecans', in R.W. Kimmerer, *Braiding sweetgrass: indigenous wisdom, scientific knowledge and the teachings of plants*. London: Penguin Random House, pp. 11–21.

Maclear, K. (2018) *Birds art life death: the art of noticing the small and significant*. London: 4th Estate.

Onwuemezi, V. (2022) 'Brother', *Granta*, 161, pp. 57–61. Available at: https://granta.com/brother-vanessa-onwuemezi (Accessed: 25 March 2024).

Sedaris, D. (2001) 'Jesus shaves', in D. Sedaris, *Me talk pretty one day*. New York: Back Bay Books, pp. 174–180.

Sethi, A. (2022) 'A trip to the countryside', in K. Lloyd (ed.) *North country: an anthology of landscape and nature*. Manchester: Saraband, pp. 243–246.

Tomlinson, B. (1986) 'Cooking, mining, gardening, hunting: metaphorical stories writers tell about their composing processes', *Metaphor and Symbolic Activity*, 1(1), pp. 57–79.

Wadham, L. (2013) *The secret life of France*. London: Faber and Faber.

Woolf, V. (2004) *A room of one's own*. London: Penguin.

Chapter 12
Dramatic techniques in poetry

Siobhán Campbell

1 Introduction

In this chapter, you will learn about several different dramatic techniques which you will then practise using. The result will be that you develop a new set of poetic tools for your writer's toolbox.

You will think of dramatic techniques as they are used in poetry in two ways. Firstly, you will think of them as the techniques that the author employs to generate tension or drama within a poem. This might be by using **dramatic irony**, by deploying misdirection or revelation, by diverting the reader's attention and surprising them, or through appealing directly to the reader's emotions. Secondly, you will learn about the techniques related to elements borrowed from drama, such as the use of scene and the use of persona (which you will study further in Chapter 14), especially when that **persona** is speaking to themselves (**soliloquy**) or to an imagined audience.

As poet Louis MacNeice said, 'all poems … in varying degrees, contain an internal conflict, cross-talk, backwash, come-back or pay-off' (MacNeice, 1987, p. 155). He may as well have spoken about how all poems are dialogic, in that they are in dialogue with you, the reader, and sometimes with a wider audience, but they can also have dialogues within themselves. Those dialogic moments often add tension: it may be that the narrator is self-revealing, creating a shared joke between the author and the reader. Or it may be that the author is using dramatic irony by having the speaker in the poem say one thing while clearly meaning something else.

2 Dramatic conflict

Figure 1 Stevie Smith (photo: Chronicle/Alamy).

Even short poems can combine the perspectives of different people or different groups and this can create dramatic conflict. Sometimes the drama lodges in a tension that we have probably all experienced: that between what is going on for a person privately and how they present their persona in public. When a poet brings these two things – the private person and the public-facing mask – into the same picture, dramatic possibilities can arise. Because dramatic conflict in poems may not be immediately obvious, it is best to read poems at least twice, or three times, and preferably aloud. In Activity 1, reading 'Not Waving But Drowning' aloud will help you to 'hear' the conflict.

Activity 1 Reading: 'Not Waving But Drowning'

Read 'Not Waving But Drowning', a poem by Stevie Smith from 1957, and then read it for a second time.

- How do you think 'they' (in 'they said') and the 'dead man' interact?
- Can you identify conflicting viewpoints in the poem?

> **Stevie Smith** lived most of her life in London. Her writing often explored themes of loneliness and despair, but her wit and human empathy is what makes the work memorable. She wrote novels as well as short stories and literary reviews, but is remembered chiefly for her poetry.

Not Waving But Drowning

Nobody heard him, the dead man,
But still he lay moaning:
I was much further out than you thought
And not waving but drowning.

Poor chap, he always loved larking
And now he's dead
It must have been too cold for him his heart gave way,
They said.

Oh, no no no, it was too cold always
(Still the dead one lay moaning)
I was much too far out all my life
And not waving but drowning.

(Smith, 2002)

Discussion

This poem uses complex techniques. You might have noticed that the first two lines are spoken by either the 'they' of 'they said' (in the last line of stanza 2) or by what we could call an omniscient narrator. But the next two lines relate to the inner, private world of the 'dead man' who seems to be trying to set the record straight. He was not waving to the indifferent 'they'; he was actually calling for help. At the start of stanza 2, we are back to the public view, and a kind of brief empathy which feels a bit false. The final stanza contradicts their idea that it was too cold in the sea, and brings the life-metaphor close to being revealed: 'it was too cold always' and 'I was much too far out all my life' imply that this man was out at sea in his own life, and that he was calling for help which never came.

The dramatic techniques here include that of combining two main perspectives, that of the dead man and that of the misunderstanding observers. As you explore the various layers of meaning, you may begin to think that the piece is satirising the stupidity and misguidedness of the public. You might even conclude that the poem is about society's indifference towards those who are different or don't seem to fit in well. The ambiguity of whether the man is actually dead, while still 'moaning', is part of Smith's ability to layer meaning onto that striking image: a person who appears to be waving, while actually drowning.

There is a hint at the layers of meaning in the intriguing title of Smith's poem. You will read about how titles can generate dramatic possibilities in the next section.

3 Titles

The title of a poem is the first thing a reader sees, and some poets consider it to be, in effect, the first line of the piece and, therefore, very important. A title can be used to add intrigue or interest, and it can also be a signpost to something in the poem. It is important to think carefully about titles and to judge what effect you want them to have. There are several ways of using a title to add drama. Two examples are:

- Surprising or intriguing titles

    Titles of poems such as 'The Comeback of Speedos' (2023) by Tishani Doshi or 'Do You Remember the Rude Nudists' (2011) by Christian Wiman have an element of surprise and, although they may be thought of as slightly rude, they do not come across as crude due to the tongue-in-cheek way in which they are phrased. A title such as 'Evel Knievel Jumps over My Family' (2014), from a poem by Jonathan Edwards, is intriguing and this author also uses a light-hearted tone in the title of the book it comes from: *My Family and Other Superheroes*.

    By contrast, titles of poems such as 'Tiptoe Lightning' (2006) by Elizabeth Willis or the 1938 poem 'Mother, among the Dustbins' (2018) by Stevie Smith bring two things into the same line that feel at odds or unexpected, setting the reader up to expect deep feelings or emotion.

- Titles which imply a dramatic story

    'Driving Home at Night with My Children after Their Grandfather's Funeral' (2023) by Bert Meyers, originally published in 1979, sets up a scenario with potential for emotional content, whereas 'On Asking My Mother about Winter 1990' (2023) by Abhijit Sarmah creates a sense of foreboding via the use of the date. That sense is played out in the **epigraph** to the poem: 'On November 27, 1990, President's rule was imposed in the Indian state of Assam and counterinsurgency operation Bajrang was launched against separatist groups. Thousands of young men were arrested, hundreds were killed' (Sarmah, 2023, p. 288).

    An example of a poem title that creates a different mood is 'For Stuart, who Accidentally Obtained a Job in the Civil Service' (2004) by Leontia Flynn; this is immediately understood as humorous via the juxtaposition of 'accidentally' and 'obtained' in relation to a job.

Activity 2 Writing: trying out dramatic techniques

Think up three or four scenarios which have some in-built problem, tension, misunderstanding or power imbalance. This will usually be between people, often two individuals or more, who want different things or who see things in different ways.

- Jot down several ideas for such scenarios. This could be where a parent and a teenager argue over appropriate dress, or where siblings have different ideas about what to do for a parent's funeral.

- Taking the scenario that you consider to be the most promising, write words, phrases or even lines or half-lines that might end up in a poem.
- Now consider whether the different perspectives at play in this potential poem can help to add drama, as in Smith's poem 'Not Waving But Drowning'. Can you use 'but' to pivot from one perspective to another, or 'they said' or 'he/she said' to help dramatise your scenario?
- Finally, think of a title for your draft poem that might intrigue, surprise or otherwise engage a reader.

Discussion

This activity asks you to use or adapt some of the dramatic techniques that you have been thinking about so far in this chapter and to think about how titles can add drama, intrigue and interest. You may find, as you read the rest of the chapter, that more ideas come to mind. Capture these as you go along, because sometimes the best writing ideas arise when you are thinking of something else. Ideas may just keep on percolating once you have begun the process.

The saying that 'Genius is one per cent inspiration, ninety-nine per cent perspiration', attributed to the American inventor Thomas Edison (Rosanoff, 1932, p. 406), is often applied by writers to their own acts of writing. In Activity 2, you engaged in the inspiration phase of writing: you will return to the early-stage notes that you produced later in this chapter, when you will find yourself in the perspiration phase – the hard graft of shaping a poem!

In the next section, you will learn how to use a favourite device of contemporary writers: irony.

4 Dramatic irony

Irony in writing is a literary device in which statements or situations reveal a reality that is different from what appears to be true. In poems, it can often take the form of the speaker revealing quite a different set of circumstances than the one they are maintaining is the case. In this way, dramatic irony exploits the device of giving the reader or spectator an item of information that at least one of the speakers or characters is unaware of, thus allowing the author to communicate directly with the reader/spectator in ways that can feel like a delicious conspiracy! This gap between the author and the speaker, when the author is in cahoots, as it were, with the reader, adds a distinctive sense of dramatic conflict.

Dramatic irony, then, arises when the reader or spectator knows something that one or more of the characters in the piece does not. In Shakespeare's play *Macbeth*, Duncan, on arrival at Macbeth's castle, observes: 'This castle hath a pleasant seat; the air / Nimbly and sweetly recommends itself / Unto our gentle senses' (Shakespeare, 2004, 1.6: 1–3). But, meantime, the audience knows that Macbeth and Lady Macbeth have been plotting Duncan's murder. Another example is when the viewer of the film *The Truman Show* (1998) is aware that Truman is on a reality television show, but the character has to learn this the hard way throughout the whole plot.

Figure 2 Dove Cottage, home of the poet William Wordsworth, Grasmere, Cumbria, 2018 (photo: Ian Dagnall/Alamy).

Activity 3 Reading: 'At the Lakes with Roberta'

Read 'At the Lakes with Roberta' (2013) by Tara Bergin.

- Take note of where you think the speaker is addressing you, or trying to influence your opinion.
- Where do you feel that the author may be having fun at the expense of the speaker?

> **Tara Bergin** grew up in Ireland before moving to England. Her poems often draw on aspects of folklore and fable, using the surreal in matter-of-fact ways. Her monologues present speakers who reveal their own attitudes, as well as the attitude of the author towards them, in incremental ways throughout the poem.

At the Lakes with Roberta

Our guide
(with whom Roberta has already been ingratiating herself
in a horribly forward manner)
has taken us to Windermere,
and tomorrow will take us to Grasmere.
Of course I am eager to see,
first-hand, as it were,
the sources of inspiration,
but I fear Roberta's behaviour
shall spoil the entire experience.

Speaking bluntly: she is far too light-hearted;
rather superficial if one may say such a thing,
and she *flatters* him, that's the point,
she flatters him with her incompetence.
I'm afraid I find it unseemly.

The fact is,
if she continues to distract our guide from his duty as guide,
there will be a breach between Roberta and me.
The fault will lie with her:
it's perfectly clear she came only to enjoy The View –
while I can hardly bear it, you see;
I can hardly bear the weight of this poetic air,
the air that WW breathed: such steep atmosphere.
There's nothing for it: one must simply never travel
with one's female companions.

And now, look:
our guide is daring to quote from 'To the Small Celandine'
(never a favourite of mine)
and Roberta's foolish gasps of pleasure hang on the mist.
It's unfortunate, really, that he has been quite so taken in,
so swallowed up by what one might call
a rather ordinary attractiveness.

And clearly I shall remain ignorant for the rest of the tour
about the more – intimate – details
of a poet's life.

(Bergin, 2013)

Discussion

The conversational, almost conspiratorial, tone of the speaker and phrases like 'Speaking bluntly', 'Of course' and 'And now, look:' all feel like an attempt by the speaker to get us on her side.

This poem is written with an air of world-weary detachment, but you may well get the impression that, in fact, the behaviours of her friend affect the speaker very much despite her matter-of-fact tone. The author is playful here in what she has the speaker choose to disclose or to withhold. The protagonist comes across as quite prudish about the flirtatiousness of Roberta with the guide, and yet she longs to know the 'intimate' details of Wordsworth's life. It's as if our speaker is only comfortable with intimacy if it's in the distant past. Additionally, the dramatic irony seems to imply that if anyone is receiving the attentions of the guide, it should be herself! The tension between what is being said and the actual jealousy she feels towards Roberta is heightened, and the reader feels they are being let in on something by the author, which is always a fun feeling.

5 The dramatic swerve

In writing, and most especially in longer forms, there is opportunity to employ other dramatic techniques such as the **cliffhanger**, **foreshadowing**, the red herring (a metaphor for when the reader's attention is drawn to irrelevant details, diverting attention from what is actually going on) and the **plot twist**.

As Sylvia Plath said, 'Poetry, I feel, is a tyrannical discipline, you've got to go so far, so fast, in such a small space that you've just got to turn away all the peripherals' (Plath, 1966, p. 171). With that in mind, for adding drama in poetry, one of the techniques akin to a plot twist, and which is economical with space, is what we can think of as a 'swerve'. This is where the poem goes to a different place than expected or has a sudden shift of **tone** or **mood**.

An example is the second stanza from my poem 'Fodder'. The first five lines of the stanza may seem whimsically romantic, but the final three swerve to undermine that by referring to corn as, first and foremost, being *food*.

Fodder

What you have seen cornfield, could make you weep.
The stories they tell from the north
would be worthless to yours.
When you were a battleground, you held your whist.
One side or another, whoever won would need to eat.
You have ears to hear the centuries whisper
but mostly you heed your own low murmur –

Cornfield, when the breeze flies through you,
makes a set dance of your bright tips,
or when a path opens up to your centre
as if a mysterious finger parts your waves,
then we could believe you hold the wisdom of the ages.
But you might not agree.
You might say instead,
    Just believe in corn.

(Campbell, 2017)

When using the swerve, it is best to consider just how dramatic the shift should be and to judge that in relation to the effect you want to elicit in the reader. If you swerve too far from the tone you've established, it may ruin the effect. In Activity 4, you will read poems by Rachel Long (Figure 3(a)) and Nessa O'Mahony (Figure 3(b)) that take two different approaches.

Figure 3 (a) Rachel Long at the Edinburgh International Book Festival, 2019 (photo: Sally Anderson/Alamy). (b) Nessa O'Mahony, 2019 (photo: Peter Salisbury).

Activity 4 Reading: poems by Rachel Long and Nessa O'Mahony

Read the two poems, 'Jail Letter' (2020) by Rachel Long and 'Deserted Village, Achill Island' (2014) by Nessa O'Mahony.

- Think about where you see the swerve in each poem.
- What do you find is the effect of the swerves on your reading of the poems?

> **Rachel Long** is a British poet and author and founder of Octavia Poetry Collective for Women of Colour. Long's writing often explores themes of identity, race and social issues, reflecting her commitment to amplifying under-represented voices in the literary world.

Jail Letter

All Saturday I sit viced between Mum's legs.
When it's dark and all my friends are inside she says,
Finished! like 'Ta-dah!' as if anything about this has been quick
or thrilling.

The corners of my eyes have been stitched into my hairline.
All the 'sheep's wool' they love to touch and say eww to at school
has been harvested into rows at the top of my head;
black crown or web.

'Mum, my scalp burns!'
'Ungrateful! Look at you, beautiful as Winnie Mandela!'
I don't know who this is,
but it doesn't sound like someone Ben Clark will fancy.

(Long, 2020)

Nessa O'Mahony was born in Dublin and – after some time in Wales – still lives there. As well as writing poems, she is a novelist, editor of anthologies and a podcaster. Her writing frequently delves into themes of history, family and Irish identity.

Deserted Village, Achill Island

in memory of my father

A gap between showers,
blue filtering half-light,
so we take our chances
on the slopes of Slievemore.

Those who'd called it home
knew about impermanence,
the reach of bog,
the gaping sockets of roofs.

Hap-hazarding lazy beds,
slip-slides of water
pouring down
the side of the mountain,
we settle for the track,
the safety of shale and quartz.

Sun wets white shards,
crystal lures us
as the track forks
to where a burnt-out digger
acts sentinel over oil slicks;
wind chimes music:
a plastic bottle
trapped by bog-*lethe*.

The quarry opens out,
slag-heaps improbably white,
as if someone had cleared snow
into neat piles,
or had scattered detergent
like there was no tomorrow,
no white sheets to be spread out,
no single rose bud to be left
beside a hospital bed.

(O'Mahony, 2014)

Discussion

In Long's 'Jail Letter', the hairstyling 'jail' takes the whole day, thereby creating a shape for the poem. She uses the finish of this styling to place a two-part swerve which brings other things into the picture for the reader. The first – the insouciant admission of not knowing who Winnie Mandela is (South African anti-apartheid activist and the second wife of Nelson Mandela, South Africa's first post-apartheid president) – performs a kind of joke for the reader who is assumed by the author to have this knowledge. The second – a charming moment of self-doubt and longing – has the effect of making the reader empathise with the speaker.

In the O'Mahony poem, the swerve is achieved with a light touch, but it is nonetheless dramatic. The reader may initially think they are in a countryside scene where the landscape bears the marks of the people's history. The final lines which bring the reader into a hospital room may come as a surprise. Has someone died? The swerve has the effect of making the reader read the poem again and, on a second reading, details such as the epigraph and words like 'impermanence' and 'gaping', along with the slightly ominous nature of the 'burnt-out digger' and 'oil slicks', may stand out. These add to the atmosphere of loss, as does the '*lethe*' of the bog, which refers to the ancient Greek word meaning 'oblivion'. The final lines, with the single rosebud left beside a hospital bed, bring all the imagery together and the poem can now be seen as a kind of **elegy**.

6 Using scenes

You read about the characteristics of scenes in Chapter 6: these include the fact that they generally happen in a particular place and time, and have a beginning and an ending. Scenes often utilise a ticking clock or timing of some sort. You have already read what could be called a scene in 'Jail Letter', with its 'ticking clock' being the time it takes to complete the hairstyle.

Other ways that poems use the idea of the scene is to have another speaker enter the poem and change the ending, sometimes breaking what we might call the mood of the scene, or to have a swerve, along the lines of those that you read about in the previous section, but one which brings the scene to a close, sometimes deliberately truncating it.

Something to consider is whether to use the present tense. This can bring the reader most fully into the **action**, meaning that they can see and feel how the scene unfolds in the moment. 'Jail Letter', for example, is written in the present tense, which makes it easy for the reader to enter into the poem alongside the speaker.

When writing a poem that is based on a scene, think about how to end the piece, whether at the end of the scene itself (as in 'Jail Letter') or with an additional flash forward or speculative moment. The poem featured in Activity 5 adds an extra moment of speculation, using 'he must have' to add an extra element at the end, for example.

Activity 5 Reading: 'Delinquent'

Read the poem 'Delinquent' (2021) by Kathryn Bevis and identify the scene, or scenes, in this poem.

> **Kathryn Bevis** was an English poet who lived in Hampshire. Her poetry often delved into themes of nature, human connection and self-discovery. Kathryn designed and delivered Poetry for Wellbeing courses for adults in mental health settings and prisons. She also edited two anthologies of poetry by new and emerging poets.

Content note: Please be aware that this reading mentions the death of a child and possible suicide.

Delinquent

Patrick McCaffery: sly-eyed, greasy-quiffed,
hands sticky blue with the BICs he liked to pull apart
in class, his mouth gobby with the spit he'd let drop
from the science block balcony on our sandwiches at break.

One assembly, his mam was there as guest. She sat
on a too-small plastic chair at the front, twisting
a tissue in her hands as she told us about the charity
she'd started in her dead daughter's name — a last wish

foundation for kids who didn't have long to live
(so they'd get to tick off one thing on their list). Patrick
only kept his face turned toward the floor, perfectly still,
silent as he'd never been, feeling our eyes aimed

into a sniper's red dot at the base of his neck. His mouth
sealed up for the rest of that day as if with Copydex,
shoulders slumped under his standard-issue, bottle-green
blazer like collapsed scoops of lukewarm, canteen mash.

He's long gone now. Overdosed at twenty six. I often
think of him arriving home that day, how he must have run
upstairs, flung himself onto his bed, how he'd worn on his face
the popped bubble-gum balloon of all our fucking pity.

(Bevis, 2021)

Discussion

Bevis structures this poem carefully. The first stanza is a mini-character sketch. She then creates the scene which forms the body of the work, that of Patrick's mother at the assembly and his reaction to this. In the penultimate stanza, she adds a kind of tail to the ending of the scene by telling us that Patrick's mouth was 'sealed up for the rest of that day'. Then comes a fast-forward. We learn that Patrick died when he was 26. The poet clinches the ending by speculating an imagined scene, at the end of 'that day' of the assembly, where Patrick shows real emotion as he 'flung himself onto his bed'. You, like me, may find that the ending – with the expletive conjoined with 'pity' – stirs up empathy for Patrick and stimulates the urge to reread the poem from the beginning.

Now that you have considered the ways in which scenes, swerves, dramatic irony and dramatic conflict can heighten a poem's sense of tension, you have the tools you need to combine some of these techniques in a poem of your own.

Activity 6 Writing: adding further dramatic elements

Using the notes you made in Activity 2, think about the characters you came up with and the problem, tension, misunderstanding or power imbalance between them.

Now, revise the draft you began in Activity 2 by using some of the following:

- dramatic irony (which might have a speaker trying to get the reader on their side)
- dramatic conflict (which might show the difference between the private and the public)
- one or two phrases such as 'they say now', 'he/she/they said' and 'I've heard that'
- a swerve to add humour or to bring in another emotion
- the shape of a scene where something ends or changes for the speaker.

Discussion

By now you are hopefully beginning to get a feel for the many ways in which tension can be a springboard in a poem to a more dramatic experience for the reader. Trying these techniques out for yourself can also enable you to 'read as a writer' more effectively, since you will be keenly aware of the ways in which other poets approach conflict and tension. Keeping notes of the more successful or surprising moves that authors make can add even more to your own store of possibilities.

As you continue your writing journey, creating new draft poems which employ the techniques you are learning, you could, in time, look back through the scenarios you created in Activity 2 and select a different one to develop. Open-ended phrases such as 'On asking my mother/father/uncle/daughter' or 'After the wedding reception/Christmas dinner/wake/funeral' can actually prove to be inspiring in themselves, bringing dramatic possibility to the poem you are writing. If you make it a habit to write a couple of sentences in your notebook about where you feel you are using dramatic techniques in any particular draft, this may help you to decide whether they are too clunky and need to be refined or, alternatively, whether you need to employ one more of the techniques you have learned to add tension to the poem.

7 Conclusion

You now have the option to use dramatic techniques including irony, the swerve and strong scene endings. Remember these when you come to write a narrative poem (as you did in Chapter 4), as they have added to your writer's toolbox. You will also find that the skills from both poetry chapters so far can be redeployed when writing prose or scripts. Understanding how writers achieve the effects they want to have on the reader will enable you to choose from an ever-widening range of possible techniques as you move forward. In this chapter, you have seen how dramatic techniques can enliven a poem or make it more memorable. In the next chapter, you will look at the persuasive techniques of analogy and rhetoric across all genres.

References

Bergin, T. (2013) 'At the lakes with Roberta', in T. Bergin, *This is yarrow*. Manchester: Carcanet Press, pp. 48–49.

Bevis, K. (2021) 'Delinquent', *Magma Poetry*, (Issue 83). Available at: https://magmapoetry.com/archive/magma-83/poems/delinquent (Accessed: 19 May 2023).

Campbell, S. (2017) 'Fodder', in S. Campbell, *Heat signature*. Bridgend: Seren Books, p. 39.

Doshi, T. (2023) 'The comeback of Speedos', *Poetry*, (January). Available at: https://www.poetryfoundation.org/poetrymagazine/poems/159260/the-comeback-of-speedos (Accessed: 3 May 2023).

Edwards, J. (2014) 'Evel Knievel jumps over my family', in J. Edwards, *My family and other superheroes*. Bridgend: Seren.

Flynn, L. (2004) 'For Stuart, who accidentally obtained a job in the Civil Service'. Available at: https://poetryarchive.org/poem/stuart-who-accidentally-obtained-job-civil-service/ (Accessed: 17 January 2023).

Long, R. (2020) 'Jail letter', in R. Long, *My darling from the lions*. London: Picador, p. 43.

MacNeice, L. (1987) *Selected literary criticism of Louis MacNeice*. Edited by A. Heuser. Oxford: Clarendon.

Meyers, B. (2023) 'Driving home at night with my children after their grandfather's funeral', *Poetry*, (January). Available at: https://www.poetryfoundation.org/poetrymagazine/poems/159253/driving-home-at-night-with-my-children-after-their-grandfathers-funeral (Accessed: 18 January 2023).

O'Mahony, N. (2014) 'Deserted village, Achill Island', in N. O'Mahony, *Her father's daughter*. Cliffs of Moher, Co. Clare: Salmon Poetry, p. 61.

Plath, S. (1966) 'Sylvia Plath'. Interview with Sylvia Plath. Interviewed by P. Orr, in P. Orr (ed.) *The poet speaks: interviews with contemporary poets conducted by Hilary Morrish, Peter Orr, John Press and Ian Scott-Kilvert*. London: Routledge & Kegan Paul, pp. 167–172.

Rosanoff, M.A. (1932) 'Edison in his laboratory', *Harper's Monthly Magazine*, 165(987), pp. 402–417.

Sarmah, A. (2023) 'On asking my mother about Winter 1990', *Poetry*, (January), pp. 288–289.

Shakespeare, W. (2004) *Macbeth*. Edited by J. Wilders. Cambridge: Cambridge University Press.

Smith, S. (2002) 'Not waving but drowning', in S. Smith, *Selected poems*. London: Penguin, p. 167.

Smith, S. (2018) 'Mother, among the dustbins', *The Poetry Archive*. Available at: https://poetryarchive.org/poem/mother-among-the-dustbin/ (Accessed: 18 January 2023).

The Truman Show (1998) Directed by P. Weir. [Feature film]. Los Angeles, CA: Paramount Pictures.

Willis, E. (2006) 'Tiptoe lightning'. Available at: https://www.poetryfoundation.org/poems/159198/tiptoe-lightning (Accessed: 18 January 2023).

Wiman, C. (2011) 'Do you remember the rude nudists'. Available at: https://www.poetryfoundation.org/poems/57359/do-you-remember-the-rude-nudists (Accessed: 3 May 2023).

Chapter 13
Persuasive techniques: using analogy and rhetoric

Emily Bullock

1 Introduction

Figure 1 A man reading (photo: Nappy. This file is licensed under the Creative Commons CC0 Public Domain Licence https://creativecommons.org/share-your-work/public-domain/cc0/).

In this chapter, you will consider the techniques of **analogy** and **rhetoric** in a number of forms: fiction, life writing, poetry and scriptwriting. You will work through reading and writing exercises to enable you both to practise using the techniques of analogy and rhetoric, and to recognise them in the work of other writers.

'Analogy' is a word or phrase that expresses a similarity between one thing and another. Analogies are usually divided into similes (where the comparison is explicit, often linking the comparison with 'like' or 'as') and metaphors (where the comparison is implied).

Rhetoric is verbal or written communication used to persuade, inform or motivate. This chapter will focus on four of the many rhetorical techniques available to writers: **repetition**, **parenthesis**, **antithesis** and **euphony**.

You will learn to use, and to develop your use of, these techniques.

2 One-word analogies

Analogies are often thought of as being phrases, but they can also consist of one word. One-word analogies are a device often used in poetry. However, examples of one-word analogies can be found in prose, as the following extract from V.S. Pritchett's short story 'The Wheelbarrow' shows:

> And when Evans waved back from the far side of the rumpled lawn where he was standing by the bonfire, she closed the window to keep out the smoke of slow-burning rubbish – old carpeting, clothes, magazines, papers, boxes – which hung about the waists of the fir trees and blew towards the house.
>
> *(Pritchett, 1984, p. 113)*

The single word 'rumpled' is used to describe the lawn, and this word is usually connected to fabric or clothes; and the firs are given 'waists' which brings them to life. By using these single words, the writer creates thought-provoking analogies that, in this instance, are closely connected to clothes, materials, and the wearing of clothes, which can be seen as significant because the short story is set at a house clearance. In the next activity, you will read a poem that uses an item of clothing as a single-word analogy.

Activity 1 Reading and writing: one-word analogies

Part 1

Read the poem 'Coat' by Vicki Feaver (1981).

- Consider how the title connects to the meaning of the poem.
- Reflect on the different emotions that are expressed in so few lines.

> **Vicki Feaver** was born in Nottingham but is based in South Lanarkshire. She is a poet and former tutor of creative writing. Her work often interrogates themes of childhood, family life and the role of women, exploring art, myths and fairy tales along the way.

Coat

Sometimes I have wanted
to throw you off
like a heavy coat.

Sometimes I have said
you would not let me
breathe or move.

But now that I am free
to choose light clothes
or none at all

I feel the cold
and all the time I think
how warm it used to be.

(Feaver, 1981)

Discussion

Did you interpret the meaning of the poem as an end of a relationship? It is a deceptively simple poem that nevertheless conveys a sense of emotion and loss. The one-word title is the focus of the whole poem, and the only analogy used. The first usage is a simile, 'like a heavy coat' (an explicit comparison), and the poem ends with a metaphor, 'how warm it used to be', an implied comparison in which the coat (or lack of) stands in for the relationship. In this analogy, the 'heavy coat' is worn in three different ways:

- with a desire for escape: 'I have wanted / to throw you off'
- as a stifling symbol: 'would not let me / breathe or move'
- and with a sense of longing for the past: 'how warm it used to be'.

These three interpretations connect to the three stages of the end of the relationship: the longing to be free, 'to throw you off'; after the relationship, being 'free to choose light clothes'; and, finally, looking back with longing or nostalgia, 'I feel the cold'. But like all good poems, it also leaves some unanswered questions. For example, what are the 'light clothes'? Is it loneliness or loss, or just nostalgia, being expressed by the end?

Maybe you came up with a different interpretation of the poem and the analogy, thinking about why the speaker might choose the wrong clothes, what that says about them and their view of the relationship. This is the power of a well-chosen analogy: it gives the reader room to interpret through the lens of their own experiences.

The way that Feaver employs the one-word analogy of the coat allows the reader to view the end of a relationship in a new and engaging way.

In the next part of this activity, see if you can develop a piece of writing using a one-word analogy.

Part 2

Pick a household object and use it as the title of a poem or a couple of paragraphs of prose. Without employing any other analogy, use the item as the focus for a piece of writing about the end of something. You may like to use one of the following ideas as a prompt:

- the end of a journey
- the end of living in a particular place
- the end of a party.

Discussion

Limitations on the subject of the exercise might appear to stifle creativity. But, as Feaver's poem demonstrates, a sense of focus and an economy of analogy can have a powerful effect. As you wrote, you may have found that it can be liberating to work within such constraints. Even if you did not enjoy the sense of constraint, it can be a useful exercise in economy to attempt to focus your writing like this, at times. Simplicity and specificity can, in fact, create great depth of emotion and universality because the constraints on the part of the writer leave room for the reader's imagination to expand and experience emotional connection.

3 The impact of analogy

An analogy should surprise and engage the reader and help to make writing come alive. In the next activity, you will read a piece of life writing from *The Grassling* (2020) by Elizabeth-Jane Burnett in order to consider the impact of analogies on the reader.

Burnett was motivated by her father's declining health and inspired by the history he wrote of his small Devon village to write *The Grassling*, a blend of memoir, nature writing and poetry. Burnett is of English and Kenyan heritage, and she considers issues of belonging, race and history from this perspective.

In the extract you will read in Activity 2, Burnett uses two different analogies in which a barn owl and a cyborg (a fictional or hypothetical creature that is part human and part machine) are used to express something about human acceptance and understanding.

Activity 2 Reading: effect of analogy on the reader

Read the extract from *The Grassling* (2020) by Elizabeth-Jane Burnett (Reading 13.1 in Part 4).

- Examine the effect of Burnett's analogies on yourself as the reader.
- Consider why the writer might have employed them.

Discussion

For me, the sighting of the barn owl starts a process of thinking about 'visitors' – who belongs and who does not. They welcome the barn owl with the words, *'Visitor, you are welcome, no worries!'* (Burnett, 2020, p. 47). The words are reworked to be more inclusive by the end of the extract, *'Nobody worry, you're all welcome'* (p. 48). This connection is established using a second analogy, involving 'cyborgs', which might on first reading have seemed out of place.

Burnett uses these two very different analogies to reimagine ideas of belonging and community: on the one hand, the wild and free barn owl that belongs in this setting and has a deep connection to father and daughter; and, on the other, the cyborg, in response to judgement from outside the family, that may startle the reader by being out of place in a narrative of nature.

These two apparently disparate analogies are finally brought together at the end of the last paragraph: 'Perhaps she would have looked at me the way my father and I had looked at that owl' (p. 48).

When you are writing and searching for ways to engage the reader or make complex emotions/ideas easier to understand, take note of what's in your scene already (the people, the place, objects, the weather) and consider whether you can use these things as the basis for your analogies, as Burnett does with the barn owl in *The Grassling*. It is worth noting that, while startling analogies (such as Burnett's cyborg) can be well-judged and have a powerful effect, it is important to use them sparingly or you risk confusing the reader.

3.1 The ordinary and the extraordinary

Consider the contrast in the extract from Burnett's *The Grassling* (2020) (Reading 13.1), with its use of the owl and the cyborg: this is a contrast between the ordinary and the extraordinary. Dictionary definitions of the term 'analogy' often refer to the idea that the device serves the purpose of making abstract concepts and ideas simple and direct. However, analogies can also be used to make the ordinary into something extraordinary, such as an encounter in a shop where a person's heritage and sense of belonging is overlooked because of the colour of their skin, by bringing in analogies of cyborgs.

This is the power of analogies: they can make the ordinary extraordinary and the extraordinary ordinary.

Figure 2 Front cover of Hannah Hodgson, *163 Days*, Bridgend, Seren, 2022. Original artwork: Sue Austin, *Over Coral*, still from *'Creating the Spectacle!'*, 2012, photographed by Norman Lomax. Photo: © We Are Freewheeling.

Activity 3 Reading: extraordinary analogies

Read this extract from the poem 'Mermaids on the Brain' (2022) by Hannah Hodgson.

Consider how and why Hodgson might have used the analogy of a mermaid.

> **Hannah Hodgson** is a writer, editor and activist living with a life-limiting illness. She uses both outpatient palliative care and hospices for respite and symptom management.

Content note: Please be aware that this reading mentions severe illness.

Mermaids on the Brain

I'm sorry to have to tell you this over the phone,
but I've got your scans in front of me,
and I'm concerned that the mermaids

we've discovered aren't receiving the care
they need. Their scales are falling off.
This can be very painful, all wounds

should be bathed in salt water.
Is there anyone at home who can help
you scrape the limpets off their skin?

Your girls are gravely ill, so they can't
look after themselves.

(Hodgson, 2022, p. 68)

Discussion

The medical and the fantastical are linked together in these stanzas. Is it that the medical news is so shocking that only a mythical analogy can provide the distance needed to examine the narrator's pain? At times the words are shocking (e.g. 'Their scales are falling off' and 'scrape the limpets off their skin'); this may suggest the bravery and endurance needed to confront these 'scans'.

The analogy of the mermaids can be seen to lift a personal medical journey into a fantastical dimension and, therefore, timeless expression of pain and suffering. The analogy is both unexpected and moving.

An extraordinary analogy can make your writing come alive, surprising and engaging the reader, but there can be a danger in overusing analogies or making them too obscure, which could make your writing harder to read. You might want to engage your reader – at times shock them and even persuade them of something – but, ultimately, as a writer, you may wish to maintain empathy not just for your characters but also your audience.

4 How much is enough?

A question like 'How much is enough?' is a matter of preference and it can relate to the development of your writerly style (which may vary depending on the piece you are writing). Some readers will be enchanted by the use of analogy and others will skim over it, determined to get to the 'story' beneath the style. As a writer, you never know who might be experiencing your work, and every reader will bring with them a unique set of experiences, opinions and values. Writers need to have an awareness of audience: for example, readers of romance and readers of hard-boiled crime will have very different expectations of the writing style. In short, there needs to be a balance between the writer's voice and the reader's expectations.

Annie Proulx's short story 'In the Pit' (1995) depicts a dysfunctional family. In the following extract, you will notice that there are a lot of explicit analogies (using 'as', 'as if', 'as though', 'like'):

> Once he had tried to grill a cheese sandwich in that toaster and the bread caught fire, black smoke as though from burning tires billowed out of the chrome. … His mother flapped the air with a towel and screamed, 'You damn little fool to try to make a sandwich in a toaster!' and his father hurled words like clods of dirt. … Blue ran up to the loft where he cried for the cheese sandwich as though it were the last one in the world, and the shouting below went on and on, and then the brown sofa creaked as though they were tearing it apart.
> … The lamp was behind the seated figure and he seemed, for a minute, to be edged in a rim of fire, with round eyeglasses glinting like circles of steel. … His face was the color of a cracker, as stiff as if it had been baked, his eyes like a hen's, yellow and ignorant.
>
> *(Proulx, 1995, p. 111)*

Proulx's analogies in the rest of the story mostly describe things such as light, colour, shape and size, movement, sensory details and the appearance of people and objects. This can be seen to be important because the story is about judgements based on appearance, and the mistaken identity of a toaster. Some readers will love this depth of detail and the opulence of the analogies, but others could find it distracting. You might want to consider your own reaction to the extract because, if you understand what you like as a reader, this can be carried forward into your writing style.

Most of Proulx's analogy choices are easily accessible to the reader. She could instead have used analogies that make the reader reach for a dictionary, and that might be something you want to try, startling the reader like Burnett does with the cyborg. But do remember the role of empathy: you don't want to scare readers away.

5 Rhetoric: a tool for reader persuasion

In the previous sections, you considered the use of analogy from the perspectives of taste and style. There are other ways to develop your style of writing: for example, rhetorical techniques can engage and persuade the reader. As stated at the beginning of the chapter, rhetoric is verbal or written communication that persuades, informs or motivates. It is usually associated with the delivery of political speeches which are meant to be heard at the time of delivery, making an impact there and then. A famous example is Martin Luther King's 'I Have a Dream' speech (Alvarez, 1988, p. 14).

There is a connection between political speeches, protests, testimony and dramatic writing and performance. All these modes of communication use rhetoric because of its ability to convey passion and power and hence provoke an emotional response in an audience. Essential to the use of rhetoric is an awareness of the audience.

Rhetoric is about employing set techniques in order to persuade a listener or reader, but this shouldn't be mistaken for manipulation. The most persuasive rhetoric works because it is emotionally honest and character-led. In this section, you will investigate how creative writers can adapt these techniques to create specific effects in their work. You will focus on four main techniques: repetition, antithesis, parenthesis and euphony.

In the next activity, you will read from Alastair Siddons and Steve McQueen's script for their screenplay *Small Axe: Mangrove* (2020). It tells the true story of Frank Crichlow, owner of a West Indian restaurant, called Mangrove, which is a lively community hub in London's Notting Hill. In 1970, in a bid to stop the discrimination and harassment of their community base, Frank and his friends take to the streets in peaceful protest, only to be met by police aggression. As a result, nine men and women are wrongfully arrested and charged with incitement to riot and affray.

Figure 3 Letitia Wright as Altheia in *Small Axe: Mangrove*, directed by Steve McQueen, BBC Studios, 2020. Photographed by Des Willie (photo: LANDMARK MEDIA/Alamy).

Activity 4 Reading: *Small Axe: Mangrove*

Read the extract from *Small Axe: Mangrove* by Alastair Siddons and Steve McQueen (Reading 13.2).

Can you spot anything that attempts to persuade you of something, or do you notice any devices that grab your attention when reading?

Discussion

There is a lot that is both shocking and moving in the scene in this script. Essentially, however, Altheia is trying to stop Frank from pleading guilty as a way of securing a more lenient sentence. You might have noticed how the language Altheia uses ranges from colloquial West Indian to standard English, traversing between familiarity and expressive eloquence to the formal language of the courtroom: 'All ya better take this fricking man out my face' (Siddons and McQueen, 2020, p. 79); 'We are the example and we must bear this responsibility' (p. 80).

Altheia uses many rhetorical devices in her attempt to convince Frank that the only right thing to do is to stand in court and have their say. But what she also does is talk directly to the audience, convincing 'us' that we would also have to stand by her if we were in that room. The speech demands that the audience understands what this choice really means. She is speaking to everyone: 'What is being called into question in this case is the right of anybody, not just black people, but the right of anybody to demonstrate' (p. 80). It is so important that it needs to be said twice.

In the extract from *Small Axe: Mangrove*, there are two audiences present: the audience of fellow characters addressed by Altheia and the audience as viewer/listener/reader. While you work through the rhetorical devices under discussion in this chapter, keep in the forefront of your mind the audience as viewer/listener/reader.

6 Repetition

You may have noted the extensive use of repetition throughout the extract from *Small Axe: Mangrove*: 'If we fold now, if we give in to them, if we let them control our decisions, then they take it all. They take it all from us. And they take it from our children, too' (Siddons and McQueen, 2020, p. 80).

Repetition is often used to emphasise a particular point or position.

Activity 5 Reading: 'Walking for My Mother'

Read 'Walking for My Mother' (2017), a short story by Jacob Ross (Reading 13.3).

Look out for repetition and note what effect it has on you, and what effect it might be supposed to have on Nella, the protagonist.

Discussion

Repetition is frequently used in the story, both in the narrative and in the dialogue. This has the effect, in dialogue, of the characters trying to impart important knowledge to Nella: 'You <u>de first</u> dis side of Old Hope Valley; in fact <u>de first</u> dis side of anywhere as far as I know to go to school in town. Once dem lil ones dere see <u>dat you kin</u> get to secandry, dey know dat <u>dey kin</u> get dere too …' (Ross, 2017, p. 37, underline added for emphasis). Here, Aunty May uses repetition to emphasise that Nella's achievement isn't just about her; she belongs to a community and this day is for them, too.

The repetitions also create a sense of the struggle that Nella's family must get through to achieve this place at secondary school – the trips to relatives, friends, the requests for money without actually asking. Repetition is especially important in oral traditions where the retaining of information cannot rely on the written word, so repeating something would make it easier to recall at a later point.

As with all the techniques you are considering in this chapter, the first rule to follow when using repetition in your work is: moderation, moderation, moderation.

7 Antithesis

This rhetorical device involves the use of words that are opposites, or noticeably different, to highlight contrasting ideas. Here are two famous examples:

> That's one small step for a man, one giant leap for mankind.
>
> *(Armstrong, 1969, quoted in NASA, 2019)*

> We must learn to live together as brothers or perish together as fools.
>
> *(King, 1964, quoted in Ratcliffe, 2016)*

The power of these lines means that they are often quoted, and we might take this to mean that the device only really works as a single line. But, consider the following excerpt from Zadie Smith's 2005 novel *On Beauty*:

> It was bright when the service began; now the sky was overcast. The congregation were more talkative departing from the church than they had been before – sharing anecdotes and memories – but still did not know *how to* end conversations respectfully; *how to* turn the talk from the invisibles of the earth – love and death and what comes after – to its practicalities: *how to* get a cab and whether one was going to the cemetery, or the wake, or both.
>
> *(Smith, 2005, p. 288, italics added)*

In this paragraph, Smith contrasts 'bright' with 'overcast', 'more talkative' against 'than before' and 'invisibles' with 'practicalities'. You may have noticed the device of repetition as well: 'how to' is used three times, which conveys a sense of uncertainty.

It is important to remember that you have a multitude of devices available to you when writing, and the more you are aware of the effect these devices can create for the audience, the more efficiently you can persuade the audience to engage with your work.

Activity 6 Reading and writing: repetition and antithesis

Read the following extract from the *Old Bailey Proceedings Online* (1759). The writing in the extract is sparse and stilted because it is taken from eighteenth-century court proceedings.

- Use either John Dean's or Elizabeth Jenkins' testimony as the basis for a piece of fiction of up to 400 words in length. The focus of the piece should be the moment of the 'crime' as experienced by your choice of either John or Elizabeth.
- When you have finished a first draft, concentrate on adding in examples of the rhetorical devices of repetition and antithesis. Don't be afraid to start out with lots of exaggerated usage of these devices. Once you have

finished the draft, return to the work and edit the piece until you are happy with the level of device usage.

113. (L.) Elizabeth Jenkins, otherwise Bateman, spinster; was indicted for stealing one man's hat, value 6 s. the property of John Dean, privately in his shop, February 14th, ++ [1759].

John Dean. I am a hatter, and live in Star-alley in Fen-church street; on Wednesday the 14th of February I was in my cellar, there is a light comes into the shop: I heard some body come into the shop; I call'd, but no body answered. I went up, and there was the prisoner; I follow'd her out of the shop, and took her at the door, and found my own wearing hat in her apron, and took it out; it is not quite new, I had left it in the shop, about three yards from the door of the shop.

Q. What was it worth when new?

Dean. It was worth 12 shillings.

Prisoner's Defence.

I was going by this gentleman's door, and saw that hat lying on the threshold; I was going to rap at the door, to know if it belong'd to the people there, and he came and took hold of me, and charged me with a robbery.

Guilty 4 s. 10 d.

(Old Bailey Proceedings Online, 1759)

Discussion

Perhaps you used repetition to establish the 'truth' of what the prisoner was saying, or you may have used antithesis to add detail to the shopkeeper's outrage at having his hat stolen. Devices like repetition and antithesis can have the effect of slowing the narrative pace, and in this way drawing the reader's attention to certain moments or events.

When you were writing the first draft, you might have included too many of the devices and, subsequently, decided to edit them out. But it's possible that some of the usage that at first felt forced or exaggerated ended up staying in the second draft. The freedom to come up with lots of repetition and antithesis makes it more likely that you could discover examples that really shine. For this reason, it can be useful to allow yourself a sense of playfulness to stimulate your imagination because surprising results can emerge; and, as the activity shows, you can always cut back during editing.

8 Parenthesis

Parenthesis involves interrupting a sentence with words that qualify what is happening or that produce the effect of an aside. These words often, but not always, appear in parentheses (brackets).

Virginia Woolf frequently uses this technique to expand on a particular line of thought, as this passage from her 1927 novel *To the Lighthouse* demonstrates:

> They had rooms in the village, and so, walking in, walking out, parting late on door-mats, had said little things about the soup, about the children, about one thing and another which made them allies; so that when he stood beside her now in his judicial way (he was old enough to be her father too, a botanist, a widower, smelling of soap, very scrupulous and clean) she just stood there. He just stood there.

(Woolf, 1971, p. 22)

The effect of parenthesis is that it can imitate a more conversational style because speakers frequently interrupt themselves and use asides. In this way, it can draw a reader closer, making them feel part of a conversation (like a listener, as well as a reader). But, of course, the passage also has repetition: 'he stood beside her', 'she just stood', 'He just stood'. Using rhetoric doesn't mean that a writer must limit themselves to one device at a time; indeed, a layering technique can be most effective.

Charles Dickens uses parenthesis on the first page of his 1843 novel *A Christmas Carol*. I have included this passage because he uses the rhetorical technique to justify his inclusion of a cliché. A cliché is an analogy that is so well worn as to have become threadbare, rarely working to engage or persuade the reader because they are overly familiar with it. But Dickens uses this knowledge to draw the reader in, and unlike Woolf in her extract, he directly acknowledges the reader's presence in the second paragraph:

> Old Marley was as dead as a door-nail.
>
> Mind! I don't mean to say that I know, of my own knowledge, what there is particularly dead about a door-nail. I might have been inclined, myself, to regard a coffin-nail as the deadest piece of ironmongery in the trade. But the wisdom of our ancestors is in the simile; and my unhallowed hands shall not disturb it, or the Country's done for. You will, therefore, permit me to repeat, emphatically, that Marley was as dead as a door-nail.

(Dickens, 2006, p. 1)

Parenthesis, as you have seen in the Dickens' extract, doesn't need to have brackets. In the Woolf example, the parenthesis is used to interrupt a sentence, whereas Dickens uses it to interrupt a thought or a statement. While I think about it – and I apologise because I am delaying you from getting to the end of this paragraph – sometimes en dashes (–) are also used to enclose a statement, as earlier in this sentence.

However you choose to present parenthesis, it is worth noting that its use can lead to unruly syntax (by using brackets, in particular, the narrative can run away with itself, diverging too far from the initial point and losing the reader in a labyrinth of sentences offering information like what your character had for breakfast, and this was toast and apricot jam, in my case) as I have just illustrated here.

9 Euphony

All the rhetorical techniques considered so far affect the way you hear as well as see the words on the page. This connects to the way that rhetoric originally developed as a form of public speech (as developed by the ancient Greeks). In literature, this is usually associated with poetry, and you might be familiar with some of these devices, like **alliteration** and **assonance**.

These echoes, although mostly used sparingly in prose, are part of a rhetorical technique called euphony that makes the work melodious ('euphony', from the ancient Greek, means 'to be pleasing to the ear'). In the following poem 'Longboat at Portaferry' (2021) by Siobhán Campbell, you will (especially if you read it out loud) find much that is 'pleasing to the ear'.

Longboat at Portaferry

At the mouth of the lough, I approach by the narrows
from fast-running tides to the place of strong currents.

I have bided my time, observing the flux,
the seals and the plover beside me beguiled.

I am still in my heart in search of safe harbor—
the wide shallow basin I've heard called a haven.

Like the waders and geese, I come back each season,
a to-ing and fro-ing since nature began.

I can see us some springtime, both newcome and native,
bathed in the light of a ferry at sunrise

when the eelgrass and thrift, the aster and thyme
are budding and thriving in warmth rearriving,

and along all the narrows are sponges and corals—
a riot of color remembering to bloom.

(Campbell, 2021, p. 88)

Perhaps you enjoyed the alliteration – 'beside me beguiled', 'see us some springtime' – or maybe the use of half rhymes on a line, such as in 'basin' and 'haven', or 'thriving' and 'rearriving' (there are three uses of 'ing' on that line which adds echo and pace). There are other examples in the poem, too. The reader is swept through the poem by these 'strong currents' of melody.

These poetic techniques can be used by all writers to create euphony in their work. In Ross's 'Walking For My Mother' (2017, p. 38), note the example 'walking as she waved, sensing with a sobering, abrupt sadness that she was also walking away from something else.' The use of euphony in such a story shouldn't be surprising when the protagonist states, 'It all sounded like music anyway' (p. 38).

However, at times your prose might call for a **discordant** or **staccato** sound. For example, in *Small Axe: Mangrove*, consider this response by Frank:

> FRANK CRICHLOW
> These people,
> they're like… vampires. Yuh think
> you beat dem but they keep coming
> back. Back at yuh again and again.
> It's like a silver bullet ain't
> enough.
>
> *(Siddons and McQueen, 2020, p. 79)*

Consider how all the words beginning with 'b' sound like expulsions of air and how this might reflect Frank's frustration. Also notice how many words end in 'k' (and contain 'k'), and the words ending in 'n' or 't' are all hard sounds that could convey a sense of anger.

The best way to decide whether you have created the desired effect in your work is to read it to yourself.

10 Conclusion

This chapter has explored the use of analogy, and how this technique can be developed for every form of writing. We've considered opinions on how analogy can add depth and excitement to a reader's experience. It's always worth considering whether an analogy you plan to use will enrich your audience's experience or confuse them.

This kind of reader/audience awareness is equally important when it comes to rhetorical devices. Usually associated with speeches, they can be deployed through specific techniques (in all forms) to persuade the reader to read on and stimulate an emotional response.

References

Alvarez, A. (1988) 'Martin Luther King's "I have a dream": the speech event as metaphor', *Journal of Black Studies*, 18(3), pp. 337–357. Available at: https://www.jstor.org/stable/2784511 (Accessed: 14 November 2022).

Burnett, E.-J. (2020) *The grassling: a geological memoir*. London: Penguin Random House.

Campbell, S. (2021) 'Longboat at Portaferry', *New Hibernia Review*, 25(2), p. 88. Available at: https://doi.org/10.1353/nhr.2021.0016

Dickens, C. (2006) *A Christmas carol*. Illustrated by G.A. Williams. Project Gutenberg eBook edition. Urbana, IL: Project Gutenberg. Available at: https://www.gutenberg.org/ebooks/19337 (Accessed: 21 November 2022).

Feaver, V. (1981) 'Coat', in V. Feaver, *Close relatives*. London: Secker & Warburg, p. 46.

Hodgson, H. (2022) 'Mermaids on the brain', in H. Hodgson, *163 Days*. Bridgend: Seren, pp. 68–69.

NASA (2019) 'July 20, 1969: one giant leap for mankind', *NASA*, 20 July. Available at: https://www.nasa.gov/history/july-20-1969-one-giant-leap-for-mankind (Accessed: 5 November 2023).

Old Bailey proceedings online (1759) 'Trial of Elizabeth Jenkins, otherwise Bateman (t17590228-1)', February. Available at: https://www.oldbaileyonline.org/record/t17590228-1?text=Trial%20of%20Elizabeth%20Jenkins (Accessed: 14 April 2023).

Pritchett, V.S. (1984) 'The wheelbarrow', in V.S. Pritchett, *Collected stories*. Harmondsworth: Penguin, p. 113.

Proulx, A. (1995) 'In the pit', in A. Proulx, *Heart songs*. London: Fourth Estate, pp. 103–114.

Ratcliffe, S. (ed.) (2016) *Oxford essential quotations*. 4th edn. Oxford: Oxford University Press. Available at: https://doi.org/10.1093/acref/9780191826719.001.0001 (Accessed: 1 November 2023).

Ross, J. (2017) 'Walking for my mother', in J. Ross, *Tell no one about this*. Leeds: Peepal Tree Press Ltd, pp. 34–38.

Siddons, A. and McQueen, S. (2020) *Small axe: Mangrove*. [Screenplay]. London: BBC Films.

Small axe: Mangrove (2020) Directed by S. McQueen. [Feature film]. London: BBC Films.

Smith, Z. (2005) *On beauty*. Harmondsworth: Penguin.

Woolf, V. (1971) *To the lighthouse*. Harmondsworth: Penguin.

Chapter 14
Voices and voicing

Emma Claire Sweeney with Derek Neale

1 Introduction

Figure 1 Amigo, a Yellow-naped Amazon Parrot singing into a microphone, Jurong Bird Park, Singapore, 2011 (photo: Nature Picture Library/Alamy).

When writing feels distinctive, it is often because fresh ideas are being expressed in language that is compelling and convincing. It is this combination of content and mode of expression that make up the voice of a text. A distinctive voice will elevate a piece of work from parrotry of other writers to something genuinely original and exciting.

To come up with fresh ideas, you often need to work out what makes you tick. What do you know a lot about? What makes you curious? What fires your imagination? To write about such topics in a way that is compelling and convincing usually involves writing in a style that is authentic to you. Perhaps you grew up surrounded by a particular dialect, or maybe you have a sharp wit, or you are especially sensitive to the melodies of language. Such matters will feed into your modes of expression even when you are writing from the perspective of fictional characters, for whom you will invent passions, preoccupations and turns of phrase.

In this chapter, you will learn how to create engaging voices for a range of characters in drama, poetry and fiction, while simultaneously remaining true to yourself.

2 The intimacy of 'I'

Poet Sinéad Morrissey claims that 'something magic happens' when you write about your own life 'so that the "I" isn't you anymore' (Solas Nua, 2021, 25:06–25:13). Whatever the form – life writing, poetry, drama or fiction – the 'I' of the narrative voice is never quite that of its author. **First-person** ('I' or, less commonly, 'we') narration is a creative construct informed to a greater or lesser extent by the author's own tastes and experiences.

Denise Saul's poetry collection *The Room Between Us* (2022) was inspired by her experiences of caring for her mother who was recuperating from a stroke. The first-person speaker in a poem of Saul's – such as 'Surrender' – might therefore appear to be closely aligned to an aspect of the poet's own voice.

> **Denise Saul** is a London-born poet and fiction writer, and fellow of The Complete Works, a mentoring scheme for Black and Asian poets that was initiated by Bernardine Evaristo in 2008 to redress lack of diversity in British poetry.

Surrender

I have grown tired of combing mother's unkempt hair. I do not know how to plait and the house is in a mess. Rather than using a comb, I pull my fingers through her hair. I tell mother to bend her head forward, *You have to lean forward if you want me to comb your hair*. Mother tilts her head back because she does not want to surrender to anyone.

(Saul, 2022)

However, the blurb on the book's back cover is careful to note that the poems are not representative of Saul's own story (Saul, 2022); rather, the poems are described as an exploration of '*a* mother's illness' and '*a* daughter's ongoing role as carer' (my italics). This suggests that some of the details in the collection could be fictional. The precise interaction described in 'Surrender', for instance, might never have occurred. But the forthright, confessional tone creates the *feeling* of a secret imparted, an emotional truth conveyed. In this way, the reader is put in the position of the speaker's trusted confidant.

Such a sense of intimacy can be achieved even when writing from a more clearly fictionalised perspective. It is this type of narration that you will investigate throughout this chapter.

3 From mind to mouth

As you will recall from Chapter 7, **monologues** in audio drama are speeches delivered by a single character. Sometimes the character will direct their words to another character or to the audience, while at other times they will simply be thinking aloud. In drama, monologue is a device commonly used for revealing a character's inner world. This is as close as a dramatist gets to the kind of first-person interior voice used by poets and prose writers to offer a glimpse inside a narrator's mind.

You learned that, to keep an audience hooked in audio drama, a monologue should:

- be expressed in a compelling and varied voice
- contain dialogic elements (e.g. the voices of other characters, an internal debate and/or an implied addressee)
- propel the story forwards.

This applies equally to monologues on stage and screen, and also to passages of first-person narration in fiction and memoir. Indeed, these principles are just as useful to writers of poetry.

It is often taken for granted that the writer of first-person drama and fiction impersonates fictional characters, while the 'I' speaker in poetry is sometimes assumed to be the voice of the writer. But, as you learned in Chapter 4, poets, too, take on the personae of characters distinct from themselves. When written in the form of a speech, this type of poetry is known as **dramatic monologue**. But to avoid confusion with the kind of monologues written for stage, screen and audio, in this chapter we will refer to the poetic form by using the broader term **persona poetry**. This term encompasses not only poems that convey a sense of an imagined character speaking aloud, but also poems that enter the interior world of an imagined character.

When writing persona poems and first-person prose, you may find it useful to think of the narration as a performance of voice – even if this voice speaks primarily in the mind of the reader rather than from the mouth of an actor.

Activity 1 Reading: *The Real Deal*

Read the screenplay of *The Real Deal* (Reading 14.1 in Part 4), Tom Wentworth's 15-minute television drama, which first broadcast in 2020 as part of *CripTales*, a series of television monologues written, directed, performed and curated by people with disabilities.

Now, jot down your responses to the following questions:

- Which aspects of Meg's voice could be described as compelling and/or varied?
- What are the dialogic elements of this monologue?
- How does Meg's voice propel the narrative forwards?

Discussion

I was struck by the way Meg's voice roams through a variety of registers: forensic ('At 14:54 precisely he limps back into his house'), humorous ('salivating like a huge, horny Doberman') and poetic ('He lets the word "assessment" fizz like a tablet dropping in water'). This very variation in voice lies at the heart of what I found compelling about Meg. She's clearly a character who cannot easily be constrained by the kind of stereotypes used at the assessment centre.

The main dialogic element of the monologue is achieved, in large part, by Meg's exchanges with her neighbour Nigel, whose informal vocabulary and turns of phrase (e.g. 'Had my eye on one of these babies on the net for a while') contrasts with Meg's more self-conscious narration. But there is also a dialogic quality to Meg's inner conflict between a feeling of gratitude to Nigel, whom she has grown to like, and her rage at the way he has cheated the system. Her stylistically varied way of expressing herself aptly represents such different aspects of her character as her strong moral compass, her sense of fun and her capacity for ruthlessness.

It is this battle between opposing impulses that propels the story forwards. The question of whether Meg will report Nigel's benefit fraud is planted at the beginning of the monologue and contributes to the building of narrative tension right until its final twist.

The Real Deal is unusual because monologues are rarely used in television for entire episodes or stand-alone dramas, as was the case in this series. Typically, monologues contribute a small part of the action, and some dramas will not contain any at all. One reason for this is the challenge they pose to the writer. Common pitfalls involved in writing monologues include:

- too much telling (summarising or explaining things) and not enough showing (demonstrating or hinting through scenes comprising action, dialogue and description)
- too much **abstraction** (words that describe thoughts and feelings) and not enough **sensory perception** (evocation of sights, sounds, smells, textures and tastes).

By making these mistakes, writers fail to propel the story forwards, and they deny audiences and readers the space to work out their own interpretations. Audiences without a job to do will grow bored quickly. As you write, remember that you are more likely to maintain the attention of your audience if you encourage them (by not telling them *everything*) to actively engage in asking questions of your characters, their motivations and the consequences of their actions.

4 Persona and impersonation

The term 'persona poem' is derived from the Latin word *persona* which refers to a theatrical mask. By donning masks, Roman actors could take on multiple roles in plays, a performative convention which built on ancient Greek theatrical practice (see Figure 3 in Section 6 for a modern-day representation of ancient Greek masks). Similarly, writers might step into the shoes of an array of different characters by impersonating a range of voices.

4.1 Stepping into someone else's shoes

Figure 2 Assorted footwear (photo: MagicBones/Shutterstock).

'Lot's Wife Speaks' is a 2017 persona poem by Malika Booker. It is written from the perspective of a figure who is said, in Judeo-Christian and Islamic scripture, to have lived in the legendary city of Sodom, which was destroyed by God for its alleged wickedness.

Booker's version of events is drawn from the disturbing account in the Book of Genesis (19: 1–38), in which a man named Lot welcomes two angels into the home he shares with his wife and unmarried daughters. That night, townsmen surround the house, demanding that Lot hand the angels over. Lot offers up his virgin daughters instead. But the angels protect Lot and his family by helping them all to escape, warning them not to look back at the city which will be burnt to the ground in their wake. According to the Book of Genesis, Lot's wife does look back, and is then punished for her disobedience by being turned into a pillar of salt.

In her persona poem, Booker relocates Lot's family to the modern-day Caribbean, reimagining Lot's wife as someone with a very different take on the traumatic encounter from that passed down in Genesis.

> **Malika Booker** is a British poet of Guyanese and Grenadian parentage. Booker also writes for the stage and radio, and was the inaugural Poet in Residence at the Royal Shakespeare Company.

Lot's Wife Speaks

That day my heart turned bitter karali.
That night they howled like rabid dogs
and pungent sulphur burned my nostrils.
I looked at my bleach floor and wept,
stood kneading the bread dough, till my hands
bled, pounding flesh over and over.
How Lot could sit and lick down domino
with them angels! I keep telling Lot,
every day bucket go ah well, one day
bam bam go stick. I say Lot boy fling out
some strong rum nuh, that go do the trick.
Drunk them into stupid sleep. I shout out
the window to that mob of carrion crow
come to gorge on innocence, *Allyuh come nuh*,
come you go see! I pulled my girls close, our shield
of three as joyful as trapped prey. We hugged up
and sank through the kitchen floor to rest we body
on moist earth. I say to myself, if he try and push
my girls out there tonight, is me and he in here,
angels or no damn angels. Then I got on my knees
and offered myself seasoned with salt, so they could be
refused. So they could have choice. Man,
pleading words vomit out of my mouth that night
as my knees bled so my daughters could blossom.
Then I who bent to no one, bowed my head
to the Lord and uttered, *Toda Lecha, Toda Lecha*,
Oh Lord Toda Lecha, till the night said, *Hush*
now woman, hush up, he hear you, we all hear you.
And as night spoke my heart turn hibiscus there and then.

(Booker, 2017)

One of the appeals of this poem is the chance it offers to hear from a character whose voice has not been heard. First-person voices can often prove effective vehicles for stories told from perspectives that have traditionally been distorted, glossed over or ignored.

To achieve such a voice convincingly, writers might draw on any relevant aspects of their own experience, conduct research and trust their imaginations. By combining these approaches, a writer can explore what kinds of topics and forms of expression feel appropriate for the speaker and their context, what fresh angle a speaker might take on a subject and how the speaker might establish a sense of intimacy with the reader. *What* might this character say, the writer must ask, and *how* might they say it?

Writers will often also ask searching questions of themselves: what makes me well placed to write from this particular perspective? Have I experienced something that resonates with a significant aspect of the life of the character I'd like to voice? Have I engaged with lots of work by and/or about the kind of figure I'd like to inhabit on the page? Are other writers better placed to give voice to this kind of experience? Which skills (listening or observing, perhaps) and processes (such as **workshopping** and revising) might help me to develop a voice that is both compelling and convincing?

There are no easy answers to such questions. It would be diminishing only to write about people just like you. The important thing is to ask yourself about your motivations for writing from a particular perspective, and to investigate whether you are well placed to create a voice that is convincing. In the next activity, you will get the chance to do just that.

Activity 2 Writing: unsung voices

- Choose any mythical, fictional or real-life figure whose perspective you feel has been distorted or ignored: for example, the monster in a fairy story, the real-life spouse of a lauded public figure or the minor servant character in a nineteenth-century novel.
- Note down which of your own experiences you could draw on to write from the perspective of such a character, what you might need to research and how you might go about doing this research.
- Now decide whether this might be a perspective you feel well equipped to fictionalise. If not, choose another figure and repeat the exercise.

Discussion

Booker's writing, for instance, is steeped in Bible stories and, having been born to Guyanese and Grenadian parents, she is familiar with Caribbean vocabulary and **idiom**. But your feeling of connection with your chosen character might be less specific than this. Perhaps your character's experience of being overlooked resonates with you because you, too, have felt overlooked, but in a different context.

The kind of research you identified as being useful for the creation of a convincing first-person voice for your chosen character will depend on the kind of figure you have chosen and the nature of the extant evidence for their life, or the lives of figures like them. For example, the footnotes in biographies or history books can provide a great springboard, and local newspapers offer a rich supply of stories to spark the imagination. Perhaps you would like to visit a museum or library or browse their websites. In the process of writing, you may have come across aspects of your character's life that you would like to investigate further. Writing tends to generate further research, which then feeds into future drafts, sometimes evolving the characterisation and plot.

4.2 Compelling voices

Whatever form you are writing in, you will want your first-person voice to capture the attention of your readers or audience. A striking sensory appeal can often help with this, especially one that might suggest a question. Next, you will want to seduce your readers or audience into keeping going. You will find that gradually revealing possible answers by showing rather than telling can be instrumental here.

For example, 'Lot's Wife Speaks', which you considered in Section 4.1, opens with a striking sensory image, which plants a question. It then segues into scenes, which gradually reveal possible answers.

The opening image ('my heart turned bitter karali') works hard to earn its place because it conveys several things at once. When an image works on multiple levels like this one does, it is sometimes referred to as layering meaning. In this case, it involves:

- grounding the voice in a particular context

    Since 'karali' is a Caribbean term for a green vegetable otherwise known as 'bitter melon' or 'bitter gourd', the speaker's voice offers a hint at the poem's surprising setting.

- engaging the senses

    The adjective 'bitter' certainly activates the sense of taste, and readers already familiar with karali will see its green skin and feel its knobbly texture.

- building a sense of intimacy

    In likening her heart to 'bitter karali', the speaker suggests that something has caused her to feel embittered. This insight into the speaker's inner world creates a sense of closeness with the reader, in whom she confides.

- hooking the reader

    The reader is invited to wonder about what might have happened to have turned the speaker's heart to 'bitter karali'. This mystery lures the reader on.

The scenes that follow gradually reveal the speaker's version of events by employing:

- action

    Note the number of **verbs** even in the first scene: 'turned', 'howled', 'burned', 'looked', 'wept', 'stood kneading', 'pounding' and 'bled'.

- description

    Through spare use of **adjectives**, Booker conveys how Lot's wife experienced these dramatic events. The air smelled 'pungent', for instance, and the earth felt 'moist' and her body 'seasoned'.

- dialogue

    The poem contains both the speaker's habitual words to her husband, and italicised phrases representing what she says to the townsmen on that particular night. Both types of dialogue contain vocabulary, phrasing and **syntax** rooted in Caribbean English. And the biblical story is invoked by the inclusion of the Hebrew phrase for 'thank you' ('*Toda Lecha*'), which reminds the reader of the poem's central dialogic purpose of complicating and challenging the version in the Book of Genesis, in which Lot's wife, who never gets to speak, is turned into a pillar of salt as divine punishment. In Booker's persona poem, however, Lot's wife testifies instead to having covered herself in salt and offering her own body to the howling men to protect her daughters from being sacrificed to this mob.

Activity 3 Writing: creating a compelling voice

- Return to the character you settled on for Activity 2. Think of an object that suggests something about when and where the character might be, and then work out which of your readers' senses this object might activate.
- Now write the title and opening 3–5 lines of a poem from the first-person perspective of your chosen character. Include in the opening the object you have just identified, establish a sense of intimacy and plant a question in the mind of the reader.
- Complete the poem by writing another 10–20 lines, making sure to include some action, description and dialogue.

Discussion

Earlier, you looked at the ways you might draw on your own experience to bring this voice to life on the page, and you considered the types of research that might be required. As you began to write, you would have employed various craft techniques, including appealing to the senses, creating intrigue, and building scenes with action, description and dialogue. Imagination comes into play, too. Although the character you impersonated was drawn from mythology, history, biography or fiction, on the page they will inevitably have become, at least in part, your own invention.

5 From ear to page

Most writers hear their first-person voices as they write them. The next trick is to render these speech sounds – or **phonetics** – on the page. There are a number of strategies that you can call on to stylise voices in this way:

- Word choice

    It is usually advisable to hone in on a few significant features of the voice you imagine for your character, rather than attempting a word-for-word phonetic imitation. The use of just one or two words fairly regularly can conjure up an entire linguistic repertoire or **idiolect**. For instance, 'mind' when used at the end of a clause – 'I was going down the road mind' – suggests a Geordie dialect; and 'dead', instead of 'very', suggests a Scouse voice. Consistency is key here. Make sure that you use the same kinds of word choices and turns of phrase for each voice throughout. You will find it easier to be consistent if you deploy fewer significant features to represent the voice.

- Syntax

    The way your character orders sentences can relate not only to their locale but also to their personality. A line such as 'I'll be coming over, will I' might bring to mind an Irish speaker. But by peppering a character's speech with a filler phrase such as 'will I' and making it into a conversational 'tic', you might also offer hints about the character's state of mind – a lack of confidence in this case, perhaps, or a desire for reassurance.

- Phonetic spelling and apostrophes

    A little tends to go a long way as far as these techniques are concerned. Take this sentence, for example: 'We wer hopin' an' prayin' thar'eed gerrit.' The overuse of apostrophes and phonetic spellings make this difficult to understand and read. Such a voice would be especially problematic over an extended narrative. But such devices can stylise a voice well when used in moderation. Take this dialled-down version of the same sentence: 'We were hopin' and prayin' that he'd gerrit.' This gives a better sense of the Scouse accent, by relying on less to do more.

Activity 4 Reading: *Be Near Me*

Read the extract from *Be Near Me*, a 2006 novel by Andrew O'Hagan (Reading 14.2), and the 2007 newspaper article in which the author talks about how his book and the character of Father David came into being (Reading 14.3).

- What do you learn of the narrator of *Be Near Me* from his voice?
- How is this first-person narrator's character different from O'Hagan's own life experience?
- How do the three voices in the passage contrast?

Discussion

Be Near Me is written in the voice of a present-day Catholic priest, Father David, a highly educated aesthete who often appears more concerned about the quality of his wine than he does about mundane reality or, indeed, about matters of right and wrong. Father David's is a voice that is self-consciously well-written. There is an aesthetic aspect to the way in which each sentence is formed. Yet this focus on artistry is also the narrator's weakness, a preoccupation which blinds him to the best way to behave in many different circumstances. Here, there is a stark contrast between the postman's bleak small-mindedness and the way Father David can only respond by musing on classical composers like Liszt and Chopin.

Father David's life history is very different from O'Hagan's, as the author admits. The problem of impersonation was one of imagining what it was like to attend a privileged public school, to be an undergraduate at Balliol College, Oxford, and to study to be a priest in the English College in Rome. Yet O'Hagan's impersonating imagination – and his research – rose to the challenge.

In terms of idiolect and idiom, all three voices are distinct. The postman's variety of Scottish dialect is rendered simply with features such as 'ae' replacing 'of', and 'didnae' replacing 'didn't'. Apostrophes are sometimes deployed, but there isn't a profusion of them. Mrs Poole uses 'aye' and 'yer' instead of 'yes' and 'your', but she is slightly more English than the postman in that she uses 'of' not 'ae'.

As you read in Reading 14.3, O'Hagan claims that 'acting' is involved when he writes. Reading work aloud can help a writer to hear whether the characters' voices sound authentic. In the next activity, you will try this out for yourself.

Activity 5 Writing: stylising voices

Revisit the title and the opening lines of the persona poem you wrote for Activity 3.

- Rewrite the poem as 200 words of first-person prose fiction, within the following parameters:
    - Retain or adapt any elements of the original that bring to life the time and place in which the character is speaking or writing, and anything that injects intrigue.
    - Stylise the voice further by employing word choices, syntax, phonetic spelling and apostrophes to offer a sense of idiolect.
- Read this passage of fiction aloud, noting any word choices or syntax that sound inauthentic or cause you to stumble. Then revise accordingly.
- Check how this version looks on the page and dial back on any phonetic spellings or apostrophes that make the passage difficult to read.

Discussion

You will likely have kept some words or phrases from your persona poem and transferred them directly into your lines of fiction. But other aspects of the poem may not have read well in prose: a half rhyme that seemed subtle in your poem, for instance, may have over-announced itself in prose. While some lines may not have made it into the fictional voice at all, you may have found that others needed to be expanded. Perhaps an image that worked in your poem precisely because of its economy of expression needed padding out to make it appear naturalistic in the voice of a character in fiction. And, no doubt, you made all sorts of other changes, too. If you adapted the context in which the character was expressing themselves, for instance, this will have had a knock-on effect on their tone and register.

The kind of decisions you had to make to translate your lines of poetry into fiction exemplify the choices any writer makes when they redraft. Essentially, writers have four options available to them in the redrafting stages: retain, adapt, add and cut. This last option is usually particularly helpful when rendering speech on to the page. When it comes to apostrophes and phonetic spellings, less tends to be more.

When O'Hagan compares writing to acting, he is not simply referring to ventriloquising how a character sounds. He mentions the need to 'inhabit' his characters in order to bring them to life. To do this, O'Hagan had to feel what the character felt. This was uncomfortable at times, but he found that he got to know himself better in the process. I can also certainly testify to this. When I was writing *Owl Song at Dawn* – a novel narrated by Maeve Maloney, an octogenarian from the northern English coastal town of Morecambe, and her twin-sister Edie, who has severe and complex learning disabilities – I had to let myself experience what my narrators went through (Sweeney, 2016). When their mother died, they had to make difficult decisions about who would care for Edie. In imagining this, I came to a better understanding of my feelings about my own sister and her care – not something I'd consciously anticipated happening.

6 Fictional communities

Figure 3 Members of the Chorus with Orestes at the rear, wearing masks designed by Jocelyn Herbert, in a performance of *Furies*, Tony Harrison's translation of the third play in Aeschylus' *Oresteia* trilogy, directed by Peter Hall, Olivier Theatre, National Theatre, London, 1981 (photo: Donald Cooper/Alamy).

The level of imaginative yet consistent impersonation in O'Hagan's *Be Near Me* (2006) has the effect of inviting the reader into a community of characters. In many ways, this is the trick that all fiction is trying to pull off. The narrator's voice, and how convincing it might appear to the reader, is the key to this invitation. It needs to be consistent with itself and its surroundings. If it fails on either of these counts, then the reader will not believe in it.

6.1 Speaking in chorus

In ancient Greek drama, the members of the chorus spoke in unison to offer commentary on the action from the sidelines (Figure 3). In contemporary fiction, the first-person plural ('we') perspective – though easier to pull off in a short story than over the course of an entire novel – can create this kind of incantatory quality.

Julie Otsuka's **novella** *The Buddha in the Attic* (2011), for instance, creates a fictional world among a community of women known as picture brides, who were shipped from Japan to San Francisco in the early twentieth century to marry men they had seen only in photographs:

SEVERAL OF US on the boat had secrets, which we swore we would keep from our husbands for the rest of our lives. Perhaps the real reason we were sailing to America was to track down a long-lost father who had left the family years before. *He went to Wyoming to work in the coal mines and we never heard from him again.* Or perhaps we were leaving behind a young daughter who had been born to a man whose face we could now barely recall—a traveling storyteller who had spent a week in the village, or a wandering Buddhist priest who had stopped by the house late one night on his way to Mt. Fuji. And even though we knew our parents would care for her well—*If you stay here in the village*, they had warned us, *you will never marry at all*—we still felt guilty for having chosen our own life over hers, and on the boat we wept for her every night for many nights in a row and then one morning we woke up and dried our eyes and said, 'That's enough,' and began to think of other things. Which kimono to wear when we landed. How to fix our hair. What to say when we first saw him. Because we were on the boat now, the past was behind us, and there was no going back.

ON THE BOAT we had no idea we would dream of our daughter every night until the day that we died, and that in our dreams she would always be three and as she was when we last saw her: a tiny figure in a dark red kimono squatting at the edge of a puddle, utterly entranced by the sight of a dead floating bee.

(Otsuka, 2011, pp. 11–12)

Even though the novel is written in the first-person plural, different individual perspectives frequently enter into the narrative, such as the woman searching for her father, whose words are italicised. Note, too, how the excerpt segues from communal experiences ('Several of us on the boat had secrets') to one character's very specific experience (the nightly dream of a three-year-old daughter 'in a dark red kimono squatting at the edge of a puddle, utterly entranced by the sight of a dead floating bee'). Although only one woman harboured this particular memory, her dream is nonetheless narrated in the first-person plural – emphasising, perhaps, that the experience of secret longing and regret is shared by the community of picture brides.

In Otsuka's novel, the 'we' emphasises the seminal shared experience that will forever draw these women together regardless of everything that differentiates them. But some fiction writers use the first-person plural to emphasise the untrustworthiness of the narration. After all, there is no such thing really as a 'we' perspective, since individuals within the group will surely see certain things differently.

6.2 Polyphonic narration

Polyphonic narration refers to a story told from a diverse range of voices and perspectives, each of them accorded more or less equal space. From William Faulkner's modernist masterpiece *The Sound and the Fury* to Barbara Kingsolver's late-twentieth-century classic *The Poisonwood Bible*, there is a rich tradition of narrating novels via multiple first-person perspectives. Although it is not impossible, it is harder to pull this off in short stories because too rapid a succession of different narrators can easily become confusing.

I Am Not Your Eve by Devika Ponnambalam (2022) is an example of a polyphonic novel. It tells the fictionalised life story of Teha'amana – a real-life Tahitian child married off in 1891 to the middle-aged French painter Paul Gauguin. The fictionalised first-person voice of Teha'amana herself interweaves and overlaps with Gauguin's unreliable musings; the diary entries of his daughter, Aline, who was the same age as his new 'wife'; and various voices drawn from Tahitian myths, Gauguin's artwork and the island's fauna.

Note the incantatory quality to Ponnambalam's impersonation of Teha'amana's voice as she addresses Gauguin, the lines rich in repetition, sensory perception, assonance and **rhyme**:

> You come to me, and whisper, I have a present for you. You show me your closed fist. It makes me flinch. But. In the palm of your hand, lies a pair of copper earrings.
>
> You wanted these, remember?
>
> You remembered. They glint, your gift, in the half-light of this half-life, for me, your half-wife.
>
> *(Ponnambalam, 2022, p. 1)*

Contrast this with Aline's fictionalised diary entry, with its syntax and vocabulary grounded in its 1890s European context:

> Dear Diary,
>
> Today, news finally arrived. Maman refused to speak a word of it, and instead, took herself to the far end of the dining table, away from our prying eyes. She read Papa's letter not once, but twice, then a third time – until I am sure she had digested every ounce of information contained within.
>
> *(Ponnambalam, 2022, p. 4)*

And see how Ponnambalam's rendering of Gauguin's voice emphasises his lasciviousness and pomposity. Here, he reflects on his marriage to Aline's mother:

> She was not my Eve, no, she was not that, but my wife, is still, strong-willed, powerful, and wise. She was good in bed too. We had an idyllic honeymoon as I recall. Didn't leave our rented rooms for a week, though we spent one sublime afternoon traipsing the Louvre, rubbing up against one another like dogs in heat, where I fell in love all over again, but this time with Delacroix.
>
> *(Ponnambalam, 2022, p. 90)*

Activity 6 Writing: evoking a sense of community

Look again at the passage of fiction you composed for Activity 5.

What kind of community does the narrator belong to?

Rewrite the passage, using either the first-person plural ('we') or three contrasting first-person perspectives.

Discussion

If you chose to write in first-person plural, did you manage to give a flavour of individual voices and viewpoints as well as the communal 'we'? If you chose to write from multiple first-person perspectives, which techniques did you use to create contrasting voices?

7 Conclusion

This chapter has focused on first-person speakers in poetry and first-person narrators in fiction. You have looked at ways of adapting some of the methods associated with dramatic monologues to create persona poems and first-person fiction. You have also seen how convincing ventriloquism depends on using vocabulary and syntax appropriate to the character and their situation. Equally important, you have learned how individual voices can create a sense of a wider community in a particular place and time. It is this temporal factor to which you will turn your attention in the next chapter.

References

Booker, M. (2017) 'Lot's wife speaks', in M. Booker, S. Olds and W. Shire, *Your family, your body*. London: Penguin, p. 34.

O'Hagan, A. (2006) *Be near me*. London: Faber and Faber.

O'Hagan, A. (2007) 'In truth: Andrew O'Hagan on the genesis of *Be near me*', *The Guardian*, 14 July, Book Club. Available at: https://www.theguardian.com/books/2007/jul/14/featuresreviews.guardianreview4 (Accessed: 13 March 2024).

Otsuka, J. (2011) *The Buddha in the attic*. London: Penguin.

Ponnambalam, D. (2022) *I am not your Eve*. Hebden Bridge: Bluemoose Books.

Saul, D. (2022) 'Surrender', in D. Saul, *The room between us*. Liverpool: Liverpool University Press, p. 29.

Solas Nua (2021) *Poetry Day Ireland 2021 – Sinéad Morrissey*. 29 April. Available at: https://www.youtube.com/watch?v=mhYNAuHcsvc (Accessed: 9 January 2023).

Sweeney, E.C. (2016) *Owl song at dawn*. London: Legend Press.

Wentworth, T. (2020) '*The real deal*', in M. Fraser (ed.) *CripTales: six monologues*. London: Nick Hern Books, pp. 39–48.

Chapter 15
Time and timing

Emma Claire Sweeney

1 Introduction

Figure 1 Hour glasses (photo: Photology1971/Alamy).

The way a piece of writing handles time and timing is a crucial and complex aspect of its structure. Just think about how a photograph freezes a particular moment, whereas a feature film shows the passage of time. Some short poems can create the illusion of freezing time, but drama, prose and narrative poetry usually function as vehicles for moving through time. It is this latter type of approach to time that you will concentrate on in this chapter, with examples drawn from novels, short stories, memoir, poetry and feature films. First, you will look at pacing techniques, examining ways to speed up and slow down time. Then you will explore the effect of sequence – in other words, the order in which you reveal information. Finally, you will consider how the way you handle the passage of time in your writing relates to decisions about a work's structure.

2 Pace

Whether you are working on fiction, life writing, poetry or drama, there are three main tools that you can use to modulate a narrative's tempo:

1. Time can be sped up.

2. The time covered by the writing can be roughly equivalent to **'real time'**.

3. Time can be slowed down.

Jill Dawson employs all three of these tools in *Wild Boy* (2003), a novel inspired by the real-life case of Victor of Aveyron. Victor was a feral child, discovered in France in 1800, and some consider that his story represents the first documented case of autism. The novel was informed by Dawson's own experience of raising a son who is on the autism spectrum.

Let's now look at these three tools in more detail, alongside examples from Dawson's novel.

1. Time can be sped up.

   Summary might allow you to cover years in only a sentence or two. You might want to offer a brief round up to conjure the sense of an entire period, or you might simply need to include an event briefly in order to transition between more important occurrences.

> The doctor narrator of Jill Dawson's *Wild Boy* uses summary to fill in **backstory** about the boy's life prior to his capture:
>
> > It does seem though, that over a period of seven years there were repeated sightings by peasants and others, of a boy, living wild in the rugged terrain of the Tarn valley and elsewhere in Aveyron. Even allowing for exaggeration, there are too many confirmed accounts for it not to be true. If, as I judge, based on height, limbs and supposition, he is now twelve years of age, the most astonishing conclusion cannot be avoided. The boy must have lived alone since he was a child of five.
> >
> > *(Dawson, 2003, pp. 16–17)*
>
> Cleverly, this summary also invites the reader to ask how the child survived seven years in the wild. By introducing this kind of question, the reader is encouraged to turn the page in the hope of unearthing an answer.

   Time jumps are another strategy for accelerating time. This is an omission from the narrative, marking a leap in time, often signified in prose by an asterisk or an additional line space.

> Here's an example of a time jump from slightly later in Dawson's *Wild Boy*:
>
> > ... A dog with an injured leg ran crookedly beside us, yelping as we flew past, but we outran that and the worst of the summer rain, arriving at Madame Guérin's in perfect time for supper.
> >
> > Here's the wild boy at Madame Guérin's kitchen table, groomed, clean, surrounded by a throng of visitors.
> >
> > *(Dawson, 2003, p. 44)*
>
> This time jump fast forwards through time, skipping the irrelevant logistics of getting Victor inside.

2. The time covered by the writing can be roughly equivalent to 'real time'.

   'Real time' describes a reading or performance time that equates to the time these events would have taken to unfold in real life. It is rare for an entire scene to occur in 'real time', but elements of a scene often do so. For example, dialogue might take the same amount of time to read or hear as it would have taken to occur in real life, particularly if there are no accompanying descriptions of gesture, manner or setting. This technique can create a sense of immediacy.

> The following exchange, again from Dawson's *Wild Boy*, is an example of 'real time' narration. The daughter of Victor's carer speaks first, and his doctor replies.
>
> > And is it true – I heard a story, so sad it was –
> >
> > Yes, it is likely that someone slit his throat. Attempted to kill him. Left him for dead in the forest, where he survived for, we believe, between five and seven years –
> >
> > Oh, it is evil, *evil*! Heartless, cruel – what wicked devil could do such a thing? They deserve – I would – pah! The guillotine is too good for them.
> >
> > *(Dawson, 2003, pp. 56–57)*
>
> While it is conventional to enclose dialogue in speech marks, writers sometimes dispense of this punctuation as Dawson has done here. The important thing to note is that the time it takes to read this dialogue exchange aloud roughly equates to the passage of time experienced by the characters having the conversation.

3. Time can be slowed down.

> In these circumstances, the scene takes longer to read than the actions, words or thoughts described would have taken to occur. For instance, if you describe what is happening in a character's thoughts as he or she listens to others talking, you are effectively going over the same time twice.

In *Wild Boy*, such a repetition of time occurs later in this same exchange. Again, the daughter of Victor's carer speaks first.

> It is *unthinkable*, a little boy of five years old, to *imagine* –
>
> But imagination is sometimes all we have! I told her. I was surprised to experience a quickening of my heartbeat as I spoke, a feeling close to anger.
>
> Nothing is unimaginable. We must never refuse to imagine … I said, with more control.
>
> *(Dawson, 2003, p. 57)*

The inclusion of the doctor's physical and emotional sensations add texture to the writing, allowing the reader time to digest the importance of the conversation.

> Alternatively, you might decelerate time by describing the same period from the points of view of more than one character.

The scene following the conversation above is narrated by Victor's carer, who offers a different perspective from the doctor's view of the exchange:

> He likes her, I can tell, our Julie. You would not say his eyes are fixed on her but then he would never be so plain as that, so *evident*. Naturally he disagreed with every word she said but that's as you would expect too, when a learned doctor meets a girl not quite sixteen whose only schooling was done by her mother and is apt to speak her mind before she has measured it. It is as if he lights up, he changes, when she's in the room.
>
> *(Dawson, 2003, p. 60)*

Such a technique for going over the same ground twice, slows down the reader, offering the chance to look at a situation from multiple angles.

Most narratives will include all three strategies for handling the passage of time. The ratio of acceleration, real time and deceleration will dictate the overall pacing of your work.

Activity 1 Reading: 'Bloodstream (1997)'

Read 'Bloodstream (1997)', a self-contained piece of memoir from *I Am, I Am, I Am: Seventeen Brushes with Death* by Maggie O'Farrell (2017) (Reading 15.1 in Part 4).

1. Note at least one occasion when the narrative:

- gives the illusion of speeding up time
- gives the impression of 'real time'
- appears to slow down time.

2. On each of the occasions that you have noted, what is the effect of this handling of the passage of time?

Discussion

You may have noticed that time is sped up on the various occasions when O'Farrell summarises, lists and omits information. Sometimes these events are sped up to create a sense of time passing and to give a general impression of the period. This is how she narrates her current life with her children in Edinburgh, for example, and her memories of the person she was in her mid-twenties. On other occasions, the events are not sufficiently important to take up too many words, but referencing them is necessary to locate the narrative within a particular timeframe or to transition from one event to another. This could be said, for example, of her arrival in London and her various temporary jobs.

The confrontation with her boyfriend includes an exchange of dialogue that gives the impression of 'real time'. This is a moment of high narrative tension, and yet the narrator finds the situation fairly clear-cut. The scene does not therefore warrant slowing down with much introspection.

The passage of time is slowed down, however, in the narration of the events that are either most dramatic or most thematically complex: the discovery of another woman's bra beneath her bed, for instance, or the visit to the sexual health clinic. In each of these cases, the action and dialogue are interspersed with memory and reflection. This gives the reader the time to digest the importance of these episodes.

When drafting high-tension events or emotionally complex issues, the instinct can sometimes be to speed up time. This, however, is usually a mistake. Counter-intuitively, you will often find that by slowing down the narration, you signal to the reader the importance of this occurrence or the complexity of the matter in hand.

2.1 Unnarrated time

Often, you will omit swathes of time because what happened during this period has little bearing on the main subject. On other occasions, though, the silence will speak volumes. Here, the unspoken aspect of the narrative might be its most significant element. The reader of 'Bloodstream (1997)', for instance, is left to imagine what might have happened to Eric between his HIV test in 1997 (where the piece ends) and his friend's family life twenty years later (where the piece begins). The real power of this memoir is contained in this unnarrated period.

Activity 2 Writing: modulating tempo

Return to any piece of fiction or life writing that you would like to redraft.

1. Identify three events in that piece of writing: one event that you may go on to speed up in the next draft, one you may cover in 'real time' and one you may narrate by creating the illusion of slowing down time.

2. In each case, make a note of why the chosen tool for modulating pace feels appropriate.

3. Next, identify the most important event in the main character's story and write (or rewrite) a passage conveying this event using one or more of the following tools: summary, time jump, repetition of time or unnarrated time.

Discussion

Whether you are working on a piece of fiction or life writing, you will have to ask yourself which events to include and which to exclude, and which warrant covering in detail and which can be summarised.

Reflect further on how you managed the acceleration, deceleration or unnarrated time in the passage you wrote or rewrote. You might make powerful use of summary. By covering, in few words, an event that clearly has a hold over your character, you might suggest that they cannot face it full on. A time jump can be a powerful tool for highlighting a period omitted from the narration, the blank space between paragraphs representing the time your character might have blocked out. At the other end of the spectrum, you might write a full scene, slowing down time and exploring the event in detail. Such an approach may well indicate that your character is finally ready to reckon with what happened.

As you write and rewrite, certain events might take on greater importance than you had predicted, while others might come to seem less significant. When this happens, you will usually need to change the tools you employ to modulate the pace.

Your decisions about pace are closely linked to what you want to convey about your characters, including which aspects of life they are ready to explore and in how much detail.

2.2 Influencing reading time

You will not be able to control how your viewers, listeners or readers engage with your writing. But, when constructing a narrative, it can be helpful to anticipate the range of possible experiences they might have in relation to the story's passage of time.

It is worth remembering that prose is made up of the following elements:

- dialogue
- action
- description
- reflection.

While dialogue and action tend to be quick to read, description and reflection tend to be slower.

Activity 3 Reading: 'Daylight Savings'

Read 'Daylight Savings' (2018) by Catherine Menon (Reading 15.2), a short story that explores a similar premise to that of O'Farrell's memoir piece: the unexpected consequences of a break-up that occurred during youth.

After you have read the story from start to finish, note which parts you read quickest, and when you most slowed down.

How effective did you find the pacing?

Discussion

My reading of this short story sped up during Amber's visit to Sarah. Their dialogue increased my reading pace because I was keen to know how they were going to respond, and how the interaction might impact on each of them. My curiosity propelled me to turn the page.

I slowed down, however, during the paragraph on mirrors. Here, the combination of description and reflection decelerated my reading pace, giving me time to digest the significance of this meeting. This postponement of the rest of their interaction heightened the narrative tension. So, for me, this modulation of pace worked well.

Most prose writers use all or most of the components listed above: dialogue, action, description and reflection. The pacing of a particular piece will depend on the specific combination of these components. As you learned in Chapter 5, drama largely comprises action and dialogue. And, as you saw in Chapter 11, life writing often allocates a fair amount of bandwidth to summary and reflection. Fiction tends to lie somewhere in between. Summary and reflection comprise only a fourteenth of the short story 'Daylight Savings' (Menon, 2018), for example, while they make up a third of the memoir piece 'Bloodstream (1997)' (O'Farrell, 2017).

Genre is key here, too. A thriller will usually contain more action and dialogue, while there is greater room for reflection and description in the kind of character- or voice-driven work that is often referred to as literary.

Activity 4 Writing: changing the pace

Stick with the piece you worked on in Activity 2.

- Overall, would you like your piece to be characterised as pacy or more languorous? With this in mind, are there any moments when the pace lags? Are there others when it races ahead too quickly?
- Rewrite one of the passages you have identified as needing a change in pace, either by introducing more description or reflection to slow it down, or adding action or dialogue to speed it up.

Discussion

Sometimes redrafting to modulate pace will involve cutting one type of narration and replacing it with another: getting rid of reflection and introducing dialogue, for example, will radically speed up a passage. At other times, however, you may want the change in pace to be less stark. In such circumstances, you might, for instance, retain some of the original action but intersperse it with description to make it a little more languorous.

It's the writer's job to find ways to propel readers through the narrative and keep them hooked. But it is usually best to resist the impulse to cram a piece full of only high-paced action and dialogue with little reflection or description. Remember, these slower-paced components give readers the chance to catch their breath. When work contains only faster elements, the pace can become unremitting and cause the reader to flag. Reflection and description are also key to creating an immersive experience for readers, offering insights into a character's mind and allowing them to experience the world of the text.

3 Sequencing

Never underestimate the power of curiosity. Whatever your form or genre, this is one of the most important tools with which you can encourage the reader to keep on turning the pages, or the viewer to keep on watching. The order in which you reveal information can heighten your reader's curiosity.

3.1 Withholding and disclosure

A writer deliberately withholds information by failing to provide it at the point when the reader wants or expects it.

There is a clear example of this in 'Daylight Savings' (Reading 15.2) when Sarah admits she is covering her tracks ahead of the visit from Amber. Will Amber find Sarah's letters, I wondered when reading this passage, and how will this meeting affect each of the women? Menon withholds the answers by inserting a scene from Amber's point of view, effectively delaying the scene of their meeting.

As in this case, the most obvious place where a writer might withhold expected information is at the end of a scene (or at the end of a chapter in book-length works). But it can also happen, in subtler ways, at other points.

Withholding information is not without its dangers, however. If the reader's desire for answers is too fully denied for too long, they might feel frustrated. And it is important to differentiate between intrigue, when the reader trusts that information is legitimately being withheld, and confusion, when the reader simply feels lost. By making the right disclosures or revelations at the right moments in the story, you will encourage readers to ask new but related questions, which will further encourage them to keep on reading.

Working this out is usually a matter of trial and error. Early readers can be a huge help here, especially if you specifically ask them to identify moments when they were confused, frustrated or intrigued.

3.2 Flashback and flashforward

Figure 2 A pocket watch swinging on a chain (photo: Olga Yastremska/Alamy).

You can build curiosity in readers and audiences by encouraging them to ask two questions: what happened to get us here and what is going to happen from here on? These questions relate to what has taken place in the past, and what might occur in the future.

The literary device of the **flashback** essentially dramatises scenes that occurred before the present time of the narration. This can prove a useful way to illuminate the events of the narrative's main timeframe and encourage the reader to ask new questions. So, although a flashback takes the reader backwards in time, it is crucial that the scene described propels the narrative forwards. In 'Daylight Savings' (Menon, 2018), for example, the flashback to the night Colin broke up with Sarah sheds light on why she enacts the strange ritual of writing to a romanticised version of Colin once a year on the night the clocks go back.

It is often fruitful to return to a significant flashback later in the text, allowing the reader to view it with a new understanding gained by the intervening plot. This device is known as a **recurring flashback**. Take care with flashbacks, though. You risk losing your reader if they are too frequent, drag on for too long or take unnecessary diversions.

The **flashforward** is a scene that occurs after the present timeframe of the narration. Used well, flashforwards can inject just the sort of pressing question that prompts a reader to turn the page. Likewise, they can create a sense of poignance by allowing the reader an unexpected insight into the character's life to come.

The literary device of the flashforward is linked to, but distinct from, the technique of foreshadowing. While **foreshadowing** involves dropping hints about the future, a flashforward comprises a scene. In 'Daylight Savings', the flashforward to Sarah's death, fifty years after the main timeframe, ends the story on an unexpected and moving note.

The flashforward is less commonly used than the flashback because it can easily cause confusion. But, used well, it can enhance intrigue and increase emotional engagement.

Activity 5 Writing: give and take, backwards and forwards

You will now formulate a question that you want your reader to ask while further developing the piece you've been working on throughout this chapter.

Choose one of the following strategies and make notes on how you might implement it when revising your piece:

- a method of delaying the answer to this question, noting also when and how you might disclose some of the information that the reader is seeking
- a scene addressing this question that could be presented as flashback
- a scene addressing this question that could be presented as flashforward.

Discussion

The aim here is to encourage you to think about how to tantalise readers: when to partially fulfil their desires and when to postpone this sense of fulfilment. A scene that answers all the questions it raises is likely to give some satisfaction, but it will not propel the reader forwards. And yet, a chapter or scene that answers none of the questions it raises is likely to be a frustrating read. Similarly, a scene that follows immediately on from the preceding one might well solve the problem you have set the reader, but it might risk providing too speedy a gratification. It is sometimes better to change time, location, focus, character – and even voice – so that the work becomes richer in texture.

As you read in Chapter 10, the process of separating strands, and setting up a tension as to where they will converge, is a means of keeping your readers intrigued, offering a delicious state of uncertainty that will encourage them to read on.

4 Time and form

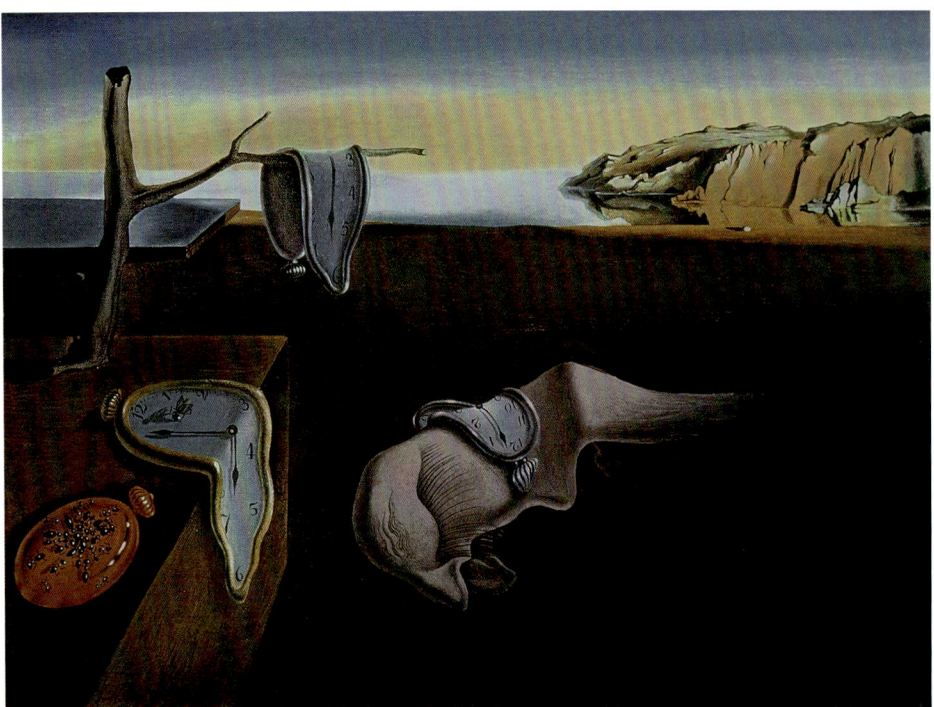

Figure 3 Salvador Dalí, *The Persistence of Memory*, 1931, oil on canvas, 24 × 33 cm, Museum of Modern Art (MoMA), New York, object number 162.1934 (photo: Bridgeman Images. © Salvador Dali, Fundació Gala-Salvador Dalí, DACS 2024).

Decisions about how to handle the passage of time in a piece of writing are intertwined with decisions about its structure. Think of structure as a particular type of vehicle for moving through time. Ask yourself what kind of vehicle might best contain the particular type of story you are trying to tell. Just as there are significant differences between cars, lorries, trains and planes, so too there are many different types of structures you can choose from.

4.1 Time and form in prose

If you are working on prose, you will want to consider when to insert chapter or scene breaks, and whether to include multiple points of view, settings or timeframes. The shorter a piece of writing, the fewer changes it can readily accommodate. Only book-length prose tends to be divided into chapters.

O'Farrell's 'Bloodstream (1997)' (2017) might initially seem as if it ends too early, finishing as it does without informing the reader of the results of Eric's HIV test. But could this be offering a hint at what happened? Might the structure mirror, perhaps, the fact that Eric's life was, similarly, cut short?

The structure of 'Daylight Savings' (Menon, 2018) could also be said to mirror its contents. The short story explores the idea that the clocks going back gives the character the chance to repeat the same mistake. The scene of Sarah in her late twenties writing to a romanticised version of her ex-boyfriend at the time the clocks go back is followed by a flashback to a scene that takes place at exactly the same hour ten years earlier. At this point, Colin has just split up with Sarah, and she ill-advisedly attempts to initiate sex. The character is repeating the same kind of mistake at the same hour, and the reader repeats on the page the experience of Sarah's mistakes.

4.2 Time and form in poetry

The marriage of form and time is perhaps most apparent in poetry.

Just as the title 'Daylight Savings' (Menon, 2018) emphasises the importance of time in Menon's short story, so too does the title 'After Closing Time' (2022) signal that time might play a significant role in Mark Pajak's poem.

> **Mark Pajak** was born in Merseyside and is a graduate of the Liverpool Everyman and Playhouse's Young Writers Programme, but is now best known for his poetry. He spent four years working on his first pamphlet, writing and reading poetry every morning between 6 a.m. and 9 a.m.

After Closing Time

We head to the edge of town,
to the black river and old stone bridge.

Two boys full of vodka,
tipping side to side like flames.

And for a laugh, we climb
the railing and hang from our arms.

Below in the deep, two boys
peer up at us over their feet.

Like drops of water
we are gathering ourselves to fall.

One of us says, *You go first*,
and we echo this back and forth.

We are here for a very long time.
Years in fact. I marry. Divorce.

> You skip all that, become a father.
> We see less and less of each other.
>
> Now we are what the world
> considers 'men'. Which is to say
>
> we've learnt that falling is inevitable.
> Yet here we are still, side by side,
>
> two boys way past closing time,
> holding on until the other lets go.
>
> *(Pajak, 2022)*

This poem is written in **free verse**. But while there might not be a fixed pattern of rhyme or rhythm, there is a pattern of stanza breaks. The poem is structured in **couplets**. This regular division of stanzas every two lines emphasises the importance of pairs in this poem: the two friends, the divorced couple, the parents, the father and child. It also perhaps highlights the two timeframes in the poem: the time of boyhood and the time of manhood.

You might have noticed that the poem includes a kind of flashforward from the youthful antics on the bridge to the choices the friends make as men. And yet the poem takes a playful approach to time, allowing the adult men to co-exist with their younger selves.

Such a playful approach lies at the heart of Tishani Doshi's poem 'Memory of Wales', reproduced below (Doshi, 2012; see Bloodaxe Books, 2013, for the poet reading this work). The title might suggest that the poem moves backwards, but it actually takes a more complex approach. Doshi's mother came from a small village in North Wales, which the family would visit from India during summer holidays. Unused to such long summer evenings, Doshi gained a new perspective on time, like 'that famous Dalí painting with the melting watches where memory and dream and reality all get mixed up' (Bloodaxe Books, 2013, 06:38–06:49; see Figure 3 for the painting she has in mind); the poem, she further explains, is about 'childhood and memory and how, in some way, you become your mother, or your mother becomes you' (Bloodaxe Books, 2013, 06:50–06:59).

> **Tishani Doshi** is a writer and dancer of Welsh–Gujarati descent who was born in Tamil Nadu, India. She writes poetry, essays, short stories and novels.

Memory of Wales

This is how it arrives, the memory
of Wales, on a day of scanty light.
I'm walking towards the playground.
I will never know newness like this,
or fear. I'm walking, and I'm eight.
I see a girl on the swing – my mother,

or at least, a version of my mother:
fair-haired, small. In the memory
of Wales it is often cold. I'm eight
and the cows are stalking light
like monsters in the playground.
I will never know newness like this.

I will never know a world like this.
This is my childhood and my mother's.
Everything begins in the playground:
beauty, decay, love, lilies. Memory
starts here on the stairs, in skylight.
Cows chew eternally. I'm eight

in this memory, I'm always eight.
There's a painting that speaks to this
malady of recurrence – an indigo twilight
of melting clocks, which shows Mother
Time as a kind of persistence, memory
and dream, coupling on the ground.

Everything we love returns to the ground.
Mother, father, childhood. When I'm eight
I know nothing of betrayal, but the memory
persists. Only once, is it different from this.
The playground is empty, and my mother,
no longer a girl, is walking a ridge of light.

Now she's at the wooden gate. Light
from Welsh stars tumbles to the ground.
Bronze cliffs in the distance sing. My mother
has met a man. She's going away. I'm eight,
but I've always known she'll leave all this.
Forsaking, after all, is a kind of memory.

My mother is eight and in Wales again.
She's in the playground of memory,
swinging towards light, towards this.

(Doshi, 2012)

This poem is a contemporary take on the **sestina**, an 800-year-old poetic form comprising six stanzas of six lines each and concluding with a **tercet** (a three-line stanza). The words at the end of the first six lines recur in a rolling pattern at the ends of subsequent lines. In the case of 'Memory of Wales', the six repeated words are: 'memory', 'light', 'ground', 'this', 'eight' and 'mother'. The sestina's structural pattern of repetition underpins the poem's exploration of memory, circularity and recurrence. 'Memory of Wales' deviates occasionally from the set pattern of repetition seen in the traditional sestina, perhaps demonstrating through the form of the poem that memories and patterns not only recur, but that they can also change. This is a subject that is investigated in the fifth and sixth stanzas which explore the mother's choice to leave.

4.3 Time and form in novels, feature films and stage plays

Writers of longer works will face the particular challenge of holding the full shape of the text in their mind. This is something you will look at in more detail in the next chapter. For now, let's zoom out to consider the five main structural choices available.

1. Linear

   Linearity is the simplest option and is ideal for plot-driven narratives in which one incident leads to another. Even in this kind of chronological cause-and-consequence narrative, there might be some limited movement within time, such as the occasional flashback.

   In a novel that is propelled more by character or voice, you might expect greater use of flashback as the character's psychology might well inform the work's structure.

   Jill Dawson's novel *Fred and Edie* (2000), for example, is based on the true story of lovers Edith Thompson and Frederick Bywaters, who were executed in 1923 for the murder of Edith's husband. In Dawson's novelised version, the present of the novel takes place from Edie's incarceration in October 1922 to her execution in January 1923. This linear narration is punctuated by snippets from real newspaper reports and court documents, which also run chronologically. But the linear narration is regularly interrupted by Edie's memories, which move around in time. So, within a broadly chronological framework, Dawson nonetheless accommodates the workings of memory.

2. Retrospective

   It is common enough to begin near the end of the timespan of a novel or film. The 'whodunnit' genre is based on the idea of moving back in time to find out the cause of a crime. Harold Pinter's play *Betrayal* (1978), about an affair, moves further back in each act, from after the break-up to before the start of the couple's adulterous relationship. This helps the audience to understand why and how the characters' affair developed.

3. Cyclical

   In this kind of structure, the ending returns to the opening. By now, the audience will be able to interpret the scene with a fuller understanding. This kind of structure can work for all kinds of forms and genres. The 1982 **biopic** *Gandhi*, for instance, begins and ends with the 1948 assassination and funeral of Mahatma Gandhi, the leader of the non-violent campaign for Indian independence. By opening with such a dramatic event, and showing the huge crowds of mourners, the film invites the audience to ask why the protagonist was killed and how he became such an influential figure.

4. Parallel

   Here, narratives that seem unrelated or only loosely so unfold in tandem. Usually, these storylines will intersect at certain points. As you saw in Chapter 10, Michael Cunningham's 1998 novel *The Hours* interweaves three strands, as does Stephen Daldry's 2002 film adaptation of the same name. Strand 1: a fictionalised version of the real-life writer Virginia Woolf during a day in 1923 when she is working on *Mrs Dalloway*, a novel set over the course of a day when the title character is throwing a party. Strand 2: Laura Brown, a woman who is reading the novel in 1949, on a day when she is throwing a party for her husband, a veteran of the Second World War. Strand 3: the 1999 narrative focuses on a character who shares the name Clarissa with the protagonist of *Mrs Dalloway*, and is also throwing a party. This event is to celebrate the major literary prize recently awarded to her dying friend. The ending of the novel reveals even closer links between the three storylines than might have originally met the eye.

5. Fractured

   A fractured narrative structure tends to be more popular in literary novels and experimental films than in more commercial works. This kind of structure requires the active engagement of readers or viewers to navigate the chronology of events presented out of order. The 1941 film *Citizen Kane* starts with the death of a newspaper tycoon, and then loops backwards and forwards in time via the recollections of those who knew him. These flashbacks offer fragmentary and conflicting details about Kane's life and are presented in a non-linear fashion.

   This structure was considered groundbreaking when the film was released, and many viewers found it confusing. Today, readers and viewers are increasingly prepared for shifts in time. However, it is important that there is a logic to the shifts. These jumps can feel contrived if they don't relate to the work's subject matter or the characters' psychologies. But, done well, moving backwards and forwards can allow you simultaneously to withhold and disclose important information, thereby increasing narrative tension.

When writing long-form work, it is easy to get lost in the intricacies of a piece and so it is helpful to zoom out periodically and examine its overall structure. If you get the outline shape of a piece right early on, it saves a lot of time in the long run. Having said this, most writers find that some of their structural decisions are made in the process of writing and rewriting, when unexpected connections might well emerge. Revisions to structure are almost always a significant part of the redrafting process.

5 Conclusion

In this chapter, you have explored a variety of ways in which time can be used. You have learned how time can manipulate the pace of a narrative, influencing the time a reader might take to experience it. You have considered how the way events are sequenced in time can inject questions in the minds of your readers. And you have seen how the structuring of timeframes, at the micro and macro levels, help to marry up form with content. In the next chapter, you will look in greater detail at approaches to shaping both short and long forms of writing.

References

Bloodaxe Books (2013) *Tishani Doshi: everything begins elsewhere*. 5 April. Available at: https://www.youtube.com/watch?v=EbihxX-KxnQ (Accessed: 17 January 2023).

Citizen Kane (1941) Directed by O. Welles. [Feature film]. New York, NY: RKO Radio Pictures.

Cunningham, M. (1998) *The hours*. New York, NY: Farrar, Straus and Giroux.

Dawson, J. (2000) *Fred and Edie*. London: Sceptre.

Dawson, J. (2003) *Wild boy*. London: Sceptre.

Doshi, T. (2012) 'Memory of Wales', in J. Kay, J. Procter and G. Robinson (eds) *Out of bounds: British Black and Asian poets*. Newcastle upon Tyne: Bloodaxe Books, pp. 165–166.

Gandhi (1982) Directed by R. Attenborough. [Feature film]. Los Angeles, CA: Columbia Pictures.

The hours (2002) Directed by S. Daldry. [Feature film]. Los Angeles, CA: Paramount Pictures.

Menon, C.G. (2018) 'Daylight savings', in C.G. Menon, *Subjunctive moods*. Leicester: Dahlia Publishing, pp. 128–138.

O'Farrell, M. (2017) 'Bloodstream (1997)', in M. O'Farrell, *I am, I am, I am: seventeen brushes with death*. London: Tinder Press, pp. 172–183.

Pajak, M. (2022) 'After closing time', in M. Pajak, *Slide*. London: Cape Poetry, p. 9.

Pinter, H. (1978) *Betrayal*. London: Eyre Methuen.

Chapter 16
The long and short of it

Emma Claire Sweeney

1 Introduction

Figure 1 Russian matryoshka dolls lined up in order of size (photo: nicodemos/ E+/Getty).

This chapter focuses on the distinctive features of prose forms of various lengths, from flashes to the novel:

- short-form: **flash fiction**; **flash non-fiction**; short story; and short, stand-alone life writing
- medium-form: novellas and equivalent-length life writing
- long-form: novels and book-length life writing.

You will work out how to tell which forms and lengths might best suit different kinds of narratives. Then you will look at some techniques from poetry and drama, which will help you to approach these different prose forms. By the end of this chapter, you will have learned, first, how to 'think short' and 'write short', and then, how to 'think long' and 'write long' – or at least plan to do so. That's the long and short of it.

2 Short-form prose

Many writers will experiment with shorter prose forms before limbering up to a novel or book-length life writing. But it would be a mistake to think of these short forms as only nursery slopes. While they offer great opportunities for experimenting with an array of fictional techniques, they are also literary forms in their own right, with their own challenges and opportunities.

Just as an artist needs one set of tools to paint a miniature portrait for a locket and another set for painting a mural on the side of a tower block, a writer takes different approaches for drafting short forms and for writing book-length narratives. Shorter-form prose has its own specific requirements, which distinguishes it from longer forms. This is because it is designed (in theory, at least) to be read in one sitting.

2.1 How short?

There is no hard and fast rule about the length of flash fiction and flash non-fiction, but these forms – sometimes known as short shorts – rarely reach the upper limit of 1500 words and are sometimes as short as 250 words (the shorter end of this range is sometimes referred to as microfiction). Indeed, even shorter varieties exist such as those comprising 100 words (known as drabbles), 55 words (nanofiction) and 50 words (dribbles).

Where does a flash end and a short story or piece of life writing begin? As with flash, it is difficult to give definitive word-count parameters for these slightly longer stand-alone forms of fiction and life writing. But, if a flash becomes overgrown at around 1500 words, then this might be a useful marker for the beginning of the short story or life writing piece.

Like flashes, these forms should be capable of being read in one sitting, and they are often published alongside other stand-alone pieces in literary magazines, anthologies or collections. It is therefore rare for a short story or life writing piece to breach the 10,000-word mark, and most shorts actually come in at 2000 to 5000 words.

There are magazines and competitions that specialise in flash. It is worth researching their requirements should you be attracted to working in this form. And, while short stories and personal essays might range from 1000 to 10,000 words, the majority of outlets suitable for apprentice writers tend to impose word limits of between 2000 and 6000 words. At first, it might be wise to practise working on this smaller canvas, as longer stories might have to be kept for a book-length collection – something that is notoriously difficult to publish, especially for debut authors.

2.2 Characteristics of flash

Tania Hershman, editor of *Fuel: An Anthology of Prize-winning Flash Fictions Raising Funds to Fight Fuel Poverty* (2023), once described flash fiction as a story 'distilled to its very essence' (Hershman, 2013, p. 169). As with much poetry, the compression of flashes means that every word has been weighed by the writer and every image designed to be interpreted in multiple ways. Every. Word. Counts. Judith Kitchen, writer and editor of flash non-fiction compares the form to a snowball. 'You have all this stuff out there called snow', she says, 'but when you gather it all up and really pack it together, you know, and you throw it off, there's a sting' (Kitchen, quoted in Moore, 2012, p. 22).

Take a look at the way the American writer of short fiction Bruce Holland Rogers packs together the flash, below, around the image of bait, and how that image causes an unexpected sting.

What Are You Using for Bait?

He comes into the Manitowish bait shop every day, asking beginner's questions and lingering at her counter. Friday he holds a fish he says he's caught. She thinks, A Salmon? In Wisconsin? She doesn't let on. He's going to grill it. Does she want to come? Her last boyfriend was a liar, too. But she likes salmon. She figures she can take the bait and spit out the hook.

(Rogers, 2009, p. 145)

Wales-based author Jupiter Jones, whose Open University Creative Writing PhD research explores flash fiction, reflects on how Rogers makes every one of those 69 words count:

- Length: This is just 69 words and whilst most flash fiction is longer, there are many features here that serve as a masterclass. In one tiny paragraph, Bruce Holland Rogers economically conjures up two characters, their motivation, a plot and reach (a before and after).
- Title: This works hard. 'What Are You Using for Bait?' establishes a context, it poses a 'beginner's question' which contributes to the formation of the character of the man, but by the end, it has taken on another layer of meaning altogether, with the salmon now dangled as bait to catch the woman.
- Beginning: Flash, being so short, is never far from either the beginning or the end and is heavily reliant on both to be effective. Here, without any preamble, the first sentence establishes who, what, where, when, and hints at why.
- Middle: There is absolute economy in the middle section, a succession of eight short sentences, such as, 'He's going to grill it. Does she want to come?' In these eight sentences, the syntax is clipped with no words

wasted, so that when Rogers uses two extra words to say, 'he holds a fish he says he's caught', the words he says become suitably weighted.

- End: The final sentence works exceptionally hard to extend the narrative into the future, to offer motivation and thus character, and to pull together the thematic threads in a way that is both surprising and satisfying. Although it is an open ending, the reader is left with a sense of completeness that comes from the insight into motivation, and from the fact that the ending feels entirely earned by everything that builds up to it.
- Sentence length: The pace of this flash is modulated in part by the length of its sentences. The long opening line has a languorous quality, appropriate to its subject: a man hanging around. This is followed by a succession of short sentences, their snappiness increasing the narrative tension. By slightly elongating the final line, Rogers manipulates rhythm to ease the reader out of the flash.
- Reach: Whilst the plot is minimal – a fisherman engages a shop assistant with possibly spurious questions, then invites her to share the salmon he claims to have caught – there is also an implied before, a **backstory** of her previous boyfriend, and possibly the fisherman's before: does he have previous history of deception? Then also, there is an implied afterwards: how does the date go? Does she manage to spit out this liar?
- Image: As with most flashes, this one comes at its subject from an oblique angle, its meaning invested in an apparently small matter that stands in for a larger truth. In this case, the bait and the catch standing in for the power dynamics in human sexual relations.

(Jones, 2023)

As you can see, 'What Are You Using for Bait?' is a self-contained, condensed piece of writing that is structured around a repeated image. This same approach can work equally well for flash non-fiction. You will now try this method for yourself to create a very rough first draft of a flash.

Activity 1 Writing: planning and writing flash

1. Identify an object that you would like to explore in a flash fiction or flash non-fiction of up to 100 words.

2. Come up with two characters (real or imaginary) who have contrasting responses to this object.

3. Devise a title that introduces the reader to the object.

4. Now write the opening lines, offering a sense of one character's relationship to the object.

5. Then, write the middle of the flash, conveying the second character's contrasting reaction.

6. Finally, draft the flash's ending. Here, the object may recur, this time in a way that hints at its wider significance.

Discussion

Flashes are rarely written in a flash, so don't worry if your draft currently reads more like preparatory notes. Their brevity makes demands that writers often need to address during a series of revisions. Should you choose to continue working on this flash, keep checking whether each word earns its place. In writing pieces of this short length, every line needs to do more than one thing simultaneously or accrue greater meaning as the piece goes on. This effect usually comes through rewriting and refinement.

The brevity of flash fiction and non-fiction lends itself to the kind of writing that warrants rereading. Just as poetry can slow down readers, asking them to turn back to previous lines, read between them and around them, so too do these short prose forms.

2.3 Characteristics of short story and life-writing pieces

These short forms embrace a wide variety of approaches. At one end of the scale, a 'slice-of-life' story might employ many of the poetic techniques you looked at in relation to flash: compression, magnification, image, layering and the evolution of meaning. At the other end of the scale, you will find plot-driven shorts, which borrow techniques from drama to propel the reader through the narrative by suggesting a series of questions: 'What happened?', for instance, or 'Who did it?' and 'How could this have come to pass?' And the spectrum from 'slice-of-life' to 'plot-driven' includes stories that blend these techniques.

Writers of pieces of different lengths need to take into account the amount of mental energy they can legitimately expect a reader to devote to the text. It is likely that the shorter the form, the more you can ask of your reader: as short story writer and novelist Jon McGregor puts it, you can expect them to do more 'of the imaginative work' to fill in the gaps (McGregor, 2017a, 03:48).

McGregor's 'Charlotte', a short story which was commissioned by BBC Radio 4 and then published as the first piece in a collection called *The Reservoir Tapes* (2018), consists of just one side of a conversation. This technique pushes to the extreme the idea of the reader (or listener) filling in the gaps. See how the opening of this story balances the demand on the reader to do a lot of 'imaginative work' with planting questions that pique curiosity:

> Could you
>
> I'd like to hear about that day, before anything happened.
> Just, from the beginning.
>
> You'd been staying in the village for how long?
>
> And you'd come back because the previous visit had gone so well, last summer?
>
> And you knew the Hunter family. You got on with them.
> So it was an easy decision, to come back for a winter break.
>
> Was it warm enough, in the cottage? I mean, the weather had been wet.
> It's quite small, isn't it, the cottage. Lovely. But small.
>
> Sorry, barn conversion.
>
> Had you been on any excursions? Had you gone for any walks?
>
> So you were maybe starting to feel a bit cooped up.
>
> *(McGregor, 2018, pp. 1–2)*

These short, fragmented lines prompt a raft of questions, which clamour in the white space that surrounds the lines. Who is the interviewer interviewing and why? Why is the interviewer tentative? What was significant about that day? What happened and to whom? Why might the interviewer be focusing on the holidaymakers feeling 'cooped up'?

The power of the white space is something poets know all about. White space is essentially a visual cue to readers, letting them know that they are expected to put in the imaginative work required to fill in the gaps.

Note, too, how this story follows the dramatist's principle of arriving late. The story does not start with a description of the interviewer, nor any backstory about how she came to be speaking to her interviewee. Rather, it starts without preamble **in medias res**, a technique that Catherine Menon employed in the opening of 'Daylight Savings' (2018), the short story you read in Chapter 15 (Reading 15.2 in Part 4). In that chapter, you also came across an example of exiting a narrative early in Maggie O'Farrell's (2017) memoir piece 'Bloodstream (1997)' (Reading 15.1), which ends without the narrator revealing the results of her friend's blood test.

As well as following the dictum of arriving late and leaving early, you would be wise when writing in these short forms to consider imposing certain other limitations as well: for example, a focus on just two or three characters, perhaps, and one setting, one narrative perspective and a short period of time. Rules are made to be broken, of course, and you might well break one of them. For example, O'Farrell's short memoir piece ranged across 22 years and Menon's short story was narrated from two perspectives. But you will likely find that the form strains at the seams if you try to overburden it with too many people, places and timeframes.

Activity 2 Planning and writing: the opening of a short story or life-writing piece

1. Imagine that the object you drew on in Activity 1 is now going to feature in a 4000-word short story or self-contained piece of life writing. Jot down notes on the following:

- Who might narrate this story? If there is more than one narrator, do you have good justification for this?
- Will you include additional characters to the two who appeared in your flash? Do they each earn their place?
- Will you include more settings now that you have many more words to play with? What are the fewest settings you need in order to tell this story in 4000 words? Are these settings relatively confined spaces (e.g. a meadow rather than a whole country)?
- What length of time needs to be covered? If it is a long stretch, are there periods of time that can be omitted?
- Which gaps will you trust your reader to fill in?
- What questions might you encourage your reader to ask?
- How will your piece 'arrive late' and 'leave early'?

2. Next, write the title and opening paragraph of this short story or life-writing piece, remembering to 'arrive late'.

Discussion

It is possible that the object from your flash didn't make it into the title or opening paragraph of your short story or life-writing piece. The whole focus of your narrative will likely have changed now that you are beginning to develop an idea for a slightly longer form. Indeed, were you to draft and redraft this 4000-word piece, you might even find that the object that kicked off your flash does not make it to the final version of your short story or life-writing piece.

As you have seen, short prose forms such as flash fiction and non-fiction, short stories and life-writing pieces range over quite a wide word count. You have looked at various creative considerations for working out how to marry the right kind of material and approach with these forms. These have included the poetic techniques of compression, magnification, image, layering and the evolution of meaning, in addition to the dramatic technique of arriving late and leaving early. You have also considered the dynamic between text and reader, and the way that the shorter forms allow you to ask the reader to put in more imaginative work.

3 Medium-length stand-alone work

Figure 2 An accordion (photo: Tat'yana Mazitova/iStock/Getty).

The general consensus is that novellas and medium-length life writing come in at between about 15,000 and 40,000 words. This leaves a no-man's land between the upper limit of the short story and equivalent-length life writing piece, which is 10,000 words, and these medium-length forms. The boundaries are indeed porous, so it is perhaps more helpful to consider the other traits that distinguish medium-length stand-alone works.

3.1 Characteristics of medium-length stand-alone works

In 1974, narratologist Judith Leibowitz attempted to differentiate the novella from its closest bedfellows, the short story and the novel:

> Whereas the short story limits material and the novel extends it, the novella does both in such a way that a special kind of narrative structure results, one which produces a generically distinct effect: the double effect of intensity and expansion.
>
> *(Leibowitz, 1974, p. 16)*

The novella form therefore makes great demands on the writer, who must be dexterous with the tools of both compression, which are so central to the short story writer; and of expansion, which are required by the novelist.

You have already looked at the way the structure of short-form prose might hang on recurring images, and the various strategies that writers of shorts use to limit their material (focusing on just one narrative point of view, for instance, or including a small cast of characters, a single setting or a short timeframe). A reverse approach allows the novelist scope for expansion: multiple points of view become possible, a larger cast of characters, various and broader settings and a longer span of time. The choices most appropriate to the writer of a novella or equivalent-length life writing might lie somewhere in between those favoured by the short story writer and those by the novelist.

Take the 39,000-word novella *Afternoon Raag* (1993) by Amit Chaudhuri, a writer who publishes fiction, poetry and non-fiction of varying lengths, for example. In *Afternoon Raag*, Chaudhuri employs the tools of the short story writer with their emphasis on image as a structural device and fruitful constraint in certain areas. The significance of image in *Afternoon Raag* is alluded to in its title. The novella is structured around Indian classical music, opening with news of the impending death of the narrator's music teacher and ending just after the death occurs. This guru had taught the main character to sing classical Indian folk songs (*raags*), and musical imagery recurs throughout the novella. In the following ways, this novella works within creative limitations: it takes place over the course of one year, for instance, and there is one main narrator. Crucially, each and every scene relates to the theme of migration, and the narrator's feeling of suspension between his family home in Bombay (present-day Mumbai) and his adopted home in Oxford.

Equally, it borrows from the novelist's more expansive choices. For example, *Afternoon Raag* ranges across various locations within the two cities. Just as in the short story 'Daylight Saving' (Reading 15.2), this text also revolves around a student love triangle. But the novella form allows for a larger array of additional characters: the narrator's friend, parents, music teachers and household staff, as well as the two women the narrator vacillates between.

This same dynamic between limitation and expansion is also a feature of medium-length life writing. In addition, both forms embrace the kind of experimentation that a reader might find wearisome over the course of a longer work.

3.2 Publishing medium-length stand-alone works

If novellas are notoriously difficult to write, they are just as tricky to publish – at least with the big publishing houses. It is especially hard to debut with a novella. In the main, the big publishers reserve their very few novella slots to authors who have already attracted a large readership for their novels. Trends do change, however, and there are always exceptions.

There isn't even a term in English for a medium-yet-potentially-book-length form of life writing. This should perhaps come as a warning! If there were a large market for such a form, there would probably be a word to describe it. A biography of under 40,000 words may well suggest to readers that there isn't enough material to furnish a full-length book, or that the writer has simply failed to conduct enough research. Novella-length life writing does sometimes get published, but such instances are few and far between. You would need a good reason to argue that your particular story was best suited to this medium length.

4 Novels and equivalent-length life writing

Yet again, there is a gap between the upper word limits of one form and the lower limits of the next: while novellas and their life-writing equivalents tend to be no longer than about 40,000 words, it is not until the 60,000-word mark that a text would usually be considered a novel or book-length life writing – at least by traditional publishing houses and literary agents. Novels published exclusively in digital format, however, are often shorter than those published in print. Traditionally, novels and memoir that range from 75,000 to 100,000 words are considered about average, and anything over 100,000 is relatively long.

The length of biographies differs somewhat from these norms, however. The greater the volume of available documentation on a subject's life, the greater the types of evidence and viewpoints for a biographer to consider incorporating into the narrative. With anything up to 200,000 words considered average for research-heavy biographies, it is perhaps unsurprising that they tend to take up to ten years to write.

Activity 3 Planning: researching length for book-length works

1. Imagine you are embarking on the process of writing a full-length book. What kind of story would you like to tell? A fictional love story, for instance, or true crime, science fiction, a historical novel, a literary biography, and so on?

2. Conduct some research on the internet, in a bookshop and/or in a library to find three books published in the past five years that are written within (or playing with) the same genre conventions as your proposed book.

3. Note down the word lengths of these books (to work this out, it helps to know that most printed books contain 250–300 words per page).

Discussion
Did a pattern begin to emerge?

Traditional romance novels are often at the shorter end of the spectrum (below 75,000 words).

Mysteries, thrillers, true crime, most memoir, and biographies of people who are not famous tend to fall into the mid-length range of 75,000–100,000 words.

Longer works tend to be those that require immersive world-building, such as science fiction, historical fiction and family sagas, as well as biographies about exhaustively documented historical figures.

Readers and publishers of certain genres come to expect work of particular lengths. If you choose to subvert these expectations, make sure that you have a good reason to do so.

4.1 Characteristics of novels and equivalent-length life writing

While the writer of a short story or piece of life writing might hope that their works could be consumed in one sitting, writers of a novel or book-length life writing must accept that their texts will battle for the reader's attention amongst all the many other demands that will inevitably have cropped up between putting the book down and picking it up again. This affects the approaches you might take when writing these longer forms.

Earlier, you learned that the novelist or author of equivalent-length life writing might find a suitable level of expansiveness by considering some or all of the following:

- a larger cast of characters than a shorter form might accommodate
- a greater number of settings or those with broader scope (so, while a flash might be set in a bait shop, a short story might take place in a lakeside town and a novel might move between Liverpool and Lagos)
- a longer span of time or more narrative points of view.

The level of expansiveness will depend in part on the overall length of the narrative.

Earlier, you read the opening lines of McGregor's short story 'Charlotte' (2018). This extract amounts to about five per cent of the overall story. Next, you will read the first five per cent of McGregor's 80,000-word novel *Reservoir 13* (2017b), which amounts to around 4000 words. The novel is set in the same community as the short story and features the same **premise** (the main idea behind a novel; in this case, a girl's disappearance).

Activity 4 Reading: the opening pages of a novel

Read the opening pages of McGregor's *Reservoir 13* (2017b) (Reading 16.1).

Now, answer the following questions:

1. In what ways is the opening of McGregor's *Reservoir 13* more expansive than the opening of his short story 'Charlotte' (see Section 2.3)?

2. Does it make fewer or more demands on its reader? If so, how?

3. To what extent does it follow the dictum to 'arrive late'?

4. What questions does it suggest, and how might they encourage you, the reader, to keep on turning the pages?

Discussion

The third-person plural ('they') perspective is an unusual choice. It certainly creates a sense of expansiveness, indicating that this novel will tell the story of an entire community. This contrasts with the more intimate conversation between two individuals in 'Charlotte', where the reader is privy to only one side. And, while the opening of the short story covers just a few moments in time, the opening of the novel spans five months, from January to May.

The novel's prose is description-heavy, which slows the reader down and demands concentration. But the narration does not require the reader to read between the lines to the same extent as the short story does. The narrative voice feels reliable, so the reader can relax into it, which creates an immersive effect.

The narrative could have opened earlier, showing the family leaving for their walk, but this would have given the reader access to events that members of the community have not seen for themselves. The reader is placed in the same position as the villagers are in. Even here, the narrative follows the dictum to 'arrive late', since the novel starts with the search party rather than the initial news of the girl's disappearance.

The questions planted by the opening are distributed rather languorously throughout the first 4000 words. But the stakes are so high that they propel the narrative, effectively buying the writer time for descriptive world-building: What has happened to the girl? Will she be discovered? Do any of the villagers hold the key to the mystery? Will the discovery of the red van really prove a game changer? Were the sightings genuine?

One of the great challenges facing writers of novel-length works is how to sustain a narrative over so many pages and how to give a sense of expansiveness without deviating into unnecessary areas. In this respect, the Aristotelian three-act structure underpinning so much Western drama, which you explored in Chapter 8, can also prove helpful to the novelist and life writer. Figure 3 outlines a common approach to applying this structure to book-length prose. The red line represents levels of dramatic tension at different points in the book.

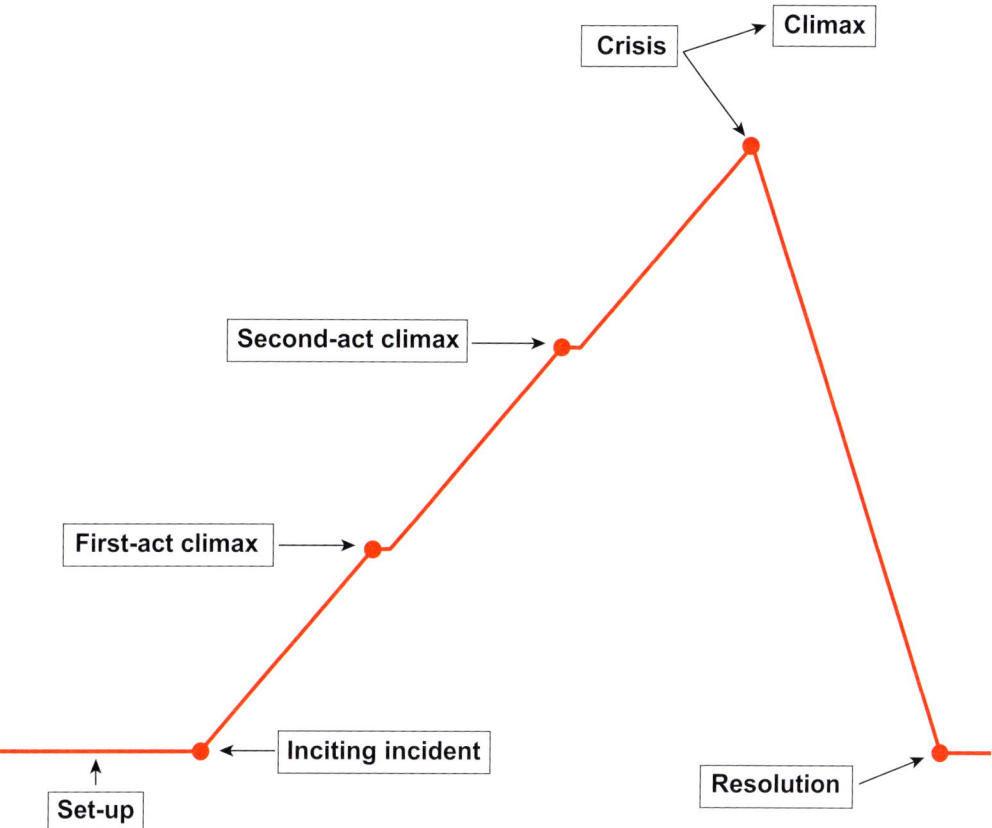

Set-up A short description or scene establishing the status quo. The set-up is sometimes omitted.

Inciting incident An event that disrupts the status quo.

First-act climax The protagonist's response to the inciting incident leads to them facing a significant problem.

Second-act climax The protagonist's response to the first-act climax causes further complications, leading to them facing an even more significant problem.

Crisis The protagonist's response to the second-act climax causes even further complications, leading to them facing their most significant problem.

Climax The crisis forces the protagonist to make a life-changing or character-defining choice.

Resolution An inevitable but unpredictable consequence of the choice made by the protagonist at the climax.

Figure 3 Annotated three-act structure model.

Books that fit neatly into popular genres such as science fiction or romance tend to be served well by the three-act structure modelled in Figure 3. *Reservoir 13*, however, plays with genre. In particular, it subverts expectations of the murder mystery novel. Many such novels open with a girl's body (the inciting incident) and end with the identification of the murderer (the resolution). By contrast, *Reservoir 13* opens with the search party and ends 13 years later, when the villagers are none the wiser about what happened and are living with the aftershocks of this lack of resolution.

Activity 5 Writing: planning for book-length works

1. First, imagine you are going to expand the 4000-word narrative that you planned in Activity 2 into an average-length novel or life-writing book (between 75,000 and 100,000 words in length for novels and memoirs, and up to 200,000 words for biography). Make notes in response to the following questions:

- Might your story lend itself to multiple perspectives?
- Will the protagonist remain the same? Is there scope to include a larger number of characters?
- Could any of your settings be broadened out?
- What timeframe might work best when you have so many more words to play with?
- Will the work include any subplots (a secondary plot that supports the main plot)?
- Which devices might you use to create a sense of narrative cohesion (a recurring image, for instance)? You might revisit this question once you have read more about theme in the next chapter.

2. Identify seven key moments when your main character might make a choice that will change the course of their story (these moments are known as climaxes or turning points).

3. Redraw the diagram in Figure 3 in your writer's notebook. Work out which of the key moments you identified above is the inciting incident, the first-act climax, the second-act climax, the crisis, the climax and the resolution. Then add this information to the appropriate labels.

4. Consider whether the traditional three-act model will best serve the kind of story you are trying to tell. If not, jot down notes on why an alternative structure might work better.

Discussion

The key here is to make use of the longer form's capacity for breadth without spreading it too thin. Finding this balance often occurs in the process of drafting and redrafting. But some sense of appropriate scope from the start can help save a huge amount of time in the long run, particularly with regard to theme. This is something you will consider in greater detail in Chapter 17.

Identifying a small number of key turning points, as you have done in this activity, can help to keep the overall structure in mind while working closely on the detail – even if you opt for an alternative to the traditional three-act model. Strategies for zooming out are particularly important when writing longer works, because it is impossible to hold a book-length narrative in your mind at once. Of course, you will almost certainly make changes as you go along, but this kind of one-page plan can help you to keep on track, and you can always update it as you draft and redraft.

5 Conclusion

You can save yourself a lot of time if you are able to identify, at an early stage, the sort of length and form that might best serve your ideas. Having said this, many a failed short story has blossomed into a novel. And plenty of writers find that they have to cut the first several thousand words of their manuscript because the narrative doesn't take off until 20 pages in. On the other hand, it is not unusual for writers to find that they need to add passages during the revision process to create a more immersive reading experience. You might find that your love story evolves into more of a mystery, or your narrative voice doesn't end up as compressed and lyrical as you planned. That is all part of the exploratory process of writing. Every so often, review the direction your writing is taking and reflect on whether your intended form and length are still appropriate to the kind of story you are trying to tell.

References

Chaudhuri, A. (1993) *Afternoon raag*. London: William Heinemann.

Hershman, T. (2013) 'Art breathes from containment', in V. Gebbie (ed.) *Short circuit: a guide to the art of the short story*. Cromer: Salt, pp. 169–178.

Hershman, T. (ed.) (2023) *Fuel: an anthology of prize-winning flash fictions raising funds to fight fuel poverty*. London: Fuel Flash.

Jones, J. (2023) Email to Emma Claire Sweeney, 26 November.

Leibowitz, J. (1974) *Narrative purpose in the novella*. The Hague: Mouton.

McGregor, J. (2017a) 'How I wrote *The reservoir tapes*'. Interviewed by S. Richardson for *BBC Radio 4*, 2 November. Available at: https://www.bbc.co.uk/sounds/play/p05lv20b (Accessed: 23 January 2023).

McGregor, J. (2017b) *Reservoir 13*. London: 4th Estate.

McGregor, J. (2018) 'Charlotte', in J. McGregor, *The reservoir tapes*. London: 4th Estate, pp. 1–16.

Menon, C.G. (2018) 'Daylight savings', in C.G. Menon, *Subjunctive moods*. Leicester: Dahlia Publishing, pp. 128–138.

Moore, D. (2012) 'Of fire and ice: the pleasing sting of flash nonfiction', in D.W. Moore (ed.) *Field guide to writing flash nonfiction: advice and essential exercises from respected writers, editors, and teachers*. Brookline, MA: Rose Metal Press, pp. 13–22.

O'Farrell, M. (2017) 'Bloodstream (1997)', in M. O'Farrell, *I am, I am, I am: seventeen brushes with death*. London: Tinder Press, pp. 171–183.

Rogers, B.H. (2009) 'Writing fixed-form narratives', in T.L. Masih (ed.) *Field guide to writing flash fiction: tips from editors, teachers, and writers in the field*. Brookline, MA: Rose Metal Press, pp. 142–149.

Chapter 17
Thematic connections

Heather Richardson with Bill Greenwell

1 Introduction

In this final chapter, you will take some time to step back and survey the writing and thinking you have done as you made your way through the book. This will give you the opportunity to notice if there are thematic threads that connect different pieces of work. Such threads can help you to understand yourself as a writer and they can also equip you with a way of narrating your projects or describing yourself for an audience. 'Audience' could mean anything from a literal audience – people hearing you read at an open mic event, for example – to an agent, publisher or theatre company whom you are approaching with your work.

Figure 1 Interference patterns of two point sources, 2004 (photo: © Richard Megna/FUNDAMENTAL PHOTOGRAPHS, NYC).

The *Oxford Dictionary of Literary Terms* defines 'theme' as 'A salient abstract idea that emerges from a literary work's treatment of its subject-matter; or a topic recurring in a number of literary works' (Baldick, 2008). Put more simply, the **theme** is the central idea of a piece of writing. It is abstract, not concrete. This is in contrast to the subject of a piece of writing.

Identifying the theme of a piece can be surprisingly tricky. One approach I find helpful is to ask of any piece, 'What's it about?', followed by, 'What's it *really* about?' For example, my poem 'Eastbourne' (Richardson, 2019), is about a surreal unexplained death – this is its subject – but it's *really* about the loss of religious faith. Loss of religious faith is, therefore, its theme.

Throughout this chapter, you will also explore some techniques used by writers to develop themes in their work. This can include self-imposed limitations, telling parallel stories and experimental approaches to form. There will be activities and readings relating to writerly approaches to theme in fiction, life writing, poetry and script, and you will have the opportunity to think about how you can apply these approaches to your own work.

2 Threads and echoes

It is one thing to identify the theme of a single piece of work, such as a poem, short story or play. However, it's only when you read several pieces by the same author that you start to recognise recurring themes. For example, the short stories of Raymond Carver are pervaded by themes of loneliness, failure and quiet despair, while the poet Mary Oliver explores themes of joy, compassion and wonder. This is not to say that everything an author publishes will address their recurring themes. It is important to remember that most authors – even highly successful ones – write a great deal of material that never gets published. This may be the writer's own choice: many of us have pieces we are very fond of, but which are too different from our usual work in their theme, tone or subject to sit comfortably in a collection. Throughout a writer's career, the themes in their work may well change to reflect their evolving preoccupations.

If you have begun to recognise recurring themes in your own work, there are some interesting techniques that you can experiment with to deepen thematic connections between separate pieces. For example, if you have written several short stories, you could introduce echoes between them, perhaps by using location, or recurring characters, or by repeating major incidents in one story as minor incidents in others.

Kate Atkinson does this in her collection of 12 short stories *Not the End of the World* (2002). The underlying theme is of transformation, or the desire for it, but this theme is built up only through subtle echoes in the structure. A car crash on the M9 motorway is incidental in the fifth story, but central to the tenth and glimpsed in the eleventh. In the third story, an incidental character is referred to as having died during dental surgery, but this incident resurfaces more centrally in the ninth story (and this pattern is repeated with many characters). A television script proposed in one story resurfaces as a programme watched in a later story. In this way, the collection is like a sound-chamber in which there are constant reverberations and, often, these are of stories from Greek mythology. Each story remains readable as a separate entity; together, they encourage readers to meditate on Atkinson's theme.

Often, it is hard to know for sure whether a writer has deliberately chosen a particular theme for a series of pieces, or if the theme has emerged unconsciously, with the writer only recognising it in retrospect. You may have noticed this in your own writing. In either case, the theme can become a kind of prompt or stimulus for further writing.

Sometimes an author will deliberately choose a single subject as a prompt for their writing and this can become a vehicle for exploring a theme. For example, in Vona Groarke's poetry collection *Other People's Houses* (1999), each poem explores some version or aspect of a house. In some of these poems, the focus is on the materiality of a house or its contents, while in others the buildings become a metaphor for the lives lived within them. The underlying themes seem to be the ephemerality of identity, and the illusion of security embodied in the home.

In a similar vein, Liam Bell's short story collection *Rare Stories* (2023a) is an A–Z of 1000-word stories inspired by words that have been designated as 'rare' by the *Oxford English Dictionary*. He said of the stories:

> I set myself a challenge of writing one a week and limited them to 1000 words. That seemed like a realistic amount to write in a week, but also the restriction (hopefully) helped to make them sharp and meant I had a 'purpose' for the almost-immediate editing I was doing. The A–Z just followed because it fitted neatly and it allowed for a six-month timescale for writing, which was ideal.
>
> In terms of theme, I didn't set out to unify them under a theme or series of themes, but I think a lot of them became quite character-led and drew on the same themes as my novels tend to – love and loss, family, political. I was very conscious, though, that I didn't want them to be one-note, so I enjoyed playing a bit with genre and trying to hit a more comedic tone with some of them too.
>
> (Bell, 2023b)

Bell did not start out with a theme in mind, but he noticed the themes that had emerged when looking at the collection as a whole.

Collections can still have thematic unity without the intricate connections constructed by Atkinson or the employment of organising principles such as those used by Groarke and Bell. For example, the 13 stories in Jane Campbell's collection *Cat Brushing* (2022a) offer readers an unsettling and unexpected insight into the inner lives of older women, revealing characters who are sensual, angry and fiercely intelligent. When interviewed about the collection, she explained, 'what I wanted to say, from quite an angry point of view, was, yes, old women are totally functioning human beings' (Campbell, 2022b). The theme of resistance to, and subversion of, the way older women are perceived and judged chimes with Campbell's own experience as an older woman writer.

As you have worked your way through this book, you will have done many writing activities, and will have produced ideas, fragments and some complete pieces of fiction, life writing, poetry and script. Perhaps it's already clear to you what themes are emerging in your writing. If you've shared your work with friends or fellow writers, they may have identified themes that you hadn't realised were there. You're now approaching the end of this book, and this is an apt moment to review the writing you've done and reflect on themes that have recurred or emerged in the process. It can be instructive to approach this quite methodically, as the next activity will guide you to do.

Activity 1 Writing: an audit of your writing

Part 1

Review the writing you have done in response to the activities suggested in earlier chapters and reflect on themes that have recurred or emerged in the process:

- List each piece of writing you have done, noting which chapter and activity it relates to.
- Give a short description of each item on the list, identifying what form it falls into, what the subject was and any themes you notice.

You may find it helpful to use a table, like the one below which includes example entries (Table 1):

Table 1 An audit of your writing: example entries

Chapter and activity number	Form	Subject	Theme
Chapter 2, Activity 5	Fiction	An unhappy couple go on a night-time ghost tour in Edinburgh	The impact of past trauma on the present
Chapter 5, Activity 3	Script	Description, from observation, of a very well-dressed man in his sixties – business suit, briefcase, expensive watch – sitting in a cheap burger bar	Pretence and self-deception
Chapter 12, Activity 2	Poetry	A teacher is trying to prepare her apathetic pupils for a school inspection	The loneliness of bereavement

Part 2

When you have completed your list of all the writing activities you have done, consider the list as a whole. Think about both your subject matter and the underlying themes: can you discern any connections or echoes running through the different pieces?

Discussion

You may have found one theme running throughout your pieces of writing, or perhaps there were multiple themes. If the latter, you may have identified potential connections between them. This kind of exercise can be useful in clarifying the themes that currently concern you in your writing which can, in turn, help you to focus your energies. For example, the themes identified in the table above all seem, in some way, to be about the long aftermath of loss, and how it can play out in a person's life. This might generate ideas for other stories, poems or scripts on the same theme.

In addition to helping you to develop your work, gaining a good understanding of your theme or themes has benefits from a professional point of view, because it can also help you to find a way of talking about yourself as a writer when engaging with editors, publishers or producers.

3 Developing themes

Once you have noticed particular themes in your work, you may want to explore different ways to develop them. One way is to create separate narratives and to allow the reader to see the connections between them. We can see this in Michael Cunningham's novel *The Hours* (1999) and its film adaptation (*The Hours*, 2002), scripted by David Hare (2003). Both book and film explore themes of existential despair, the constraints of the roles imposed by society, and what makes life worth living. There are three narrative strands set in different time periods, but they all explore these themes in ways that echo across the strands. Only once does a character from one of the three narratives meet one from another, but the stories are held together by comparisons, echoes and similarities. The writer encourages the audience to link the stories by using visual devices – the flowers in the film version of *The Hours*, for instance. The repetition of images encourages the viewer to speculate on what brings the three stories together.

Another device that you can use to bring out a theme is the setting, or place, as in Adam Thorpe's rural environment in his novel *Ulverton* (1992). The novel contains 12 chapters which range over more than 350 years, but each chapter is set in the same rural community. Thorpe (1996) testified that his theme became the rural world of England, its 'secret history, the hidden history'. He explained: 'I think part of the political programme of *Ulverton* was bound up with allowing voices that have been suppressed or are suppressed even now, when you look at history, to have their say' (Thorpe, 1996).

A single setting can be both an effective structural device and an opportunity to explore a particular theme. Hotels (and other locations such as hospitals, boarding-houses, aeroplanes and stations) are often used in fiction and drama to explore the theme of loneliness because they bring strangers together under one roof; being unmoored from their normal lives, characters in these locations are given an unusual equality of status.

William Trevor's *The Boarding-house* (1965), Emma Tennant's *Hotel de Dream* (1976) and Ali Smith's *Hotel World* (2001) are just three fictional examples. In Terence Rattigan's pair of linked one-act plays, *Separate Tables* (1955), each play is set in the same location (a Bournemouth hotel) and with the same minor characters. However, the protagonists of each play, in each case a woman and a man, have no direct connection with the protagonists of the other. What the two couples have in common is loneliness. Placing the plays side by side helps Rattigan to emphasise his theme: the private, uncertain worlds of the characters.

Writers of poetry must think about the order in which their poems are presented in a sequence or collection because this is an important way to communicate their theme to the reader. It can be useful to look at the running order of poems in a number of poetry collections, or sequences within collections, and analyse what the poet may be trying to convey about their theme through the choices they have made. In Carol Ann Duffy's collection

The Other Country (1990), the poems hold a kind of restless conversation with the reader. Having found her theme – 'otherness' – she seems to have shuffled her pack of poems until they were in the most interesting and suggestive order. However, there are many other ways of exploring a theme through a sequence: one way is to take a set of characters, and another is to focus on a group of naturally related phenomena or objects. The pressure of the structure can help you to locate your ideas. For instance, Frieda Hughes bases her sequence *Waxworks* (2002) on wax models at Madame Tussauds museum in London. *Waxworks* presents over 50 figures from myth and history, ordered in such a way as to imply a growing darkness, finishing with images of apocalypse and hell. The order of poems in a sequence or collection will help communicate the theme, whether it is developed incrementally, as with Hughes's *Waxworks*, or whether it seems more apparently random, as with Duffy's *The Other Country*.

It can be interesting to observe your own process as your themes emerge: does it gradually dawn on you what your themes are, or do you have a sudden flash of insight? Did you start with one theme in mind, and then find a different one surfacing? Or perhaps some aspect of your reading, such as the types of work that resonate with you, helped you to recognise the themes that are significant to you in your writing.

Activity 2 Writing: discovering thematic connections in your work

For this activity, look again at the list you produced for Activity 1. You may find it helpful to use a technique like **mind mapping** or **storyboarding** to consider how separate pieces of your writing might fit together. For instance, the table of examples in Activity 1 might generate all sorts of connections: the schoolteacher could be one half of the unhappy couple on the Edinburgh ghost tour, and the businessman in the burger bar could be the estranged father of her partner. In this way, you could connect the three separate pieces.

- Consider any thematic clusters, and how you might bring separate pieces of work together in ways that would bring out the themes more markedly.
- Looking at some of the techniques employed by the authors mentioned above, consider whether you could adapt these to use with your own work.
- Make notes about the process you use, any conclusions you come to, and new ideas that emerge.

Discussion

Doing this kind of activity can sometimes make you realise that pieces of writing that you thought of as quite separate from each other gain power and impact by being brought together. Here's an example from Heather Richardson's own practice: I had two short pieces of life writing about very different aspects of my mother's and my father's lives. One was my reimagining of an episode from my father's young adulthood, when he climbed up the outside of a church spire with his steeplejack brother and found himself so terrified that he could not move. The other was a meditation on my mother's love of travel and sunshine, and the way her life gradually shrank and darkened as she developed dementia. Looking at these vignettes together, I realised I could assemble them into a larger, two-part piece that would draw out themes of memory, grief and love.

4 Thematic life writing

In the previous chapters on life writing, you encountered many examples of the topics writers address, such as going on a journey, returning 'home', or family. Often, when a writer's work is looked at as a whole, over the span of several essays or books, the reader can identify a recurring theme, such as overcoming adversity, or identity.

Even conventional biographies which take a birth-to-death approach to a well-known figure will often take a particular line on their subject or concentrate on particular aspects. For instance, Claire Tomalin's *Thomas Hardy: The Time-torn Man* (2006), a biography which starts, significantly, with his first wife Emma's death, not with Hardy's own birth, depicts him as a novelist and poet whose response – as a man and as a writer – to her death reveals an energetic, romantic and lyrical individual – a man who is steeped in the music of his childhood.

Dan Richards' *Outpost: A Journey to the Wild Ends of the Earth* (2019) explores remote or isolated places that have attracted artists and writers over the centuries. In the opening chapter, he explains how his interest stems from an artefact that his Arctic-explorer father brought home from an expedition to a remote part of Norway, and sets out the organising principle of the book:

> This book is not designed to be a definitive tour but rather an odyssey inspired by a world of possibilities and wonder embodied by a polar bear pelvis brought home to South Wales one wet and blustery night.
>
> Every chapter will explore a particular situation or structure, each location a stop in an ongoing narrative, each examining a different facet, perspective and approach to the experience of wilderness.
>
> *(Richards, 2019, p. 13)*

Outpost, like much contemporary life writing, blends personal reflection and encounters with some part of the outside world. Life writing can also focus on themes which are explicitly personal. Anne Enright's *Making Babies* (2004) combines a memoir of her early years of motherhood with a section called 'Babies: A Breeder's Guide', which humorously subverts the conventions of parenting manuals. Miranda Doyle's *A Book of Untruths* (2017) tells her family's troubled history through a series of short chapters focused on lies she was told when growing up, such as 'We don't have favourites' and 'School is really nice'.

Maggie Nelson's *Bluets* opens with the lines, 'Suppose I were to begin by saying that I had fallen in love with a color. Suppose I were to speak this as though it were a confession; suppose I shredded my napkin as we spoke' (Nelson, 2009, p. 1). Over the course of 240 sequentially numbered paragraphs (some of which are very short), Nelson meditates on life, loneliness and beauty, addressing her words to an unnamed 'you', her former lover. She remembers the passion and pain of their relationship and the trauma of its ending. Another strand of the book is Nelson's support of a friend who has suffered a life-changing accident and who must adapt to a new life with limited mobility. Nelson quotes from philosophers and poets who have written about the colour blue, and the paragraphs flit between different aspects of her experience of blueness. In one section, she picks up a book called *The Deepest Blue* assuming it to be a treatise on colour, only to find it's a self-help book for women experiencing depressive illness. This finding leads to further reflections on her own state of mind:

> 88. Like many self-help books, *The Deepest Blue* is full of horrifyingly simplistic language and some admittedly good advice. Somehow the women in the book all learn to say: *That's my depression talking. It's not 'me'*.
>
> 89. As if we could scrape the color off the iris and still see.
>
> 90. Last night I wept in a way I haven't wept for some time. I wept until I aged myself. I watched it happen in the mirror. I watched the lines arrive around my eyes like engraved sunbursts; it was like watching flowers open in time-lapse on a windowsill. The tears not only aged my face, they also changed its texture, turned the skin of my cheeks into putty. I recognized this as a rite of decadence, but I did not know how to stop it.
>
> 91. Blue-eye, archaic: 'a blueness or dark circle around the eye, from weeping or other cause.'
>
> *(Nelson, 2009, pp. 34–35)*

Nelson's approach here is very different from the more conventional narrative form of Richards' *Outpost* or Enright's *Making Babies*. It is much more fragmentary, and it is not always immediately clear how one paragraph relates to the next, but the whole work does follow a dramatic arc.

Figure 2 Graham Dean, *Blue Mirror 2*, 2009, watercolour and colour dye, 98 × 112 cm. Private collection (photo: © Graham Dean. All rights reserved 2024/ Bridgeman Images).

Activity 3 Writing: connected fragments

The colour blue was one of Nelson's subjects in *Bluets*, but it also acted as a thread connecting different aspects of her themes of brokenness and pain. Pick a colour other than blue and write a series of short fragments (around 500 words in total) that are, in some way, connected to the colour of your choice. This could include memories associated with the colour, observations from the world around you and snippets of facts that you know or find out through research. You could also look through writing you have done in the past to see if any fragments resonate with the colour in some way.

If you prefer, you can choose a different connecting thread relating to another sense: for example, a sound, a smell or a physical sensation such as heat or cold.

When you have written and compiled your fragments, consider the best order for them to be presented.

Discussion

This approach of writing thematically connected fragments can be an interesting and more experimental way to explore life writing. If you confined yourself to writing about your own experience, what themes did you find emerging? Did you organise your fragments chronologically, or in some other way? If you included quotations from other writers, how did these connect with the fragments written from your own perceptions?

5 Theme in the poetry sequence

Writing a sequence of poetry invariably involves the use of echo and resonance, sometimes with more emphasis on the structural similarity of the poems which the sequence contains. A sequence is designed to develop a theme and to explore ideas through images, often by shifting and altering the perspective of each successive poem. Sequences are often self-contained within a collection – for example, the sequence 'The Wasting Game' (1998) from Philip Gross's collection of the same name, which recounts his daughter's experience of anorexia. However, poets can also interweave a theme throughout a collection. In Kei Miller's *A Light Song of Light* (2010), there are three poems called 'Some definitions of light' at separate points in the collection, each of which deals with the body, illness, death and beauty. Other poems also use the 'Some definitions of …' construction, while many others are 'songs', for example 'The Longest Song' and 'A Praise Song for Sudden Lights'.

Activity 4 Reading: poets and their themes

Read an interview with poets Siobhán Campbell and Jane Yeh (2023) (Reading 17.1 in Part 4), in which they discuss the ways they have worked with theme and sequence in their own poetry collections; they also suggest some examples of other contemporary poets who have taken interesting approaches to the sequence.

As you read, take note of any of the suggested ways of working with sequence that chime with your own approach, or that you might want to explore further.

Discussion

Neither Campbell nor Yeh deliberately set out to write sequences. However, they sometimes find that when they have produced a body of poems, there are recurring subjects, themes or moods which begin to suggest a sequence. They are both drawn to the idea of the 'scattered sequence', where thematically connected poems are dispersed throughout a collection, rather than collected together in the way that the sequence has more traditionally been understood.

They also discussed the way a sequence can have two different manifestations. An example of this is Michael Symmons Roberts' 'Last Words', which was originally broadcast in its entirety on BBC Radio 4, but which later appeared in his collection *The Half-healed* (Symmons Roberts, 2008), where it was interspersed with other poems.

6 Theme in drama

As you have seen in this chapter, authors often find themselves returning to particular themes in their writing. Dramatists are no exception to this. For example, Oladipo Agboluaje, whom you encountered in Part 2 of this book, tends to write on themes related to his experiences as a person of Nigerian heritage living and working in Britain.

One interesting example of this is American playwright Suzan-Lori Parks, who wrote a very short play every day for a year in her project *365 Days/365 Plays* (Parks, 2006). In her 1994 essay, 'Possession', Parks says she sees her work as:

> a way of creating and rewriting history through the medium of literature. Since history is a recorded or remembered event, theatre, for me, is the perfect place to 'make' history – that is, because so much of African-American history has been unrecorded, dismembered, washed out, one of my tasks as playwright is to – through literature and the special strange relationship between theatre and real-life – locate the ancestral burial ground, dig for bones, find bones, hear the bones sing, write it down. […] I'm working theatre like an incubator to create 'new' historical events.
>
> *(Parks, 1994, p. 12)*

Figure 3 Suzan-Lori Parks, on a break during a rehearsal of *Father Comes Home from the Wars*, American Repertory Theatre, Cambridge, Massachusetts, 2018. Photographed by Joanne Rathe (photo: Boston Globe/Getty).

In her preface to the published version of *365 Days/365 Plays*, she says she 'wrote what came' (Parks, 2006, p. vii) each day. Although, according to her own account, she did not set out with a specific theme or themes in mind, it is clear on reading the plays that certain themes and motifs recur. Some of these speak to Parks' rewriting of history, such as several plays that explore, invent or subvert aspects of Abraham Lincoln's life. Many of the plays feature a man and a woman at odds in some way, and simmer with the threat of violence. For example, 11 of the plays are titled *Father Comes Home from the Wars*, and these often feature a female character attempting to contain the violent impulses of a male character through deflection and distraction. Given the pressure of writing a play every day for a year, with little time for self-censorship or self-curation, it makes sense that Parks' preoccupations manifest themselves in the work she generated.

When reviewing the writing activities that you worked through in Part 2 of this book, be alert to the recurrence of your own preoccupations, and consider how you could lean into these as you develop the pieces or write new work.

7 Theme and the reader

Developing a theme does not mean that you need to explain it to the reader. Adam Thorpe did not set out with a theme for *Ulverton*, or even with a novel in mind: he began with a single short story. As his theme came to him, he developed it through a succession of styles, from stream of consciousness to letters, to the final chapter which is a film script. It is, in fact, perfectly possible to read *Ulverton* as a succession of short stories. Thorpe testified that he wanted the reader to have to work hard: 'I don't see much point in writing a novel unless the reader works because there's so much in life and culture at the moment that's just for easy consumption' (Thorpe, 1996). If you are writing a sequence of pieces, it is important to let images resonate and to assist the echoes you are creating.

You can see a different approach to theme in anthologies in which the editor chooses a selection of pieces from multiple authors. It is important that the theme of an anthology can be clearly communicated to, and understood by, readers – indeed, this will often be a key point in the marketing of the book. Although the different authorial voices are unique, there is a sense of the anthology as a unified text.

Activity 5 Reading: themed anthologies

Read extracts from editors' introductions to four very different anthologies (Reading 17.2). *The Black Dreams* (Chamberlain-King, 2021) is a collection of uncanny short fiction set in Northern Ireland. *The Good Immigrant* (Shukla, 2016) brings together 21 reflections on race in contemporary Britain. In *Cast a Long Shadow* (Stansfield and Oakley, 2022) the focus is on short crime fiction by Welsh women writers, while *Antlers of Water* (Jamie, 2020) features nature writing about Scotland.

In their introductions, the editors reveal the themes of their anthologies through their discussions on the impulses that brought them into being, their hopes or expectations for how they might be received and what they might achieve.

As you read, consider again the themes that have emerged from your own reflections throughout this chapter.

Discussion

In all of these anthologies, there is an overlap between themes and organising principles. The first is where the authors live (Northern Ireland, England, Wales and Scotland, respectively), and the second is the subject of their writing – 'weird' fiction; the experience of people of colour in contemporary Britain; crime fiction and nature writing. Also, with the exception of *Antlers of Water*, there is consistency in the form within each anthology: both *The Black Dreams* and *Cast a Long Shadow* are fiction, while *The Good*

Immigrant is non-fiction. *Antlers of Water*, on the other hand, contains poetry, prose, song lyrics and visual art.

8 Conclusion

This chapter has explored the subterranean nature of theme in fiction, life writing, drama and poetry sequences. The novelist Nigel Watts compares theme to 'a unifying thread, a line of thought that leads through a story upon which the plot events are strung like beads' (Watts, 1996, p. 115). The thread, no matter what the form, should not be too visible. If you prefer a musical metaphor with which to describe theme, then you might say that it is important that theme's echoes are not too loud. The most interesting sequences are connected in a surreptitious and imaginative way so that the reader can delight in glimpsing the thread, sensing the echo. Whether you are compiling a collection of stories, dramatic episodes or poems which are united by theme, take great pleasure in finding the best order – the richest, most tantalising and most powerful order or sequence. Laying the trail of your theme, as you discover it, is one of the most enjoyable experiences for any writer – and following the trail will engross your reader.

References

Atkinson, K. (2002) *Not the end of the world*. London: Doubleday.

Baldick, C. (2008) 'Theme', in *The Oxford dictionary of literary terms*. 3rd edn. Available at: https://www.oxfordreference.com/display/10.1093/acref/9780199208272.001.0001/acref-9780199208272-e-1141 (Accessed: 26 May 2023).

Bell, L. (2023a) *Rare stories*. Manchester: Bridge House.

Bell, L. (2023b) Email to Heather Richardson, 31 May.

Campbell, J. (2022a) *Cat brushing*. London: riverrun.

Campbell, J. (2022b) 'She's 80 years old, she's furious, and she just published her first book'. Interview with Jane Campbell. Interviewed by H. Schwedel for *Slate*, 15 October. Available at: https://slate.com/culture/2022/10/octogenarian-debut-author-jane-campbell-cat-brushing-book.html (Accessed: 14 March 2024).

Campbell, S. and Yeh, J. (2023) Interview with Siobhán Campbell and Jane Yeh. Interviewed by H. Richardson for the Open University module A363 *Advanced creative writing*, 24 April.

Chamberlain-King, R. (ed.) (2021) *The black dreams: strange stories from Northern Ireland*. Belfast: The Blackstaff Press.

Cunningham, M. (1999) *The hours*. New York, NY: Farrar, Straus and Giroux.

Doyle, M. (2017) *A book of untruths*. London: Faber & Faber.

Duffy, C.A. (1990) *The other country*. London: Anvil.

Enright, A. (2004) *Making babies*. London: Jonathan Cape.

Groarke, V. (1999) *Other people's houses*. Oldcastle: The Gallery Press.

Gross, P. (1998) 'The wasting game', in P. Gross, *The wasting game*. Tarset: Bloodaxe Books, pp. 10–17.

Hare, D. (2003) *The hours, based on the novel by Michael Cunningham*. [Screenplay]. London: Faber.

The hours (2002) Directed by S. Daldry. [Feature film]. Los Angeles, CA: Paramount Pictures.

Hughes, F. (2002) *Waxworks*. Tarset: Bloodaxe Books.

Jamie, K. (ed.) (2020) *Antlers of water: writing on the nature and environment of Scotland*. Edinburgh: Canongate.

Miller, K. (2010) *A light song of light*. Manchester: Carcanet.

Nelson, M. (2009) *Bluets*. Seattle, WA: Wave Books.

Parks, S.-L. (1994) 'Possession', in S.-L. Parks, *The America play and other works*. New York, NY: Theatre Communications Group, pp. 11–12. Available at: https://ebookcentral.proquest.com/lib/open/detail.action?docID=939916 (Accessed: 24 March 2024).

Parks, S.-L. (2006) *365 days/365 plays*. New York, NY: Concord Theatricals.

Rattigan, T. (1955) *Separate tables*. London: Hamish Hamilton.

Richards, D. (2019) *Outpost: a journey to the wild ends of the earth*. Edinburgh: Canongate.

Richardson, H. (2019) 'Eastbourne', *Poetry Ireland Review*, 127, p. 69.

Shukla, N. (ed.) (2016) *The good immigrant*. London: Unbound.

Smith, A. (2001) *Hotel world*. London: Hamish Hamilton.

Stansfield, K. and Oakley, C. (eds) (2022) *Cast a long shadow: Welsh women writing crime*. Aberystwyth: Honno Press.

Symmons Roberts, M. (2008) 'Last words', in M. Symmons Roberts, *The half-healed*. London: Jonathan Cape, pp. 6, 14, 17, 21, 23, 28, 31, 36, 40, 45, 48, 50.

Tennant, E. (1976) *Hotel de dream*. London: Gollancz.

Thorpe, A. (1992) *Ulverton*. London: Secker & Warburg.

Thorpe, A. (1996) 'An Interview with Adam Thorpe'. Interview with Adam Thorpe. Interviewed by S. Hagenauer for *Erfurt Electronic Studies in English 3*, 10 November. Available at: https://webdoc.sub.gwdg.de/edoc/ia/eese/artic96/hagenau/3_96.html#Ulver (Accessed: 19 March 2024).

Tomalin, C. (2006) *Thomas Hardy: the time-torn man*. London: Viking.

Trevor, W. (1965) *The boarding-house*. London: The Bodley Head.

Watts, N. (1996) *Writing a novel and getting it published*. London: Hodder & Stoughton.

Part 4
Readings

Chapter 1 readings

Reading 1.1 'A Real Durwan'

Jhumpa Lahiri

> Jhumpa Lahiri was born in Britain and moved to the United States as a child with her Bengali parents. She is a writer, editor and translator of fiction, essays and poetry, and has written in both English and Italian. In her work, she writes the voices of many different characters and explores issues including love, identity and immigrant experiences.

BOORI MA, sweeper of the stairwell, had not slept in two nights. So the morning before the third night she shook the mites out of her bedding. She shook the quilts once underneath the letter boxes where she lived, then once again at the mouth of the alley, causing the crows who were feeding on vegetable peels to scatter in several directions.

As she started up the four flights to the roof, Boori Ma kept one hand placed over the knee that swelled at the start of every rainy season. That meant that her bucket, quilts, and the bundle of reeds which served as her broom all had to be braced under one arm. Lately Boori Ma had been thinking that the stairs were getting steeper; climbing them felt more like climbing a ladder than a staircase. She was sixty-four years old, with hair in a knot no larger than a walnut, and she looked almost as narrow from the front as she did from the side.

In fact, the only thing that appeared three-dimensional about Boori Ma was her voice: brittle with sorrows, as tart as curds, and shrill enough to grate meat from a coconut. It was with this voice that she enumerated, twice a day as she swept the stairwell, the details of her plight and losses suffered since her deportation to Calcutta after Partition. At that time, she maintained, the turmoil had separated her from a husband, four daughters, a two-storey brick house, a rosewood *almari*, and a number of coffer boxes whose skeleton keys she still wore, along with her life savings, tied to the free end of her sari.

Aside from her hardships, the other thing Boori Ma liked to chronicle was easier times. And so, by the time she reached the second-floor landing, she had already drawn to the whole building's attention the menu of her third daughter's wedding night. 'We married her to a school principal. The rice was cooked in rosewater. The mayor was invited. Everybody washed their fingers in pewter bowls.' Here she paused, evened out her breath, and readjusted the supplies under her arm. She took the opportunity also to chase a cockroach out of the banister poles, then continued: 'Mustard prawns were steamed in banana leaves. Not a delicacy was spared. Not that this was an extravagance for us. At our house, we ate goat twice a week. We had a pond on our property, full of fish.'

By now Boori Ma could see some light from the roof spilling into the stairwell. And though it was only eight o'clock, the sun was already strong enough to warm the last of the cement steps under her feet. It was a very old building, the kind with bathwater that still had to be stored in drums, windows without glass, and privy scaffolds made of bricks.

'A man came to pick our dates and guavas. Another clipped hibiscus. Yes, there I tasted life. Here I eat my dinner from a rice pot.' At this point in the recital Boori Ma's ears started to burn; a pain chewed through her swollen knee. 'Have I mentioned that I crossed the border with just two bracelets on my wrist? Yet there was a day when my feet touched nothing but marble. Believe me, don't believe me, such comforts you cannot even dream them.'

Whether there was any truth to Boori Ma's litanies no one could be sure. For one thing, every day, the perimeters of her former estate seemed to double, as did the contents of her *almari* and coffer boxes. No one doubted she was a refugee; the accent in her Bengali made that clear. Still, the residents of this particular flat-building could not reconcile Boori Ma's claims to prior wealth alongside the more likely account of how she had crossed the East Bengal border, with the thousands of others, on the back of a truck, between sacks of hemp. And yet there were days when Boori Ma insisted that she had come to Calcutta on a bullock cart.

'Which was it, by truck or by cart?' the children sometimes asked her on their way to play cops and robbers in the alley. To which Boori Ma would reply, shaking the free end of her sari so that the skeleton keys rattled, 'Why demand specifics? Why scrape lime from a betel leaf? Believe me, don't believe me. My life is composed of such griefs you cannot even dream them.'

So she garbled facts. She contradicted herself. She embellished almost everything. But her rants were so persuasive, her fretting so vivid, that it was not easy to dismiss her.

What kind of landowner ended up sweeping stairs? That was what Mr. Dalal of the third floor always wondered as he passed Boori Ma on his way to and from the office, where he filed receipts for a wholesale distributor of rubber tubes, pipes and valve fittings in the plumbing district of College Street.

Bechareh, she probably constructs tales as a way of mourning the loss of her family, was the collective surmise of most of the wives.

And 'Boori Ma's mouth is full of ashes, but she is the victim of changing times' was the refrain of old Mr. Chatterjee. He had neither strayed from his balcony nor opened a newspaper since Independence, but in spite of this fact, or maybe because of it, his opinions were always highly esteemed.

The theory eventually circulated that Boori Ma had once worked as hired help for a prosperous *zamindar* back east, and was therefore capable of exaggerating her past at such elaborate lengths and heights. Her throaty impostures hurt no one. All agreed that she was a superb entertainer. In exchange for her lodging below the letter boxes, Boori Ma kept their crooked stairwell spotlessly clean. Most of all, the residents liked that Boori Ma, who slept each night behind the collapsible gate, stood guard between them and the outside world.

No one in this particular flat-building owned much worth stealing. The second-floor widow, Mrs. Misra, was the only one with a telephone. Still, the residents were thankful that Boori Ma patrolled activities in the alley, screened the itinerant peddlers who came to sell combs and shawls from door to door, was able to summon a rickshaw at a moment's calling, and could, with a few slaps of her broom, rout any suspicious character who strayed into the area in order to spit, urinate, or cause some other trouble.

In short, over the years, Boori Ma's services came to resemble those of a real *durwan*. Though under normal circumstances this was no job for a woman, she honored the responsibility, and maintained a vigil no less punctilious than if she were the gatekeeper of a house on Lower Circular Road, or Jodhpur Park, or any other fancy neighborhood.

On the rooftop Boori Ma hung her quilts over the clothesline. The wire, strung diagonally from one corner of the parapet to the other, stretched across her view of television antennas, billboards, and the distant arches of Howrah Bridge. Boori Ma consulted the horizon on all four sides. Then she ran the tap at the base of the cistern. She washed her face, rinsed her feet, and rubbed two fingers over her teeth. After this she started to beat the quilts on each side with her broom. Every now and then she stopped and squinted at the cement, hoping to identify the culprit of her sleepless nights. She was so absorbed in this process that it was some moments before she noticed Mrs. Dalal of the third floor, who had come to set a tray of salted lemon peels out to dry in the sun.

'Whatever is inside this quilt is keeping me awake at night,' Boori Ma said. 'Tell me, where do you see them?'

Mrs. Dalal had a soft spot for Boori Ma; occasionally she gave the old woman some ginger paste with which to flavor her stews. 'I don't see anything,' Mrs. Dalal said after a while. She had diaphanous eyelids and very slender toes with rings on them.

'Then they must have wings,' Boori Ma concluded. She put down her broom and observed one cloud passing behind another. 'They fly away before I can squash them. But just see my back. I must be purple from their bites.'

Mrs. Dalal lifted the drape of Boori Ma's sari, a cheap white weave with a border the color of a dirty pond. She examined the skin above and below her blouse, cut in a style no longer sold in shops. Then she said, 'Boori Ma, you are imagining things.'

'I tell you, these mites are eating me alive.'

'It could be a case of prickly heat,' Mrs. Dalal suggested.

At this Boori Ma shook the free end of her sari and made her skeleton keys rattle. She said, 'I know prickly heat. This is not prickly heat. I haven't slept in three, perhaps four days. Who can count? I used to keep a clean bed. Our linens were muslin. Believe me, don't believe me, our mosquito nets were as soft as silk. Such comforts you cannot even dream them.'

'I cannot dream them,' Mrs. Dalal echoed. She lowered her diaphanous eyelids and sighed. 'I cannot dream them, Boori Ma. I live in two broken rooms, married to a man who sells toilet parts.' Mrs. Dalal turned away and looked at one of the quilts. She ran a finger over part of the stitching. Then she asked:

'Boori Ma, how long have you slept on this bedding?'

Boori Ma put a finger to her lips before replying that she could not remember.

'Then why no mention of it until today? Do you think it's beyond us to provide you with clean quilts? An oilcloth, for that matter?' She looked insulted.

'There is no need,' Boori Ma said. 'They are clean now. I beat them with my broom.'

'I am hearing no arguments,' Mrs. Dalal said. 'You need a new bed. Quilts, a pillow. A blanket when winter comes.' As she spoke Mrs. Dalal kept track of the necessary items by touching her thumb to the pads of her fingers.

'On festival days the poor came to our house to be fed,' Boori Ma said. She was filling her bucket from the coal heap on the other side of the roof.

'I will have a word with Mr. Dalal when he returns from the office,' Mrs. Dalal called back as she headed down the stairs. 'Come in the afternoon. I will give you some pickles and some powder for your back.'

'It's not prickly heat,' Boori Ma said.

It was true that prickly heat was common during the rainy season. But Boori Ma preferred to think that what irritated her bed, what stole her sleep, what burned like peppers across her thinning scalp and skin, was of a less mundane origin.

She was ruminating on these things as she swept the stairwell – she always worked from the top to bottom – when it started to rain. It came slapping across the roof like a boy in slippers too big for him and washed Mrs. Dalal's lemon peels into the gutter. Before pedestrians could open their umbrellas, it rushed down collars, pockets, and shoes. In that particular flat-building and all the neighboring buildings, creaky shutters were closed and tied with petticoat strings to the window bars.

At the time, Boori Ma was working all the way down on the second-floor landing. She looked up the ladderlike stairs, and as the sound of falling water tightened around her she knew her quilts were turning into yogurt.

But then she recalled her conversation with Mrs. Dalal. And so she continued, at the same pace, to sweep the dust, cigarette ends, and lozenge wrappers from the rest of the steps, until she reached the letter boxes at the bottom. To keep out the wind, she rummaged through her baskets for some newspapers and crammed them into the diamond-shaped openings of the collapsible gate. Then on her bucket of coals she set her lunch to boil, and monitored the flame with a plaited palm fan.

That afternoon, as was her habit, Boori Ma reknotted her hair, united the loose end of her sari, and counted out her life savings. She had just woken from a nap of twenty minutes, which she had taken on a temporary bed made from newspapers. The rain had stopped and now the sour smell that rises from wet mango leaves was hanging low over the alley.

On certain afternoons Boori Ma visited her fellow residents. She enjoyed drifting in and out of various households. The residents, for their part, assured Boori Ma that she was always welcome; they never drew the latch bars across their doors except at night. They went about their business, scolding children or adding up expenses or picking stones out of the evening rice. From time to time she was handed a glass of tea, the cracker tin was passed in her direction, and she helped children shoot chips across the carom board. Knowing not to sit on the furniture, she crouched, instead, in doorways and hallways, and observed gestures and manners in the same way a person tends to watch traffic in a foreign city.

On this particular afternoon Boori Ma decided to accept Mrs. Dalal's invitation. Her back still ached, even after napping on the newspapers, and she was beginning to want some prickly-heat powder after all. She picked up her broom – she never felt quite herself without it – and was about to climb upstairs, when a rickshaw pulled up to the collapsible gate.

It was Mr. Dalal. The years he had spent filing receipts had left him with purple crescents under his eyes. But today his gaze was bright. The tip of his tongue played between his teeth, and in the clamp of his thighs he held two small ceramic basins.

'Boori Ma, I have a job for you. Help me carry these basins upstairs.' He pressed a folded handkerchief to his forehead and throat and gave the rickshaw driver a coin. Then he and Boori Ma carried the basins all the way up to the third floor. It wasn't until they were inside the flat that he finally announced, to Mrs. Dalal, to Boori Ma, and to a few other residents who had followed them out of curiosity, the following things: That his hours filing receipts for a distributor of rubber tubes, pipes, and valve fittings had ended. That the distributor himself, who craved fresher air, and whose profits had doubled, was opening a second branch in Burdwan. And that, following an assessment of his sedulous performance over the years, the distributor was promoting Mr. Dalal to manage the College Street branch. In his excitement on his way home through the plumbing district, Mr. Dalal had bought two basins.

'What are we supposed to do with two basins in a two-room flat?' Mrs. Dalal demanded. She had already been sulking over her lemon peels. 'Who ever heard of it? I still cook on kerosene. You refuse to apply for a phone. And I have yet to see the fridge you promised when we married. You expect two basins to make up for all that?'

The argument that followed was loud enough to be heard all the way down to the letter boxes. It was loud enough, and long enough, to rise above a second spell of rain that fell after dark. It was loud enough even to distract Boori Ma as she swept the stairwell from top to bottom for the second time that day, and for this reason she spoke neither of her hardships, nor of easier times. She spent the night on a bed of newspapers.

The argument between Mr. and Mrs. Dalal was still more or less in effect early the next morning, when a barefoot team of workmen came to install the basins. After a night of tossing and pacing, Mr. Dalal had decided to install one basin in the sitting room of their flat, and the other one on the stairwell of the building, on the first-floor landing. 'This way everyone can use it,' he explained from door to door. The residents were delighted; for years they had all brushed their teeth with stored water poured from mugs.

Mr. Dalal, meanwhile, was thinking: A sink on the stairwell is sure to impress visitors. Now that he was a company manager, who could say who might visit the building?

The workmen toiled for several hours. They ran up and down the stairs and ate their lunches squatting against the banister poles. They hammered, shouted, spat, and cursed. They wiped their sweat with the ends of their turbans. In general, they made it impossible for Boori Ma to sweep the stairwell that day.

To occupy the time, Boori Ma retired to the rooftop. She shuffled along the parapets, but her hips were sore from sleeping on newspapers. After consulting the horizon on all four sides, she tore what was left of her quilts into several strips and resolved to polish the banister poles at a later time.

By early evening the residents gathered to admire the day's labours. Even Boori Ma was urged to rinse her hands under the clear running water. She sniffed. 'Our bathwater was scented with petals and attars. Believe me, don't believe me, it was a luxury you cannot dream.'

Mr. Dalal proceeded to demonstrate the basin's various features. He turned each faucet completely on and completely off. Then he turned on both faucets at the same time, to illustrate the difference in water pressure. Lifting a small lever between the faucets allowed water to collect in the basin, if desired.

'The last word in elegance,' Mr. Dalal concluded.

'A sure sign of changing times,' Mr. Chatterjee reputedly admitted from his balcony.

Among the wives, however, resentment quickly brewed. Standing in line to brush their teeth in the mornings, each grew frustrated with having to wait her turn, for having to wipe the faucets after every use, and for not being able to leave her own soap and toothpaste tube on the basin's narrow periphery. The Dalals had their own sink; why did the rest of them have to share?

'Is it beyond us to buy sinks of our own?' one of them finally burst out one morning.

'Are the Dalals the only ones who can improve the conditions of this building?' asked another.

Rumors began spreading: that, following their argument, Mr. Dalal had consoled his wife by buying her two kilos of mustard oil, a Kashmiri shawl, a dozen cakes of sandalwood soap; that Mr. Dalal had filed an application for a telephone line; that Mrs. Dalal did nothing but wash her hands in her basin all day. As if this weren't enough, the next morning, a taxi bound for Howrah Station crammed its wheels into the alley; the Dalals were going to Simla for ten days.

'Boori Ma, I haven't forgotten. We will bring you back a sheep's-hair blanket made in the mountains,' Mrs. Dalal said through the open window of the taxi. She was holding a leather purse in her lap which matched the turquoise border of her sari.

'We will bring two!' cried Mr. Dalal, who was sitting beside his wife, checking his pockets to make sure his wallet was in place.

Of all the people who lived in that particular flat-building, Boori Ma was the only one who stood by the collapsible gate and wished them a safe journey.

As soon as the Dalals were gone, the other wives began planning renovations of their own. One decided to barter a stack of her wedding bracelets and commissioned a white-washer to freshen the walls of the stairwell. Another pawned her sewing machine and summoned an exterminator. A third went to the silversmith and sold back a set of pudding bowls; she intended to have the shutters painted yellow.

Workers began to occupy this particular flat-building night and day. To avoid the traffic, Boori Ma took to sleeping on the rooftop. So many people passed in and out of the collapsible gate, so many others clogged the alley at all times, that there was no point in keeping track of them.

After a few days Boori Ma moved her baskets and her cooking bucket to the rooftop as well. There was no need to use the basin downstairs, for she could just as easily wash, as she always had, from the cistern tap. She still planned to polish the banister poles with the strips she had torn from her quilts. She continued to sleep on her newspapers.

More rains came. Below the dripping awning, a newspaper pressed over her head, Boori Ma squatted and watched the monsoon ants as they marched along the clothesline, carrying eggs in their mouths. Damper winds soothed her back. Her newspapers were running low.

Her mornings were long, her afternoons longer. She could not remember her last glass of tea. Thinking neither of her hardships nor of earlier times, she wondered when the Dalals would return with her new bedding.

She grew restless on the roof, and so for some exercise, Boori Ma started circling the neighbourhood in the afternoons. Red broom in hand, sari smeared with newsprint ink, she wandered through markets and began spending her life savings on small treats: today a packet of puffed rice, tomorrow some cashews, the day after that, a cup of sugarcane juice. One day she walked as far as the bookstalls on College Street. The next day she walked even farther, to the produce markets in Bow Bazaar. It was there, while she was standing in a shopping arcade surveying jackfruits and persimmons, that she felt something tugging on the free end of her sari. When she looked, the rest of her life savings and her skeleton keys were gone.

The residents were waiting for Boori Ma when she returned that afternoon at the collapsible gate. Baleful cries rang up and down the stairwell, all echoing the same news: the basin on the stairwell had been stolen. There was a big hole in the recently whitewashed wall, and a tangle of rubber tubes and pipes was sticking out of it. Chunks of plaster littered the landing. Boori Ma gripped her reed broom and said nothing.

In their haste the residents practically carried Boori Ma up the stairs to the roof, where they planted her on one side of the clothesline and started screaming at her from the other.

'This is all her doing,' one of them hollered, pointing at Boori Ma. 'She informed the robbers. Where was she when she was supposed to guard the gate?'

'For days she has been wandering the streets, speaking to strangers,' another reported.

'We shared our coal, gave her a place to sleep. How could she betray us this way?' a third wanted to know.

Though none of them spoke directly to Boori Ma, she replied, 'Believe me, believe me. I did not inform the robbers.'

'For years we have put up with your lies,' they retorted.

'You expect us, now, to believe you?'

Their recriminations persisted. How would they explain it to the Dalals? Eventually they sought the advice of Mr. Chatterjee. They found him sitting on his balcony, watching a traffic jam.

One of the second-floor residents said, 'Boori Ma has endangered the security of this building. We have valuables. The widow Mrs. Misra lives alone with her phone. What should we do?'

Mr. Chatterjee considered their arguments. As he thought things over, he adjusted the shawl that was wrapped around his shoulders and gazed at the bamboo scaffolding that now surrounded his balcony. The shutters behind him, colorless for as long as he could remember, had been painted yellow. Finally he said:

'Boori Ma's mouth is full of ashes. But that is nothing new. What is new is the face of this building. What a building like this needs is a real *durwan*.'

So the residents tossed her bucket and rags, her baskets and reed broom, down the stairwell, past the letter boxes, through the collapsible gate, and into the alley. Then they tossed out Boori Ma. All were eager to begin their search for a real *durwan*.

From the pile of belongings Boori Ma kept only her broom. 'Believe me, believe me,' she said once more as her figure began to recede. She shook the free end of her sari, but nothing rattled.

Source: Lahiri, J. (1999) 'A real durwan', in J. Lahiri, *Interpreter of maladies: stories*. London: Flamingo, pp. 70–82.

Chapter 2 readings

Reading 2.1 Extract from the novel *The Water Dancer*

Ta-Nehisi Coates

> Ta-Nehisi Coates is an author and journalist. He has written essays and articles, as well as fiction, non-fiction and comic books. His work often draws on his experiences as an African American male in the United States.

Content note: This reading alludes to slavery and abduction.

Note: Although *The Water Dancer* is set in the south of pre-Civil War America, Coates rarely uses the word 'slave' to describe the people he names in the book as 'Tasked'.

ALL MY LIFE I had wanted to get out. I was unoriginal in this—all the Tasked felt the same. But, separate from them, separate from all of Lockless, I possessed the means.

   I was a strange child. I talked before I walked, though I never talked much, because more than anything, I watched and remembered. I would hear others speak, but I did not so much hear them as see them, their words taking form before me as pictures, chains of colors, lines, textures, and shapes that I could store inside of me. And it was my gift to, at a moment's beckoning, retrieve the images and translate them back into the exact words with which they had been conjured.

…

… It had happened when I was nine years old, the day after my mother was taken and sold. I awoke that cold winter morning knowing she was gone as a fact. But I had no pictures, no memory, of any goodbye, indeed no pictures of her at all. Instead I recalled my mother in the secondhand, so that I was sure that she had been taken, in the same way that I was sure that there were lions in Africa, though I had never seen one. I searched for a fully fleshed memory, and found only scraps. Screams. Pleading—someone pleading with me. The strong smell of horses. And in the haze of it all, an image flickering in and out of focus: a long trough of water. I was terrified, not simply because I had lost my mother, but because I was a boy who remembered all his yesterdays in the crispest colors, and textures so rich I could drink them. And there I was, awakening with a start to nothing but ephemera, shadows, and screams.

Source: Coates, T.-N. (2020) *The water dancer*. London: Penguin, pp. 10–11.

Reading 2.2 Extract from the novel *The Power*

Naomi Alderman

> Naomi Alderman is a novelist from London who has also written for gaming and podcasts, and often presents radio programmes on science. Her fiction ranges across a variety of genres, often exploring themes relating to gender, power and religion.

There's a girl on the beach at high tide, lighting up the sea with her hands. The girls from the convent watch her from the clifftop. She's waded into the ocean up to her waist, higher. She's not even wearing a bathing suit – just jeans and a black cardigan. And she's setting the sea on fire.

It's coming on to dusk, so they can see it clearly. Threads of kelp are spread in a fine, disorderly mesh across the surface of the water. And when she sends her power into the water, the particulate and debris glow dimly, and the seaweed brighter yet. The light extends in a wide circle around her, lit from beneath, like the great eye of the ocean gazing at the sky. There's a sound like popping candy as the branching limbs of the sargasso plants smoulder and the buds swell and burst. There's a marine scent, salt and green and pungent. She must be half a mile away, but they can smell it from the clifftop. They think at any moment she must have used out her power, but it goes on; the flickering luminescence in the bay, the scent as the crabs and small fish rise to the surface of the water.

Source: Alderman, N. (2017) *The power*. London: Penguin, p. 99.

Reading 2.3 Extract from the novel *Neverwhere*

Neil Gaiman

> Neil Gaiman is a prolific author of fiction, non-fiction and graphic novels, whose writing crosses genres and audiences. Many of his works have been adapted for film, television, theatre and radio. He grew up in Sussex and credits the county's local librarians with fostering in him a lifelong love of reading.

Content note: Please be aware that this reading makes passing reference to slavery.

Richard stood there, alone in the throng, drinking it in. It was pure madness. Of that there was no doubt at all. It was loud, and brash, and insane, and it was, in many ways, quite wonderful. People argued, haggled, shouted, sang. They hawked and touted their wares, and loudly declaimed the superiority of their merchandise. Music was playing – a dozen different kinds of music, being played a dozen different ways on a score of different instruments, most of them improvised, improved, improbable. Richard could smell food. All kinds of food: the smells of curries and spices seemed to predominate, with, beneath them, the smells of grilling meats and mushrooms. Stalls had been set up all through the shop, next to, or even on, counters that, during the day, had sold perfume, or watches, or amber, or silk scarves. Everybody was buying. Everybody was selling. Richard listened to the market cries as he began to wander through the crowds.

'Lovely fresh dreams. First-class nightmares. We got 'em. Get yer lovely nightmares here.'

'Weapons! Arm yourself! Defend your cellar, cave or hole! You want to hit 'em? We got 'em. Come on darling, come on over here …'

'Rubbish!' screamed a fat, elderly woman, in Richard's ear, as he passed her malodorous stall. 'Junk!' she continued. 'Garbage! Trash! Offal! Debris! Come and get it! Nothing whole or undamaged! Crap, tripe and useless piles of shit. You know you want it.'

A man in armour beat a small drum, and chanted as he did so, 'Lost Property. Roll up, roll up, and see for yourself. Lost property. None of your found muck here. Everything guaranteed properly lost.'

Richard wandered through the huge rooms of the store, like a man in a trance. He was unable to even guess how many people there were at the night market: a thousand? Two thousand? Five thousand?

One stall was piled high with bottles, full bottles and empty bottles of every shape and every size, from bottles of booze to one huge glimmering bottle that could have contained nothing but a captive djinn; another sold lamps, and candles, made of many kinds of wax and tallow; a man thrust what appeared to be a child's severed hand clutching a candle towards him, as he passed, muttering 'Hand of Glory, sir? Send 'em up the wooden hill to Bedfordshire. Guaranteed to work.' Richard hurried past, not wishing to find out what a Hand of Glory was, nor how it worked; he passed a stall selling glittering gold and silver jewellery, another selling jewellery made from what looked like the valves and wires of antique radios; there were stalls that sold every manner of book and magazine; others that sold clothes – old clothes patched, and mended, and made strange; several tattooists; something that he was almost certain was a small slave market (he kept well clear of this); a dentist's chair, with a foot-operated manual drill, with a line of miserable people standing beside it, waiting to have their teeth pulled or filled by a young man who seemed to be having altogether too good a time; a bent old man selling unlikely things that might have been hats and might have been examples of modern art; something that looked very much like a portable shower facility; even a blacksmith's …

Source: Gaiman, N. (2013) *Neverwhere*. London: Headline Publishing Group, pp. 109–111.

Reading 2.4 Extract from the memoir *Russian Journal*

Andrea Lee

> Andrea Lee is an American author of memoirs, short fiction and novels. Often drawing on her childhood in a middle-class, Black family, her writing creates an ongoing dialogue around the places where cultures, races and imaginations intersect. *Russian Journal*, Lee's account of a year spent in Russia, was published in 1981.

Note: *Russian Journal* was published before *perestroika*, during a time of change in Russia following the decline of communism. *Perestroika* was a political movement for reformation within the Communist Party of the Soviet Union during the 1980s and is widely associated with the Soviet leader Mikhail Gorbachev and his *glasnost* (meaning 'openness') of policy reform.

Last week, three days before Easter, I went to the peasant market near the Byelorussian train station and found it thronged with people shopping for the holiday, the day the State grudgingly permits to be celebrated but does its best to suppress. Instead of durable winter vegetables – big pale cabbages, waxed turnips, giant, mud-covered carrots – the counters were heaped with the fresh spring greens that were just beginning to make their frail way into the world: sorrel, dill, dandelion leaves. A *babushka*, perhaps the oldest in the world, with earth-colored wrinkles closing in on themselves so that her tiny gleaming eyes were scarcely visible, and skinny fingers as yellow as beeswax, sold me a bunch of herbs, mumbling, 'Now, this will make you a fine Easter soup!' After her trembling fingers had counted out the kopecks in change, she crossed herself.

At outdoor booths in the sunny market courtyard, vendors were selling brightly painted Easter eggs; I bought several from a short man with cheerful blue eyes and frostbite marks on his cheeks. The eggs are all exuberantly painted with naive scenes that suggest a religious and secular rejoicing at the fullness of new life awakening in the world: they show squat onion-domed Orthodox churches, ducklings in baskets, young suitors hurrying along with bouquets of flowers, bearded peasants clutching enormous sturgeons. All of the eggs bear the inscription XB, the Russian abbreviation for *Khristos Voshes* – Christ Is Risen. One of my most amusing eggs bears the XB inscription and, underneath it, the message: 'Happy Easter, dear Comrades!' Wishful thinking. Easter and comrades in fact don't mix at all. It was pleasant to walk out into the balmy afternoon with my net bag filled with green leaves and Easter eggs, but on the subway I began to notice the people staring at the colorful paint, and I started to feel that I was openly carrying contraband. Later I heard that the market had been raided, and the Easter eggs, absurdly enough, seized by the police.

Source: Lee, A. (1993) 'Russian journal', in M. Morris and L. O'Connor (eds) *The Virago book of women travellers*. London: Virago, pp. 456–457.

Chapter 3 readings

Reading 3.1 'Getting High in the Low Countries'

David Webster

> David Webster is a philosopher and specialist in pedagogy. He writes about Buddhism, the nature of belief, the blues and death. He had a stroke in 2012 and, after rehabilitation, climbed the Excalibur tower, a climbing wall in Groningen in the Netherlands, for a charity event.

Content note: Please be aware that this reading briefly mentions the experience of a stroke.

Middle-age, it seems, is full of surprises. Of twists and turns that befuddle attempts at prediction and sense-making. These thoughts run though my head as I fiddle with my harness at the base of the 'Excalibur' climbing tower in Groningen, Holland. I glance at my companions. My climbing partner, D, is, carefully, checking the 80-metre rope we have borrowed from the friendly, laid-back staff. He's not looking very laid-back though. My teenage son has his harness on, in seconds, and is taking in his surroundings seemingly unaffected by the rising 'why did we agree to this madness' sensation that I am failing to ignore. Further away, a non-climbing friend readies a camera and offers vaguely encouraging gestures.

The journey to this tower began years before. In my 30s, my path seemed marked out. Work. Marriage. Two young kids. Pretty amazing. Happy. I hadn't exercised since my teenage pushbike was stolen in the 1980s. Good living was incrementally swelling my bulk, but I barely noticed. Until I did. A predictable late 30s male turn of events – albeit somewhat startling to me. Whether it was merely shock at failed-to-avoid-mirror reflections, or an existential foreshadowing of mortality, I started my mid-life crisis slightly ahead of schedule, and traded the pleasures of sloth, booze, cake and cigarettes with the pleasures of exercise-generated endorphins, and even more cake. I even ran (if that's the right word) a marathon in the year I turned 40. Fairly predictable in terms of demographics and mass behaviour, but, as I say, exceptionally startling to me. It was a change of direction, but one where I felt I could accurately envisage the road ahead. As usual, I was wrong.

By now, I can detect a slight quiver in my hands. The route we have chosen up the 37m tower is the easiest grade they have, and we are on the nicely reclining side. The climb is fairly small in terms of what people achieve in everyday, multi-pitch excursions in the hills. Nonetheless, the starkness of the contrast between the flatness around Groningen, the flatness we saw as the train from Amsterdam sped us here last night, and the looming tower, is remarkable. Having checked my harness seventeen times, I concentrate on tying on to the rope, and affecting a chirpy nonchalance. I decide I need to think some better thoughts. People have sponsored us – so bottling out is not an option. It is an organised climbing centre. With opening hours and a café. With cake. As I ask D to check my knot, and as I check his belaying arrangements, I can feel a settling. Not an absence of fear, but a more balanced form of it; balanced by faith in our training, and in the modesty of our ambitions here today.

When you are new to parenting, it all seems about the next day, the next decent night's sleep, the plans for the coming weekend's farm park trip. You know you're in for supermarket tantrums, drinking overpriced, repulsive tea at soft-play centres, making packed lunches for school, having odd patches (either sick or yoghurt, who knows?) on your smartest clothes, and never not being slightly tired. With two kids, this part of life seemed to go on and on. Not in a bad way. Far from it. But nonetheless, the rounds of city-farms, children's menus with broken colouring-in pencils, booster seats and school-gate small talk was firmly established as the new normal. Then it isn't the case. In line with my tendency to have no clue what is about to happen in life, children start to get older and you start to find unexpected (if like, me you weren't thinking ahead) fragments of free time. As this began to emerge in my own experience, it was paralleled by other unforeseen occurrences.

Like millions of idiot parents before me, I had imagined that my children would engage in the hobbies or interests that I had, or tried to cultivate in them. I learnt a lesson there. Both my daughter, and then her younger brother, J, seemed oddly obstinate about choosing their own path in life. For my son, this meant a total disinterest in competitive sports (and competition generally), and a rejection of my youth time preoccupation – cycling. Like solidly anxious parents, we cast about for something non-video-game based that he might actually enjoy like, the fight between biking vs running failed for a long time. Then we found climbing. Our local climbing wall has an atmosphere most climbers will recognise: jokey, but (other than a few topless supermen) non-competitive, and hugely supportive. The kids' club had an ethos that seemed to suit his character. He was soon going twice a week, and I was drinking a lot of tea in their café. Given my mid-life adoption of endorphin-based recreation, it was only matter of time before I had taken their introductory course, and was scraping up F6a routes, staring at comparative harness reviews in magazines, and taking tentative steps towards sport climbing outdoors.

My harness is on properly. My knot is safe. Cameras are pointed at me. Time to stop thinking and start doing. The first clip is near to the ground, and I can clip the rope into it while barely stepping off the lovely, safe, woodchip-covered ground. The familiar action of pushing the rope into a karabiner steadies me further, as I grin and reach. The first few moves are easy. Actually, all the moves are easy. It is an easy route from a technical stance. No problems. This lasts about three further moves. Then I begin to notice what should have been obvious from the ground. The friendly line of red holds, so many that it is almost embarrassing when I look back at the photos, is actually quite near the left-hand edge of the tower. When you look left, you see air, and your stomach does some kind of flip thing. So, I think, don't look left. Don't. Look. Left. Looking mostly to my left, I decide momentum is the key here. Clip, breathe, move, look left, panic a bit, charge like a crazy person to next clip and pull the slack up. Repeat. The climb has a section in the centre where the tower sort of leans back (when climbed from this friendly side). This seems easy. It is all going fine. I'll be at the top before you can say 'middle-aged man in moderately impressive, but ultimately pointless, achievement'. But the flatter section, of course, then kicks up for the final third. The looking left is really getting on my nerves now, as I feel my back move to an undeniably vertical alignment. The notion that I won't actually finish the climb, the one I have been harassing colleagues to sponsor me for, that everyone is aware of via endless social media, hasn't occurred to me till this point. Time to stop thinking again, and breathe.

If previous changes in my life's direction had felt like changing tracks on a train journey, like a set of points taking me to a slightly unforeseen destination, through similar, but largely predictable terrain, what happened to me in later June 2012 felt like a derailment. One evening I was bouldering outdoors with my friend. By the next, I was in the Stroke ward of my local hospital. I had experienced a stroke on waking, and lost control of the right side of my body. That evening, I couldn't walk, my arm refused to obey my brain, and my speech was slurred. I won't drag it out, but I was lucky. I began to hobble by the next day, pacing the ward corridor, generally getting in the way, and over the following months my control over my arm and leg improved. My speech went from what one friend called a 'two-cocktail slur' to a slight impediment only a few now notice. In the September I had a heart procedure to reduce the risk of further strokes. I had rehab. Lots of rehab. The NHS gave me occupational therapy, speech therapy and physiotherapy. I moved pegs in little boards (badly), I balanced on Swiss balls, and I stood on one leg a lot. I read tongue twisters from cards.

In between rehab, I looked at the internet. A lot. I don't remember which online rabbit hole I'd fallen down, but I found myself looking something like 'ten buildings you won't believe are real', or some such click-bait title, and there it was. A curving tower, a short-hop to Holland away, that seemed both doable (familiar fake climbing holds, quickdraws all in place, a café and nearby city), but also dramatic and something I would need to train for. So, after my September operation, I was allowed to resume exercise in early 2013. I still had symptoms, and my right hand is still pretty unreliable when carrying a full mug of tea, but repetition seemed to be what the rehab therapists recommended. Bouldering helped a lot. I would stand two big holds, and just see how many holds I could use. I fell off a lot, but to be honest, I fell off a lot before my stroke too. I talked to my climbing partner D, who I'd climbed with since that first 'intro' course. He was up for it, as was my now-teenage son. So we decided to raise money for the Rehab centre that I'd been so helped by. The rest is what you'd expect. An online sponsorship service, Facebook posts, plane tickets, emails to the climbing centre in Holland (http://www.bjoeks.nl/), trying to do more and more routes at the local wall, trying to lose some of the cake-weight I'd gained while not exercising. In a flash, it was October 2013, and we found ourselves at the base of the Excalibur tower, digesting a hotel breakfast, and hiding nerves under excessive photography and feigned ease.

A few more breaths and only a handful of minutes after clipping into that first quickdraw, I am clipping into the descending point at the top of the climb. I had planned to hoik myself up onto the top of the tower (apparently they will let you bivvy on top for the night if you ask), and take a good look round. That is not going to happen. I fumble my old, not-a-disaster-if-destroyed digital camera from my harness and manage to fake-smile for a selfie; though looking at the picture now – I'm fooling no one. I am flooded with adrenaline, even though I am safe. Harness, rope, bomb-proof industrially-tested anchors; safer than crossing the road. But the adrenaline is something else. It's the whole business. In my mind, in my intentions, this climb is a full-stop to the episode of ill-health in my life. But we are not safe. By the time I had my stroke, I lived a ridiculously healthy life. Running, cycling and a healthy diet (cake excepted) – but it still happened. I lowered down and belayed (with great care, my wife having made very clear threats about what might happen if I allowed my son to be hurt) J and D, while they fled up and down the tower with (what seemed from the outside) ease and rapidity.

The climb was memorable because it was a trip, a spectacle, a dramatic event, but I was wrong to think of it as a something I could use to close off, to bracket out, the fear and loss of control that my illness had brought me. As we sat on trains and planes back to the UK, and the adrenaline faded, I was struck that safety is only ever relative. The unpredictability of life is neither intrinsically good nor bad, but the inevitability of change, of the mutability of what we take as stable is something we'd be wise to acknowledge, before it leaves us dizzy with vertigo, while stood on solid ground. I've heard it said that old age is no place for wimps, but it seems middle-age can also be pretty hazardous terrain.

Source: Webster, D. (2016) 'Getting high in the Low Countries', *Dispirited: how contemporary spirituality makes us stupid, selfish and unhappy*, 25 November. Available at: https://dispirited.org/2016/11/25/getting-high-in-the-low-countries/ (Accessed: 12 February 2024).

Reading 3.2 Extracts from the memoir *Once Upon A Time in the East: A Story of Growing up*

Xiaolu Guo

> Xiaolu Guo is a novelist, memoirist and filmmaker who was born and raised in China before moving to Britain in her late twenties.

Content note: Please be aware that the first extract in this reading briefly mentions capital punishment and the second extract briefly mentions the death of a grandparent.

Village of Shitang

Some people said Shitang was an island, others a peninsula. It lay soaking in the salty water between mainland China and Taiwan, three hundred kilometres from the Taiwanese coast, the first place on the mainland to receive the dawn's rays every morning. In 2000, Shitang was in the news because a ceremonial sun statue had been built on a cliff facing east. The statue didn't look anything like the sun, but more like a tall, thin monolith out of *2001: A Space Odyssey*. It turned the village into a tourist attraction. But for the people of Shitang, it was odd. They had always known their village lay further to the east. Why, suddenly, was it such a big deal?

Shitang literally means stone pond. The word pond in old Chinese was associated with fish. Perhaps thousands of years ago, the area had been a salt-water lagoon next to the sea, before inhabitants built up the land along the seafront, just as Hong Kong or Macau had grown up on reclaimed marsh and swamp. Our family house was a small, green-coloured stone dwelling right on the horn of the peninsula. My grandfather lived upstairs, where he could look straight out to sea through a small window by his bed. In my memory, the sea was always yellow-brown, whether seen from my grandfather's window or from the beach. This yellow-brownness was to do with the large kelp beds growing in the shallow water by the shore. The kelp – we called it *haifa*, the hair of the sea – had tough stalks with broad leaf-like palms and long green-brown stripes. A swarm of shapeless sea snakes, they entangled themselves in the space between land and water. Despite its monstrous shape, we loved the taste. We either stewed it in eel soup or fried it with pork. We never tired of it, along with the tiny kelpfish we harvested from among the algae.

The soil was very salty in Shitang. It was not land suited to agriculture. There were barely any trees growing in the village. But gardenia trees are a determined species. They grew between rocks, their white flowers swirling in the salt-laden wind. It was the only type that could face the sea's yellow foam. I loved their strongly scented flowers. Women picked the buds to tie in their plaits. One day, thirty-odd years later, I stumbled across a gardenia in northern Europe. I breathed in the familiar scent under a clear European sky and cried. This tree didn't belong in my Western life. It was a sorrowful smell, if tinged with a warm feel of nostalgia. It took me straight back to my childhood on the typhoon-ridden coast of the East China Sea.

In that house, only my grandfather had a view over the kelp beds and the foamy sea. My grandmother and I lived downstairs, where the windows on two sides were blocked by our neighbour's washing lines, dried squid and salted ribbonfish hanging from poles. I couldn't say then whether I loved or hated that house. I lived there until I was seven and a half. It was simply our house, our village. There was no comparison, no alternative. But years later, after I had left the village, I felt that Shitang had killed all tenderness in my heart. It had become a rock in my chest. Those hard corners, those jagged stone houses had turned me to stone too. The landscape made me merciless and aggressive.

Our street was originally called Anti-Pirates Passage. In the 1980s, the name was changed to Front Barrier Slope by the local authorities. The original name came from the Ming Dynasty. During that time, the area was under constant attack by pirates from the East Pacific, such that the local militia armed themselves with home-made guns and bombs for protection. Eventually, the village was returned into local hands. But that was four hundred years ago. It felt to me that nothing significant had happened since then, apart from when the local government replaced the Buddha posters in their offices with images of Mao. It had been a backwater, from the days of China's dynasties until now. The only dramatic stories came from the sea, from being close to Taiwan.

In the sixties and seventies, some local fishermen and villagers tried to cross the Taiwan Strait in secret, hoping they would be rewarded by the Nationalist government with gold and farmland as promised. Some succeeded, but very often they were recaptured and punished: some-one's uncle and his brother were caught on the edge of international waters and sentenced to death. 'Shot at dawn' and 'life sentence' came regularly through the village loudspeakers. In the 1970s, no one had private radios or televisions. All news was announced at high volume in the street. Our house directly faced an electricity pole adorned with two loudspeakers. Every so often, in the early morning, we were woken by Communist songs followed by a 'shot at dawn' announcement. Even though capital punishment was normal at that time, hearing these statements still horrified me. I had never witnessed anyone be shot, but the village gossip alone was enough to make me shiver.

Our street doubled as a market, with one end starting in the mountains where a Buddhist temple had been built, and the other end finishing at the beach and the open sea. From our little house we could always hear chatting, crying, arguing, haggling, cockerels crowing, children screaming, pigs oinking from day to night. There was never a moment of peace and quiet. It was simply the sound of China. There were always people everywhere, life everywhere, noise everywhere, for better or for worse.

My grandparents knew everyone in the village. They could spot an outsider instantly. My grandfather was always grumpy, so even though he knew everyone he never greeted anyone in the street. People would greet him and ask: 'How is your boat, Old Guo?' or 'Have you eaten today?' Local longhand for hello. But he never bothered to answer. He would just grunt, or pass them without even raising his eyebrows. My grandmother was the opposite, and greeted everyone she passed. But she also knew that her friendliness could not stop the village gossip about her relationship with her husband. No wonder, as gossip was the only form of entertainment available.

Source: Guo, X. (2017) *Once upon a time in the east: a story of growing up*. London: Vintage, pp. 14–16.

The Return

But the sea was calling me. Swaddled in a warm blanket, we took Moon to visit my grandparents' fishing village. The bus trip to Shitang was easy and quick compared with when I was a child. As we arrived, I discovered that even the station had been relocated. Standing on the asphalted promontory, I breathed in the familiar air. It had the same fishy salty taste, and the same perfume of kelp and ribbonfish hung in the air, but now this was mixed with a strong odour of petrol. As we walked down the hill towards the open sea, I spotted large industrial fishing boats parked in the harbour and my heart leapt. They were different to the ones of my youth, but I loved the sight of them, creating elaborate ripple patterns in the water. As we got closer, I could hear the workers speaking Mandarin Chinese to each other. 'How are the fish today?' I asked one of them in Shitang dialect. He didn't react, so I tried another question. 'Did you catch any big snapper?' But everyone stared back at me with blank expressions. They were migrants, I realised, they didn't know the local tongue. Of course Shitang had always been home to migrant fishermen. My grandfather had been one. I had forgotten, somewhere in the thirty years since his death.

As we stood by the churning waves, Moon woke up in the sling and opened her eyes. Her small head stretched out a little from my jacket, and seemed to peer out at the vast body of water in front of her. What did she see? I wondered. Was it the grey waves of my childhood? Would this picture survive into her later life to form a dim memory of the past? Or, was the sea nothing more than another part of her mother's body and being?

Carrying Moon in the sling, we tried to find our way back to my grandparents' house, but we were soon lost in a maze of new buildings and streets. Whenever I passed some old people sitting out on the street, I wondered if they recognised me. Yet I couldn't recall any of these wrinkled faces. And neither could I find my childhood home. We stopped and I asked a white-haired man if he knew a street named Front Barrier Slope. The old man stared at me for almost half a minute, not responding but only sucking on his cigarette. I then tried again in the local dialect: 'Front Barrier Slope, it used to be called Anti-Pirate Passage.' An obscure smile squeezed itself out across his face and he pointed with his nicotine-stained finger.

Finally, I spotted the old stone house, squashed in between two new premises. It was *our* house. My feet slowed as we approached. The outside hadn't changed at all, although now it was a hair salon filled with fashionable teenagers. Standing outside for a while, I wasn't sure if I should go in and introduce myself to the owner.

After some hesitation, I entered with Moon in my arms. A middle-aged man was cutting the hair of a young girl. Two teenaged boys sat on a bench playing with their phones. I introduced myself to the man: my name, and my family name, Guo.

'Guo?' The man's eyes sparkled, as if he might just recognise me.

'Yes. We owned this house twenty-five years ago, or more actually, twenty-seven years ago, when my grandmother was still alive.'

The man holding the scissors immediately understood who I was. 'I know! I know! Your father sold this house to us! How is he? All well?'

I nodded. I didn't want to explain. He dropped what he was doing, leaving his customer on the chair, and called to his wife to say hello to me. It was an awkward situation. We were invited inside for tea. The sofa we sat on was where my grandmother used to have her old bamboo bed, and where we had slept every night. This was also where, on the very night my grandmother died, I sat with my parents and watched over her coffin under candlelight. As I sat on the edge of the sofa, holding the teacup, I wondered about the upstairs room. My grandfather's room. There was no sound coming from the top floor.

'Oh, the ceiling upstairs has been leaking for a while. We don't use that room,' the wife said, as if she could read my thoughts.

Sunset cast a golden light across the wavy sea and the grey sand. We took the bus back to Wenling before nightfall. Despite my mother's illness, I was longing to return to Britain. There was no use in us staying here with her. We had nothing more to say to each other. Physical closeness hadn't brought us together in any way emotionally. Our minds had occupied different universes for too long, and we couldn't bridge the chasm that had been created. Our relationship had always gone unacknowledged. It was just a fact, like breathing air, or rain in typhoon season. It was unconscious. As if we were performing a script which neither of us had written. We never wanted or liked it, but it had been handed to us by fate. Perhaps I had never looked into my mother's eyes with the hope of understanding her situation, and she had never done the same for me. I had no memory of a motherly look. There was only the culturally programmed habits of duty, hers of a mother and mine of a filial child. That programme had replaced any true understanding between us. It had conditioned me, indeed, had made me guilty from the very beginning, as the unworthy, wayward daughter. It had killed any natural love I might have had for my birth family. It had never been there in the first place. Of course, I was aware of how my own child would feel about all this when she grew up, since her childhood would take place in the West – a totally different reality from mine. I will have to wait and see how our relationship turns out.

A few days later we said goodbye to my mother. We stood by the taxi, which was about to take us to the airport, and I looked at my mother. She looked back at me, but somehow our eyes didn't meet. I took in her broad face, aged and wrinkled, but still childlike in some way. I could tell she felt miserable. My heart was pained by a coldness, a feeling that there was no love in me. There was just a kind of weight, unbearable weight, and a lethargy of the spirit. In the next life, I would be a good daughter, I thought. She wore her wig, like an actor performing one of the opera roles of her youth, and kept up a stream of simple comments about catching the flight and breastfeeding Moon. I nodded but said nothing. Both of us knew, I guessed, that there would be no next time.

Source: Guo, X. (2017) *Once upon a time in the east: a story of growing up*. London: Vintage, pp. 310–313.

Chapter 5 readings

Reading 5.1 Extract from the screenplay of *Little Miss Sunshine*

Michael Arndt

> Michael Arndt is a screenwriter and film producer based in New York. His debut screenplay was *Little Miss Sunshine*, the film of which was released in 2006.

Content note: Please be aware that this reading briefly mentions attempted suicide.

Sheryl enters with a big bottle of Diet Sprite.

>   SHERYL
> You guys, go on and start. Frank,
> some Sprite? I want everyone to
> have at least a little salad.
>
>   FRANK
> Thanks, Sheryl.

She pours him a cup, sits down, and starts opening containers of cole slaw and mashed potatoes.

Richard returns to the table, sits, and grabs a piece of chicken from the bucket. Dwayne follows suit, as does Frank.

The meal begins. Three seconds of silence.

>   FRANK (cont'd)
> So, Sheryl… I couldn't help
> notice Dwayne has stopped speaking.
>
>   SHERYL
> Oh! I'm sorry. Dwayne's taken a
> vow of silence.
>
>   FRANK
> You've taken a vow of silence?!

Dwayne nods.

                    SHERYL
He's gonna join the Naval Academy and become a fighter pilot. He's taken a vow of silence until he reaches that goal.

                    FRANK
                (to Dwayne)
You're kidding…!

Dwayne stares at Frank. He's not kidding. Olive enters the dining room, with Grandpa following.

                    OLIVE
Hi, Uncle Frank!

                    FRANK
Olive. Boy, you're gettin' big!
                (to Sheryl)
Is she big for her age?

Sheryl nods. Olive, unprompted, walks over and gives him a kiss on the cheek. She sees the bandages on Frank's wrists.

                    OLIVE
What happened to your arms?

                    SHERYL
Olive …

                    FRANK
No, it's okay. I had a little accident. I'm okay now.

                    RICHARD
How's the new routine coming?

                    OLIVE
It's good.

                    RICHARD
When're you gonna let us see it?

> OLIVE
> I dunno. It's up to Grandpa.

> GRANDPA
> A couple of days. It needs a polish.

Olive sits. Grandpa walks to the table.

> GRANDPA (cont'd)
> What is this?! Chicken?! Every day it's the chicken! Holy God almighty! Is it possible, just one time, we could have something for dinner except the goddamn fucking chicken?!

Sheryl ignores him. Richard tries to cut him off.

> RICHARD
> Dad… Dad… Dad… Dad!!!

> GRANDPA
> I'm just saying…!

> RICHARD
> If you want to cook or buy your own food, you're more than welcome…

> GRANDPA
> Christ. Y'know, at Sunset Village…

> RICHARD
> If you liked Sunset Village so much maybe you shouldn't have gotten yourself kicked out of there…!

> GRANDPA
> (waves dismissively)
> Ahhhh…!

He takes out a piece of chicken and starts eating. A tense silence. Frank tries to get things going again.

FRANK
When did you start? With the vow?

Dwayne shrugs. He doesn't care to comment.

RICHARD
It's been nine months. He hasn't said a word. I think it shows tremendous discipline.

SHERYL
Richard…

RICHARD
I'm serious! I think we could all learn something from what Dwayne's doing! Dwayne has a goal. He has a dream. It may not be my dream, or your dream, but still… He's pursuing that dream with focus and discipline. In fact, I was thinking about the Nine Steps…

GRANDPA
Oh, for crying out loud…!

RICHARD
(evenly)
…About the Nine Steps, and how Dwayne's utilizing at least seven of them in his journey to personal fulfillment.

SHERYL
Richard. Please.

RICHARD
I'm just saying! I've come around! I think Dwayne deserves our support.

Frank looks at Dwayne. Dwayne rolls his eyes. Olive addresses Frank.

OLIVE
How did it happen?

FRANK
How did what happen?

OLIVE
Your accident...

SHERYL
Honey...

She shakes her head: 'Don't go there.'

FRANK
No, it's okay. Unless you object…

SHERYL
No, I'm pro-honesty here. I just think, you know… It's up to you.

FRANK
Be my guest...

SHERYL
Olive, Uncle Frank didn't really have an accident. What happened was: he tried to kill himself.

OLIVE
You did? Why?

RICHARD
I don't think this is an appropriate conversation.
        (to Olive)
Let's leave Uncle Frank alone.

A beat. Olive has stopped eating.

OLIVE
Why did you want to kill yourself?

RICHARD
Frank. Don't answer that question.

Frank stares at Richard. He turns back to Olive.

FRANK
I tried to kill myself because I was very unhappy.

RICHARD
(overlapping)
Don't listen, honey, he's sick and he doesn't know what he's…

SHERYL
Richard… Richard… Richard…

RICHARD
What?! I don't think it's appropriate for a six year old!

SHERYL
She's gonna find out anyway. Go on, Frank.

OLIVE
Why were you unhappy?

Frank glances at Richard – deadpan victorious – and continues.

FRANK
Well, there were a lot of reasons. Mainly, though, I fell in love with someone who didn't love me back…

OLIVE
Who?

FRANK
One of my grad students. I was very much in love with him.

OLIVE
Him? It was a boy? You fell in love with a boy?

FRANK
Yes. I did. Very much so.

This is new to Olive. She thinks it over.

                    OLIVE
          That's silly.

                    FRANK
          You're right. It was very, very
          silly.

                    GRANDPA
          There's another word for it…

                    RICHARD
          Dad...

                    OLIVE
          So… That's when you tried to
          kill yourself…?

Source: Arndt, M. (2007) *Little Miss Sunshine: the shooting script*. [Screenplay and notes]. New York, NY: Newmarket Press, pp. 12–16.

Reading 5.2 Extract from the script of the stage play *Summer Rolls*

Tuyền Đỗ

> Tuyền Đỗ was born in Vietnam and raised in East London. Her debut play *Summer Rolls* is considered the first major work of theatre by a British Vietnamese writer to be staged in the UK. Đỗ co-founded VanThanh Productions, which collaborates with artists from minority groups to enable them to tell their own stories.

Content note: Please be aware that this reading includes themes of war and family separation.

Vietnam, 1976. Near the Mekong river.

Under the cover of darkness, further camouflaged by overgrown banana leaves, a heavily pregnant WOMAN scuttles from tree to tree lit only by moonlight. Close behind her is a boy, 11 but small. Her SON. She tugs at his hand and pulls him near to her. A fishing vessel is waiting. He's sobbing.

WOMAN: Don't trust anybody. They will take everything you have.

SON: I don't want to / go.

WOMAN: When a chance comes along, you have to take it. Understand?

There is a noise. Flashlight. WOMAN gestures into the darkness that they are ready. She holds her SON, suddenly softer.

SON: I want to stay here / with you.

WOMAN: If you stay here, they will take you and make you fight for them. As soon as you're old enough, you'll be made to kill. I cannot lose you too.

SON: What will happen to you?

WOMAN: Don't worry about me.

SON: What will happen to her? *(Gestures at her tummy.)*

WOMAN: Her?

SON: I know it's a girl.

She pulls out a wad of dollars in plastic sewn into her áo bà ba (simple Vietnamese blouse) and starts to shove it down his pants.

WOMAN: I've sewn a pocket inside your pants. It can double up as an arse cushion. Everyone speaks the language of dollars.

SON: What if it the boat sinks?

WOMAN: It won't sink.

SON: What if I fall?

WOMAN: You know how to swim.

SON: What if I don't make it.

She shakes him.

WOMAN: Fear is just a sign telling us we have to try harder.

SON nods.

You have to raise yourself up, my son. When you get to the other side. Say you're ten instead of eleven, no, nine, eight, the younger the better. They look after children… My prayers will keep you safe. I will wait for you. Even if it take a thousand years. Now go.

She pushes him away. He refuses to leave.

SON: Mum.

WOMAN: You have a lucky number, my son.

There is another noise. Flashlight.

She shoves him hard away from her. He runs back and they embrace.

He runs into the darkness. WOMAN is left standing alone.

Her heart shatters and she lets out a stifled groan.

A swelling of sound.

The sea, mixed with sounds of human distress, the sound of a baby crying morphing into the indistinct sound of a crowd. Flashes of photographs of the future family and other Vietnamese faces litter the stage.

Source: Đỗ, T. (2019) *Summer rolls*. London: Bloomsbury Publishing, pp. 9–10.

Reading 5.3 Extract from the script of the stage play *Sanctuary*

Tanika Gupta

> Tanika Gupta was born in London to parents from Kolkata, India. She has written over 25 stage plays and her work has been produced in many of the leading theatres in the UK. She has also written numerous scripts for television and radio.

Content note: Please be aware that this reading mentions death of children.

Act 1, Scene 1

We are outdoors in the corner of a graveyard – a small Eden-like, neat patch of luscious green packed with shrubbery, ornate flowering plants (orchids) and small tubs of herbs etc. There is a wall to one side and a large tree, which overhangs the wall into the road outside. There is a shed to the other side and an old bench under the tree. The shed is covered in rambling roses and clematis, all in bloom. In the background we can see row upon row of gravestones, which stretch into the distance. A few bits of rubbish litter the otherwise beautiful garden.

It is a bright day. MICHAEL enters and sits on the bench beneath the tree, fashioning a piece of wood into a spoon. He works diligently whilst listening to the cricket commentary on the radio. MICHAEL is casually but smartly dressed. He looks completely engrossed in his work. SEBASTIAN wanders in and sits next to MICHAEL. He is shabbily dressed and dishevelled looking.

At first, he simply sits there in silence. Then he takes interest in what MICHAEL is doing.

Sebastian: What're you working on?

Michael: (*African accent*) It is going to be a spoon.

Sebastian: Ahhh…

SEBASTIAN watches him attentively.

You're good with your hands.

Michael: My father was a carpenter.

Sebastian: Family trade?

Michael: Not really. He was good. He made all the furniture in our village. I just do it to pass the time.

SEBASTIAN looks around.

Sebastian: I like it here.

Michael: Yes.

Sebastian: You like it here?

Michael: Yes.

Sebastian: Lots of dead people. Makes you feel lucky.

Michael: Eh?

Sebastian: That we're alive, man! However bad things are out there, at least we're not fucking six feet under. Know what I mean?

Michael: (*Polite*) I certainly know what you mean.

Sebastian: Too right. Especially when you look at all those gravestones. Young people – half my age. Cut off in the prime of their lives.

MICHAEL continues with his work.

It's the baby ones that always get me. Tiny little coffins.

Michael: Yes, that is sad.

Sebastian: Sad? It's fucking tragic.

Michael: Yes. Tragic. That is what I meant.

Sebastian: Still, like I said. Makes me feel lucky to be drawing breath. The Good Lord up there saw it fit to spare my life.

SEBASTIAN looks heavenward.

(*Shouts*) Thank you God. Not that I'm any fucking good to anyone.

The two men sit in silence.

What's your name again?

Michael: Michael.

Sebastian: Pleased to meet you, Michael. Put it there brother –

MICHAEL gingerly slaps palms with SEBASTIAN.

The name's Seb.

MICHAEL smiles a greeting. SEBASTIAN gets up and staggers around. He looks at the plants.

Very pretty.

We hear voices. A woman vicar wearing a dog collar, JENNY, and an Asian man, KABIR, enter. KABIR is pushing a wheelbarrow full of fresh rolls of turf.

Kabir: They are having the petition in their hands?

Jenny: Yes. I delivered it myself.

Kabir: They will be seeing sense.

Jenny: Yes, I'm sure they will.

Kabir: It is still being beyond all reasoning. They converted St Mary's into luxury apartments.

Jenny: Can't imagine the yuppies moving in round here. I'm going to speak to the bishop this afternoon. He's on our side. Oh – and don't forget, that journalist's coming in on Friday.

Kabir: Eh?

Jenny: You know, from *The Post*. Said she'd be here for most of the afternoon. (*Preoccupied*) Hello Michael. Seb.

SEBASTIAN grunts.

Michael: It is a beautiful morning.

Kabir: Hey, Mikey – what's the score?

Michael: Pakistan are still batting. 223 for three wickets.

Kabir: Good. Have you seen Mumtaz this morning?

Michael: No.

Jenny: She's probably hiding in her nest somewhere.

Kabir: She is always coming to greet me in the mornings – quackety – quack – but only silence today.

Jenny: She'll turn up. She usually does.

MICHAEL continues with his work.

Anyway, this journalist's going to be interviewing people – maybe even you.

Kabir: I will be telling her. This place, it is being a community asset – yes?

Jenny: Very good.

Kabir: People are coming here to pray, to mourn, to grieve and to be with their loved ones. I will be introducing her to people to speak with. Mikey?

Michael: Please Kabir – leave me out of it.

Jenny: Your testament would be useful.

Kabir: You must be helping us, Mikey.

A mobile phone rings.

Jenny: This is important. The coverage would be good for us. The more people read about this place, the better our case.

JENNY answers the phone.

Jenny Catchpole? Edith … of course … he's gone into that nursing home … I took him there myself last week. Coming here? Shit.

JENNY moves aside to have a more private conversation.

SEBASTIAN undoes his flies to have a pee. KABIR spots him.

Kabir: Oy, oy, oy … don't you dare be pissing on my plants. And in front of a lady! (*He points at JENNY*) Shame on you! Put it away.

SEBASTIAN hesitates and then puts it away.

JENNY comes off the phone.

Sebastian: Sorry man. I wasn't thinking.

SEBASTIAN looks a bit shame-faced and staggers off. The others watch him go.

Kabir: Jenny – did you see what he was doing? People are thinking this is being a public toilet! The whole place always smelling of piss.

Michael: (*To JENNY*) He's a bit of a mess.

Jenny: But the kids love him and his classes at the church hall are very popular.

Kabir: I would not be trusting him with the charge of my children. In his last lesson he was having them all wandering around the graveyard taking photographs of baby graves. Isn't that being a little bit odd?

Jenny: He's an artist. Probably just being creative.

Kabir: Artist – my foot.

Jenny: What's the new turf for?

Kabir: The area by the pond. Especially for your baby photographers and my ducks.

Jenny: Wonderful. I thought that patch was looking a bit rough.

Kabir: Too many people stepping around there. Churning it up into mud – especially you ladies, with your thin pin like heels.

Jenny: Don't blame me. I don't wear shoes like that.

Source: Gupta, T. (2002) *Sanctuary*. London: Bloomsbury Publishing, pp. 15–20.

Chapter 6 readings

Reading 6.1 Extract from the screenplay of *The Power of the Dog*

Jane Campion

> Jane Campion is a writer and director from New Zealand. Her films often focus on the struggle of creative expression in the face of brutality.

Content note: In this reading a character makes a racist remark.

8   INT – THE RED MILL/STAIRS/HALL/BEDROOM – DAY   8

Rose walks up the wooden stairs and along the hallway to her son's bedroom. PETER 17 years old sits at a desk near the window. He covers up the exercise book where he was busy gluing magazine pictures. He is neat and extremely thin with a slightly enlarged forehead and wide deep set eyes, that appear to see both everything and nothing.

>   ROSE
> We are going to need your room, all
> the rooms up here – what are you
> doing?

>   PETER
> Nothing.

Rose moves over to his table with its black leather bound Medical Text Books in a neat row and magazines and clippings, scissors and glue.

>   ROSE
> Is it an album?

>   PETER
> Not really.

>   ROSE
> What's in it?

She begins to turn the pages. There are magazine pictures of cruise ships and home designs, jewelry and automobiles all characterising luxury and affluence.

>   PETER
> Nothing, just things I like.

Rose is looking at a picture of a woman like herself in a living room with a rock feature wall. In another picture a couple are in a luxury cruise liner dancing in moonlight. Beside the album Rose notices some handmade paper flowers, intricately folded and pleated with clipped and rolled frills for stamen. Rose examines one.

>   ROSE
> Oh that's clever Peter.

>   PETER
> Not really.

But he nonetheless shows her a decorated milk bottle with several paper flowers together. She turns it about.

>   ROSE
> For the tables? They're lovely.

She puts it down.

>   ROSE (CONT'D)
> I need three more chickens. Can you
> do them?

>   PETER
> Yes Mother.

Rose starts pulling Peter's sheets off his bed.

>   ROSE
> Can you put your things in the
> shed? I'll make a bed for you on
> the floor.

                    PETER
            Where will you sleep?

                    ROSE
            I'll put a cot up in the kitchen.

9   EXT/INT – THE RED MILL/CHICKEN COOP/KITCHEN/   9
    DINING – DAY

    In the chicken coop Peter quietly corners a suitable fryer.
    Rose in the kitchen closes the window and stops her ears as
    she walks through to the dining room and sits at the Pianola
    playing 'The Red Mill' loudly and well to drown out the
    squawking.

10 EXT – THE RED MILL/CHICKEN COOP – DAY   10

    Peter takes the bird suddenly by the neck, twists his wrist
    just so; the body twirls twice and falls headless to the
    ground where it hops and flops and the discarded head beside
    it gazes with bright astonished eye at its own jerking body.
    Only when the body falters and lays quiet does the lid come
    down over the eye.

11 INT/EXT – THE RED MILL/BEDROOM/GRAVEYARD – DAY 11

    Rose walks upstairs with an armful of sun dried sheets. From
    the window in the hall she sees Peter with his strange
    mechanical gait climb up the bald hill to a small haphazard
    graveyard, bordered with a single strand of rusted barbwire.

12 EXT – TOWN OF BEECH/GRAVEYARD – DAY   12

    Peter passes several untended graves before kneeling in front
    of one with a newer headstone. He wipes the dust off the
    engraved name. DOCTOR JOHN GORDON, BELOVED
    HUSBAND AND FATHER to Rose and Peter Gordon.

    Peter sticks a posy of his paper flowers into the earth and
    places on top an upturned large pickle jar as protection.

    Peter makes his way down the hill squinting in the afternoon
    sun as he sees the first line of the Burbank outfit reach the
    edge of the town, Beech.

13 EXT – TOWN OF BEECH/ENTRANCE – DAY   13

    The lead steers spook at the sight of the first buildings,

straightening their front legs and sniffing the ground until pushed on by Cowhands.

RESIDENTS watch admiring from their windows and Phil keeps his eyes peeled for any fool wandering out to spook the cattle.

14   EXT – BEECH STOCKYARDS – EVE/DAY   14

OTHER RESIDENTS look on as the last of the Burbank cattle are corralled within the Stockyards adjacent to the railway yards. Two Cowhands and George look on down the tracks over a flat endless plain. No train yet. The Cowhands lead their horses across to the horse yards where a lump of hay awaits them.

15   INT/EXT – THE SALOON/BEECH STREET – EVENING   15

The whole Burbank Outfit stands along the bar small spirit glasses in front of each man. Phil is holding everyone off, Jock is standing lookout on the street.

      PHIL
  He there?

      JOCK
  Nope.

Phil is put out. He beckons for Jock to come in.

      PHIL
  Well we can't wait forever the
  cattle are in the yards. So drink
  up.

      JOCK
  You going to say something?

      PHIL
  No. Not without my brother.

The boys lift their little glasses and drink. Phil is not a pretender he's miffed and not drinking. The Barkeep refills. George walks in and over to Phil.

> PHIL (CONT'D)
> Where were you? I couldn't hold the boys back forever.

> GEORGE
> That's fine. Checked the power it's held up, not coming till morning.

Phil passes George his shot glass expecting a brotherly toast.

> GEORGE (CONT'D)
> No thanks Phil. They're ready for us over at The Red Mill.

This brush-off digs deep.

> GEORGE (CONT'D)
> Dinner boys.

Nobody listens.
Phil's in a hell of a mood.

> PHIL
> Twenty-five years ago, where were you Georgie boy? I'll tell you, a chubby know-nothing, too dumb to get through college. People helped you Fatso, one person in particular taught me and you ranching so we damn well succeeded.

George looks down and nods.

> GEORGE
> Yes, yes Bronco Henry.

> PHIL
> So to us brothers, Romulus and Remus and the wolf who raised us.

George picks up his glass, clinks with Phil.

GEORGE	PHIL (CONT'D)
To Bronco.	Il Lupo.

George drinks the spirits in two even sips while Phil downs his in one. Phil's eyes water with emotion. He turns to the bar and gives a piercing whistle. The Burbank Boys look over at Phil who is headed to the door. Glasses are put down the Burbank Boys follow.

16 EXT – BEECH MAIN STREET – EVENING   16

The Burbank Outfit, all twelve walk down the main street towards The Red Mill.

17 INT/EXT – BEECH MAIN STREET/THE RED MILL/DINING –   17
    EVENING

Rose in the kitchen an apron over a twenty's frock and low heels, her hair held back with pins stops her washing up as she sees the men approaching. Rose meets them in the dining room.

                    ROSE
              This is your table.

Rose leans over and lights the candles melted into the wine bottles. George sits down at one end, Phil remains standing. He looks at a table of six next to their table where JEANIE (30's) is drinking wine and telling a story loudly, she puffs on her cigarette something Phil finds repulsive in a female. Then Phil notices the paper flowers on his table.

                    PHIL
           Well, well, ain't that purdy.

Phil bends to sniff. The Cowhands cowered by the prissiness of the roadhousey atmosphere and the napkins look at Phil admiring his poise and ease.

                    ROSE
              Everything alright?

GEORGE
Yes fine.

As Rose goes back to the kitchen Jeanie calls after her loudly.

JEANIE
Play us something, please Rosie.

The others take up the chant 'Play'. Rose shakes her head. They are drunk and she's busy.

Phil finally sits as Peter comes out in his white waiter's shirt and black pants, combed wet hair and a white cloth draped over his stiffly folded left arm. He walks past Phil to the table of six where he starts to clear their plates. Phil leans back on the legs of his chair eyeing Peter with rising distaste.

PHIL
Where's our service boy? Are we black or something?

Peter looks across anxiously but continues with his plate piling. Phil turns to his table and his eyes light again on Peter's paper flowers. He leans forward and with his gnarled dirty hands, still bloody from a small cut on his palm, he takes the flowers in his fist and regards them closely, poking a finger into the paper flower corolla.

PHIL (CONT'D)
My goodness I wonder what little lady made these?

Peter turns, his hands full of plates.

PETER
I did actually sir. My mother you see trained as a florist.

                    PHIL
          Well do pardon me, they're as real
          as possible.

Phil puts them back in the jar pretending to arrange them.

Peter is paused, realising he's being ridiculed. A couple of Cowhands giggle. Phil hasn't finished.

                    PHIL (CONT'D)
          Oh look here gentlemen, that's what
          you do with the cloth.

Four or so of the Cowhands innocently mimic Peter's waiter affectation draping their napkins over their arm. Rose hearing the laughter, opens the door and sees Phil offering the jar of paper flowers to the Cowhands to take mock sniffs. Rose's heart sinks. Peter looks trapped and in hell as Cowhands CRICKET and SANDY masquerade with their napkins.

                    PETER
          It's really only for wine drips.

                    PHIL (MIMICKING PETER'S LISP)
          Got that boys, only for drips now
          get us some food.

Peter looks down ashamed, his eyes smart, he continues into the kitchen. Phil and the Cowhands laugh. Phil looks at George who does not 'join' he wears his napkin on his lap and sits.

18   INT – THE RED MILL/KITCHEN/DINING ROOM – NIGHT   18
     A flustered Rose serves delicious looking fried chicken and wilted lettuce on the twelve waiting plates, Peter now expressionless carries them out two at a time.

19   INT – THE RED MILL/DINING ROOM – NIGHT   19

                    BOBBY
          Did Bronco ever eat here?

                    PHIL
          He did not.

                    BOBBY
          So where did you eat?

                    PHIL
          Back then we had herrings at the
          Saloon and a lot of alcohol. Once
          Bronco Henry made a wager that he
          could take any horse and jump the
          tables and chairs of the Saloon
          piled out on the street. We chose
          him a nag all right it didn't
          bother him. He took off its saddle,
          walked the horse up to the tables
          talking to him. Stroking its big
          ugly head while it sniffed. Then he
          swung on, rode back and...

Phil has meanwhile rolled himself a cigarette, he takes a paper flower and flames it up on the candle then lights his tight slim smoke.

                    BOBBY
               What?

Phil pulls a disaster face. The Cowhands wait.

                    PHIL
          Flew over.

Peter enters with more plates stunned to see his flower burning. Phil slowly shakes it out.

                    JOCK
          But to get a nag to jump...

Phil nods blowing smoke. Rose brings to the table two steaming platters of biscuits deftly removing Peter's paper flowers.

                                PHIL
                    Put it down to amour. What do you
                    say George?

The Cowhands turn to George who is head down eating.

                                GEORGE
                    What?

Phil stares at George. The Cowhands slowly begin to laugh. George's inattention throws Phil. Suddenly he is aware of the loud revelling behind him on the Pianola. Phil turns sharply.

                                PHIL
                    Do you mind quietening, we're
                    eating.

The MAN on the Pianola lifts his hands as the keys amusingly play on.

                                PHIL (CONT'D)
                    Shut that down, or I will.

Phil stands. The Man stops the Pianola and the party assemble to leave. Peter serves the last two plates, one to Phil. He blows out the candles on the departed table.

Source: Campion, J. (no date) *The power of the dog*. [Screenplay], pp. 9–16. Available at: https://deadline.com/wp-content/uploads/2022/01/The-Power-Of-The-Dog-Read-The-Screenplay.pdf (Accessed: 5 May 2024).

Reading 6.2 Extract from the novel *Small Island*
Andrea Levy

> Andrea Levy was a British writer of Jamaican heritage who was born in London. Her novels explore the complex experiences of people from the Caribbean who settled in the UK from the mid-twentieth century onwards. London often features as the setting for her stories and novels.

I had to grab the banister to pull myself up stair after stair. There was hardly any light. Just one bulb so dull it was hard to tell whether it was giving out light or sucking it in. At every turn on the stairs there was another set of steep steps, looking like an empty bookshelf in front of me. I longed for those ropes and pulleys of my earlier mind. I was groping like a blind man at times with nothing to light the way in front of me except the sound of Gilbert still climbing ahead. 'Hortense, nearly there,' he called out, like Moses from on top of the mountain. I was palpitating by the time I reached the door where Gilbert stood grinning, saying: 'Here we are'.

'What a lot of stairs. Could you not find a place with fewer stairs?'

We went into the room. Gilbert rushed to pull a blanket over the unmade bed. Still warm I was sure. It was obvious to me he had just got out of it. I could smell gas. Gilbert waved his arms around as if showing me a lovely view. 'This is the room,' he said.

All I saw were dark brown walls. A broken chair that rested one uneven leg on the Holy Bible. A window with a torn curtain and Gilbert's suit – the double-breasted one – hanging from a rail on the wall.

'Well,' I said, 'show me the rest, then, Gilbert.' The man just stared. 'Show me the rest, nah. I am tired from the long journey.' He scratched his head. 'The other rooms, Gilbert. The ones you busy making so nice for me you forget to come to the dock.'

Gilbert spoke so softly I could hardly hear. He said, 'But this is it.'

'I am sorry?' I said.

'This is it, Hortense. This is the room I am living.'

Three steps would take me to one side of this room. Four steps could take me to another. There was a sink in the corner, a rusty tap stuck out from the wall above it. There was a table with two chairs – one with its back broken – pushed up against the bed. The armchair held a shopping bag, a pyjama top, and a teapot. In the fireplace the gas hissed with a blue flame.

'Just this?' I had to sit on the bed. My legs gave way. There was no bounce underneath me as I fell. 'Just this? This is where you are living? Just this?'

'Yes, this is it.' He swung his arms round again, like it was a room in a palace.

'Just this? Just this? You bring me all this way for just this?'

The man sucked his teeth and flashed angry eyes in my face. 'What you expect, woman? Yes, just this! What you expect? Everyone live like this. There has been a war. Houses bombed. I know plenty people live worse than this. What you want? You should stay with your mamma if you want it nice. There been a war here. Everyone live like this.'

He looked down at me, his badly buttoned chest heaving. The carpet was threadbare in a patch in the middle and there was a piece of bread lying on it. He sucked his teeth again and walked out the room. I heard him banging down the stairs. He left me alone.

He left me alone to stare on just this.

Source: Levy, A. (2004) *Small island*. London: Headline Publishing, pp. 20–21.

Reading 6.3 Extract from the script of a stage play adaptation of *Small Island*

Helen Edmundson

> Helen Edmundson is a dramatist from London who writes primarily for theatre. She has also written television and radio dramas. Her plays, many of them adapted from literary sources, often use intimate personal stories to address bigger political and historical themes.

A grey, starkly realistic world.

A small room at the top of QUEENIE*'s house in Earl's Court. A single bed, a small table and two chairs – one of which has a broken leg and rests on an old book. There is a gas fire and an armchair. A suit hangs on a hanger on the back of the door. In one corner there is a gas ring, a sink and a kettle. A very small window looks out onto rooftops. It is a late afternoon in November and the sky is already growing dim.*

GILBERT, *fully-dressed, is asleep on the bed. Downstairs, the front-door bell rings. After a moment it rings again.* GILBERT *suddenly sits up.*

GILBERT. Oh, no.

He checks his watch.

No! No, no, no!

The bell rings again as GILBERT *frantically pulls on his shoes and fastens the loose buttons on his shirt.*

No!

Female voices can be heard in the hall now. GILBERT *rushes from the room, tripping over his not-quite-done-up shoelaces, and we hear the sound of him running down the stairs. We hear his voice joining those of the others, loud at first and then quiet. We hear a rat running over the roof of the room, scratching and scurrying.*

Footsteps approach on the stairs.

(*Off.*) Not much further now.

More footsteps. GILBERT *appears in the doorway and holds the door open for* HORTENSE *to enter. She is dressed in a pristine white coat with the white hat and gloves she wore for her wedding. She has a handbag over her arm. She is a little breathless.*

Here we are.

HORTENSE *stands in the doorway, taking in the room. She is disorientated, shocked, inwardly afraid, but she is determined to cover it.* GILBERT *rushes to pull the covers over the unmade bed – a move which does not escape* HORTENSE*'s notice. He looks at her, smiling nervously. She swallows.*

HORTENSE. Well. Show me the rest.

She looks at him and he stares at her.

Show me the rest, nah. I am tired from the long, long journey. The other rooms, Gilbert. The ones you say you so busy making nice for me that you forget to come and meet me at the dock.

GILBERT. But... this is it.

HORTENSE. I beg your pardon?

GILBERT. This is it. This is the room I am living.

HORTENSE *stares around at the room again in shocked silence.*

HORTENSE. Just this?

She suddenly has to sit down on the edge of a chair so that her legs don't give way. GILBERT *swings his arms as though to suggest how spacious the room is.*

GILBERT. Yes. This is it.

HORTENSE. Just this?

GILBERT. What you expect? Yes, just this. There has been a war. Houses bombed. I know plenty people live worse than this.

Footsteps are heard on the stairs.

QUEENIE (*off*). Gilbert!

HORTENSE *stands as* QUEENIE *enters. She is flushed and breathless. She looks a little rounder, but is not obviously pregnant.*

Sorry. You're going to have to move that trunk, you know? You can't just leave it by the steps.

GILBERT. Course. I come nah.

QUEENIE. I would say someone'll make off with it except it's that bloody heavy.

GILBERT *glances at* HORTENSE*'s shocked face.*

GILBERT. I come nah. I get Winston to help me.

QUEENIE. Oh, I don't think that's Winston in his room. I think it's Kenneth. (*To* HORTENSE.) They're twins, you see. But the one who's in there now just looked up my skirt so I'm pretty sure it's Kenneth.

GILBERT. Right. I get Kenneth to help me then. (*To* HORTENSE.) I won't be long.

GILBERT *leaves.* QUEENIE *smiles at* HORTENSE. *She sits down on the edge of the bed – needing a moment's rest.* HORTENSE *is confused – why is this woman making herself at home in her room?*

QUEENIE. So you're Gilbert's wife. What's your name again?

HORTENSE. Hortense.

QUEENIE. Hortense. Funny name. My name's Mrs Bligh, but you can call me Queenie if you like? Everyone here does. Would you like that?

HORTENSE *hesitates to reply.*

Cat got your tongue?

HORTENSE. What cat?

QUEENIE. Oh. No, it's just an expression. It means you're not saying much. Don't worry, you'll soon pick up English.

He didn't come to meet you then? Men, eh? I'm sure he meant to. He told me he was going to. So how long have you and Gilbert been married? (*Loudly and slowly.*) How... long... have...?

HORTENSE. Gilbert and I have been married for six and a half months.

QUEENIE. Six? Six months?

HORTENSE. That is what I said.

QUEENIE. What – altogether? But Gilbert's been here for about four. Ah. You're newlyweds then. Sweet.

HORTENSE. I suppose so.

QUEENIE. Did you say 'I suppose so'? You don't sound too pleased about it.

There sounds of footsteps on the stairs now and some bumping and cursing.

Oh, no, what are they doing?

QUEENIE *leaves*.

(*Off.*) You know that bannister's dodgy, don't you?

Watch out for the paintwork!

HORTENSE *goes into the kitchen area. She stares at the dirty sink. She runs a finger of her white glove along the window pane and it turns black. She stares back at the room in disbelief.*

KENNETH *bursts through the door holding one end of* HORTENSE'S *trunk.* GILBERT *follows him in with the other. They are straining under the weight of it.*

KENNETH (*to* HORTENSE). Man, what you got in here? Your mother?

HORTENSE. You may place it in that corner and please be careful.

KENNETH *looks at* GILBERT *and they drop the trunk where they stand.*

Careful! That is a very expensive trunk!

KENNETH *is staring at* HORTENSE. *He is a shifty-looking, scruffy young man.*

GILBERT. Kenneth, this is Hortense. My wife.

HORTENSE. How do you do?

KENNETH. What part of the island you from?

HORTENSE. I have been living in Kingston but...

KENNETH. What your name before you marry him?

HORTENSE. My name was Roberts...

KENNETH. What ship you come on?

HORTENSE. I...

KENNETH. You meet a man on the ship from Buff Bay? His name Clinton.

HORTENSE. No, I...

KENNETH. So what you got in the trunk? Apart from your mother.

KENNETH *chuckles at his own joke.*

HORTENSE. I have my possessions in that trunk...

KENNETH. Any rum? Mango? Guava? Tell me you got guava. Guava fetch a good price right now. I know one of the boys give me half his wage to place him tongue in a guava.

HORTENSE is looking at him with disdain.

GILBERT. Thank you for your help, Kenneth.

KENNETH. What? Surely you got something for me?

GILBERT. I tell you what – you can take a shilling off the six shilling you already owe me.

KENNETH sucks his teeth.

KENNETH (*to* HORTENSE). You sure you haven't got any rum, nah? (*To* GILBERT.) Cha, why don't you tell her to bring some rum with her?

GILBERT. Goodbye, Kenneth.

KENNETH. You goin', man?

GILBERT signals that he wants to be alone with HORTENSE – staring at HORTENSE and then shifting his eyes towards the door repeatedly.

Oh. (*Nodding and grinning.*) Oh. I must be gone. Leave you two alone. Five months – that a long time.

He chuckles again – pleased with himself, and then he leaves. His footsteps are heard going down the stairs.

HORTENSE. That man is your friend?

GILBERT. Why you no sit down nah?

HORTENSE. Why would you choose such a friend?

GILBERT. Any boy from back home a friend here, believe me.

Take off your coat. The fire is on so... Oh – it gone out. I have to put more money in the meter. (*Checking his pockets.*) Where I put that shilling?

(*Searching through the bedcovers.*) Had it put aside special.

HORTENSE. You keep your money in the bed?

GILBERT. No. But when I was sleeping it must have fallen out me pocket...

HORTENSE. Oh. So you were sleeping then?

GILBERT stops still – caught out.

GILBERT. No. I just lie for a minute and...

HORTENSE. So that why you no there to meet me.

GILBERT. No. I came but...

HORTENSE. What is it you write in your letter? 'I will be at the dockside to meet you. You will see me there, jumping and waving and calling your name with longing in my tone.'

GILBERT. Hortense, Hortense, let me tell you. I worked a shift at the post office last night. In the morning I went straight to the dock but there was no ship. So they tell me to come back later when the ship will arrive. So I go home to take the opportunity of fixing the place up nice for you...

HORTENSE. Oh, yes. see how nice it is.

GILBERT. And I just lie for a minute and I fall asleep. I so tired. And next thing I know you are ringing the bell and...

HORTENSE. Do you know what a fool I feel waiting on that dock? Waiting and waiting...

GILBERT. I know...

HORTENSE. And everyone else is meeting people or going off in little twos and threes...

GILBERT. I'm sorry...

HORTENSE. And then the taxi driver could not understand what I am saying when I tell him this address, and I begin to wonder if this place even...

GILBERT. Sorry. I'm sorry. Hortense, I am glad you are here. Man, I look forward to this day so long.

HORTENSE (*unconvinced*). Really?

GILBERT. Yes! Of course. I have my wife with me at last.

HORTENSE *is silent.* GILBERT *spots the coin on the floor and picks it up sheepishly.*

Let me sort the fire out nah. Let me show you how to put the money in the meter.

HORTENSE. You think I don't know how to put money into a meter?

GILBERT *tries to put the coin in the meter but it jams. He kicks the meter, but still it does not go in.* HORTENSE *watches with disdain as he stands back and kicks the meter again. The coin goes in.* HORTENSE *turns away and sucks her teeth.* GILBERT *lights the fire.*

GILBERT. You wan' a cup of tea? I'll make you a nice cup of English tea. Yes?

She assents with the slightest of nods. GILBERT *goes into the kitchen area and puts the kettle on.*

Take off your coat nah.

HORTENSE *takes off her coat reluctantly. She leaves her hat and gloves on. She is wearing the white dress which she wore for the wedding.* GILBERT *goes to her and takes her coat from her. He hangs it over the suit – his wedding suit – on the back of the door.* HORTENSE *is still taking in the room.*

HORTENSE. Only one bed.

GILBERT. Yes. But nights here very cold, yah know? And we...

HORTENSE. At least you will have a chair to sleep on.

GILBERT *almost protests but decides not to.* HORTENSE *sits down.*

Who is that woman downstairs?

GILBERT. Queenie. She own the house. She is the landlady.

HORTENSE. She married?

GILBERT. Her husband lost in the war.

HORTENSE. She on her own?

GILBERT. Yes.

HORTENSE. You friendly with her?

GILBERT *freezes and thinks for a moment before answering.*

GILBERT. I knew her during the war. She was kind to me. Lucky I remember her address. Lucky she still here. Places hard to come by, especially for coloured boys.

HORTENSE. She seem to know all your business.

GILBERT. What? No. She just friendly.

HORTENSE. Who else live in this house?

GILBERT. Winston. Him exactly like Kenneth but honest. And a white woman called Jean. You won't see her much. She work nights.

HORTENSE. She a nurse?

GILBERT. Something like that. Come – I show you how to use the gas ring. It only small but it surprising what you can cook up on it.

HORTENSE. I will cook in the kitchen.

Pause.

GILBERT. This is the kitchen.

HORTENSE. Where?

GILBERT. This ring. This sink. This is the kitchen.

HORTENSE. Just this? There is no kitchen down the stairs?

GILBERT. Not for us to use. This is the kitchen. (*Pointing to the table and chairs.*) That is the dining room. I thought you...

HORTENSE, aghast, takes this in.

HORTENSE. And what about the lavatory? Tell me we have our own lavatory.

GILBERT. No. The lavatory is on the ground floor. It's a shared lavatory.

HORTENSE. Do you mean to tell me, that every time I need the lavatory, I must go all the way down those stairs and then come all the way back up again?

GILBERT. Yes. (*Suddenly.*) No! No –

Excited, he goes to the bed and pulls a potty out from underneath.

Sometimes I use this.

He shows it to her. But the potty is full and some of the contents slop over the side. HORTENSE *jumps back in disgust.*

Oh!

HORTENSE. Disgusting! What are you doing?!

GILBERT. Sorry! I forgot it was... Oh, no...

HORTENSE. This place is disgusting! How you bring me here?!

GILBERT. Hush!

HORTENSE. I caan believe you bring me all this way for a place like this! You tell me you have somewhere nice to live. You want me to live like this?!

GILBERT (*moving towards her and forgetting the potty*). Hush nah. No need to tell the whole...

HORTENSE. Get it away from me! I caan believe you bring me here. You live like an animal!

Source: Edmundson, H. (2019) *Small island*. London: Nick Hern Books, pp. 79–87.

Chapter 7 readings

Reading 7.1 Extract from the script of the radio play *Breaking Up with Bradford*

Kamal Kaan

> Born in Bradford, West Yorkshire, Kamal Kaan's work for stage, screen and radio aims to interrogate lazy stereotypes of minorities. His writing explores how one experience can impact a wide spectrum of society and serves to remind audiences of the power of stories to create positive change.

<u>SCENE 1.
INT. CAMBRIDGE. BEDROOM. DAY.</u>

<u>SFX: A FLOWING RIVER OUTSIDE THE WINDOW ACCOMPANIED BY BIRDSONG. MUSIC PLAYS. KASIM TYPING A LETTER ON HIS LAPTOP.</u>

KASIM: Cambridge. Dearest,

I watch the sun lower into the earth, for [the] last time,
melting as dark oil into the river outside my window.
It was love at first sight with you
seduced by your gothic spires.
I was just a boy from Bradford,
walking through your cobbled streets,
then we'd nest in the secrecy of the great Christopher Wren library.

Alas. A thing of beauty can't be a joy forever,
I'm leaving, broken, by you
returning back to the one who will love me unconditionally.
Infinitely with devotion
for the shape of you
will always be printed on me.

Yours truly,

                        Kass
                        Oh. And kiss kiss.

                        THE MUSIC THEN TRANSFORMS INTO…

                        SCENE 2.
                        INT. TRAIN. DAY.

                        SFX: A TRAIN SPEEDING ALONG. MUSIC
                        PLAYS.

                        INSIDE, KASIM IS SAT, LOOKING OUT.

TRAIN
ANNOUNCER: Thank you for travelling with us today.
                        The final destination is Bradford Interchange,
                        please take all your belongings with you.

                        SFX: KASIM GETTING OFF THE TRAIN,
                        FOLDING BICYCLE IN ONE HAND AND
                        SUITCASE BEING LUGGED BEHIND.

STATION
STAFF: Ey up lad! Wanna come through this way with
                        that bike?

KASIM: Thanks!

STATION
STAFF: Av a luvly day!

                        SFX: KASIM GOING THROUGH THE
                        TICKET BARRIER.

SCENE 3.
INT/EXT. BRADFORD INTERCHANGE.
TRAIN STATION. DAY.

SFX: THE BUSYNESS OF A TRAIN STATION.

KASIM: Sid?

SID: KASIM, broooo!

SFX: KASIM AND SID EMBRACING.

KASIM: Honestly, so good to see you!

SID: Calm down, it's not that exciting…

KASIM: Missed you man!

SID: Softy. Wait –

KASIM: What?

SID: Your voice! (IMITATING KASIM'S ACCENT) 'So good to see you'.

KASIM: Ey?

SID: Ya sound like ya swallowed the queen?

KASIM: (IN A THICK BRADFORD ACCENT) Don't mess about broo. *You've* changed.

SID: Noo. DFA man!

KASIM: Been gymming?

SID: Oh right. Yeh, benching 150 now. Feel em?

(KASIM FEELS SID'S BICEPS)

SID:	Solid! Birds love em. Come gymming with me. I'll get you discount innit – looks like you need it bro! Why's ya jumper so baggy?
KASIM:	This? … oh …it's not mine.
SID:	OMG. From a charity shop?
KASIM:	…Err…a friend's… It's cashmere?!
SID:	From Pakistan? You converted? I thought you were Bengali?
KASIM:	The wool? Feel it…
SID:	You want me to caress ya, in public?
KASIM:	(ALARMED) What?
SID:	I'm joking broo!
KASIM:	Duh…(BEAT) Where are you parked?
SID:	Over here. Hang on, where's all ya stuff?
KASIM:	Just finished my exams but I'm still at uni?
SID:	So you going back ta your Cambridge-land then?
KASIM:	Just for graduation in a months time. Then, I'll be home for good!
SID:	Eh? You see my confused face bro? You're gunna move *back* ta Bratfud, full time, after graduation?
KASIM:	Why not?
SID:	People who leave never come back! Look what happened to 'r bro Zayn Malik?
KASIM:	But I'm not a member of a teen pop boyband am I?

SID:	Ya got the looks and ya don't need any talent?
KASIM:	Better than having neither?
SID:	Go back. I'll drop you off?
KASIM:	(LAUGHING) No chance. This is home.

> SFX: KASIM AND SID WALKING, WITH A SUITCASE BEING ROLLED, THE BELL ON KASIM'S BIKE PINGS.

Source: Kaan, K. (2017) *Breaking up with Bradford*. (Produced and directed by C. Riches. BBC Radio 4, 17 August, 14:15) [Script], pp. 2–6. Available at: https://www.bbc.co.uk/writers/documents/breaking-up-with-bradford-kamal-kaan.pdf (Accessed: 18 March 2024).

Reading 7.2 Extract from the script of the audio monologue *The Dead Dad Show*

Annalisa Dinnella

> Annalisa Dinnella is a writer for TV, film and radio who began her writing career in TV documentaries. She is also a stand-up comedian. As a visually-impaired writer (with about five per cent vision), Dinnella is an alumnus of the BBC Writers' Access Group (for disabled writers).

> MUSIC – STEVE REICH, SIX MARIMBAS 0.00 –.

> FX   APPLAUSE FROM A COMEDY CLUB AUDIENCE.

Hello Edinburgh Chortle Awards, thank you for having me.
My name is James and I'm…
(HESITATES)
And I'm…
(HESITATES)
I'm…
(A BEAT OF AWFUL SILENCE)

<u>FX   A SHARP MECHANICAL SCREECH AND MUSIC STOPS ABRUPTLY AT 0.37.</u>

I wake up, this time, because I'm thrown against the wall. I'm somewhere between midnight and six am, somewhere between London Paddington and Edinburgh Waverley.

<u>FX   THE ROAR AND RATTLE OF A SLEEPER TRAIN.</u>

I flip my pillow and fumble around for my water bottle but it must have rolled off the mattress. I'll never find it. I emptied my rucksack all over the floor last night – spreading myself out to fit all the available space.

I told the organizers I had to have my own cabin on account of my sleep issues. They accepted without question. Some of the others had to share.

I don't really have sleep issues.

I'm lying. I do have sleep issues. I mean historically. I have historical sleep issues. They can reappear in times of stress. And this is a time of stress.

I go through my set – Reasons Why It's OK For Me To Love Hugh Grant, Annoying Doorbells, Things You Learn About Your Mates In An Escape Room, New And Better Names For All The Classic Haribos … I'm going to die on my arse tomorrow if I don't sleep. I can't die on my arse. I can't die in front of everyone.

I feel across the wall behind my head for the A/C switch and turn it off. Cold air is still blowing at me so I sit up and feel for the switch by the top bunk but there's something in the way. Don't remember putting anything up there. It's heavy, round, sort of warm. I try and move it.

… and realize that I am cupping the heel of a human foot.

My hand is on a human foot.

The foot springs away from me. I spring away from it and, above me, a body begins very slowly to shift its weight.

> FX   A WHEEZY SORT OF SIGH, SHEETS RUSTLE.

There's a body in my cabin.

> FX   LIGHT SNORING.

There's a body in my cabin.

I locked my door. (I can be a bit obsessive about these things and I remember locking my door) I locked my door.

Could I have gone for a piss and left it unlocked? Don't remember doing that. Did I sleepwalk? Haven't done that since I was six years old. Haven't wet myself since I was six either. And, no, I haven't wet myself. But thanks for asking.

I'm breathing – just breathing – and thinking that probably the best thing to do in this situation is to… pretend it's not happening. Just pretend it's not happening. I'm going to go back to sleep because that's the priority here – sleep. The most important thing is sleep. I'll deal with this douchebag (CONSIDERS) Douchbag? I'll deal with this douchbag in the morning. It could be a funny story. Could be material. I mean he might be a nice guy. He might be a dick. He's probably a dick. Right. Come on. Sleep. Sleep now.

> FX   WHEEZY BREATHING, LIP SMACHING.

Sleep.

> FX   WHEEZY BREATHING, A BODY MOVING UNDER BEDSHEETS.

Sleep.
He's a dick.

FX A FART.

I am not making this up. This is a sealed cabin. The windows don't open.

FX ANOTHER FART.

I'm not in the mood for this. This is not the time. This is not the moment.

'Hey buddy' I hear myself saying... Not too loudly. 'You got the wrong cabin mate. Excuse me, mate. But you're in my cabin.'

FX BREATHING CONTINUES.

'I've got a gig tomorrow. I need to sleep. Can you hear me?'

FX BREATHING CONTINUES.

So I'm on my feet now, flicking the lights on. Turns out douchbag bunk invader is a man with grey-hair. He's wearing an eye-mask and green tartan pyjamas. He's sleeping like the dead. Foetal position.

FX MORE BREATHING.

I prod him on the arm. No dice. Prod him again.
(EXASPERATED SIGH)

MUSIC – STEVE REICH, SIX MARIMBAS 8.44 – 8.54.

Source: Dinnella, A. (2019) *The dead dad show.* (Directed by M. Beeby. BBC Radio 3, 11 June, 22:45) [Script], pp. 1–4. Available at: https://www.bbc.co.uk/writersroom/documents/music-monologues-the-dead-dad-show-annalisa-dinnella.pdf (Accessed: 18 March 2024).

Chapter 8 readings

Reading 8.1 Extract from the script of the stage play *Talking in Tongues*

Winsome Pinnock

> Winsome Pinnock is a playwright from London who has won numerous awards for her work. She was the first woman of Black British heritage to have a play staged at the National Theatre.

Scene Three

Leela, **Claudette** and **Curly** *are hiding under coats.*

Curly   We'll miss the countdown.

Claudette   Who cares? This party is so dry. I can't stand the thought of watching those people trying to enjoy themselves.

Curly   We should have brought a bottle up with us. I'll go and get a bottle, shall I? You've got to toast the New Year in, haven't you?

Leela   I've never liked parties. People get so desperate at parties, don't they?

Curly   You like parties. We used to go to a party every Saturday when we were younger.

Leela   I never liked those either. I only went because there was nothing else to do. What else do you do on a Saturday night when you're sixteen?

Curly   I thought you enjoyed them. We were the bees knees, weren't we? I loved getting dolled up, trotting around on high heels – we wore high heels!

Leela   Getting stuck with your nose up the armpit of some bloke you never fancied.

Claudette   Or doing something stupid like this just so that you had something to tell your mates on Monday morning.

Curly   I'll get those drinks, shall I?

Leela   We don't need drinks.

Curly   It's bad luck to be without a drink when the clock strikes twelve. What do you fancy? I don't suppose we'll have much choice, anyway. I'll just get what I can find.

Claudette   Don't let anyone see you coming up, Curls. Before you know it they'll be up here getting us to join them in the bloody conga.

Curly *goes.*

Claudette What a lot of coats. I'll dream coats. (*Picks one up, tries it on.*) Suit me?

Leela It's not your colour.

Claudette How much do you think a coat like this costs?

Leela Enough.

Claudette You and Bentley know some smart people.

Leela Take it off, Claudette.

Claudette I think I'll keep it on. It suits me.

Leela Do what you like.

Claudette You can't slouch in a coat like this. You've got to walk upright, haven't you? Did you have a nice Christmas?

Leela All right. You?

Claudette What did you do?

Leela We stayed at home.

Claudette Just the two of you?

Leela We wanted it quiet.

Claudette That's nice. Exchanged presents in the morning?

Leela Yes.

Claudette What did he get you?

Leela I can't remember.

Claudette It was only last week.

Leela A chain – a necklace, some perfume.

Claudette What kind of perfume?

Leela Claudette –

Claudette I tried to get in touch with you, left messages on your answering machine.

Leela Yes, thanks, it was good to hear from you. The song 'Jingle Bells' – it made me laugh.

Claudette I thought you might ring me back.

Leela I meant to. I was busy. I write the message down on a bit of paper and it gets lost.

Claudette Things have been happening. I needed to talk.

Leela I'm here now.

Claudette It passed.

Leela   People have to get on with their lives.

Claudette   Their men.

Leela   I don't have to apologise, Claudette.

Claudette   I was always around for you.

Leela   Curly lives near you.

Claudette   Curly doesn't know me. You know me inside out.

Pause. They hear the countdown to the New Year, then cheers, whistles and people singing.

Claudette   Watching's becoming a habit with me. I can't walk down a street at night without stopping to look through someone's window. I'm becoming obsessed. Honestly, I don't care whether they're in there or not. I stop in the middle of the road to listen to couples quarrelling and listen in on people's conversations in restaurants. The other day I was listening to this couple arguing about whether she ought to go away or not. I must have been staring at them without realising it. He turns to me and says 'Do you mind?' It's becoming embarrassing.

Leela   Poor Claudette.

Claudette   I can cope.

There's a knock on the door. **Claudette** *puts her fingers to her lips. They both sit still.*

Curly (*off*)   Quick, it's me. Curly.

Claudette *goes to the door and lets* **Curly** *in, helping her with bottles and cups.*

Curly   They're going mad down there. Streamers everywhere. I got caught up in the conga. Did I miss anything?

Claudette   You didn't miss anything.

Leela   We were talking about Christmas.

Curly   I'd rather put Christmas behind me, wouldn't you? All I could find was Babycham.

Claudette   Which cheapskate brought Babycham to a party?

Curly   We used to have a lot of laughs, though, didn't we? We were always giggling, remember? We didn't even need a reason, just laughed for the sake of laughing. I reckon we should all make a New Year's resolution to see more of each other.

Claudette   I'm all for that.

Leela   Me too.

Curly   Let's drink to it.

They raise their cups. There's the sound of someone approaching.

Man (*off*) I don't understand what's wrong with you.

Woman (*off, bitter laugh*)   You wouldn't, would you?

Claudette Under the coats.

They hide under the coats.

Curly It's just like being back at school.

Leela *and* **Claudette**   Sssh.

Silence. **Fran** *and* **Bentley** *enter.* **Bentley** *tries to hold* **Fran**, *but she moves away and locks the door.*

Fran   I can see why you chose her. She has a certain charm, a certain passive charm.

Bentley Come on, Fran.

Fran Though I'd always pictured you with someone a bit more dynamic. A real go-getter. Like you.

Bentley *tries to take her hand. She pulls it away.*

Fran   No. (*Slight pause.*) Do you want to end it?

Bentley Why would I want to end it?

Fran   You might be bored.

Bentley No. Are you?

Fran What do you think?

Bentley *kisses* **Fran**. *They lie on the floor.* **Fran** *traces her finger along* **Bentley**'s *face. He strokes her shoulders, removes her panties. They make love. It's tender, noiseless, furtive. They look at each other all the time. Afterwards, they lie still. Then* **Fran** *sits up on her elbows.* **Bentley** *stands, adjusting his clothes.*

Bentley Happy New Year.

They laugh.

Fran Close your eyes.

Bentley What for?

Fran Go on. Don't you trust me?

Bentley *closes his eyes. A moment passes.* **Bentley** *opens his eyes again.*

Bentley What?

Fran I just wanted to look at you.

Bentley Crazy woman. (*He kisses* **Fran**'s *cheek.*)

Fran Let's make love again.

Bentley What if someone comes in?

Fran Good. Let them come in.

Bentley Crazy.

Fran She's your guilty conscience, isn't she?

Bentley What?

Fran This is hardly politically correct, is it?

Bentley Come on. Let's get dressed.

Fran I am dressed. Is it?

Bentley Politics doesn't come into it.

Fran Politics comes into everything.

Bentley Even fucking?

Fran Especially fucking.

Bentley Get dressed.

Fran I agree politics shouldn't come into it. Whatever happened to *amor omnia vincit* and all that stuff?

Bentley What do you want me to do?

Fran A little honesty would be nice.

Bentley I'm always straight with you.

Fran I'd leave Jeff tomorrow, you know that. We're finished anyway.

Bentley It's not that easy, Fran. You know that.

Fran Tell me, do all black men let their heads rule their hearts?

Bentley Every evening she comes home she needs to talk. I mean really talk. She never does, though. She just potters around, makes pleasant conversation: 'had a nice day at the office dear?' Underneath it all you can hear this, like a grating sound, you can hear what she really wants to say struggling to get out. But she won't let it out.

Fran Let what out?

Bentley You wouldn't understand.

Fran I see. It's a black thing.

Bentley No. (*Slight pause.*) Yes. She's fighting to make something of herself. I know how hard that is even though I do believe that it's up to the individual to rise above all the shit. That's all that matters. Work hard and you can achieve anything. You're judged by what you do these days, aren't you? Not that she doesn't work hard. Do a good job and no one can touch you. (*Slight pause.*) So the small talk goes on and on. Worse thing is you stop listening and she knows you've stopped listening and she can't help resenting that. So there's that between you. Sometimes you – I can't bring myself to look at her, say I've got a lot of work to do. So it gets worse. You can't rest. You're so busy trying…to cope with it, deal with it. To be decent. You can't rest. I owe it to her…find the right time…explain…or… (*He shrugs hopelessly.*)

Fran (*rolls over on to her tummy*)   I don't want to make trouble, but I don't want to be hemmed in. I want to be free. I think people should be free.

Bentley (*takes her hands, pulls her up*)   And we will be. Soon.

They go. After a short while **Leela**, **Claudette** *and* **Curly** *come out from underneath the coats. Silence.*

Curly   Sorry, Leela.

Leela   What for? It's not your fault.

Claudette   The bastard.

Curly   Claudette.

Claudette   Fucking bastard.

Claudette   What do you want us to do?

Leela   I want us to go downstairs, that's all.

Claudette   Let's go downstairs then.

Source: Pinnock, W. (2013) 'Talking in tongues', in L. Goddard (ed.) *The Methuen Drama book of plays by black British writers*. London: Methuen Drama, pp. 185–189.

Reading 8.2 Extract from the script of the stage play *The Christ of Coldharbour Lane*

Oladipo Agboluaje

> Oladipo Agboluaje is a London-based playwright of Nigerian heritage. He has written plays for Oval House Theatre, the Soho Theatre, the Arcola, the Unicorn and West Yorkshire Playhouse, as well as radio dramas for the BBC.

Soundscape: The music from the gentleman's club morphs into the sound of the underground. All that remains from the previous scene is the pole.

OMO, in the tube. PASSENGERS jammed up around the pole, some with their heads stuck in the newspapers, magazines, novels. The rest hold on to the pole. They all avoid making eye contact with each other. Those reading newspapers or magazines shake them in unison. Those reading novels turn the page in unison.

PASSENGERS: (*To the sound of the train.*) 'Grin and bear it. Grin and bear it. Moan and Groan. Grin and bear it. Grin and bear it…'

The train grinds to a halt. PASSENGERS sway and halt in unison.

DRIVER: (*Over the PA.*) This is your driver speaking. Sorry for the delay. There is a signal failure at Victoria Station. We're being held here until further notice.

PASSENGERS groan collectively. They shake their newspapers and continue reading, avoiding making eye contact with each other.

Source: Agboluaje, O. (2016) *The Christ of Coldharbour Lane*. London: Oberon Books, pp. 44–45.

Chapter 9 readings

Reading 9.1 Extract from the novel *Small Island*

Andrea Levy

> Andrea Levy was a British writer of Jamaican heritage who was born in London. Her novels explore the complex experiences of people from the Caribbean who settled in the UK from the mid-twentieth century onwards. London often features as the setting for her stories and novels.

Content note: Please be aware that this reading explores racist attitudes towards the narrator.

Three women sitting neatly at desks perused me as I came through the door. In a puppet dance all three quickly glanced to each other then returned to staring on me.

'Good day,' I said.

Two dropped their heads returning to their business as if I had not spoken, leaving just an older woman to ask, 'Yes, do you want something?' This woman smiled on me – her countenance gleaming with so much joy that I could do nothing but return the welcome. Her beaming smile was so wide I had trouble stretching my own lips to match the delight. She bathed me in this greeting for several moments before breath sufficient enough for a reply returned to me.

'I am a teacher,' I said, intending to carry on with some further explanation. But I was startled to find myself timorous in this woman's friendly presence. My voice faltered into a tiny squeak. I took a moment to cough into my hand. Having composed myself I began again. 'I am a teacher and I understand this is the place at which I should present myself for a position in that particular profession.' Through this woman's warm smile I detected a little confusion. Too well bred to say 'What?' she looked a quizzical eye on me, which shouted the word just as audibly. I repeated myself clearly but before I had completed the statement the woman asked of me sweetly, 'Did you say you are a teacher?'

'I am,' I said. My own smile was causing me some pain behind my ears but still I endeavoured to respond correctly to her generosity. I handed her the two letters of recommendation which I had taken from my bag in anticipation of their requirement. She politely held out her slim hand, took them, then indicated for me to sit. However, instead of studying the letters she merely held them in her hand without even glancing at their contents.

'What are these?' she asked with a little laugh ruffling up the words.

'These are my letters of recommendation. One you will see is from the headmaster at—'

Interrupting me, her lips relaxed for just a moment before taking up a smile once more, 'Where are you from?' she asked. The letters were still held in mid-air where I had placed them.

'I am from Jamaica,' I told her.

She was silent, we both grinning on each other in a genteel way. I thought to bring her attention back to the letters. 'One of the letters I have given you is from my last post. Written by the headmaster himself. You will see that—'

But once more she interrupted me: 'Where?'

I wondered if it would be impolite to tell this beguiling woman to read the letter in her hand so all her questions might be answered. I concluded it would. 'At Half Way Tree Parish School,' I told her.

'Where's that?'

'In Kingston, Jamaica.'

She leaned back on her chair and instead of opening the letters she began playing with them – flicking the paper against her fingers. 'And where did you train to be a teacher?' she asked me.

Her comely smile belied the rudeness of her tone. And I could not help but note that all gladness had left her eye and remained only at her mouth. 'I trained at the teacher-training college in Constant Spring, under the tutelage of Miss Morgan.'

'Is that in Jamaica?'

'Yes.'

It was relief that tipped her head to one side while she let out a long breath. I eased myself believing everything was now cleared between us. Until, leaning all her ample charm forward, she told me, 'Well, I'm afraid you can't teach here,' and passed the unopened letters back to me.

I was sure there had been some misunderstanding, although I was not clear as to where it had occurred. Perhaps I had not made myself as understood as I could. 'If you would read the letters,' I said, 'one will tell you about the three years of training as a teacher I received in Jamaica while the other letter is concerned with the position I held as a teacher at—'

She did not let me finish. 'The letters don't matter,' she told me. 'You can't teach in this country. You're not qualified to teach here in England.'

'But...' was the only sound that came from me.

'It doesn't matter that you were a teacher in Jamaica,' she went on, 'you will not be allowed to teach here.' She shook the letters at me. 'Take these back. They're of no use.' When I did not take them from her hand she rattled them harder at me. 'Take them,' she said, so loud she almost shouted. Her smile was stale as a gargoyle. My hand shook as it reached out for the letters.

And all I could utter was 'But—'

'Miss, I'm afraid there really is no point your sitting there arguing with me.' And she giggled. The untimely chortle made my mouth gape. 'It's not up to me. It's the decision of the education authority. I can do nothing to change that. And, I'm afraid, neither can you. Now, I don't mean to hurry you but I have an awful lot to do. So thank you for coming.'

Every organ I possessed was screaming on this woman, 'What are you saying to me?'

She went back about her business. Her face now in its normal repose looked as severe as that of the principal at my college. She picked up a piece of paper, wrote something at the top. She looked to another piece of paper then stopped, aware that I was still there.

'How long is the training in England?' I asked her.

'Goodbye,' she said, pointing a finger at the door.

'Must I go back to a college?'

'Really, miss, I have just explained everything to you. You do speak English? Have you not understood me? It's quite simple. There is no point you asking me anything else. Now, please, I have a lot to do. Thank you.'

And she smiled on me – again! What fancy feigning. I could not stand up. My legs were too weak under me. I sat for a little to redeem my composure. At last finding strength to pull myself up, I told this woman, 'I will come back again when I am qualified to teach in this country.'

'Yes,' she said, 'you do that. Goodbye.'

Source: Levy, A. (2004) *Small island*. London: Headline Publishing, pp. 451–455.

Reading 9.2 Extract from the script of a stage play adaptation of *Small Island*

Helen Edmundson

> Helen Edmundson is a dramatist from London who writes primarily for theatre. She has also written television and radio dramas. Her plays, many of them adapted from literary sources, often use intimate personal stories to address bigger political and historical themes.

The following day. A miserable, bomb-damaged London street. A crooked signpost points directions to different council offices – 'Education Department', 'Planning Department'. GILBERT is waiting. He looks worried. He is holding his hat in his hands, turning it round and round. From time to time, someone (white) hurries by.

After a moment, HORTENSE comes from the direction of the offices. She is wearing her pristine white coat, hat and gloves. She is holding her handbag and clutching some letters in her hand. She reaches the street, hesitates for a moment, confused, panicky, then begins to walk away. GILBERT sees her –

GILBERT. Hortense!

> *He rushes towards her. HORTENSE changes direction and begins to walk another way. GILBERT goes after her.*

How you get on? They say you have a job?

HORTENSE. Why are you here? I told you not to wait for me.

GILBERT. Wait! What they say?

HORTENSE. What business is it of yours? Leave me alone!
I don't want you here!

HORTENSE *hurries purposefully away in another direction.*

GILBERT. You don't even know where you are!

A MAN *(white) passes her, almost bumps into her.*

MAN. Watch where you're going!

HORTENSE *stops very still and lowers her head.* GILBERT *approaches her carefully.*

GILBERT. Hortense? Hortense, no more cuss me. Tell me what happen.

She is silent for a moment, trying to recover her composure.

HORTENSE. They say I can't teach.

GILBERT. What they mean?

HORTENSE. They say I would have to train all over again. None of my qualifications count for anything. None of my letters of recommendation. They speak to I like I am a fool.

GILBERT. Man, that…

He shakes his head. A WOMAN *(white) passes by and stares at them. She tuts as she walks on.* GILBERT *waits for* HORTENSE *to speak.*

HORTENSE. I walk into a cupboard.

GILBERT *takes this in for a moment.*

GILBERT. Why you do that?

HORTENSE. Because I thought it was the door to leave by.

GILBERT. Oh.

HORTENSE. But it was a cupboard. The office women… they all laugh on me.

GILBERT. Oh dear. I see. And tell me, what was this cupboard like?

HORTENSE *looks at him – trying to read his intention.*

HORTENSE. There was a bucket and a mop.

GILBERT. Ah. Now that is a broom cupboard. I have walked into many broom cupboards. I walk into a broom cupboard, a stationery cupboard…

HORTENSE. This one had paper also.

GILBERT. Did it? Ah. Two functions. Now that is an interesting cupboard.

She stares at him. His eyes twinkle at her a little.

HORTENSE. Are you teasing me, Gilbert Joseph?

GILBERT. And what do you do when you come from the cupboard?

HORTENSE. I left the room.

GILBERT. You no say anything to the women who was laughing on you? You should have told them it was an interesting cupboard.

HORTENSE. It was a dirty cupboard.

GILBERT. Well then. Cha, you should tell them that you are used to clean cupboards where you come from.

HORTENSE. I am.

GILBERT. Oh, I don't doubt it, Miss Spitfire.

She looks at him sharply. He smiles, and for a moment it seems that she might smile back. But then her face falls back into despair.

Tell you what – you wan' see the King?

HORTENSE. What are you talking about…?

GILBERT. You ever been on a London bus?

HORTENSE. No.

GILBERT. We will take a ride on a red London bus. We will sit on the top deck. I will show you Buckingham Palace and the Houses of Parliament. Big Ben. Piccadilly Circus. All the fine sights. You like that?

She nods. But then her eyes fill with tears. She fights against them. GILBERT *moves to put his arm around her but then decides he'd better not.*

HORTENSE. I dreamed of coming to England.

GILBERT. And you are here. Not many people have their dream come true.

HORTENSE. But what am I to do now? If I can't teach.

GILBERT. Don't worry. Don't worry, Hortense. I can look after you.

HORTENSE. I don't need looking after!

Pause. GILBERT *thinks.*

GILBERT. Well then. What else can you do? Can you sew?

HORTENSE. Of course.

GILBERT. Is that 'of course' like you can cook? Or can you actually sew?

Source: Edmundson, H. (2019) *Small island.* London: Nick Hern Books, pp. 107–109.

Chapter 10 readings

Reading 10.1 Extract from the autobiography *An Angel at My Table*

Janet Frame

> Janet Frame was a New Zealand writer from a working-class background who wrote novels, short stories and poetry. Some of her fiction addresses her experience of time spent in mental hospitals after a misdiagnosis of schizophrenia. Her autobiography, *An Angel at My Table*, was originally published in three volumes in 1982–85.

Content note: Please be aware that this reading briefly mentions corporal punishment.

One morning, during my first week at school, I sneaked into Mum and Dad's bedroom, opened the top drawer of the duchesse, where the coins 'brought back from the war' were kept, and helped myself to a handful. I then went to Dad's best trousers hanging behind the door, put my hand in the pocket (how cold and slippery the lining!), and took out two coins. Hearing someone coming, I hastily thrust the money under the duchesse and left the room, and later, when the coast was clear, I retrieved my hoard and on my way to school stopped at Heath's store to buy some chewing gum.

   Mr Heath looked sternly at me. 'This money won't buy anything,' he said. 'It's Egyptian.'

   'I know,' I lied. Then, handing him the money from Dad's pocket, I asked, 'Will this buy me some chewing gum?'

   'That's better,' he said, returning yet another of the coins, a farthing. Armed with a supply of chewing gum, I waited at the door of the Infant Room, a large room with a platform or stage at one end and double doors opening on to Standard One, and as the children went into the room, I gave each a 'pillow' of chewing gum. Later, Miss Botting, a woman in a blue costume the same colour as the castor-oil bottle, suddenly stopped her teaching and asked, 'Billy Delamare, what are you eating?'

   'Chewing gum, Miss Botting.'

   'Where did you get it?'

   'From Jean Frame, Miss Botting.' (I was known at school as Jean and at home as Nini.)

   'Dids McIvor, where did you get your chewing gum?'

   'From Jean Frame, Miss.'

   'Jean Frame, where did you get the chewing gum?'

   'From Heath's, Miss Botting.'

   'Where did you get the money?'

   'My father gave it to me.'

Evidently Miss Botting did not believe me. Suddenly she was determined to get 'the truth' out of me. She repeated her question. 'Where did you get the money? I want the *truth*.'

I repeated my answer, substituting *Dad* for *father*.

'Come out here.'

I came out in front of the class.

'Go up on the platform.'

I went up on to the platform.

'Now tell me where you got the money.'

Determinedly I repeated my answer.

Playtime came. The rest of the class went out to play while Miss Botting and I grimly faced each other.

'Tell me the truth,' she said.

I replied, 'Dad gave me the money.'

She sent for Myrtle and Bruddie, who informed her with piping innocence that Dad did not give me the money.

'Yes, he did,' I insisted. 'He called me back when you had both gone to school.'

'He didn't.'

'He did.'

All morning I stayed on the platform. The class continued their reading lessons. I stayed on the platform through lunchtime and into the afternoon, still refusing to confess. I was beginning to feel afraid, instead of defiant, as if I hadn't a friend in the world, and because I knew that Myrtle and Bruddie would 'tell' as soon as they got home, I felt that I never wanted to go home. All the places I had found – the birch log in Glenham, the top of the climbers in Edendale, the places in the songs and poems – seemed to have vanished, leaving me with no place. I held out obstinately until mid-afternoon, when the light was growing thin with masses of dark tiredness showing behind it, and the schoolroom was filled with a nowhere dust, and a small voice answered from the scared me in answer to Miss Botting's repeated question. 'I took the money out of my father's pocket.'

While I'd been lying, I had somehow protected myself; I knew now that I had no protection. I'd been found out as a thief. I was so appalled by my future prospects that I don't remember if Miss Botting strapped me. I know she gave the news to the class, and it spread quickly around the school that I was a thief. Loitering at the school gate, wondering where to go and what to do, I saw Myrtle and Bruddie, carefree as ever, on their way home. I walked slowly along the cocksfoot-bordered road. I don't know when I had learned to read, but I had read and knew the stories in the primer books, and I thought of the story of the fox that sprang out from the side of the road and swallowed the child. No one knew what had happened or where the child had gone, until one day when the fox was walking by, a kind person heard 'Let me out, let me out!' coming from the fox's belly, whereupon the kind person killed the fox, slit the belly open, and lo, the child emerged whole, unharmed, and was taken by the kind person to live in a wood in a cottage made of coconut ice with a licorice chimney …

I finally arrived at our place. Myrtle was leaning over the gate. 'Dad knows,' she said, in a matter-of-fact voice. I went up the path. The front door was open and Dad was waiting with the strap in his hand. 'Come into the bedroom,' he said sternly. He administered his usual 'hiding', not excessive, as some children had, but sharp and full of anger that one of his children was a *thief*. *Thief, thief*. At home and at school I was now called *Thief*.

Source: Frame, J. (2008) *An angel at my table*. London: Virago Press, pp. 22–24.

Reading 10.2 Extract from the screenplay of *An Angel at My Table*

Laura Jones

> Laura Jones is an Australian scriptwriter who has written original film screenplays, as well as adaptations of high-profile novels and memoirs for the screen. She has adapted both classic and contemporary texts, and worked with film directors such as Jane Campion, Gillian Armstrong, Sarah Gavron and Alan Parker.

Janet's hand slides into Dad's best trousers hanging on a hook behind the bedroom door. There is the chink of coins.

Janet stands at the door of the Infants room. She hands each child who comes in a pillow of chewing-gum, naming them: Marjorie, Joy, Billy, and so on.

The children sit at desks in rows, all chewing gum. Two monitors walk up and down the aisles giving out green-covered copy books.
   Miss Botting turns from the board where she has lettered the day and date.
   Not all the children stop chewing as she turns.
MISS BOTTING: Billy Delaware. What are you eating?
BILLY: Chewing-gum, Miss Botting.
MISS BOTTING: Where did you get it?
BILLY: From Jean Frame, Miss Botting.
MISS BOTTING: Dids McIvor, where did you get your chewing-gum?
All the chewing has now stopped, everyone transfixed by the scent of trouble.
DIDS: From Jean Frame, Miss.
MISS BOTTING: Jean Frame, where did you get the chewing-gum?
JANET: From Heath's, Miss Botting.
MISS BOTTING: Where did you get the money?
JANET: My father gave it to me.
MISS BOTTING: Where did you get the money? I want the *truth*.
JANET: Dad gave it to me.
MISS BOTTING: Come out here.
Janet gets up from her desk and goes to the front of the class.
MISS BOTTING: Come up here.
Janet climbs up on to the raised platform, where Miss Botting's desk and

chair stand, in front of the blackboard.
MISS BOTTING: Now tell me where you got the money.
JANET: My father gave me the money.
MISS BOTTING: I want the *truth*.
JANET: Dad gave it to me.
MISS BOTTING: Face the blackboard.
Janet turns and faces the blackboard. Miss Botting puts her hand on Janet's back and moves her closer to the board, so she is only a few inches away from the cloudy green board.
MISS BOTTING: Now you'll stay there until you tell me the *truth*.

Later, Janet is now alone in the classroom. She is still in the same position, on the platform, in front of the blackboard. The board is now covered in words and simple Infants sentences, in Miss Botting's perfect ball-and-stick lettering.
  The high sound of the school at lunch in the playground can be heard.
  Janet's eyes roam across the pattern of words and numbers on the board.

Miss Botting, the class seated behind her, stands in front of the platform. Late afternoon sun lights the columns of dust and chalk floating in the air.
MISS BOTTING: Turn around, Jean Frame.
Janet turns around.
MISS BOTTING: Are you ready to tell me the *truth*?
Janet pauses; then finds herself saying, in a small voice.
JANET: I took the money out of my father's pocket.
Miss Botting is pleased; the class gasps.

The next day, Janet walks through the school playground: all the games of hopscotch, jacks, ball, and chasings are going on around her.
  We hear a chorus, like cicadas, saying THIEF THIEF THIEF THIEF THIEF. They are not children's voices, but Janet's imagination telling her what everyone must be saying and thinking.
  BLACK SCREEN

Source: Jones, L. (1990) *An angel at my table: the screenplay, from the three volume autobiography of Janet Frame*. [Screenplay]. London: Pandora, pp. 4–6.

Reading 10.3 Extract from the novel *The Hours*
Michael Cunningham

> Michael Cunningham is an American writer of novels, short stories and screenplays. Cunningham acknowledges that the novelist Virginia Woolf is a huge influence on his work. This is apparent in his writing, where he often presents the fleeting thoughts, associations and states of consciousness of his characters.

Content note: Please be aware that this reading briefly mentions suicide.

Mrs. Dalloway said she would buy the flowers herself.

For Lucy had her work cut out for her. The doors would have to be taken off their hinges; Rumpelmayer's men were coming. And then, thought Clarissa Dalloway, what a morning—fresh as if issued to children on a beach.

It is Los Angeles. It is 1949.

Laura Brown is trying to lose herself. No, that's not it exactly—she is trying to keep herself by gaining entry into a parallel world. She lays the book face down on her chest. Already her bedroom (no, *their* bedroom) feels more densely inhabited, more actual, because a character named Mrs. Dalloway is on her way to buy flowers. Laura glances at the clock on the nightstand. It's well past seven. Why did she buy this clock, this hideous thing, with its square green face in a rectangular black Bakelite sarcophagus—how could she ever have thought it was smart? She should not be permitting herself to read, not this morning of all mornings; not on Dan's birthday. She should be out of bed, showered and dressed, fixing breakfast for Dan and Richie. She can hear them downstairs, her husband making his own breakfast, ministering to Richie. She should be there, shouldn't she? She should be standing before the stove in her new robe, full of simple, encouraging talk. Still, when she opened her eyes a few minutes ago (after seven already!)—when she still half inhabited her dream, some sort of pulsating machinery in the remote distance, a steady pounding like a gigantic mechanical heart, which seemed to be drawing nearer—she felt the dank sensation around her, the nowhere feeling, and knew it was going to be a difficult day. She knew she was going to have trouble believing in herself, in the rooms of her house, and when she glanced over at this new book on her nightstand, stacked atop the one she finished last night, she reached for it automatically, as if reading were the singular and obvious first task of the day, the only viable way to negotiate the transit from sleep to obligation. Because she is pregnant, she is allowed these lapses. She is allowed, for now, to read unreasonably, to linger in bed, to cry or grow furious over nothing.

She will make up for breakfast by baking Dan a perfect birthday cake; by ironing the good cloth; by setting a big bouquet of flowers (roses?) in the middle of the table, and surrounding it with gifts. That should compensate, shouldn't it?

She will read one more page. One more page, to calm and locate herself, then she'll get out of bed.

What a lark! What a plunge! For so it had always seemed to her, when, with a little squeak of the hinges, which she could hear now, she had burst open the French windows and plunged at Bourton into the open air. How fresh, how calm, stiller than this of course, the air was in the early morning; like the flap of a wave; the kiss of a wave; chill and sharp and yet (for a girl of eighteen as she then was) solemn, feeling as she did, standing there at the open window, that something awful was about to happen; looking at the flowers, at the trees with the smoke winding off them and the rooks rising, falling; standing and looking until Peter Walsh said, 'Musing among the vegetables?'—was that it?—'I prefer men to cauliflowers'—was that it? He must have said it at breakfast one morning when she had gone out on to the terrace—Peter Walsh. He would be back from India one of these days, June or July, she forgot which, for his letters were awfully dull; it was his sayings one remembered; his eyes, his pocket-knife, his smile, his grumpiness and, when millions of things had utterly vanished—how strange it was!—a few sayings like this about cabbages.

She inhales deeply. It is so beautiful; it is so much more than ... well, than almost anything, really. In another world, she might have spent her whole life reading. But this is the new world, the rescued world—there's not much room for idleness. So much has been risked and lost; so many have died. Less than five years ago Dan himself was believed to have died, at Anzio, and when he was revealed two days later to be alive after all (he and some poor boy from Arcadia had had the same name), it seemed he had been resurrected. He seemed to have returned, still sweet-tempered, still smelling like himself, from the realm of the dead (the stories you heard then about Italy, about Saipan and Okinawa, about Japanese mothers who killed their children and themselves rather than be taken prisoner), and when he came back to California he was received as something more than an ordinary hero. He could (in the words of his own alarmed mother) have had anyone, any pageant winner, any vivacious and compliant girl, but through some obscure and possibly perverse genius had kissed, courted, and proposed to his best friend's older sister, the bookworm, the foreign-looking one with the dark, close-set eyes and the Roman nose, who had never been sought after or cherished; who had always been left alone, to read. What could she say but yes? How could she deny a handsome, good-hearted boy, practically a member of the family, who had come back from the dead?

So now she is Laura Brown. Laura Zielski, the solitary girl, the incessant reader, is gone, and here in her place is Laura Brown.

One more page, she decides; just one more. She isn't ready yet; the tasks that lie ahead (putting on her robe, brushing her hair, going down to the kitchen) are still too thin, too elusive. She will permit herself another minute here, in bed, before entering the day. She will allow herself just a little more time. She is taken by a wave of feeling, a sea-swell, that rises from under her breast and buoys her, floats her gently, as if she were a sea creature thrown back from the sand where it had beached itself—as if she had returned from a realm of crushing gravity to her true medium, the suck and swell of saltwater, that weightless brilliance.

She stiffened a little on the kerb, waiting for Durtnall's van to pass. A charming woman, Scrope Purvis thought her (knowing her as one does know people who live next door to one in Westminster); a touch of the bird about her, of the jay, blue-green, light, vivacious, though she was over fifty, and grown very white since her illness. There she perched, never seeing him, waiting to cross, very upright.

For having lived in Westminster—how many years now? over twenty,—one feels even in the midst of the traffic, or waking at night, Clarissa was positive, a particular hush, or solemnity; an indescribable pause; a suspense (but that might be her heart, affected, they said, by influenza) before Big Ben strikes. There! Out it boomed. First a warning, musical; then the hour, irrevocable. The leaden circles dissolved in the air. Such fools we are, she thought, crossing Victoria Street. For Heaven only knows why one loves it so, how one sees it so, making it up, building it round one, tumbling it, creating it every moment afresh; but the veriest frumps, the most dejected of miseries sitting on doorsteps (drink their downfall) do the same; can't be dealt with, she felt positive, by Acts of Parliament for that very reason: they love life. In people's eyes, in the swing, tramp, and trudge; in the bellow and the uproar, the carriages, motor cars, omnibuses, vans, sandwich men shuffling and swinging; brass bands; barrel organs; in the triumph and the jingle and the strange high singing of some aeroplane overhead was what she loved; life; London; this moment of June.

How, Laura wonders, could someone who was able to write a sentence like that—who was able to feel everything contained in a sentence like that—come to kill herself? What in the world is wrong with people? Summoning resolve, as if she were about to dive into cold water, Laura closes the book and lays it on the nightstand. She does not dislike her child, does not dislike her husband. She will rise and be cheerful.

At least, she thinks, she does not read mysteries or romances. At least she continues to improve her mind. Right now she is reading Virginia Woolf, all of Virginia Woolf, book by book—she is fascinated by the idea of a woman like that, a woman of such brilliance, such strangeness, such immeasurable sorrow; a woman who had genius but still filled her pocket with a stone and waded out into a river. She, Laura, likes to imagine (it's one of her most closely held secrets) that she had a touch of brilliance herself, just a hint of it, though she knows most people probably walk around with similar hopeful suspicions curled up like tiny fists inside them, never divulged. She wonders, while she pushes a cart through the supermarket or has her hair done, if the other women aren't all thinking, to some degree or other, the same thing: Here is the brilliant spirit, the woman of sorrows, the woman of transcendent joys, who would rather be elsewhere, who has consented to perform simple and essentially foolish tasks, to examine tomatoes, to sit under a hair dryer, because it is her art and her duty. Because the war is over, the world has survived, and we are here, all of us, making homes, having and raising children, creating not just books or paintings but a whole world—a world of order and harmony where children are safe (if not happy), where men who have seen horrors beyond imagining, who have acted bravely and well, come home to lighted windows, to perfume, to plates and napkins.

What a lark! What a plunge!

Laura gets out of bed. It is a hot, white morning in June. She can hear her husband moving around downstairs. A metal lid kisses the rim of its pan. She takes her robe, pale aqua chenille, from the newly reupholstered chair and the chair appears, squat and fat, skirted, its nubbly salmon-colored fabric held down by cord and salmon-colored buttons in a diamond pattern. In the morning heat of June, with the robe whisked away, the chair in its bold new fabric seems surprised to find itself a chair at all.

She brushes her teeth, brushes her hair, and starts downstairs. She pauses several treads from the bottom, listening, waiting; she is again possessed (it seems to be getting worse) by a dreamlike feeling, as if she is standing in the wings, about to go onstage and perform in a play for which she is not appropriately dressed, and for which she had not adequately rehearsed. What, she wonders, is wrong with her. This is her husband in the kitchen; this is her little boy. All the man and boy require of her is her presence and, of course, her love. She conquers the desire to go quietly back upstairs, to her bed and book. She conquers her irritation at the sound of her husband's voice, saying something to Richie about napkins (why does his voice remind her sometimes of a potato being grated?). She descends the last three stairs, crosses the narrow foyer, enters the kitchen.

She thinks of the cakes she will bake, the flowers she'll buy. She thinks of roses surrounded by gifts.

Her husband has made the coffee, poured cereal for himself and their son. On the tabletop, a dozen white roses offer their complex, slightly sinister beauty. Through the clear glass vase Laura can see the bubbles, fine as grains of sand, clinging to their stems. Beside the roses stand cereal box and milk carton, with their words and pictures.

'Good morning,' her husband says, raising his eyebrows as if he is surprised but delighted to see her.

'Happy birthday,' she says.

Source: Cunningham, M. (1999) *The hours*. London: Fourth Estate, pp. 37–43.

Reading 10.4 Extract from the novel *The Inheritance of Loss*

Kiran Desai

> Kiran Desai is an Indian writer who was educated in India, England and the United States. Her second novel *The Inheritance of Loss* investigates rural life in India alongside the migrant experience in the United States.

The judge took a spoon from a bowl of cream and thwacked a white blob into the red.

'Well,' he said to his granddaughter, 'one must not disturb one another. One's had to hire a tutor for you—a lady down the hill, can't afford a convent school—why should one be in the business of fattening the church …? Too far, anyway, and one doesn't have the luxury of transport anymore, does one? Can't send you to a government school, I suppose … you'd come out speaking with the wrong accent and picking your nose. …'

The light diminished now, to a filament, tender as Edison's first miracle held between delicate pincers of wire in the glass globe of the bulb. It glowed a last blue crescent, then failed.

'Damn it!' said the judge.

In her bed later that evening, Sai lay under a tablecloth, for the last sheets had long worn out. She could sense the swollen presence of the forest, hear the hollow-knuckled knocking of the bamboo, the sound of the *jhora* that ran deep in the décolleté of the mountain. Batted down by household sounds during the day, it rose at dusk, to sing pure-voiced into the windows. The structure of the house seemed fragile in the balance of this night—just a husk. The tin roof rattled in the wind. When Sai moved her foot, her toes went silently through the rotted fabric. She had a fearful feeling of having entered a space so big it reached both backward and forward.

Suddenly, as if a secret door had opened in her hearing, she became aware of the sound of microscopic jaws slow-milling the house to sawdust, a sound hard to detect for being so closely knit unto the air, but once identified, it grew monumental. In this climate, she would learn, untreated wood could be chewed up in a season.

Source: Desai, K. (2006) *The inheritance of loss*. London: Hamish Hamilton, p. 34.

Chapter 11 readings

Reading 11.1 Extract from the memoir *Biting through the Skin*

Nina Mukerjee Furstenau

> Nina Mukerjee Furstenau is a journalist, author and editor. She was born in Thailand to Indian parents, and her family moved to Kansas when she was a child. As a young adult, she served in the US Peace Corps and was one of its delegates for the UN World Conference on Women in Nairobi, Kenya, in 1985.

I am six and sitting alone on a black bus seat. My legs swing, almost kicking the back of the seat in front of me. The windows have a horizontal bar to slide them open or shut and there is a small wedge open at the top of mine. Ahead of me about five rows are the backs of the heads of my family: wispy hair, surprisingly gray for a fortyish father, flies about in streaks of sun slanting through the windows and reveals glimpses of a smooth, bald brown pate. This, the very top of my *baba*, is a head and shoulders above the tidy bun sitting quietly on my mother's neck, and stair-stepped down from her is just the tip of my wavy-haired brother's head. I lift my chin to watch as others leave the bus to buy papaya juice or a mango, or to stroll around the small highway pull-off until the driver is ready to continue on the switchback road up, up, and nauseatingly up through the blue Nilgiri Hills near Chennai. My stomach feels queasy from sickness, but I have been told to eat, hence my bully separateness from the rest of my family.

    I have a banana in my lap, the small brown Indian kind full of flavour, and have just finished a sandwich my mother packed this morning. A crowd has gathered around the bus and far below me, I see a small child standing and looking straight into my eyes. He wears shorts and a buttoned shirt of some indeterminate color and he stands as tall as the elbows of the older children near him. No one else in the crowd looks at my window. His eyes stay steady though the crowd jostles him and the ragged hem of his shirt rucks up. I startle as I realize he has seen me eat the last bites of my bread. He has watched me swallow. I look at him more closely and see his hands are cupped.

    I suddenly feel the bulkiness of the gummed bread still in my throat and stare at the banana in my lap. I want a drink but do not call out for one. My mother is talking earnestly, using her hands and tipping her head, making a point that causes my father to chuckle. *Do not waste your food, Nin*, she would admonish, and I look back to the boy and lift my banana to peel it. But I cannot do it. I feel the black vinyl seat stick to the backs of my thighs as I lift my torso up. Not high enough. I stand and the vinyl pulls free of my skin. I reach out the top of my window, toss the banana out, and watch as it drops and wobbles through the hot air. All else freezes as it makes its diver's arc, end over end. The sounds of vendors, of the driver's radio, of talking tourists, fade. The milling people themselves, in their colorful saris, with their turbans and beards pulled tight under the chin, blur. Then, just before the boy's outstretched hand can close around the fruit, the smell of the idling bus engine reaches my nose and I sit back quickly. My grandparents said just last night not to 'encourage them,' so I glance up to make sure no one saw.

Now, the bread in my throat goes down and I swallow audibly. I hope I will not be hungry later, and I look down once more at the boy. He has deftly caught the banana, though sometimes I imagine it dropping in the dirt first before he snatches it up. He takes quick bites straight through the bitter peel, as if someone might get to it still. I imagine what banana peel tastes like and what the soft, fleshy fruit would feel like beneath it on my tongue. I rub my tongue behind my front teeth and grimace. Then, I am frantic. What if my mother sees that the peel is not in my trash? Will she ask what became of the fruit? She walks back to check on me and never looks into the wilted paper sandwich wrapping. She pats my head and goes back to her seat as the bus pulls away.

I realise now how paralyzed I was seeing a child beg for food. I had seen beggars in India asking for money, but none had affected me as much as that boy. During our meals around a shellacked wooden table in Kansas, I spent inordinate amounts of time hiding foods that I didn't like. Peas were pushed under crusts of bread, and *korola*, a gourd that my father and I called 'blood purifier' to indicate its bitterness, I mashed with my fork to subdue. After the parts I didn't like were sorted to satisfaction, I ate the comfort foods, like potatoes with black pepper, or rice with minced meat, with such relish that I would finish in five minutes the meal my mother wanted us to linger over. Every dinnertime, at exactly 5:30, my father would turn on the national news with Huntley and Brinkley. All conversation stopped so he could hear. My back was to the television so I had nothing to do but stare at the foods my mother had prepared and rest my head on my hand.

The cautionary stories of starving children in India bandied about in Kansas to force kids to finish their peas did not apply to my life until that moment on the bus. Now I understand I had formed an acute sense of privilege in being born who and what and where I was. My family lived with this dichotomy all their lives, but that's when I saw it first. My grandfather felt that the economy ran by families hiring a cook, a driver, a gardener. They kept order by separating people into groups that served and supervised. In many ways, I think that moment on the bus was the impetus behind my later development work in the Peace Corps, behind my teenage squabbles with my family over politics after I began turning around and watching the news unfold each night on TV. In the end, for me, there was that boy, eating a fruit with absolute concentration and no quibbling, peel and all.

Source: Furstenau, N.M. (2013) *Biting through the skin: an Indian kitchen in America's heartland*. Iowa City: University of Iowa Press, pp. xvi–xviii.

Reading 11.2 Extract from an interview with Nina Mukerjee Furstenau

Lania Knight

LANIA KNIGHT (LK):

How were you able to write moments from long ago with such rich detail?

NINA MUKERJEE FURSTENAU (NMF):

That's a good question, and I think a lot of people who write non-fiction struggle with this. And I personally think that when you start focusing on a period in your life, a memory might emerge that's familiar and that you've thought of from time to time, but when you continue to consider it specifically, it might lead into other tangents of memory. Or you might be lucky enough to have people who are still in your life who could talk about that same event with you.

Things will sift through that maybe you hadn't considered before as part of that memory. I think that more and more things surface as you give yourself time to consider it. There will be an emotional truth that comes up. Often, I think, we all understand that memory is different, depending on who's thinking about it. Everybody brings a different view to the same event.

So, you have to consider what's true to you. And when you're writing, I think it's fair enough that that is the part that emerges in your writing because you are hopefully prefacing the whole work with something that says this is your angle or your view of the events that happened.

It's really nice to enrich the context of what you're doing. Let yourself probe those memories a little bit more. It's kind of surprising how many will arise if just given a little focus and a little bit of time.

LK:

About reflection and insight, my question is: what was the process for realising and writing about the banana scene [in *Biting through the Skin*] as a pivotal moment in your life?

NMF:

That was a event in my life that I spent a lot of years thinking was a dream. It came to me a lot, you know. I thought it was just something that, you know, came up in dreams, but I asked my mother. I said, 'Were we on that bus?' Because our family didn't take buses very often. So, could that have actually been the case? Were we in the Nilgiri Hills going up on a bus to see tea plantations? And we were. And I asked her, 'Would the bus driver have stopped at a fruit stand halfway up?' 'Yes, they did that all the time.' And every answer she gave me sort of built the scene that I was already seeing in my mind.

So, it was a process of just sort of discovering that that was not a dream. And the more I think about that scene, you know, I realise it was so vivid, you know. The young boy, he was probably my age, but he was small because he probably didn't have the nutrition I had had. He had an indeterminate khaki-colour shirt on. There was two boys standing next to him. I remember his large, beautiful, big brown eyes. And I remember just being sort of paralysed at that moment thinking, 'That could be me'. And I was five or six.

So, it was a moment that pivoted everything for me. It was a moment that probably has determined a lot of my life choices.

And I think for students who, especially who want to explore the world through artistic means, maybe writing, maybe other creative outlets, it's important to let yourself feel important and weighted moments that happen to you.

Because I think that if you write from that place – and for me, I have been; ever since I started writing from that place, that boy, and what that meant in my life, then and how it influenced all my decisions since – then you are writing something that no one else can write. It becomes your superpower.

And I think that identifying that for me, I was just sort of taken aback. I was like, 'Oh, my goodness! I think that's why I went into the Peace Corps.' I think that boy is why I started teaching about food systems journalism, to explore how foods are presented to our plate. I started working on food security and food and identity. And I've done that ever since.

Every single decision I've ever made, I really think was influenced by that young boy. And I really wish I could find that young man, find out what happened to him. I guess, of course, you know, never will. But he was pivotal in my life. And I think that every one of us has moments perhaps like that.

Source: Furstenau, N.M. (2023) Interviewed by L. Knight for The Open University, 27 June.

Reading 11.3 Extract from the essay 'Jesus Shaves'

David Sedaris

> David Sedaris is an American humour writer. Sedaris's pieces appear regularly in *The New Yorker* and have twice been included in *The Best American Essays* yearly anthology. There are over ten million copies of his books in print and they have been translated into 25 languages.

'Easter is a party for to eat of the lamb,' the Italian nanny explained. 'One too may eat of the chocolate.'
   'And who brings the chocolate?' the teacher asked.
   I knew the word, so I raised my hand, saying, 'The rabbit of Easter. He bring of the chocolate.'

'A rabbit?' The teacher, assuming I'd used the wrong word, positioned her index fingers on top of her head, wriggling them as though they were ears. 'You mean one of these? A *rabbit* rabbit?'

'Well, sure,' I said. 'He come in the night when one sleep on a bed. With a hand he have a basket and foods.'

The teacher sighed and shook her head. As far as she was concerned, I had just explained everything that was wrong with my country. 'No, no,' she said. 'Here in France the chocolate is brought by a big bell that flies in from Rome.'

I called for a time-out. 'But how do the bell know where you live?'

'Well,' she said, 'how does the rabbit?'

It was a decent point, but at least a rabbit has eyes. That's a start. Rabbits move from place to place, while most bells can only go back and forth — and they can't even do that on their own power. On top of that, the Easter Bunny has character. He's someone you'd like to meet and shake hands with. A bell has all the personality of a cast-iron skillet. It's like saying that come Christmas, a magic dustpan flies in from the North Pole, led by eight flying cinder blocks. Who wants to stay up all night so they can see a bell? And why fly one in from Rome when they've got more bells than they know what to do with right here in Paris? That's the most implausible aspect of the whole story, as there's no way the bells of France would allow a foreign worker to fly in and take their jobs. That Roman bell would be lucky to get work cleaning up after a French bell's dog — and even then he'd need papers. It just didn't add up.

Nothing we said was of any help to the Moroccan student. A dead man with long hair supposedly living with her father, a leg of lamb served with palm fronds and chocolate; equally confused and disgusted, she shrugged her massive shoulders and turned her attention back to the comic book she kept hidden beneath her binder.

I wondered then if, without the language barrier, my classmates and I could have done a better job making sense of Christianity, an idea that sounds pretty far-fetched to begin with.

In communicating any religious belief, the operative word is *faith*, a concept illustrated by our very presence in that classroom. Why bother struggling with the grammar lessons of a six-year-old if each of us didn't believe that, against all reason, we might eventually improve?

Source: Sedaris, D. (2001) 'Jesus shaves', in D. Sedaris, *Me talk pretty one day*. New York, NY: Back Bay Books, pp. 178–179.

Chapter 13 readings

Reading 13.1 Extract from the memoir *The Grassling*

Elizabeth-Jane Burnett

> Elizabeth-Jane Burnett is a poet, academic and author of the nature writing memoir *The Grassling: A Geological Memoir* (2020). A writer of English and Kenyan heritage, she was born in Devon and her work is inspired by the landscape in which she was raised.

But one of the first seeds for this writing came from the barn owl. The flush of white, so much purer than any other in the landscape, came first. Then the unnatural craning of the head. *Unnatural only to humans*, I self-correct before the word is fully out. It is the unexpectedness – when these birds, these animals appear – that shakes us out of our usual scripts. My father, midway through his upstairs walk, had joined me on the landing. Minutes passed. Minimal words, in whispers, though the window and several feet stood between us and it, taking care not to frighten. We tried to establish how long it had been there, how long we had left before it would go. *Visitor, you are welcome, no worries!*

…

And I felt that, the last time I visited; when I wasn't recognized, when I wasn't noticed. When I tried to speak, but was looked over, as you do look over things that do not matter, that bear no connection to you. Just as the bare branches of the hedge I had walked along had given nothing away as to their species, so my skin had seemed unfathomable. And not for the first time I had wondered when we will be able to tell more about each other at a glance than we do now. Perhaps as cyborgs evolve, we'll be able to download each other's information at the click of a switch, with the blink of an eye. If we could reveal our histories through our eyes, then perhaps she would have looked at me with more interest, more warmth – that woman in the village I had tried to talk to. Perhaps she would have looked at me the way my father and I had looked at that owl. *Nobody worry, you're all welcome.*

Source: Burnett, E.-J. (2020) *The grassling: a geological memoir*. London: Penguin Random House, pp. 47–48.

Reading 13.2 Extract from the screenplay of *Small Axe: Mangrove*

Alastair Siddons and Steve McQueen

> Alastair Siddons is a British screenwriter, producer and director who has worked across documentary, original TV drama and film, and adaptation.

> Steve McQueen is a British director, producer, screenwriter and video artist, whose work in both film and visual art often explores intense subject matters. The *Small Axe* anthology is a particularly personal project as it portrays the larger community that he grew up in.

Content note: Please be aware that this reading mentions race discrimination.

She quickly slips off a shoe, picks it up, and starts hitting MR CROFT with it, over and over.

                    ALTHEIA JONES-LECOINTE
          Oh shut your... Huh? All a' ya
          wicked. You flipping... What you
          say? Plead what?
                    MR CROFT
          Guilty.

FRANK gently tries to stop ALTHEIA, who's wound up now.

ALTHEIA wriggles free from FRANK, hits him with her shoe before chucking it at MR CROFT.

She sits down, too wound up.

                    ALTHEIA JONES-LECOINTE
          All ya better take this fricking
          man out my face. Move out my face!
          Is that what you gon' do? You can't
          be doing that. Not now, you can't,
          Frank. He trying to divide us. For
          four-hundred years people like him
          trying to divide our people,
          undermine us. This trial is another
          way of doing that. Of destroying a
          strong black movement in this

country. We have to stick together.
As a collective. The Mangrove Nine.
As a people. It's what you telling
me boy. That's all that matters.

FRANK has tears in his eyes.

FRANK CRICHLOW

I don't get it, nah. You wanna sit in a courthouse for another six week to get more time in jail? Me don't want no jail, man. Yuh understand me? These people, they're like… vampires. Yuh think you beat dem but they keep coming back. Back at yuh again and again. It's like a silver bullet ain't enough. You haff to stake them through de heart, den get de garlic and chop their head off too. It's never enough.

No one says a word. He abates, composing himself a little.

FRANK CRICHLOW (CONT'D)

De best we can hope for is ah draw. Ah draw. De system rigged. It rotten and we're fighting it for what? Fuh what, Altheia?

ALTHEIA JONES-LECOINTE

For my unborn child. That's what.

This is news to everyone. We hear a pin drop. FRANK rooted to the spot.

ALTHEIA JONES-LECOINTE (CONT'D)

All of this, all of our… fight. It counts beyond us here. It does, y'know. This trial is about more than just our freedom. What is being called into question in this case is the right of anybody, not just black people, but the right of anybody to demonstrate. So I'm not here just defending myself, but trying to defend us all. If we fold now, if we give in to them, if we let them control our decisions, then they take it all. They take it all from us. And they take it from our children, too.

She pauses to let this sink in.

ALTHEIA JONES-LECOINTE (CONT'D)
We are the example and we must bear
this responsibility. But please, if
anyone wants to take a plea, you
take it? As is your right to.

FRANK shakes his head, just enough to answer.

ALTHEIA walks over to her shoe. Picks it up, puts it back on.

Source: Siddons, A. and McQueen, S. (2020) *Small axe: Mangrove*. [Screenplay]. London: BBC Films, pp. 79–80.

Reading 13.3 'Walking for My Mother'
Jacob Ross

> Jacob Ross was born in Grenada and now lives in Britain. He is a writer of novels and short stories, and he is also an editor and creative writing tutor.

Old Hope turned out their children to watch Nella go. It was wonderful and frightening because the quiet in the air was all for her. All for her, the gifts, the utterances of pleasure, the sideway glances and sweat-rimmed smiles. Like they were seeing her properly for the first time.

Ken had gone into the bushes and brought back two glistening guavas. White and rare, they smelled of the last days of the Dry Season. Even the wrapping was unusual – a dasheen leaf, shaped like a heart and patterned with a web of purple veins. Her uncle placed the guavas on the table beside the bread they'd baked specially for her.

Aunt Gigelle had brought her a boiled egg. She came swaying down the hill, balancing one in each palm as if they were the globes of life.

'Pretty peee-ople!' she sang, bending low and curving her very, very long fingers around her face and Liam's. 'One from Bucky and one from me. One for Liam and one for you.' Then, preciously, she placed them on the flowered tablecloth.

Uncle Ian had polished the new black patent leather shoes till they shone like pools of water in the morning light, while Gran Lil moved around her strangely. Her grandmother had taken off her headwrap and allowed her white hair to uncoil and settle like a halo round her face.

Even her twin brother seemed amazed. Liam had promptly offered her the other egg. Every now and again, he examined the brilliant white polyester shirt, passed the back of his hand against the dark-blue skirt and lifted the tip of the gold-striped, carmine tie.

They'd already begun preparing her. Aunty May had bathed her with the

Cussons Imperial Leather soap they'd bought for the occasion. A new toothbrush that matched the ochre wrapping of the soap exactly and a little packet of Colgate toothpaste waited on the table while she ate in brand new socks and underwear. Occasionally, her mother glanced at her and then at Liam, furtively.

Breakfast over, her mother dressed her. Her hands were trembling slightly.

Over the weeks she'd seen her mother take complete command of everything. Her moment had arrived and she'd slipped into it like a garment cut especially for her. She'd become strange and secretive and oddly compelling, for her Mammy now ruled the yard with worry.

Mammy had worried for a month about the money she didn't have, might never have, but had to have in order to buy the books and uniform. And gradually the yard began to worry too. She fretted for another week – her voice low, complaining, and very mildly accusing – till one Sunday, moody and fed up, Aunty May sent her, Nella, off to take the good news to a friend of hers in some place named La Tante.

She had returned home with fifteen dollars, which Mammy promptly took off her.

Gran Lil had also had enough, and spent an entire day rummaging her memory for names of distant cousins, nephews, nieces and great aunts up north. She then sent the good news off through friends, by bus. Soon, crumpled packets began to arrive with pairs of socks and underwear; and bags with beautiful, obscure books – whose only purpose had been to sit on shelves near Bibles because they looked important. Sometimes they came wrapped on top of sacks of provision or between a couple of live chickens.

That was good, but not enough, her mother fretted. What the child needed most was money. 'Mooneeey.' Her voice drifted with the word, reluctant to let it go.

So over the evening meal, they helped each other recall ancient favours to old-time friends and once they'd settled on some names, they sent her off again, on her own. It was always on her own. Never, they warned, to mention money, or to remind them of the favours, just to pass the good news on.

Then one Sunday morning, with a long, momentous sigh, Mammy sat down on the steps, plunged her hand down her bosom and pulled out a handful of notes. She kept dipping and dropping fistfuls at her feet while they looked on fascinated.

'T'ree hundred dollars an…' She paused abruptly, her face rigid with anxiety. She beat a frantic tattoo on her chest, thrashed her skirt, stomped and heaved herself, before bringing her nose down to the stones in the yard. Finally, fingers poised as if to pick up a needle, her mother retrieved something, grinned a large democratic grin, and muttered fervently, victoriously, '…an one cent!' which raised a wave of laughter.

Then she left the money there for anyone to examine it, as if to say that her figure was, well, just that – hers! – a mere probability – and they, after counting it themselves, might just as easily come up with a different but equally legitimate sum.

Some stared at the notes, others prodded them with their fingers, or nudged them with a marvelling toe, or, not uncommonly, brought their noses down to them. For nothing on earth smelled as satisfying as three hundred EC dollars, and one cent.

With that money, her mother had bought her everything, including the breakfast of bacon, the bowl of steaming Quaker oats, and the Milo drink she hated but felt obliged to drink because it was what eddicated children was s'posed ter have on their first day at any secondary school, anywhere in the world.

Now that she was about to set out, something tight and warm had settled in her stomach. A hush had settled over the valley. The neighbours had brought their children to the side of the road and placed the younger ones directly in front, holding them there with hands firmly on their shoulders.

The new bag of books dangling from her shoulders, and a few dollars stuffed down her pocket, she made her way down the track to the road. Aunty Paula had set off in front, clearing the path of leaves and stones and whatever else she thought might make her trip and bruise her dignity.

'Yuh modder don't want you to take de bus from here,' Aunty May whispered.

She nodded – she would have nodded to anything. Aunty May also told her that Mammy, at the last minute, had decided not to come with her. 'She ain got nothing to put on,' her aunt explained. 'Never mind, she going ter be watching you. Everybody goin be watching you.' Then she'd paused a while. 'An I not comin eider, so don't bodder look at me.'

'People getting on as if I not comin back!'

'You intend to?' Aunty May grinned cheerlessly at her.

'Is just a secondary school I going to, dat's all.'

The woman stopped wiping her face with her hand. 'You de first dis side of Old Hope Valley; in fact de first dis side of anywhere as far as I know to go to school in town. Once dem lil ones dere see dat you kin get to secandry, dey know dat dey kin get dere too, by de hook or by de crook. Dem tinkin mongst demself dat if Hannah girl-chile kin do it, deir own chile kin do it too. Jealousy,' she chuckled loudly. 'Dat kind o jealousy is good.'

'People talk as if I deadin o someting.'

'Hush you mouth, you always complainin. Deadin me tail! I hope you not going ter talk like dat when you reach inside dem people hifalutin, low-fartin school. You go to speak proper. Deadinggg – pronounce your G proper, hear? You got your handkerchief? 'Kay! Hold orrrn, Hannah! Stop frettin at me! You can't see I fixin 'er?' She gasped and laughed and stepped away. 'Gwone chile, we give you broughtupsy, now go and get de eddication.'

'And Liam? I want Liam to walk wit me, I want…'

'Never mind Liam, Liam goin to be awright. Liam always goin to be awright. Liam is a boy!'

Aunty May moved up close. She did a strange thing. She licked a finger and made a circle on Nella's forehead. She then kissed the spot she'd marked.

'When you reach Cross Gap, you stop an wave, okay? Cos all o we goin be watchin over you.'

She knew straight away where they would be standing. Glory Cedar Hill was the only spot from which the whole snaking thread of asphalt could be seen all the way to Cross-Gap Junction.

'Walk, Nella. Walk tall an proudful like you never walk befo. Gwone gyul! Start walkin for your modder.'

She lifted a querying face at her aunt, 'Walkin for my…?' Then she understood.

Aunty May turned and hurried back up the hill.

Miss Ticksy broke away from the crowd lining the roadside, wiped her hand on her dress and handed her a dollar bill. The woman stepped back and wiped her hand again. 'Hannah is me friend,' she explained. 'An Nella is she daughter.' And she laughed a laugh that was loud enough for all of them.

She heard Missa Ram's dry voice. 'You break away, gyul! Look at my crosses! De lil gyul break away!' It was one of the rare times she had seen the old man off his donkey.

She took her time, feeling lost and not a little awkward. The new unfamiliar leather shoe made walking appropriately difficult. Shereen called her softly from the verge. She smiled back, shyly, uncomfortably, from the distance that her friend was placing her. Their faces were open and friendly, but they were not reaching out to her. They seemed to be taking her in with a new interest.

Half an hour later, still dazed, still drifting, she arrived at Cross-Gap Junction. Turning, she squinted up at Glory Cedar Hill.

Shapes they were, just shapes: her granny, Mammy and Aunty Paula and Aunty May and Shereen and Miss Ticksie and the rest of them. Shapes, dancing against the morning sky.

She thought she heard them singing. Or perhaps they were shouting something down to her. It all sounded like music anyway.

She waved back, walking as she waved, sensing with a sobering, abrupt sadness that she was also walking away from something else.

Source: Ross, J. (2017) 'Walking for my mother', in J. Ross, *Tell no one about this*. Leeds: Peepal Tree Press Ltd, pp. 34–38.

Chapter 14 readings

Reading 14.1 'The Real Deal'

Tom Wentworth

> Tom Wentworth is a dramatist who identifies as disabled. His work for theatre and television pushes boundaries, especially around diversity.

Note: 'The Real Deal' was first performed by Liz Carr in 2020 as part of the BBC Studios Scotland production *CripTales* on BBC America and BBC Four, directed by Ewan Marshall. The formatting below follows that used when the script was published in book form. As such, you might notice variations from the guidance in Chapter 8 on formatting screenplays.

MEG *lives in a pristine shoebox. There is a window overlooking the street (where her phone sits on a tripod).*

MEG *sits in her wheelchair at her laptop, furiously typing time-coded entries into a benefit-fraud form.*

It was when he winked at me; I knew he had to be stopped. I'm not a snitch. But there comes a point and it's a sharp one – where you can't ignore things any longer.

Sniper-like, she spots something outside.

14:52. White Vest is back on the dot as usual. Say what you like about him (and I do), the one thing that I can't fault is his timekeeping.

(Lining up the shot. To her phone.) 'Shoot.'

'Shoot!' for God's sake.

It clicks.

Every day the same agonising performance: a slow, painful walk around the block with that stick of his. Every afternoon the same.

At 14:54 precisely he limps back into his house, pulling his trousers up over his (considerable) backside as he goes. I know a faker when I see one. We're all meant to be good little lambs tripping off to slaughter, but it's a criminal act we're talking about here. I simply can't let him get away with it.

Something catches her eye.

He's back out again. He never comes out at this time.

'Shoot.'

14:55. White Vest walking with stick. See, it's not even touching the ground, there's no weight on it at all. He's wearing a jacket over that vest of his. Going somewhere smart, are we?

Hm, if I didn't know any better, I'd say someone was off to meet a lady friend.

MEG's *doorbell rings. She freezes.*

Later. MEG *looks frail. Her wheelchair is gone.*

He looms over me like a shadow on stilts. Despite watching him day in, day out, we've hardly ever spoken. 'Alright,' he says, trying to make it sound casual.

'Yes, Mr Giles? Were you and your stick just passing?

'Look, I know it's a big favour,' he says, gripping his stick tighter. And I wonder if he might strike me. 'But could I borrow your wheelchair?'

'It's broken, sorry.'

This isn't a lie, the battery's kaput, and I haven't had the energy to get another one. Some days I just can't be bothered. Rage and fatigue fight it out in my body, and the fatigue wins. Fatigue always wins.

White Vest comes straight back with, 'No problem. I can soon get it fixed up for you. What are neighbours for?'

I don't know what to do with my face, how I study the carpet intensely as he barges his way in. His eyes are gleaming now.

'Had my eye on one of these babies on the net for a while.' He says. 'But then I thought, why don't I go and see my old friend Sue.'

'Meg,' I correct him. 'But my name's Miss Davies.' White Vest plays with a bit of mucus on his finger as he studies my chair and me in it.

'I can soon get her fixed up. Even got a battery at home. Just don't ask what lorry it fell off.'

I want to shout, 'Look here, Mr Giles. My wheelchair is not a "baby"! It's functional. To get me from one place to another.'

But before I even realise what's happened White Vest has literally taken my chair from under me.

'You're a brick, Sue!' he says.

'Good thing I came over isn't it? Your knight in shining armour.'

Bloody cheek.

'You haven't said why you want it,' I say.

'Did I not mention?' White Vest tries to look innocent. 'I've got my face-to-face PIP assessment tomorrow and well, you gotta up your game, haven't you?' He lets the word 'assessment' fizz like a tablet dropping in water.

God, I need some painkillers.

My whole body burns. 'But you don't need a wheelchair,' I say.

'Not at the moment,' he says dramatically, 'but in a year, who knows? They don't know how degenerative this condition of mine might be.'

I feel sick.

'I'll bring it back,' he shouts, pushing it down the drive. 'A deal's a deal.'

'Thank you,' I call, as if he's done me the favour. Why the hell did I say thank you?

Beat.

White Vest makes me feel like they did at the assessment centre. From the moment the X-Ray-eyed receptionist smiled at me, I knew I'd lost. I tried so hard to look capable; smart, even though I felt like an imposter. When my letter arrived, I knew what it said without opening it…

'Just be yourself, Meg. Sit tall. Smile.' My mother's voice comes through, as always. But as I sit there I think of how it was because I attended her funeral that I lost my benefits. I chose her over them. And now I'm paying for it.

Of course, X-Ray Eyes sees right through me. My guilt. The fact that I felt I didn't deserve it.

For hours the night before I made a list of all the things I couldn't do and in the morning I felt worthless.

I held it tightly in my hand, but the more questions they asked me, the more my hand went into spasm and the paper crumpled. I crumpled.

Later. MEG*'s back at her desk again, holding her PIP letter…*

The next day you-know-who is back, zooming down the road, running down my new battery.

'King of the road, me!' He shouts from the street, like a pitbull with two tails. I want to punch those yellow teeth of his as he jumps nimbly from my wheelchair. There's not a shred of decency in the man.

I brandish my assessment letter at him. 'Look!' I shout. 'It's so bloody unfair. I go to them, and they give me nothing, you go to them, they hand it to you on a plate. Just leave me alone.'

He lands on the assessment letter like a hungry vulture. And for the first time, I see a genuine light shining in his eyes. 'You can appeal,' he said. I feel all the air go out of me like a deflated balloon. 'It's so humiliating,' I say.

'You have to fight.' White Vest grabs me by the shoulders. 'You know your trouble: you simply don't look disabled enough.'

My jaw hits the floor.

'You dress too smart.'

'I have my pride!' I shout, but he just shakes his head.

'And where's pride ever got you?'

Without warning, he waltzes in and starts rummaging through my dirty-washing basket.

I desperately try to stop him as bras and knickers fly but finally, he holds up my oldest, dirtiest blouse.

'This is the one,' he says, salivating like a huge, horny Doberman.

'Wear this to your next assessment, and they'll never be able to turn you down.'

Then White Vest tips the whole basket onto the floor, going through it like a like a pig searching for truffles.

Out comes some sweatpants I'd wet myself in last week and hadn't been able to wash.

'Lovely,' he says, smelling the crotch.

She rubs her hands with antibacterial gel at the memory.

What White Vest is suggesting is terrible. Horrible. Wrong…

But they are my clothes, after all.

I mean, it's not exactly lying.

Stop it, Meg. Don't even think of it. But in that terrible moment, I just know… White Vest is right.

Beat.

'You need to be more disabled!' he shouts at our daily training session.

'I am disabled!' I screamed in his face (and I felt it).

'I don't think you really want this,' he said. I wanted to forget I even existed. I could feel my old friend fatigue taking over, and White Vest was ready to take full advantage.

While MEG *speaks as White Vest, we see her turn into what he describes.*

'Don't sit tall. Slump.'

'Dribble a bit. Aw, they love that.'

'Slump more. More. Look pained.'

'Look vacant. Don't shake hands.'

'No make-up. No sleep the night before. Now you're the real deal. But most important of all, don't speak. I'll do all the talking.

The easiest part of White Vest's plan was the not sleeping. By going blithely along had I made myself exactly like him? A good little lamb to the slaughter…

Later. MEG *sits at her desk with a bottle of fizz and two glasses. She has a few blurry shots of White Vest pinned up on the wall, like an incident room.*

White Vest told a pack of lies, of course. But they believed every word that came from his silver tongue.

'No, Miss Davies can't wipe her own arse.'

'No, Miss Davies can't fold her own sheets.'

'No, Miss Davies can't cook a meal.'

'Miss Davies can't stand up, sit down, or do the Hokey Cokey.'

'Don't you understand, Miss Davies couldn't even open the envelope your letter arrived in.'

When we got out, we celebrated. Actually we celebrated all afternoon.

White Vest even bought me champagne – okay, it's cheap supermarket stuff, but I'm not complaining. When it was time for him to go I said, 'Mr Giles, thank you.' And he said, 'Call me Nigel.'

She smiles. Drains her glass.

And then he winked at me again. That was your mistake, Nigel. You've made me see things clearer than I have done for weeks… You've made me feel alive again… You've reminded me that you can't get away with it and that I am the real deal.

We see MEG *submit the benefit-fraud form. She smiles.*

Fade to black.

Source: Wentworth, T. (2020) '*The real deal*', in M. Fraser (ed.) *CripTales: six monologues*. London: Nick Hern Books, pp. 41–46.

Reading 14.2 Extract from the novel *Be Near Me*
Andrew O'Hagan

> Andrew O'Hagan, who was born in Glasgow and grew up in a working-class housing estate in Ayrshire, is a novelist and non-fiction writer interested in the relationships between fact and fiction, writer and reader.

Before we'd started the soup, the postman came to the door and hammered on it with his usual disregard. 'Nothing gets your attention like a knock at the door,' said Mrs Poole, and she went out. I spent a moment playing a phrase on the piano, placing my foot on a dull brass pedal. Then I stopped and cocked an ear before putting Chopin into the CD player; I could hear very clearly what the postman was saying to Mrs Poole.

'How's yer English priest getting on then?'

'He's not English,' she said. 'He was born in Edinburgh.'

'Don't kid yerself,' said the postman. 'Yer man's as English as two weeks in Essex. Get a load ae that rug lying there!'

'What are you talking about?'

'That thing under yer feet,' he said. 'They didnae have that in Father McGee's day. That's a pure English rug, that.'

'Just go about your business and stop coming round here talking nonsense,' said Mrs Poole. 'This is a Persian rug.'

'That's Iran or Iraq,' he said. 'You want to get rid ae that.'

As he laughed he sent a menacing splutter into the hall. 'There's blood in they carpets. Our troops are over in that place and they're not buildin' sandcastles. There's young men dying out there. You have to watch out for the Iraqis.'

I'm sure there's an essay in which Liszt writes of Chopin's apartment on the chaussée d'Antin, the room with a portrait of Chopin above the piano, and the belief of the younger musician that the painting must have been a constant auditor of the sound that once flamed and lived in that room, bright and brief as a candle.

'The postman?' I said.

Mrs Poole put a letter into its envelope and folded the whole thing in three. She creased it as people do who never file their letters, holding the stiff paper in her hand like a small baton. 'Aye,' she said. 'Just another of yer local idiots.'

'Isn't Good Friday a bank holiday? Don't they get the day off?'

'Not in Scotland,' she said. 'That's an English thing.'

She seemed more than slightly annoyed with the postman, as if his careless and brash way of talking had added some terrible degree of insult to the letter he had given her, the letter she now stuffed into the front pocket of her apron.

'Are you all right?'

She smoothed one lip against the other. 'In this country,' she said, 'they prefer to have an extra holiday on the second of January. They ignore Good Friday but they don't ignore the second of January.'

'Really?'

'Of course,' she said. 'The second is the day after New Year's Day, and they'd much sooner have an extra day with alcohol than an extra day with God.'

'You're very severe, Mrs Poole.'

'No wonder,' she said. 'The idea of a person like that being responsible for bringing the post.'

Source: O'Hagan, A. (2006) *Be near me*. London: Faber and Faber, pp. 12–13.

Reading 14.3 'In truth: Andrew O'Hagan on the genesis of *Be Near Me*'

Andrew O'Hagan

I was alone in a cafe near the Rue Balzac when the first seeds of *Be Near Me* were planted. I hardly ever go to Paris, but it was one of those blue nights that make you think you ought to go to Paris more often, and the room was bustling and crowded in the way of those famous paintings. I remember noticing a grey-haired priest who was sitting alone at a table beneath the window. He stared at his hands and after a while he stirred his coffee and a tear rolled down his cheek.

Back home, I began to hear the voice of Father David at the shaving mirror. There was something lovely but annoying in his voice – something both wise and deluded at the same time. I could hear he liked wine and poetry, cared for gardening and music, and quickly I decided he went to school at Ampleforth and came from a long line of recusants. After some months, I resolved that he went to Balliol College, Oxford, and the English College in Rome. None of these things had happened to me personally, so I went in search of the facts and the dates and the flavours. I walked through the parks in Rome where he would have walked and I took notes at the bases of statues and dreamed of his boyhood hours on the Lancashire coast. In Scotland, I took a boat to Ailsa Craig and was forced back by the weather.

Writing a novel is an act of self-annihilation as much as self-discovery. You can kill whole appetites and flood whole depths while plumbing them, but if you are serious about it you also get to put something into the world that wasn't quite there before. I've been asked which of the other arts novel-writing is most like, and I have come to believe it is acting. Of course, in terms of pattern it can be like music, in terms of structure it can be like painting, but the job to me is most like acting. You give life to these characters and you inhabit them at some cost to yourself, while also realising yourself in the process.

Be Near Me really came alive when I went to the scene of a mob demonstration in the north of England. There were people outside a priest's house – placards, cameras, ice-creams – and looking up at one of the bedrooms I saw the net curtain twitch. There is a human being up there, I thought. And suddenly I knew this story was about a very human struggle – a struggle of individuals and communities in various guises – and I knew, too, that the book was asking for everything I had. After some weeks, I could see each of my characters in their exact colours: some knew how to live naturally and practically, while others lived opportunistically; some had faith and a care for the beauty of life, while others simply hid in tradition or eloquence, or existed defensively or in company with ugliness. I worked with each character in relation to the others, and I began to feel the novel was my own. I knew Mark and Lisa; I knew Mrs Poole. And my greatest job was to help readers to know my narrator, Father David, better than he knows himself.

There's a horrible fallacy that exists in the popular discussion of fiction these days: the idea that a successful central character need be 'likeable' or 'sympathetic'. It is surely more important that they be human, no? More crucial that they breathe? The idea that people in novels should be more sympathetic than people in life simply baffles me. The characters I have loved most in Dickens, in Evelyn Waugh, or F Scott Fitzgerald have been, at best, morally ambiguous, and that state of being can only add to the joy of the book for me. Father David, as I say, had something not quite right about him from the beginning: he could be lovable and terrible, an enabler and a snob, a poet and a holy fool, and that made him just the perfect person to narrate this particular story.

A novel is a machine made up of pure essentials, where every part is crucial to the overall effect. My narrator surprised me at first, but then possessed me. I worked hard to protect his narration from my own arguments: the sentences I gave him don't express an editorial or form a manifesto (only fools think novels do that), but they may animate a true moral drama in the mind of a sensitive reader. I say true, and I mean that. A novel that is any good will know how to be true to itself if nothing else.

Source: O'Hagan, A. (2007) 'In truth: Andrew O'Hagan on the genesis of *Be near me*', *The Guardian*, 14 July, Book Club. Available at: https://www.theguardian.com/books/2007/jul/14/featuresreviews.guardianreview4 (Accessed: 13 March 2024).

Chapter 15 readings

Reading 15.1   The memoir piece 'Bloodstream (1997)'

Maggie O'Farrell

> The novelist Maggie O'Farrell was born in Northern Ireland, and grew up in Wales and Scotland. Her memoir, *I Am, I Am, I Am*, chronicles a series of near-death experiences, from her own life-threatening childhood illness to that of her young daughter.

Content note: Please be aware that this reading mentions severe illness and needles.

Occasionally, but not that often, I think about the person I was in my mid-twenties. I consider her. I try to recall how it felt to be that age. What were the frameworks of her days, the patterns of her thoughts? I am as far from her now as she was from her childhood. She is the median line between me and my birth.

Sometimes it's hard to capture her essence, impossible to remember what it was like to keep forging ahead in the face of such flux and instability. Other times, however, I might be walking down a street with my children, holding one by the hand while trying to catch up with another and simultaneously listening to what the third is saying about the Scottish referendum (my children have divergent and incompatible walking styles – one likes to lag behind, another to sprint ahead, and the other to walk right next to me, so close that I'm often tripped by our tangling feet). We will be moving along in our assorted fashions, when I will be hooked by something – the specific timbre of a decelerating underground train, a particular guitar riff coming out of the window of a basement café, the feeling of cold fingertips curled inside a pocket – and I will sense her as if she is on the pavement with us.

There she goes, walking by, in her weather-insufficient tights, short skirt and bright blue trainers. She has cut off her hair – it doesn't entirely suit her – and bleached the asymmetric fringe. She has a pager in her belt, a book in her bag and a lidless pen leaking ink into the lining. She walks fast; she is probably late. She needs a multi-vitamin, a square meal, a place to live. She has moved no fewer than nine times since she arrived in London. She can fit her possessions into a single backpack. She gets sore throats, swollen tonsils. She stays out late, doesn't sleep much, fails to purchase even the most basic of groceries. She runs out of money before payday every month.

She has recently left the man she'd been living with, shouldering her bag and walking down the stairs. The circumstances were dismayingly pedestrian, soap-operatic in their mundanity: she had knelt beside the bed to search for a shoe and seen instead the loop and catches of a bra. She knew before she touched it. A flesh-coloured bra, not her size, not a style she ever wore, bought from a shop to which she had a particular aversion. A surprisingly practical bra, under the circumstances – no wiring, no embellishment – and ingrained with the sanitised scent of fabric softener. The kind of bra that a sporty, organised, no-nonsense girl might wear under a smart blouse. A girl who does her laundry on a regular basis, buys clothes to last and takes herself on healthy outdoor excursions. A girl who is, in short, her diametric opposite, in every way.

She confronted him, in a lowered voice, so as not to alert their flatmates to the situation. At first her boyfriend tacked wildly. He'd never seen the bra before, it was nothing to do with him. He had no idea where it had come from. It was probably hers. Could she have forgotten she'd bought it? It belonged to a visitor. It arrived here by mistake. It must be his sister's.

Pausing in the act of cramming sweaters and dresses and books into her bag, she laughed. Bullshit, she said loudly, momentarily forgetting the other people in the rooms around them. That, she pointed at the bra, flung wide on the boyfriend's desk, wouldn't fit your sister in a million years.

He stopped disowning the bra. He stood up. He got defensive, angry. He said, yes, all right, there has been a woman. There have, in fact, been several. He accused her of always working or reading or sitting at her desk writing (or, as he put it, 'typing'). She never had any time for him. If she wasn't out, she was distracted by something else. He was losing his sense of self, his sense of worth, and needed to find himself again. He ended this speech with the words: 'I did it for us.'

This closing sentence has provided her and her friend Eric with much comedic mileage during the more boring moments of their jobs (of which there are many). They like to tack the phrase on to acts of an entirely self-serving nature, the more selfish the better. Extra points are awarded for slipping it into conversation in front of a more senior colleague, which isn't hard to do because pretty much everyone is senior to them.

'I ate a sandwich,' Eric will murmur into his phone from across the office, 'and I did it for us.'

'I bought some new shoes in my lunch-hour,' she will message him, 'for us, of course.'

'I went to the gym last night,' he will say in a loud voice, 'and I want you to know that I did it for us.'

It has been two years since she got off the twenty-four-hour bus from Prague in a damp bus station in London. It has taken her this long to find a job that doesn't seem like a cul-de-sac. She is working as an editorial assistant on a newspaper. She answers phones, she opens post, she calls critics to remind them that their copy is due, she tracks down the IT man if computers misbehave, she fetches page proofs, she checks captions, she visits the picture desk to find photographs, she tidies – cupboards, shelves, in-trays, chairs, desks, drawers. She does whatever people ask of her and, in return, she badgers them gently, politely, to let her write something for the paper. She counsels editors, assistant editors, critics, sub-editors on the phone, in the smoking room, in the alcove by the photocopier that everything is going to be all right. It is a job with long hours, indistinct boundaries, diva-ish personalities, twists and turns of panic, steep learning curves, feverish in-house gossip, urgent deadlines, days with no lunch and then days when she is taken out of the office for hours at a time by an older colleague, who will ply her with expensive food, then quiz her about something that's happening in her section. Her days are filled with changes of management, made over everyone's heads, dry sandwiches, redundancy paranoia, coffee machines, security passes, rides in lifts, slews of book proofs, late-night tube rides home at the end of press day, peculiar freebies (a reflective bag, paperweights with the heads of authors inside, wellington boots that don't quite fit, chocolate toolkits and once, out of the blue, an astonishingly expensive German fountain pen – which I still have).

So, her ex is right, in a way. She is out at work a great deal. She is distracted. When she is at home, which isn't often, she is usually writing ('typing'). She has started something that she is telling herself is a short story. Just a short story. It is, the last time she checked, more than twenty thousand words and getting longer all the time.

When she meets her friend Will for a coffee – they are friends at this point, good friends, very good friends, friends who call each other every day, who see each other once or twice a week, friends who perhaps take a shade too much interest in the ups and downs of each other's love lives – and he asks her what she's been writing, she tells him about her short story, her long short story. He looks at her, in his penetrating way, narrowing his eyes, and says: you're writing a novel.

No, she says, shaking her head, of course not, I could never do that, absolutely not, whatever gave you that idea?

Late at night, when her soon-to-be ex-boyfriend calls for her to come to bed, for God's sake, she murmurs absently, in a minute. The house is so quiet, the flatmates all asleep, the work of the story so absorbing, so satisfying in a way that nothing else ever has been, the words scrolling out from under the flashing cursor, the paragraphs opening out from each other, like Matroyshka dolls. Then, suddenly, it's three a.m. and she's blindsided by exhaustion and exhilaration, and she crawls into bed, thinking about her story, unable to find the path to sleep, listening to the sounds of the city waking up.

She has waited the requisite time: she knows it takes months for the virus to appear in your blood. (Does it hide somewhere, she wonders, like a pantomime villain, behind a door, up a chimney, in the leaves of a tree?) As with anyone who grew up in the 1980s, she knows the rules, the risks, the causes. She still remembers the grim governmental warnings on TV, with falling tombstones and rock-flaying chisels.

So, she is taking herself off to a clinic for the blood test. Not a prospect to relish, this, but something to be got through. She wants to be sure that her ex-boyfriend hasn't passed anything on to her, hasn't deposited anything sinister in her bloodstream.

She has persuaded Eric to come with her, to get tested alongside her. Eric walks the distance from the tube station to the clinic door, talking, gesturing, tugging at the ends of her scarf.

At the clinic, there is an administrative fluster. The receptionist cannot countenance that Eric has arrived without an appointment. 'The thing is,' he said, snatching off his sunglasses, 'my need is greater than hers.'

She sees the receptionist about to argue, to insist, to stick to her guidelines and to deny him a test, but then she sees her look at Eric, properly and for the first time.

There is a slight pause.

The receptionist nods, finally, to the pile of forms and they walk away together, towards the waiting area.

'"Write down a list of the people you have slept with in the past five years",' Eric reads aloud from the form – a little too aloud. 'Do you think you're allowed to ask for extra paper? Like in an exam?'

'Ssh,' she says, and he is saying an affronted 'What?' and she is trying not to laugh because it seems a sacrilegious thing to do here, in a sexual-health clinic, where other people are sitting with their heads bowed, avoiding each other's eyes, working their way through these labyrinthine forms.

Eric sighs, fidgets, says they need to line up some sort of treat for afterwards. 'What if you don't know their names?' he is asking, tapping his pen on the clipboard. 'Do you just write Man One, Man Two? Or, if I'm being brutally honest, Man Ninety-nine, Man One Hundred?'

At that moment, someone calls her name and she gets up, lifting her clipboard, and walks towards a woman in a green overall. Eric is behind her, hissing that he isn't going to let her forget she made him do this, that she put him through it, even though she knows how much he hates needles. She moves in her blue trainers over the carpet, and as she does so, she considers the gravity of the possible outcome. Could it be that her ex has passed on something destructive, something stealthy and corroding? That his body scooped up something from the wearer of the flesh-coloured bra – or one of the others – and deposited it in hers? She hasn't allowed herself to dwell on who these women were, whether she knows them, whether they looked at her clothes draped on the chair, her books stacked up beside the bed, her make-up and toothbrush in the bathroom, the photos on the walls of her sisters, her nieces, her coat hanging by the door, whether they thought, I wonder who she is. She tries not to imagine them, what they looked like, how he touched them, what they might have said together, how he could not have said anything the first time it happened, how he could turn from them to her, without giving himself away. Infidelity is as old as humanity: there is nothing about it you can think or say that hasn't been thought or said before. You go back and back over the days, the conversations, the walks you took, wondering why on earth you hadn't seen it, how you could have missed it, how you could not have known. The pain of it is interior, humiliating, infinitely wearying.

She knows this; Eric knows this. It's why they joke about it all day long, with a gleeful irreverence that probably annoys everyone else in earshot. Sometimes being flippant is the only way forward, the only way to get through.

Perhaps this attitude, however, has been preventing her from entertaining the possibility that these tests might be positive. She realises this as she walks towards the nurse. She made this appointment mostly for show, so she could tell Eric as she dialled the number, so he could listen as she made the appointment, so she could say to him, as she headed out from work, why don't you come too? You could keep me company. We could take the blood test together.

She is on a tightrope as she makes her way to the consulting room, Eric behind her, the nurse in front. What, she is asking herself, will she do if something comes up on this test? If her show-appointment turns out to be needed after all? She tries out the scenario of going round to see her ex. She thinks about taking the tube and walking the very familiar route past the cricket ground, across the bus terminus, ascending the stairs to the door whose threshold she swore she'd never cross again and saying – what, exactly? I need to talk to you? I've got some news for you? What would anyone say in these situations? How do you broach such a subject?

But mostly, as she rolls up her sleeve, as she makes a fist, as she turns her head away – because she never likes to see the needle slide in, the flesh yield beneath its point – she's not thinking about her ex or the other women or the flat they used to share. She's not thinking about the plants she had to abandon there, plants she's sure he never waters, the walls she painted, the curtains she installed, standing precariously on a stepladder to do so. She's thinking about Eric, about his ochre-tinged skin, the cornflake-sized scab on his face that won't heal, the opal-pale moons of his fingernails as he types across the office from her. She is seized with an irrational urge to say to the nurse, make it all right. Please. For him. Make it OK.

Source: O'Farrell, M. (2017) 'Bloodstream (1997)', in M. O'Farrell, *I am, I am, I am: seventeen brushes with death*. London: Tinder Press, pp. 172–183.

Reading 15.2 'Daylight Savings'
Catherine Menon

> Catherine Menon is an Australian–British writer of Malaysian heritage, who combines writing fiction with her work as a computer scientist.

At just past two in the morning Sarah switches off her alarm, buttons her dressing gown, and sits down to write to Amber's husband. This isn't, she understands, quite a normal thing to do. It's less normal, say, than going for after-work drinks. It's less normal than wearing M&S knickers and standing in bus queues and tracking the FTSE index, all of which she does quite regularly. She has an excuse, though. This is not exactly a normal night.

She takes a biscuit from the pack on her desk and sucks at the chocolate coating. Tonight is the end of daylight savings, and she's riding on the back of a night-time stammer, an hour when the clocks go back and nothing counts, not biscuits nor diets – nor adultery, she thinks with determination, and applies herself to the task of telling Colin exactly what she's wearing.

'A rose-patterned chemise, love,' she writes. 'And those silky stockings you bought me.' She touches the knot of her flannel dressing gown, slipping her fingers inside. It's a lie, but it won't last long. In twenty minutes her extra hour will be over, and then she'll happily admit to wearing her comfortable old nightgown. A few more minutes and she'll even confess that Colin hasn't, in fact, bought her any stockings. And not long after that, the final truth. He isn't, in any way, her lover.

She nibbles at the corner of another biscuit and contemplates toast. She hadn't quite finished her letter, but she still heaves herself out of the chair and pads down the sea-green gloom to her kitchen. In a horror film this is the point where she'd be found, where she'd be ravished while the camera lingered on that wonderful chemise. She looks about the kitchen hopefully, but Sarah has never been the kind to be found. Not by the right person anyway. She carves herself a ragged slice off a white loaf.

Colin spends most of the year consigned to a blurred stack of photographs tucked into her university leavers' book. She remembers the photographs at odd intervals but has long since forgotten the events. Punting in summer, and Colin's hand inching up underneath her shirt. When his fingers encounter the roll of her stomach he will flinch, beat a hasty retreat. Sticky skin against hers under the thin sheets of his bed in halls, her back to the cold brick wall separating them from next door's showers and the groans of splashing students. Awkward silences in the pub, her wrists clamming from resting on beermats sodden with someone else's happiness. No, she decides. She doesn't remember those things.

They'd broken up one night in September after an anaemic fight, a bloodless battle dangling limply from *ifs* and *buts* and *it's for the bests*. She could take a hint, she'd told him with dignity, she wasn't the sort to go where she wasn't wanted. Ten years later, Sarah finds this bewildering. She must have thought it was a virtue, at the time.

Colin had been pleased, relief shining from his freckles and his gangly limbs twitching with *I told you so*.

'So that's it then,' he'd said, triumphantly. At that moment his golden hair had begun to fade, dimming to an unappealing mouse-brown. He'd offered to walk her to the bus stop, where she'd stood with chilled feet and bruised dignity until it became clear the last bus had gone. She trailed three paces behind him – and had he always been so skinny? Had he always had dandruff? – back to his hygienic room in halls.

She remembers what followed, the glowing numbers on his alarm clock rolling back as her fingers scuttled under the blankets. Daylight saving. A hiccup, a scratched record, a chance to make the same mistakes twice. An hour that didn't count; an hour for Colin to reclaim his gorgeous, golden-brown beauty. He hadn't, though. He'd plucked himself free after a single aching minute. She had no sense, he'd informed her, of the decencies.

He'd gone on to date and marry Amber, two years younger than Sarah and sopped through and through with decency. By then, to Sarah, his hair was definitely brown and his teeth a filmy yellow. And that's how he stayed for almost ten years, installed in a Croydon semi-detached with Amber by his side. But once a year, when the clocks go back, she still writes to him. It's her private hour, sixty stolen minutes when he's beautiful again, when he rolls naked under her pen and sprawls across her desk.

She swallows the last of the cocoa, stows the mug and glances at the clock. It's all over now, and she wishes Amber joy of him.

The next morning, Sarah adds one more page to the small stack of letters in her desk. Last night's words catch her eye. *A rose-patterned chemise, love*. She's never sent any of the letters. They aren't for Colin, not the real Colin with his thinning hair and golf-buggy paunch, with his normal wife and normal baby and his almost-certainly-normal decencies.

Sarah slips off her dressing gown in the bedroom, bleached by morning light. A mirror hangs on the back of the door, with another propped beside it on the dressing table. Mirror-Sarah looks back at her, slab-pale, jellied with fat and swags of flesh. Before Sarah turns away, she gives her mirror-self a slick of make-up, a tighter waist, a rose-patterned chemise. They don't suit her.

Sarah looks away as she pulls on her trousers. She makes sure her desk is clear and all the toast crumbs brushed away. Amber's coming to visit this afternoon, and Sarah – snuffling around her house, padding through rooms and nosing at smells – is covering her tracks.

In her gloss-emulsion bedroom in Croydon, Amber pulls out a pair of ballet flats and fluffs the dust from the diamante buckles. Her feet are still swollen and the shoes too tight, but she wants to dress up. She prods at her lipstick, edges it with careful liner, but it makes no difference. The paint's feathering, bleeding into cracks in much the same way that everything else is for Amber these days.

She's off to see Sarah, though, which always cheers her up. Sarah – poor Sarah, she qualifies kindly – used to pal around with Colin at university, long before Amber knew either of them. Amber's kept in touch with Sarah; she's sent pre-printed Hallmark cards at Christmas and offered to introduce her to some really *nice* men. Divorced, but you can't be too choosy, she thinks. Not when you're Sarah.

Amber lives on a raw-boned estate new as an egg, and today she's taking Poppy out for the first time. Poppy's two months old and Amber's still not sure what to make of her. She picks the baby up, adjusts her pink ribbons and settles the damp weight onto her hip. Amber doesn't have many achievements but – unlike poor Sarah – she hasn't made many mistakes either. Poppy, at this stage, could turn out to be either.

'Amber, how nice to see you.' Sarah pulls the door wider. Amber still hasn't quite lost the baby weight, looks older and more formidable in those silly shoes of hers. Diamante, thinks Sarah. *Honestly*.

'Sarah, darling, you look wonderful!' Amber kisses Sarah twice, once on each meaty cheek. She's charming, thinks Sarah, who isn't. Sarah accepts the pecks, but mistrusts charm.

'And Poppy, too. How lovely to meet her.' Sarah takes them through to the living room, where she's set out plates of cakes iced in lurid pink. The room's reflected in two mirrors, giant ones that came with the house and which Sarah's never dared to remove. For someone of her size, throwing out mirrors can hardly be a neutral act. She'd be taking a side, taking up arms against mirror-Sarah, and she isn't at all sure who would win. Instead, she narrows her eyes at the glass as a multitude of Ambers beam simultaneously down.

'It was wonderful, Sarah. The birth, I mean. Almost orgasmic, and I was in the birthing pool and just felt so… so nurturing, and –' Amber, nipping at frosting and dabbing her lipstick, launches herself on a description. Sarah listens with polite interest. She's not the sort of person to whom these things would happen.

'And how's Colin?' Sarah asks eventually. By now they've exhausted childbirth, Amber's maternal instincts and her sore nipples and her five stitches which tore right through. Where else is there to go?

Amber tucks her legs up and leans closer in a waft of perfume and baby powder. 'Well, it's hard for men at first, isn't it? Adjusting.'

Colin has been distant since Poppy's birth, and Amber wants to complain. She wants to luxuriate in feminine woe and to make those slights bitter, wry observations about men which she thinks would be appropriate. She'd like Sarah to tell her she doesn't need a man, an observation she plans to cap indulgently by noting that she seems to be stuck with one. Sarah, however, does nothing of the sort.

'I suppose so.' Sarah leans forward, picks at a cake and puts it back. Amber's reflection, looking down on her, nods in approval.

Sarah's done well, thinks Amber. She's dieting and denying herself; she's *getting there*. Yes, Amber thinks. If Sarah lost some weight, if she smartened herself up... perhaps a really *nice* divorced man. She feels almost fondly towards Sarah right now. Confessional, in a way.

'Last night, though... well, that was different.' Amber smiles. She means to be kind; she means to confide.

'I gave Poppy a bottle about two. And then Colin said we had an extra hour, so' – she licks her lips, pulpy as oysters, and Sarah thinks briefly of her own extra hour, of gold and roses and lovers at dawn – 'we were at it for an hour.' She finishes with a giggle. 'I didn't think he could keep it up.'

Sarah feels a lurch, a jab of malice that whips down her spine and coils out to those diamante flats. Amber has just appropriated her hour, has climbed right into it with a baby and a milk bottle and a husband she can fuck without even losing sleep. And that husband is Colin, and if Sarah thinks too hard about *that* then she knows her own rose-and-gold lover will vanish, will climb unceremoniously out the window and leave nothing but dank sheets and white-brick walls and an alarm clock ringing out her mistakes. She is dimly aware of betrayal, and of Poppy beginning to cry.

Amber bends over her daughter, pulling her top down so that Poppy can suck. Sarah's mirrors obligingly reflect her: Madonna and child. And mirror-Sarah, too, sitting lumpish and charmless by herself without even a rose-patterned chemise for comfort. She should have stuck with the M&S knickers, she thinks, with the toast and the FTSE index and the virtues of going where she's wanted.

'And what about you?' Amber tucks a neat breast back into her top. These are the rules; Sarah has to confess, too. 'What's the gossip?'

Sarah, with nothing to confess, resents the question. She's under a lot of stress that afternoon, what with Colin's wife and his baby and his unexpectedly fulfilling sex life, and so she feels she has some excuse, at least, for what happens next.

'I've been seeing someone, too. An old flame from university.' Mirror-Sarah grins at these words. Like everything in a mirror, she can't quite be trusted, and is egging Sarah on disgracefully.

'Oh, but Sarah!' Amber, ensconced on the sofa with knees together and

Poppy slipping like a battered handbag to the floor, gives a delicious little giggle. 'Who is it? Anybody I'd know?'

This, as Sarah will determine later, is where she makes a mistake. It's true that malice is still churning inside her, and true that Amber is insufferable and true that it is, after all, an unseasonably hot afternoon and tempers are frayed. But nonetheless, as she will later conclude, she makes a mistake.

'Oh, no,' she says. 'He's quite before your time.' She gets to her solid feet and crosses the room to her desk. 'He's been sending me letters.'

Amber smiles. 'Oh, look at *you*,' she coos. Letters, she thinks. How appropriate, how perfect. She can think of nothing better – for Sarah. 'What does he say?' she asks with a savage kind of curiosity.

So much, Sarah thinks, for the decencies. She wonders if Colin knows what he's married, and decides that he probably does. She takes up one of the sheets of paper and begins to read.

'I miss you so much tonight, Sarah. I miss licking your lips before we kiss.' She looks up, notes a gleam of memory flash over Amber's face.

'I miss our nights in halls, that second-floor room next to the showers.'

Amber's face is puzzled. She knows the halls; she lived there for three years herself. There was only one room next to the showers, as Amber knows very well. White-brick walls, hygienic, with Colin's alarm clock rolling back just as it ought. No trace left of Sarah under those thin sheets, not by the time Amber came along.

'I miss you pulling my hair,' Sarah continues. 'Rough. The way I like it. The way wives don't do.'

It's a gamble, that last line. For all she knows, wives do. Judging by Amber, wives are the vicious sort. The sort who might very well indulge in hair-pulling, in little pinches and slaps. Sarah wouldn't put anything past them.

But Amber's smile is collapsing. She's floundering to her feet, a dark red flush mottling her pretty face and smearing her lipstick.

Amber is full of suspicions and swollen, tender thoughts edged with jealousy. She tumbles Poppy into her arms with a defensive, protective shrug. She won't expose her child to Sarah's mind, to those… to those *obscenities*, Amber thinks indignantly. She doesn't ask to see Sarah again, or offer her cheek for a goodbye kiss.

And that night, too, Amber has a row with Colin.

'Writing letters?' he says. 'To Sarah? Don't be ridiculous.' There's an uncomfortable pause as the baby monitor begins to wail.

'But she was so… so gloating,' Amber bleats. 'And all the things she said… such things.' Things which Amber wouldn't dream of discussing, herself.

'Look, can't you do something with Poppy?' Colin asks. The howling from the baby monitor is giving him a headache; Amber's getting on his nerves, and, quite frankly, he thinks as he watches his wife climb the stairs, he wouldn't mind having *had* this damn affair. Not with Sarah, of course. Never with Sarah.

Meanwhile, Sarah is climbing her own stairs, on a fruitless hunt for cocoa, or biscuits, or anything that will distract her. She's been sitting at her desk since Amber left, watching the afternoon fade and chewing on slices of toast.

Everything's been fine, while the light lasted. But by evening, something is badly wrong.

Every time she passes a mirror, someone lurks behind mirror-Sarah, just out of sight. He's mouse-brown and short-sighted, he wears M&S underpants, he has a paunch and a bald spot and an entirely unsuitable wife. And although Sarah hasn't yet realised this, he will never leave.

From now on she'll spend that extra hour each autumn sleeping or eating or watching pale shadows in the dark, until fifty years later her sister will visit her in the hospice and dreamily add a touch of lipstick to that champing mouth that won't stop asking – will never stop asking until she dies five days later – for a rose-patterned chemise.

Source: Menon, C.G. (2018) 'Daylight savings', in C.G. Menon, *Subjunctive moods*. Leicester: Dahlia Publishing, pp. 128–138.

Chapter 16 readings

Reading 16.1 Extract from the novel *Reservoir 13*

Jon McGregor

> Nottinghamshire-based writer Jon McGregor writes short stories and novels, sometimes combining the two forms to produce a composite form known as a novel-in-stories.

Content note: Please be aware that this reading mentions the disappearance of a child.

1.

They gathered at the car park in the hour before dawn and waited to be told what to do. It was cold and there was little conversation. There were questions that weren't being asked. The missing girl's name was Rebecca Shaw. When last seen she'd been wearing a white hooded top. A mist hung low across the moor and the ground was frozen hard. They were given instructions and then they moved off, their boots crunching on the stiffened ground and their tracks fading behind them as the heather sprang back into shape. She was five feet tall, with dark-blonde hair. She had been missing for hours. They kept their eyes down and they didn't speak and they wondered what they might find. The only sounds were footsteps and dogs barking along the road and faintly a helicopter from the reservoirs. The helicopter had been out all night and found nothing, its searchlight skimming across the heather and surging brown streams. Jackson's sheep had taken the fear and scattered through a broken gate, and he'd been up all hours bringing them back. The mountain-rescue teams and the cave teams and the police had found nothing, and at midnight a search had been called. It hadn't taken much to raise the volunteers. Half the village was out already, talking about what could have happened. This was no time of year to have gone up on the hill, it was said. Some of the people who come this way don't know how sharply the weather can turn. How quickly darkness falls. Some of them don't seem to know there are places a mobile phone won't work. The girl's family had come up for the New Year, and were staying in one of the barn conversions at the Hunter place. They'd come running into the village at dusk, shouting. It was a cold night to have been out on the hill. She's likely just hiding, people said. She'll be down in a clough. Turned her ankle. She'll be aiming to give her parents a fright. There was a lot of this. People just wanted to open their mouths and talk, and they didn't much mind what came out. By first light the mist had cleared. From the top of the moor when people turned they could see the village: the beech wood and the allotments, the church tower and the cricket ground, the river and the quarry and the cement works by the main road into town. There was plenty of ground to cover, and so many places she could be. They moved on. There was an occasional flash of light from the traffic on the motorway, just visible along the horizon. The reservoirs were a flat metallic grey. A thick band of rain was coming in. The ground was softer now, the oily brown water seeping up around their boots. A news helicopter flew low along the line of volunteers. It was a job not to look up and wave. Later the police held a press conference in the Gladstone, but they had nothing to announce beyond what was already known. The missing girl's name was Rebecca Shaw. She was thirteen years old. When last seen she'd been wearing a white hooded top with a navy-blue body-warmer, black jeans, and canvas shoes. She was five feet tall, with straight, dark-blonde, shoulder-length hair. Members of the public were urged to contact the police if they saw anyone fitting the description. The search would resume when the weather allowed. In the evening over the square there was a glow of television lights and smoke rising from generators and raised voices coming from the yard behind the pub. Doubts were beginning to emerge.

At midnight when the year turned there were fireworks going up from the towns beyond the valley but they were too far off for the sound to carry and no one came out to watch. The dance at the village hall was cancelled, and although the Gladstone was full there was no mood for celebration. Tony closed the bar at half past the hour and everyone made their way home. Only the police stayed out in the streets, gathered around their vans or heading back into the hills. In the morning the rain started up once again. Water coursed from the swollen peat beds quickly through the cloughs and down the stepped paths which fell from the edge of the moor. The river thickened with silt from the hills and plumed across the weirs. On the moor there were flags marking where the parents said they'd walked. The flags furled and snapped in the wind. At the visitor centre television trucks filled the car park and journalists started to gather. In the village hall the trestle tables were laid with green cups and saucers, the urns rising to the boil and the smell of bacon cobs drifting out into the rain. At the Hunter place there were voices coming from the barn conversion where the parents were staying, loud enough that the policeman outside could hear. Jess Hunter came over from the main house with a mug of tea. A helicopter flew in from the reservoirs, banking slowly along the river and passing over the weir and the quarry and the woods. The divers were going through the river again. A group of journalists waited for the shot, standing behind a cordon by the packhorse bridge, cameras aimed at the empty stretch of water, the breath clouding over their heads. In the lower field two of Jackson's boys were kneeling beside a fallen ewe. There was a racket of camera shutters as the first diver appeared, the wetsuited head sleek and slow through the water. A second diver came round the bend, and a third. They took turns ducking through the arch in the bridge and then they were out of sight. The camera crews jerked their cameras from the tripods and began folding everything away. One of the Jackson boys bucked a quad bike across the field and told the journalists to move. The river ran empty and quick. The cement works was shut down to allow for a search. In a week the first snowdrops emerged along the verges past the cricket ground, while it seemed winter yet had a way to go. At the school in the staffroom the teachers kept their coats on and waited. Everything that might be said seemed like the wrong thing to say. The heating pipes made a rattling noise that most of them were used to and the mood in the room unstiffened. Miss Dale asked Ms French if her mother was any better, and Ms French outlined the ways in which she was not. There was a silence again in the room and the tapping of the radiator. Mrs Simpson came in and thanked them for the early start. They all said of course it wasn't a problem. Under the circumstances. Mrs Simpson said the plan was to follow their lessons as normal but be ready to talk about the situation if the children asked. Which it seemed likely they would. There was a knock at the door and Jones the caretaker stepped in to say the heating would be working soon. Mrs Simpson asked him to make sure the yard was gritted. He gave her a look which suggested there'd been no need to ask. When the children were brought to school Mrs Simpson stood at the gate to welcome them. The parents lingered once the children had gone inside, watching the doors being locked. Some of them looked as though they could stand there all day. At the bus stop the older children waited for the bus to the secondary school in town. They were teenagers now. It was the first day back but they weren't saying much. It was cold and they had hoods pulled tightly over their heads. All day they would be asked about the missing girl, as if they knew anything more than they'd heard on the news. Lynsey Smith said it was a safe bet Ms Bowman would ask if they needed to chat. She did finger-quotes around the word *chat*. Deepak said at least it would be a way of getting out of French. Sophie looked away, and saw Andrew waiting at the other bus stop with Irene, his mother. He was the same age as they were but he went to a special school. Their bus pulled up and James warned Liam not to make up any bullshit about Becky Shaw. It snowed and the snow settled thickly. There was a service at the church. The vicar asked the police to keep the media away. Anyone was welcome to attend, she said, but she wanted no photography or recording, no waving of notebooks. She wanted no spectacle made of a community caught in the agony of prayer. The wardens put out extra chairs, but people were still left standing along the aisles. The men who weren't used to being in church stood with their hats bent into their hands, leaning against the ends of the pews. Some folded their arms, expectantly. The regulars offered them service books opened to the correct page. The vicar, Jane Hughes, said she hoped no one had come looking for answers. She said she hoped no one was asking for comfort. There is no comfort in the situation we find ourselves in today, she said. There is no comfort for the girl's parents, or for the family members who have travelled to the village to support them. No comfort for the police officers who have been involved in the search. We can only trust that we might meet God among us in these times of trouble. Only ask that we not allow ourselves to be overcome by a grief which is not ours to indulge but instead be uplifted by faith and enabled to help that suffering family in whatever way we are called to do. She paused, and closed her eyes. She held out her hands in a gesture she hoped might resemble prayer. The men who had their arms folded kept them folded. The warden rang the bell three times and the sound carried out through the brightening morning and along the valley as far as the old quarry. At the end of the month the sun came out and the fields softened. The still air shook to the thump of melting rooftop snow. There were rumours and only rumours of where the parents might be now. They were beside themselves, it was said.

In February the police arranged a reconstruction, bringing actors over from Manchester. There had been no leads and they wanted to make a fresh appeal. The press were allowed up to the Hunter place and given instructions on what to film. The day was clear and edged with frost. The press officer asked for quiet. The door of the barn conversion opened and a couple in their early forties appeared, followed by a thirteen-year-old girl. The woman was slim, with blonde hair cropped neatly around her ears. She was wearing a dark-blue raincoat, and tight black jeans tucked into calf-length boots. The man was tall and angular, with wiry dark hair and a pair of black-framed glasses. He was wearing a charcoal-grey anorak, walking trousers, and black shoes. The girl looked tall for thirteen, with dark-blonde hair to her shoulders and a well-acted look of irritation. She was wearing black jeans, a white hooded top, a navy body-warmer, and canvas shoes. The three of them got into a silver car which was parked outside the barn conversion, and drove slowly down to the road. The photographers ran alongside. At the visitor centre the actors waited for the photographers to get into place before climbing out of the car and setting off towards the moor. The girl lagged behind and three times the actors playing her parents turned and called for her to hurry up and join them, and three times the girl responded by kicking at the ground and slowing a little more. The two adult actors held hands and walked ahead, and the girl quickened her pace. This sequence of events had been drawn from police interviews, it was later confirmed. The two adults kept walking until they'd gone over the first rise and dropped out of sight, and a few moments later the girl dropped out of sight as well. The cameras photographed the empty air. The press officer thanked everyone for coming. The three actors came back down the hill. Work started up at the cement works again and the roads were silvered with dust. The freight trains came shunting through the hill and around the long bend between the trees. A pale light moved slowly across the moor, catching in the flooded cloughs and ditches and sharpening until the clouds closed overhead. On the riverbank towards the weir at dusk a heron stood and watched the water. A slow fog came down from the hills overnight. At four in the morning Les Thompson was up and bringing the cows across the yard for milking. Later in the day the vicar was seen driving to the Hunter place. She was inside for an hour with the missing girl's parents, and she didn't speak to anyone when she left.

The investigation continued. By the end of March the weather had warmed and the parents were still at the Hunter place. There was no news. Jane Hughes went up to see them again one morning, and on her way past the Jackson place she saw Jackson and the boys out front of the lambing shed. They wore the looks of men who've been working hard but see no need to admit it. They had mugs of tea and cigarettes. The smell of breakfast being cooked came from inside the house. It was only when they saw the first children on their way to school that Will Jackson remembered he was due at his son's mother's house, to fetch the boy for school. The van wouldn't start so he took the quad bike, and he knew before he got there that the boy's mother wouldn't be happy about this; that it would be one more thing for her to hold against him. When they got back to the school the gates were locked and Will had to call Jones out of the boilerhouse to let them in. He took the boy down to his class. Miss Carter accepted his apologies, and settled the boy down, and asked Will if he might think about the class coming to visit at lambing time. He told her they'd started lambing already and she looked surprised. She asked if there weren't more to come and he said if she wanted to arrange a school trip she'd have to put something to his father in writing. It was the most she'd heard him say in weeks. When he got back to the yard his brothers were all inside the shed. They'd lost a ewe while he'd been gone. There was a meeting of the parish council. Brian Fletcher had trouble keeping people to the agenda, and eventually had to concede that it was difficult to pay mind to parking issues at a time like this. The meeting was adjourned. The police held a press conference in the function room at the Gladstone, and announced that they wanted to trace the driver of a red LDV Pilot van. The journalists asked if the driver was considered a suspect, and the detective in charge said they were keeping an open mind. The girl's parents sat beside the detective and said nothing. In the afternoon the wind was high and the clouds blew quickly east. A blackbird dipped across Mr Wilson's garden with a beakful of dead grass for a nest. There were springtails under the beech trees behind the Close, feeding on fragments of fallen leaves. At night from the hill the lights could be seen along the motorway, the red and the white flowing past one another and the clouds blowing through overhead. The missing girl had been looked for. She had been looked for all over. She had been looked for in the nettles growing up around the dead oak tree in Thompson's yard. Paving slabs and sheets of ply had been lifted before people moved away through the gates. She had been looked for at the Hunter place, around the back of the barn conversions and in the carports and woodsheds and workshops, in the woodland and in the greenhouses and the walled gardens. She had been looked for at the cement works, the huge buildings moved through with unease, people nosing vaguely behind pallets and forklifts and through the staffroom and canteen, their hands and faces slick with white dust when they ghosted on down the road. At night there were dreams about where she might have gone. Dreams about her walking down from the moor, her clothes soaked and her skin almost blue. Dreams about being the first to reach her with a blanket and bring her safely home.

By April when the first swallows were seen the walkers were back on the hills. At the car park as they hoisted their packs they could be heard speculating about the girl. Which way she might have headed, how far she might have gone. North and she'd have been over the motorway by nightfall. East and the reservoirs would have been in her way. West and she'd have come to the edges, where the heather and soil frayed out into air and the gritstone rolled away from the hill. The weather she'd have been walking through. And in those shoes. There were so many places to fall. How was it she hadn't been found, still, as the days got longer and the sun cut further into the valley and under the ash trees the first new ferns unfurled from the cold black soil. In the evenings the same pictures were shown on the news: an aerial shot of the search party strung across the moor; the divers moving through the water; the girl's parents being driven away; the photograph of the girl. In the photograph she matched the description of what she'd been wearing and her face was half-turned away. It made it look as though she wanted to be somewhere else, people said. The girl's mother was again visited by detectives. Sometimes there were new questions. At the school before the children arrived Miss Carter filled aluminum jugs from the dinner hall with water and arranged in them cut branches of willow tight with buds. On the allotments the purple broccoli was sprouting, the heads snapping off cleanly and too sweet on the tongue to get a decent harvest home. Surveyors were seen up on the land around the Stone Sisters. There were rumours they worked for a quarrying firm. The annual Spring Dance was almost cancelled, but when Irene suggested holding it in aid of a missing-children's charity it became difficult for anyone to object. Sally Fletcher offered to help organise it, once Irene had looked pointedly at her for long enough. The divers roped up again, slipping into the reservoir while the herons sloped away overhead. The trees came back into leaf. A soft rain blew in smoky clouds across the fields.

At the butchers for May Day weekend there was a queue but nothing like there once would have been. Nothing like the queue Martin and Ruth needed to keep the shop going. Martin had been keeping this to himself, although it was becoming obvious and nobody asked. Irene was at the front of the queue telling everyone what she knew about the situation at the Hunters'. She did the cleaning there, and knew a thing or two. You can imagine what it's like for the girl's parents, she said. Having to watch us all down here just getting on with things. Ruth saying but surely the village couldn't be expected to put life on hold. Austin Cooper came in with copies of the *Valley Echo* newsletter and laid them on the counter. Ruth wished him congratulations, and he looked confused for a moment before smiling and backing away towards the door. Irene watched him go, and asked if Su Cooper was expecting. Ruth said yes, at last, and from the back of the queue Gordon Jackson asked would there be any chance of getting served before the baby was born. A breakdown truck came slowly down the narrow street, with a red LDV Pilot van hoisted on the back and a police car following. The van was wrapped in clear plastic. Martin wiped his hands on his apron and stepped outside to watch it pass. Gordon came out with him and lit a cigarette. Martin nodded. That changes things, he said. Fucking breakthrough is that, Gordon said. The swallows returned in number, and could be seen flying in and out through the open doors of the lambing shed at the Jacksons' and the cowsheds over at Thompson's, and the outbuildings up on the Hunters' land. The well-dressing committee had a difference of opinion about whether to dress the boards at all this year. Under the circumstances. There'd never been a year without a well dressing that anyone could remember. But there'd never been a year like this. In the end it was agreed to make the dressing but to keep the event low-key. There were sightings of the girl. She was seen by Irene, first, on the footbridge by the tea rooms, walking across to the other side. Quite alone she was, Irene said. Her young face turned half away and she wouldn't look me in the eye. Gone before I got to her and I couldn't see which way she went. I knew it was her. The police were told, and they went searching but they found nothing. There were lots of young families in the area that day, a police spokesperson said. But I know it was her, Irene said again. There was rain and the river was high and the hawthorn by the lower meadows came out foaming white. The cow parsley was thick along the footpaths and the shade deepened under the trees. Stock was moved higher up the hills and the tea rooms by the millpond opened for the year. In the shed Thompson's men were working on the baler, making sure they'd be ready when the time came for the cut. The grass was high but the weather had been low for days. The rain on the roof was loud and steady. The reservoirs filled.

Source: McGregor, J. (2017) *Reservoir 13*. London: 4th Estate, pp. 1–14.

Chapter 17 readings

Reading 17.1 Interview with Siobhán Campbell and Jane Yeh

Siobhán Campbell and Jane Yeh, interviewed by Heather Richardson

> Siobhán Campbell is a poet and critic. She was born in Dublin, and has lived in London and Belfast. Her interest in creative writing for social cohesion has led to community-based work with a diverse range of groups, including social workers and NHS workers.

> Jane Yeh is a poet. She was born in the United States and has lived in London since 2002. In addition to poetry, she also writes on books, theatre and fashion.

Content note: Please be aware that this reading briefly mentions alcoholism.

HEATHER RICHARDSON (HR):

It seems to be quite difficult to find an official definition of what a poetry sequence is, and I guess we all have our own understanding of what it means. I wondered each of you how you would define a poetry sequence?

SIOBHÁN CAMPBELL (SC):

I suppose what comes to mind first is that the reader recognises it even if it's not signposted. The reader begins to think 'Oh, I know now what's going on', poem after poem, so whether that's thematically – what's in the poems – or something else. Michael Symmons Roberts's sequence in *Drysalter* is a hundred and fifty poems of fifteen lines, so that's more a sequence based on form, although there are some thematic links as well. I suppose even if it's not labelled a sequence a reader might understand it as a sequence because it starts to declare itself bit by bit.

JANE YEH (JY):

For the simplest definition I would say it's a series of poems that are thematically connected, or maybe have a narrative connection. There are probably exceptions, but I think most people nowadays would say a poetry sequence is a series of individual poems that have some kind of connection or link to each other.

SC:

Numbering in contemporary poetry seems to be one way of showing you're doing a sequence. They're helpfully numbered, like Michael Symmons Roberts, again, his 'Last Words' 1–12. Each of those poems is about the anniversary of the attacks of 9/11. Even though they're quite different, they're all individual pieces, but they're numbered helpfully which declares itself to us as a reader, as a sequence.

HR:

Just thinking about *Drysalter*, he has other poems in the collection that all have the same title, there are no numbers and they're scattered throughout the collection. Is that a sequence within sequences?

SC:

I think that's maybe a variation on it, to put the sequence within a collection scattered through. There are various ways to do this sequence thing. Tying it down is actually a bit tricky.

JY:

Another kind that's similar to that is the American poet Terrance Hayes who has a book called *American Sonnets for My Past and Future Assassin*, and every poem in the collection is actually a sonnet whose title is 'American Sonnet for My Past and Future Assassin'. They're not numbered and they don't have subtitles either so that's the most extreme case. I think that clearly signals the fact that it's a sequence of poems because they've all been given the exact same title.

HR:

I sometimes find it difficult to distinguish between an organising principle and a thematic connection. When we're talking about sequences it seems a grey area, doesn't it? If you take something like the 9/11 poems, there's an organising principle there, isn't there, as well as the sequence of it?

SC:

There probably are some sequences in poetry that are not thematically connected, at least their 'top note' is not thematically connected, so that the content doesn't immediately appear to be connected. But there's a sensibility. It's the same poet, and so there's a sensibility connection coming through, although when you first read them there mightn't appear to be. As opposed to that, there are ones that veer more towards the very connected, telling a full story. There's a collection out at the moment by Liz Berry called *The Home Child* which is being reviewed as a sequence. You could review it potentially almost as a verse novel, but each poem is separate at the same time. It's the story of the forced emigration to Canada of Berry's great aunt in the early 1900s. The UK sent poor or orphaned children to Canada to be billeted out, and adopted and put to work often by farming families. So that's another way of looking at it.

HR:

It's useful to unpick it a bit and to know that there isn't actually a simple and straightforward definition, I think it's important to be aware of that, isn't it? That there are traditions, but it also seems to be an extremely malleable concept that poets can use as they wish to.

SC:

It could be something very simple. Richard Price has a sequence called 'A Spelthorne Bird List', and each one is about a bird except it gets more complex. The birds are also standing in for people. You could say there's an organising principle – at least that's the initial thing it appears to be.

HR:

So, what about within your own work? I know you both have used sequences in different ways, sometimes in that traditional way, numbering the poems one, two, three, four, but also sometimes with poems scattered throughout a collection.

JY:

Whenever I've deliberately set out to write a sequence it doesn't really work. A sequence has to be three poems or more because otherwise it's just a poem and a sequel, so even when I've tried to write a second poem as sequel to a first one in some way it almost never seems to work out for me. But in my last collection I ended up with what you'd probably call a series or sequence of five poems that all have titles that are almost the same but with variation. The formula for the title is 'Self-portrait as X,' so 'Self-portrait as Klaus Nomi in New York' [...] and those are scattered throughout the book.

They were maybe subliminally influenced by poems from Kaveh Akbar's collection *Calling a Wolf a Wolf*. He has ten poems scattered throughout it, and they're all titled 'Portrait of the Alcoholic X', so, 'Portrait of the Alcoholic with Doubt and Kim Fisher', 'Portrait of the Alcoholic with Moths and River', 'Portrait of the Alcoholic Stranded Alone on a Desert Island' and so on. I thought that was cool, and it was quite interesting as a way of linking these poems together even though each one is very distinctive and different. With my self-portrait poems, at the time I was writing them I wasn't considering them as part of a sequence, so some of them I only titled self-portrait after they were totally finished. I was looking at them as a group already, so the title was added afterwards to make them into more of a sequence. I started thinking of them as linked in a non-linear way, not in a narrative way, because they're totally not. They don't form an extended narrative at all. I thought of them in terms of their approach or their voice. They're all written in the first person, but aren't exactly lyric in that traditional sense of lyric as a poem that is spoken by the poet themselves about their own thoughts and experiences. To me they're linked because they're all a hybrid of lyric and dramatic monologue, where the poem is spoken by another character not the poet themselves. If you're looking for a way that they're linked thematically as a sequence, I guess they concern ideas about otherness or being an outsider or the nature of identity or identity as a kind of artifice or persona.

I've actually continued to write more of these 'Self-portrait as X' poems as I'm working on my next book. Only sporadically, not one after the other. It's having a very loose framework for some of my poems, or a lens to view them through. It's a very capacious framework that almost anything can fit into actually, but it's one I do consciously allow to guide me at times when I'm writing. Previously I never had anything so this concept of having a sequence of poems, I think, has been helpful to me.

SC:

I don't usually start off with the idea of writing a sequence, and in my present book that I'm finishing a sequence has emerged in effect which is of cow poems. They have different moods from each other, but cows are the linking feature. So I was considering, well, do I batch these together? There's about eleven of them at this point although some are quite short. Or do I put them throughout the collection? In the end I think they will probably be throughout the collection because what has happened as part of the writing process is other animals started to arrive. So now I have sheep, I have horses, I have owls, I have a whale or two, sharks, so actually I'm gathering other animals in. And I had a friend who's also a poet, we peer review each other's work, and she called it 'the bestiary' immediately, and she saw the whole thing as a sequence, so this was an eye-opener to me. However, there are other poems in there, so I don't consider it a bestiary. At the same time, it just shows you that once you put something down and you try and make some coherent whole of it other people may see sequences.

It's part of the writing process to discover how poems talk to each other. And I think that is key even if you're just making it a short sequence of say four or five poems. It's good to think about quite abstractly initially. If I had to pick a colour for these poems, what colour would it be? Or perhaps take an adjective, what adjective would it be? Because you can then see sometimes, 'Ah, this one doesn't fit in some way', and it could come out. And another question to ask to make a short sequence is 'Which is the key poem of this sequence?' The one that captures as much of the feeling that might be done in different ways in the other poems but is the key poem. You might then decide where to put that key poem. Do you end with that? Or do you put it at the beginning, as a lead into the sequence? It starts very much being about the feel and the atmosphere of the poem as much as about the content.

HR:

Do you want to say anything else about your approaches, or the different conventions that you might have experimented with or tried out or have used in collections in the past?

SC:

Yeah, there's something about numbering, which I used to hate but which I now quite like. You have to decide whether you use Arabic numerals – 1, 2, 3 – or you're going to use Roman, the little 'i's with the dots on them … There's something about the Roman, and because you can keep it lower case as well it feels a bit more inviting to me, although it could be quite off-putting for some people. I've come to appreciate numbered sequences rather than titling each poem. Especially if they're very short, titling each can feel a bit heavy but just numbering each one and allowing them to segue into each other can create a different experience.

JY:

I wouldn't use numbering, but a lot of contemporary poets use titles that are almost the same but with variation. Another example of a book that influenced me a lot was a different book by Terrance Hayes, *Lighthead*. He has one poem in each of three sections called 'Lighthead's Guide to X'. So 'Lighthead's Guide to the Galaxy' and stuff like that. And then in the same collection he also has six other poems scattered throughout that all have the word 'head' in them in a major way, so one is called 'Anchor Head', one is called 'Tank Head', and one is called 'Puzzle Head'. It's a way of naming things to show that they're part of a sequence but they're scattered throughout the collection. I guess there's something that appeals to me about that. In my own collections where I've scattered these poems throughout, I want to avoid the reader being bored. I think if you put say six poems in a row in a book that are titled 'Self-portrait as X' it might seem repetitive even if they're all totally different. That's part of the reason I would scatter them around. But it's also about placing a poem where it fits best in a collection in terms of the poems that come before and after it. They create this environment that an individual poem is sitting in, so that's what people are thinking of in terms of placing these poems in different positions in a collection.

I have two analogies for that. The first is that when you scatter a sequence of poems throughout a collection then they act as a leitmotiv or motif, to use terms from music. It's something recurring that the book keeps returning to, although it's also different each time. The second analogy is a little bit involved: if you think of this structure of a US TV programme, what they call a procedural, the structure has existed for a long time and still exists. Each series of a TV programme consists of usually 22 weekly episodes. There are a number of episodes that are essentially stand-alone, self-contained stories, even though they have the same recurring characters. But there's also a larger narrative arc that extends across the whole series. A number of episodes scattered throughout the year are concerned with the larger narrative story or arc. In each series of 22 episodes there's this balance between narrative continuity that extends the arc, and the stand-alone episodes. For me, because I don't write narrative poems or have over-arching narratives, it's more about continuity, and the sequence might be a theme or approach or attitude. And then there's variety in the individual poems that aren't part of a sequence, much more variety in terms of content or voice or style.

HR:

It seems to me that there are a couple of different things going on. For example, if a poet doesn't sit down to write a sequence, but writes and a sequence emerges. Let's say for the sake of argument that they end up with three, four or five poems and they think 'Yes, this is a sequence, this is the order I'd have them as a sequence.' And this is the piece of work, but then something different can happen when it's put into the context of a collection and, in fact, it might be appropriate to disassemble the sequence at that point. In a way the sequence can have two different lives, first as the initial artefact itself, and then as it's used within a collection.

SC:

Yes, that's very true. Some do something slightly different. For example, Ian McMillan has a pamphlet, *This Lake used to be Frozen*, and in it there's a little mini sequence which is eight poems numbered zero to seven. They're about a walk he has taken all his life, so there's childhood, adulthood and even an imagined old age along the same walk, taking in nature, obviously, but embedding a lived life in there. It's sort of time-travelling, which is something that poetry can do, and to some extent imaginative travel. Carrie Etter's book *Imagined Sons* has a narrator who tells different stories about imagined sons, because the narrator, it turns out, gave up a son for adoption in her teenage years and then imagines these different lives for that son. There's an overarching organising principle, but within that it allows each imagined son to be quite different and they all do different things. One sells the *Big Issue*, one is a used car salesman and so on.

JY:

I wonder if those Ian McMillan poems are meant to allude to that famous Shakespeare soliloquy 'The Seven Ages of Man' from *As You Like It*? Seamus Heaney used to have this exercise for students where he would ask them to write a poem that covers the seven ages of man, and it's a little bit what you're describing in a way.

SC:

I wouldn't be surprised, Jane, I'd say you might well be right there.

JY:

You could write a sequence and have them all in a certain order and you see them as a sequence, but then when you decide to include them in a whole book you might separate them or change around a sequence. One example is Hala Alyan in her book *The Twenty-Ninth Year*. One of the themes running throughout the book is her experience of alcoholism and recovery. She has four poems that are named for four steps from the Alcoholics Anonymous '12 steps', so one is titled 'Step One: Admit Powerlessness', one is titled 'Step Two: Higher Power', and so on. Those are the shorthand for the steps, but actually there are only four of the poems in the book, not all twelve, and they're not in order. It's not steps one to four, there's one, two, four and eight. They don't even appear in numerical order in the book. I don't know if she did this on purpose – I don't know the origin behind it all – but it seemed to me that she didn't want it to be so neat or tidy, grouping them all together, having them all in the order of one to twelve. It makes it more interesting, I think, the way she's arranged them. Each of them is very different and very unique, so it's not some dull, plain thing like 'Here's how I did step eight and made amends'.

HR:

Are there any other contemporary poets that you think are worth having a look at to see what they do with the sequence?

SC:

I suppose we should mention something else – researched sequences, for want of a better way of putting it. This could be where the poet goes and talks to or interviews a group of people and feeds that into their poems. I'd find it really difficult because I feel the poems could become dead, but people can manage this. One writer that comes to mind is Zeina Hashem Beck's 'There Was and How Much There Was'. In effect it's a room full of women talking about their lives, their children, their husbands and their bodies, that's the premise for the book. I'm nearly sure Zeina Hashem Beck did research and took verbatim words and did interviews. And so she's basically made this room of the book, but different characters and different voices and different stories are in there in the different poems. And then there's *Dart* by Alice Oswald. She spent three years talking to people all along the River Dart in Devon. But I don't know if people consider that to be a sequence or a long poem.

JY:

I have two more examples. One is a book by Solmaz Sharif, *Customs*, where she has three poems that are all titled identically 'Dear Aleph'. There's no numbering but they're quite clearly a sequence. They're scattered throughout the book, and each of them is very different formally and stylistically or by content. But you could say they share the themes of a critique of US mainstream ideology, and they concern experience of otherness. The other example I was thinking of is by Rachel Long in her collection *My Darling from the Lions*. The book is divided into a couple of sections: the first section is titled 'Open' and within it there are five poems scattered throughout it that are each identically titled 'Open', so again that's very clearly a sequence. A lot of the words from them are identical, it's almost the same poem repeated five times but with small variations, and each poem is so short – they're all five lines each, except the last one which is seven lines – but basically, they're these tiny poems punctuating this section of the book. It's almost the way in a silent movie there used to be title cards to separate sections or to punctuate the movie, or maybe I think of them as places where the reader can pause for thought between the longer poems that are in there. To me that was a really interesting device that I hadn't seen anyone use before really in quite that way.

HR:

Just thinking about this chapter title – 'Thematic connections' – I get the sense that sequence is a way of the poet suggesting to the reader, that 'Yes, we have several different poems, but I want you to pay attention to the fact there is some kind of connection between them'. Does that ring true?

SC:

Yes, definitely, that sounds right.

JY:

That seems very apt, I think.

HR:

It feels much less instrumental than just saying 'Here is a sequence', one, two, three. It's about thinking of the purpose of sequence. Not so much *how* a poet might use it, but *why* a poet might use it. I think you've both come up with some really fascinating insights into the sequence. Is there anything you would like to add?

JY:

Going back to something Siobhán said earlier, you're saying it's a way of a poet telling the reader 'Here are poems that are linked in some way', and asking them to look at them in that way. I wonder if it's also a way for the poet to do that to themselves. I was saying I didn't really realise my self-portrait poems were linked until after the fact. I was talking about how you discover it as you're in the process of writing, or soon after writing, so it's a signpost both to yourself and to the reader, especially this use of titles to mark out a sequence.

Source: Campbell, S. and Yeh, J. (2023) Interview with Siobhán Campbell and Jane Yeh. Interviewed by H. Richardson for the Open University module A363 *Advanced creative writing*, 24 April.

Reading 17.2 Extracts from editors' introductions to themed anthologies

17.2(a) *The Black Dreams*

Reggie Chamberlain-King

> Reggie Chamberlain-King is a writer and editor of fiction and non-fiction, with a particular interest in the weird and unusual. He also presents documentaries on the strange for BBC Radio 4. He lives in Northern Ireland.

Content note: Please be aware that this reading mentions gun violence.

I don't recall if I saw my first gunman in my childhood nightmares or on my childhood streets. There were plenty in both and they looked very much like each other. The things my mother warned would happen to little boys who spoke to soldiers or travelled by taxi soon happened to other people – it was frequently in the news. She was anxious about many things, and stories were her way of sharing them with me. Her warnings were partway between fairy tale and premonition, a magical act of manifestation. It became easy to believe, then, all the other stories. For example, there were devil worshippers sacrificing dogs on Black Mountain. And when it was suggested that those stories were actually planted by the military as part of British psy-ops, that was easy to believe as well. Everything was possible. I borrowed *The prophecies of Nostradamus* many times from the Falls Library and was able to match each news headline with one of its vague quatrains. Fear is a function of imagination and one lives in it as fully as a dream – the same laws apply. There is something inside the mind stronger than everything outside it and physics only asserts itself on the occasions when the dream meets the reality, when bomb scare becomes bomb.

...

When I came to compile this collection of strange stories, it was my dream – at once a desire and a delusion – to capture my uneasy feeling of growing up in Northern Ireland, the same feeling that was safely contained in a bank holiday horror film or *Tales to Tremble By*: things are not as they seem. That the authors of these stories have managed to distil that uncertainty in many different ways, in many different parts of Northern Ireland, at different times, shows just how much that feeling permeates the imagination here. We all have our own anxieties.

Source: Chamberlain-King, R. (2021) 'Introduction: dreaming the black dream', in R. Chamberlain-King (ed.) *The black dreams: strange stories from Northern Ireland*. Belfast: The Blackstaff Press, pp. xi–xii, xxii.

17.2(b) *The Good Immigrant*
Nikesh Shukla

> Nikesh Shukla is a novelist, screenwriter and editor, based in Bristol. He is an advocate for diversity and inclusion in the arts.

Content note: Please be aware that this reading explores the effects of racism.

This book emerged out of a comment on a *Guardian* article. I know, I know, it's easy to say, don't read the comments. But I do. Because I want to know my enemy. The commenter took umbrage at an interview a journalist had done with five authors (including me) about their writing process. The journalist (Asian) had interviewed five or six people of colour. The commenter wondered why there wasn't a more prominent author interviewed for this piece. He supposed (for it is almost always a 'he') that perhaps we were all friends of the journalist, given we too were all mostly Asian. This constant anxiety we feel as people of colour to justify our space, to show that we have earned our place at the table, continues to hound us. For while I and the 20 other writers included in this book don't want to just write about race, nor do we *only* write about race, it felt imperative, in the light of that comment (and the many others like it), the backwards attitude to immigration and refugees, the systemic racism that runs through this country to this day, that we create this document: a document of what it means to be a person of colour now. Because we're done justifying our place at the table.

Source: Shukla, N. (2016) 'Editor's note', in N. Shukla (ed.) *The good immigrant.* London: Unbound, p. xix.

17.2(c) Cast a Long Shadow

Katherine Stansfield and Caroline Oakley

> Katherine Stansfield is a poet and novelist. She grew up on Bodmin Moor in Cornwall, and now lives in Wales. In addition to novels published under her own name, she co-writes crime/fantasy novels as D.K. Fields.

> Caroline Oakley has had a long career in publishing, and was publisher/editor at Honno, which specialises in work by Welsh women writers, from 2005 to 2021.

Content note: Please be aware that this reading mentions violence against women and girls.

This rich field of contemporary crime writing is one in which women are extremely well-represented – as writers and as readers. But also as victims – a reflection, it must surely be argued, of horrifying levels of real-world male violence against women and girls. For all their trappings of fiction, crime stories often have at their heart a shocking realism, and this is true for this anthology. A number of contributions centre on women and girls as the victims of male violence. Putting together this book in the period in which Sarah Everard was abducted and murdered by a serving police officer in London, resulting in a very public conversation about the safety of women in society, means that the stories women tell of violence, power and justice are more urgent than ever.

Narratives of women as victims do not preclude those that cast women as defenders, seeking justice and to restore order in their world, as they define it. Such characters are plentiful in *Cast a Long Shadow*, in recognisably realist modes as well as in re-imaginings of myths new and old. Women also feature strongly among the culprits, taking the law into their own hands and not always for the good. A similar plurality can be seen in the nature of crime explored within these covers. Murder plots sit alongside those involving fraud, drug production, theft and issues of consent. And the anthology points forward to transgressive acts that should preoccupy us all, now and in the years to come: crimes against the environment.

The women writers of Wales have risen to the challenge of this narrative form and the number of submissions for this anthology confirmed the popularity of the genre here, as well as the wealth of talent: crime writing, in all its myriad styles and preoccupations, is a hugely active field in Welsh writing in English. *Cast a Long Shadow* offers a snapshot of the Welsh women crime writers at work today, with the promise of much more to come.

Source: Stansfield, K. and Oakley, C. (2022) 'Introduction', in K. Stansfield and C. Oakley (eds) *Cast a long shadow: Welsh women writing crime.* Aberystwyth: Honno Press.

17.2(d) *Antlers of Water*

Kathleen Jamie

> Kathleen Jamie is a Scottish poet, essayist and editor. Much of her work focuses on travel, the natural world and archaeology. She has also written for BBC Radio 3 and Radio 4.

Antlers of Water is a collection of specially commissioned writing which concerns our relationship with the more-than-human world. It announces a 'new Scottish nature writing' and brings together, for the first time, a fine selection of our country's hugely talented contemporary nature and environmental writers. It features prose and poetry which is by turns personal, celebratory, political, frightened and hopeful. All the writers in this book are alive in this difficult moment; all reside, or have resided, in Scotland; and all are writing here about some aspect of the country they call home. Their work addresses the realities of our times, and examines our relationship with our fellow creatures, our beloved and fast-changing landscapes, our energy futures, our ancient past.

...

We invite you to read not as a passive recipient, but as an active participant in this vital work, this noticing. If by reading you are encouraged or confirmed in your love of the natural world, if your interest is piqued, if you're inspired simply to put the book down and look outside, then our job is done. When we read and write, when we love our fellow creatures, when we walk on the beach, when we just listen and notice, we are not little cogs in the machine, but part of the remedy.

Source: Jamie, K. (2020) 'Introduction', in K. Jamie (ed.) *Antlers of water: writing on the nature and environment of Scotland.* Edinburgh: Canongate, pp. xi and xvii.

Glossary

abstraction
in creative writing, this word often refers to the quality of dealing with ideas and feelings rather than events and details.

action
when something happens in front of the reader rather than being described or recounted via **exposition**.

action line
a way of describing the dramatic arc in a story by focusing solely on the actions, or events, of the story.

adjective
a word that describes the quality of a person, place or thing.

allegory
a story that can be interpreted to have a hidden meaning.

alliteration
when words that begin with the same sound are put in close proximity to each other.

analogy
a word or phrase that expresses a similarity between one thing and another.

antithesis
the use of words that are opposites, or noticeably different, to highlight contrasting ideas.

assonance
the recurrence of similar-sounding vowels in a group of words or lines of poetry.

aural
refers to anything that is related to the sense of hearing.

autobiography
an account of someone's life written by that person, usually in the first person and giving the impression of encompassing the whole life (see also **memoir**).

backstory
the history of events prior to the dramatic present or the 'now' of the story.

ballad
a poem or song narrating a story in short stanzas. Traditional ballads are typically of unknown authorship, having been passed on orally from one generation to the next.

beat sheet
a document that sets out all the story beats in a script according to the order in which they occur.

biography
an account of someone's life written by someone else.

biopic
a film based on the life of a real person.

blank verse
poetry written in unrhymed but metrically regular lines, usually, but not always, in iambic pentameter with five stressed and five unstressed syllables.

cliffhanger
a plot device in fiction or film/TV which often features a main character in a precarious situation or confronted with a shocking revelation just as the episode or chapter ends.

close-up
in films or TV drama, when the camera focuses on a subject, magnifying it to many times its natural size.

conflict
when a character, in creative writing, faces an obstacle to their wants or needs, or finds themselves in trouble or opposition. Conflict can come in the form of other characters or natural events; it can also be internal – in other words, a character can experience a clash of opposing feelings.

couplet
a stanza of two lines.

dialect
a variety of language usage which is peculiar to a limited district, ethnic group, class of people or section of society.

dialogic
often describes how a character engages with the audience as though they are speaking directly to them. This can be achieved through exchanges with other characters, as well as through implied exchanges with an audience.

dialogue
a conversation between two or more characters, revealing aspects of the characters' backgrounds and personality traits. This is often presented using quotation marks.

discordant
having a quality of sound that lacks harmony and, so, being harsh or jarring.

dramatic action
a shift, which may be just a transition in a set of relationships or a change in emotional state, that is enacted and manifest in the events and elements of the story.

dramatic irony
a plot device often used in theatre, literature, film and television to highlight the difference between a character's understanding of what is occurring, and that of the audience.

dramatic monologue
a type of **persona poem** written in the form of a speech.

dystopia
an imagined world, usually set in the future, characterised by injustice and suffering.

elegy
a poem of serious reflection, typically a lament for the dead.

emotion line
a way of describing the dramatic arc in a story by focusing on the emotional journey of a character.

enjambment
in poetry, the continuation of a sentence or phrase across a line break into the next line, without punctuation at the end of the line (sometimes called a run-on line).

epic
a long poem, typically derived from ancient oral tradition, narrating the deeds and adventures of heroic or legendary figures.

epigraph
a quotation, phrase, poem or small extract that appears at the beginning of a text.

episodic
in literature, this refers to the way in which a story is told by focusing in turn on a different character, location or theme in a longer work. It may also apply in a shorter work that looks at a sequence of events or episodic happenings in turn.

epistolary
a type of fiction that is written in the form of letters, emails or other types of text communication.

euphony
having the quality of being melodious or pleasing to the ear.

exposition
declaring, describing or announcing either in speech or in writing (see **telling**).

fantasy
a genre of fiction in which the settings and scenarios are imaginary and not primarily realistic representations of the known world.

figurative language
language used for something other than its literal meaning, including **personification**, **simile** and **metaphor**.

first-person narration
a narrative usually told by a character or characters within the story, using the pronouns 'I' or 'we' rather than 'he', 'she' or 'they'.

flashbacks
retrospective leaps to dramatic moments in the backstory (see also **recurring flashback**).

flash fiction
stories that have a short word count (sometimes referred to as 'microfiction', 'short short stories' or 'short shorts').

flashforward
a leap forwards to a dramatic moment that occurs after the present timeframe of the narration.

flash non-fiction
stand-alone pieces of non-fiction that have a short word count (sometimes referred to as 'micro non-fiction').

foreshadowing
hinting at events that will happen later in the narrative.

form
this term encompasses (a) modes of artistic expression, such as fiction, poetry, life writing and drama; (b) types of text, such as short stories, novels, epic poems, lyric poems, memoirs, biographies, stage plays and feature films; and (c) types of traditional poetic forms such as sonnet, sestina and pantoum.

free verse
poetry written without a fixed pattern of rhythm or **rhyme**, often without any rhyme.

freewriting
a way of allowing your 'writing mind' to freely associate thoughts and feelings that are expressed as words and phrases. There is no attempt to link these deliberately but on rereading, patterns of thought often emerge.

genre
in fictional forms, especially films and novels, this can be taken to mean a particular type of story, such as an action adventure, science fiction, romantic comedy or crime thriller, for example.

Gothic novel
a genre or mode of narrative writing characterised by the use of terror and suspense, often accompanied and heightened by elements of the supernatural and by a claustrophobic atmosphere. Writing of this type has appeared in many different periods and places; it was particularly popular in the UK from the 1760s to the 1820s.

half rhyme
words that only partially **rhyme**.

historical fiction
a genre of fiction that takes place in the past and where real historical events, settings and people may be a major component of the story.

idiolect
a person's unique way of speaking or writing.

idiom
an expression or group of words that, through established usage, produces a meaning that is more than the literal definition of its individual component words; it can be a form of expression peculiar to a specific person or group of people. In dramatic dialogue, idiom usually refers to these forms of expression in relation to a given character or group of characters.

imagery
a description that involves a **sensory perception** (i.e. that appeals to at least one of the five senses: taste, touch, hearing, sight or smell).

impersonation
identifying and using key elements of behaviour and language used by a particular character or characters, to imitate (in narrative or performance) their actions and way of speaking and thinking.

inciting incident
the event that propels the rest of the action in a story.

in medias res
in the middle of the action.

intercutting
switching between different narrative strands.

internal rhyme
rhyme that occurs in the middle of lines of poetry, instead of at the ends of lines. Internal rhyme is often half rhyme rather than full rhyme (see also **half rhyme**).

intertextual
an adjective describing writing that relates to, and often references, other literary and artistic works, or biographical and historical narratives.

life writing
writing based on the experiences, facts and lives of real people, but that uses fiction writing techniques so that it reads more like a story than journalism or a report. This includes **autobiography**, **memoir** and **biography**.

lyric poem
usually refers to a short poem, often with songlike qualities, which typically expresses powerful feelings via the presence, in the poem, of the poet themselves.

magic realism
a genre of literature that blurs the boundaries between fantasy and reality by introducing magical or surreal elements into an otherwise realistic narrative.

memoir
usually an account of part of someone's life (for example, a specific time or thematically connected events) written from the personal knowledge or experience of the author.

metaphor
an implicit comparison of likeness between two things, without using the word 'like' or 'as'.

metre
a pattern of rhythm in a line of poetry, usually the pattern of stressed and unstressed syllables.

mind map
a visual diagram to develop an idea, often with a central concept in the middle, in which lines are used to connect associated concepts, and new concepts can be added as part of the process.

monologue
in drama, an extended speech delivered by one character, voicing their thoughts to other characters or as if alone.

montage
when two dissimilar images are placed side by side to create a new meaning and move the story along.

mood
the general feeling or atmosphere that a piece of writing creates in the reader.

morality tale
a story or narrative from which one can derive what is right or wrong.

motion capture
the process or technique of digitally recording patterns of movement from an actor's performance so that it can be translated into the action of a computer animation.

narrative
a structured account of a series of events (see **story**).

narrative arc
the complete progression (beginning/middle/end) of a story.

narrative strands
different storylines within the overall story, each often associated with a specific character and/or place.

non-linear
in relation to plot, this describes a course of events that does not progress smoothly, from one stage to the next, in a logical way.

novella
a form of prose fiction that is longer than a short story but shorter than a novel, usually between 15,000 and 40,000 words.

offstage action
any dramatic action that is crucial to the story but is not shown to the audience. This action is often reported in dialogue between characters.

omniscient narrator
an all-knowing narrator (usually not a character in the story) with access to the mind of every character, and knowledge about the story's events (past, present and future).

parenthesis
the interruption of a sentence with words that qualify what is happening or that produce the effect of an aside.

parentheticals
descriptive words and phrases, often adverbs, which appear in parentheses (brackets) within sections of dialogue in a script. They describe how an actor moves, responds or delivers a line.

persona
an invented perspective that a writer uses. The assumed point of view might be entirely different from the writer's own.

personal essay
an essay that focuses on the writer's own experiences and is explicitly shaped by the personality of the author.

persona poetry
a poem written from the perspective of a character created by, and distinct from, the poet. **Dramatic monologues** are a type of persona poem.

phonetics
analysis of the sounds of human speech.

plot twist
a technique that introduces a radical change in the direction or expected outcome of the plot which the audience is not expecting.

point of view
the position of the narrator in relation to the story being told.

polyphonic narration
a story told from a diverse range of voices and perspectives, each of them accorded more or less equal space.

premise
the cornerstone of a novel's plot or the main idea explored in book-length life writing.

protagonist
the main character in a piece of writing.

realism
used to describe literary works characterised by their authors' interest in representing human life and experience 'as they really are'.

'real time'
a reading or performance time that equates to the time these events would have taken to unfold in real life.

recurring flashback
a significant flashback that is returned to later in the text, allowing the reader to view it with a new understanding gained by the intervening narrative.

repetition (in narrative prose)
repeated images, actions or other elements – a structural tool that helps reinforce the dramatic action.

rhetoric

verbal or written communication used to persuade, inform or motivate.

rhyme

repetition of the same or similar sounds, often between the final syllables or groups of syllables of multiple words.

romance

a prose or verse narrative in which unlikely events occur, usually involving love and/or adventure. Many medieval romances, like *Sir Gawain and the Green Knight*, focus on the adventures of King Arthur and his knights. The term has been used to refer loosely to many different kinds of fantastical writing. Romance, in these circumstances, is often contrasted with **realism**.

romance fiction

a genre of fiction in which romantic relationships form a major component of the story, typically culminating in a happy ending – not to be confused with the kinds of fantastical narratives known as **romances**.

scene

an episode of continuous action set in a particular time and place.

science fiction

fiction set in an imagined future, usually including futuristic scientific or technological advances.

screenplay

a dramatic text (the script) that is written for a screen-based dramatic medium, such as film, TV drama or streamed content. It is formatted in a particular layout: see Chapter 8 of *A Creative Writing Handbook*.

sensory perception

experiencing the world through one or more of the senses.

sequence

a group of scenes that form a continuous segment in a narrative.

sestina

a poetic form comprising six stanzas of six lines each and concluding with a three-line stanza. The words at the end of the first six lines recur in a rolling pattern at the ends of subsequent lines.

short documents

the documents that summarise the narrative and features of a script in a simplified and shortened form.

showing

the use of scene to allow the reader or audience to experience the story through the characters' **sensory perceptions**.

simile

a comparison of likeness between two things, using the words 'like' or 'as'.

social realism

a type of fiction that is often contemporary and deals with lived, day-to-day situations.

soliloquy
in literature, a dramatic device where a character speaks to themselves, rather than to another character. Soliloquies often reveal the otherwise hidden thoughts of a character while they speak as if thinking aloud.

staccato
a quality of sound that is short, sharp and clipped.

stanza
a group of lines which a poem is divided into. Stanzas are usually arranged with white space between them, which can feel like a moment of progression or change to the reader.

step outline
a document that describes, in order, every step in the dramatic action of a script.

story
a narrated account of events.

story beats
crucial points in the story progression.

storyboard
images or drawings displayed in sequence to visualise scenes in, for example, a feature film.

stream of consciousness
a style of narration that emulates the way in which the mind of a character flits from one thing to the next.

subtext
parts of dialogue or interaction between characters where meaning is implied rather than stated outright.

summary
when events are summarised rather than dramatised.

synopsis
a condensed retelling of a narrative that details the main events in simplified form.

syntax
the arrangement of words into phrases, clauses and sentences.

telling
the use of exposition, explanation, summary, reflection or description to recount or consider aspects of a story.

tension
a literary device that creates a sense of suspense, anxiety or uncertainty in the reader. Tension is produced via the highlighting of characters' conflicting desires or via the threat of something ominous happening to the characters.

tercet
a three-line stanza.

theme
the central idea of a piece of writing.

third-person narration
a narrative told by a character or characters within the story or external to it, using the pronouns 'he', 'she' or 'they', rather than 'I' or 'we'.

thriller
a genre characterised by its use of plot twists, fast pace and heightened suspense, which can encompass genres such as crime and horror.

time jumps
omissions from the narrative, marking a leap in time, often signified in prose by an asterisk or an additional line space.

tone
commonly understood to be the mood created by the author in a literary work and how this is experienced by the reader (e.g. intimate or formal); this can be achieved via word choice and atmosphere, or via the author supplying a speaker with a particular voice. The formal literary definition of tone as an authorial device refers to the attitude of the author to the content of the work, particularly when that stance is ironic, satiric or heightened via humour.

treatment
a document that sets out the plot of a script, and also provides details about its setting, mood, genre, and any other aspects that convey its intended effects on an audience.

verb
a word that indicates a physical action, a mental action or a state of being: for example, 'drive', 'think', 'exist'.

vernacular
in general, the informal, ordinary language spoken in, for example, different regions or countries.

workshopping
exchanging creative work with fellow writers.

world-building
the creation of a new fictional world.

Acknowledgements

Grateful acknowledgement is made to the following sources for permission to reproduce material within this book:

Chapter 1

Reading 1.1: Lahiri, J. (1999) 'A Real Durwan', from 'Interpreter of Maladies: Stories', HarperCollins Publishers.

Chapter 2

Gaiman, N. (2013) 'Neverwhere', BBC Sounds, https://www.bbc.co.uk/sounds/play/p015s82k.

Baldick, C. (2008) 'dystopia', in The Oxford Dictionary of Literary Terms, Oxford University Press. Reproduced with permission of the Licensor through PLSclear.

Baldick, C. (2008) 'fantasy', in The Oxford Dictionary of Literary Terms, Oxford University Press. Reproduced with permission of the Licensor through PLSclear.

Reading 2.1: Excerpt(s) from THE WATER DANCER: A NOVEL by Ta-Nehisi Coates, copyright © 2019 by BCP Literary, Inc. Used by permission of One World, an imprint of Random House, a division of Penguin Random House LLC. All rights reserved. From 'The Water Dancer' by Ta-Nehisi Coates published by Hamish Hamilton. Copyright © BCP Literary, Inc., 2019. Reprinted by permission of Penguin Books Limited.

Reading 2.3: Gaiman, N. (2000) Neverwhere, Headline Publishing Group Limited. Reproduced with permission of the Licensor through PLSclear.

Chapter 3

Reading 3.1: Webster, D. (2016) 'Getting High in the Low Countries', Dispirited: how contemporary spirituality makes us stupid, selfish and unhappy. https://dispirited.org/2016/11/25/getting-high-in-the-low-countries/.

Reading 3.2: From Once Upon A Time in the East by Xiaolu Guo published by Chatto & Windus. Copyright © Xiaolu Guo, 2017. Reprinted by permission of The Random House Group Limited.

Chapter 4

Extracts from the Poem '"Out, out—"' from THE COLLECTED POEMS by Robert Frost © 1969 Holt Rinehart and Winston, Inc., published by Vintage Books. Extract reproduced by permission of The Random House Group Ltd.

Sebastian Matthews, 'Buying Wine' from We Generous. Copyright © 2007 by Sebastian Matthews. Reprinted with the permission of The Permissions Company, LLC on behalf of Red Hen Press, redhen.org.

Acknowledgements

Etter, C. (2009) 'Divorce', from 'The Tethers', Seren. Reproduced with permission of the Licensor through PLSclear.

Jackie Kay, 'Darling: New & Selected Poems' (Bloodaxe Books, 2007) by permission of the publisher. Reproduced with permission of Bloodaxe Books. www.bloodaxebooks.com @bloodaxebooks (twitter/facebook) #bloodaxebooks.

Mid-Term Break from OPENED GROUND: SELECTED POEMS 1966-1996 by Seamus Heaney. Copyright © 1998 by Seamus Heaney. Reprinted by permission of Farrar, Straus and Giroux. Reprinted by permission of Farrar, Straus and Giroux & Faber and Faber Ltd. All Rights Reserved.

"What I Did With Your Ashes" from SCATTERED AT SEA by Amy Gerstler, copyright © 2015 by Amy Gerstler. Used by permission of Penguin Books, an imprint of Penguin Publishing Group, a division of Penguin Random House LLC. All rights reserved.

Johnson, R.B. (2006) 'What I Do', from 'Jubilee', Anhinga Press.

Mueller, L. (1996) 'When I Am Asked', from 'Alive Together: New and Selected Poems', Louisiana State University Press.

Chapter 5

Reading 5.1: Arndt, M., Dayton, J. and Faris, V., Little Miss Sunshine: The Shooting Script, Newmarket Press (2007).

Reading 5.2: © Tuyen Do, 2019, 'Summer Rolls', Oberon, an imprint of Bloomsbury Publishing Plc.

Reading 5.3: © Gupta, T. (2002) 'Sanctuary', Oberon Books, an imprint of Bloomsbury Publishing Plc.

Chapter 6

Reading 6.1: Campion, J., The Power of the Dog, See Saw Films, BBC Films, New Zealand Film Commission, Max Films, Bad Girl Creek City Films (2021).

Reading 6.2: Excerpt from SMALL ISLAND by Andrea Levy. Copyright © 2004 by Andrea Levy. Reprinted by permission of Picador. All Rights Reserved. Reproduced with permission of Headline Publishing Group Limited through PLSclear.

Chapter 7

Reading 7.1: Kaan, K. (2017) 'Breaking Up With Bradford', BBC Radio 4, https://www.bbc.co.uk/writers/scripts/radio-drama/breaking-up-with-bradford.

Reading 7.2: Dinnella, A. (2019) 'The Dead Dad Show', Music Monologues, BBC Radio 3. https://www.bbc.co.uk/writersroom/documents/music-monologues-the-dead-dad-show-annalisa-dinnella.pdf.

Chapter 8

Volger, C. (2007) 'The Writers Journey: Mythic Structure for Writers', Michael Wiese Productions.

Acknowledgements

Reading 8.1: Talking in Tongues © 1991 by Winsome Pinnock. Talking in Tongues was first presented at the Royal Court Theatre Upstairs, London, on 28 August 1991. All rights whatsoever in this play are strictly reserved and application for performance etc., must be made before rehearsal to Casarotto Ramsay & Associates Ltd., 3rd Floor, 7 Savoy Court, Strand, London WC2R 0EX (info@casarotto.co.uk). No performance may be given unless a licence has first been obtained.

Chapter 9

Reading 9.1: Excerpt from SMALL ISLAND by Andrea Levy. Copyright © 2004 by Andrea Levy. Reprinted by permission of Picador. All Rights Reserved. Reproduced with permission of Headline Publishing Group Limited through PLSclear.

Reading 9.2: Edmundson, H. (2019) 'Small Island', adapted from Levy, A. 'Small Island', Nick Hern Books.

Chapter 10

Reading 10.1: AN ANGEL AT MY TABLE by Janet Frame. Copyright © 1984, Janet Frame, used by permission of The Wylie Agency (UK) Limited. Reproduced with permission of the Licensor through PLSclear.

Reading 10.2: Jones, L. (1990) 'An Angel At My Table: The Screenplay', Pandora Press.

Reading 10.3: Excerpt from THE HOURS by Michael Cunningham. Copyright © 1998 by Michael Cunningham. Reprinted by permission of Farrar, Straus and Giroux. All Rights Reserved. Reprinted by permission of HarperCollins Publishers Ltd © 1998 by Michael Cunningham.

Chapter 11

Reading 11.1: Mukerjee Furstenau, N. (2013) 'Biting through the Skin: An Indian Kitchen in America's Heartland', University of Iowa Press.

Reading 11.2: From Me Talk Pretty One Day by David Sedaris, copyright © 2000. Reprinted by permission of Little, Brown, an imprint of Hachette Book Group, Inc & Little Brown Book Group Limited. Reproduced with permission of the Licensor through PLSclear. David Sedaris ME TALK PRETTY ONE DAY; First published in Esquire Magazine; Reprinted by permission of Don Congdon Associates, Inc. Copyright ©; 2000 by David Sedaris.

Chapter 12

Bergin, T. (2013) 'At the Lakes with Roberta', from 'This is Yarrow', Carcanet Press.

Bevis, K. (2022) 'Delinquent', Magma 83, Magma Poetry.

O'Mahony, N. (2014) 'Deserted Village, Achill Island', from 'Her Father's Daughter', Salmon Poetry.

Campbell, S. (2017) 'Fodder', from 'Heat Signature', Seren Books.

Acknowledgements

Long, R., 'Jail Letter'. From My Darling from the Lions, first published in 2020 by Picador an imprint of Pan Macmillan. Reproduced by permission of Macmillan Publishers International Limited. Text copyright © Rachel Long 2020.

'Not Waving But Drowning', by Stevie Smith, from ALL THE POEMS, copyright © 1937, 1938, 1942, 1950, 1957, 1962, 1966, 1971, 1972 by Stevie Smith. Copyright © 2016 by the Estate of James MacGibbon. Copyright © 2015 by Will May. Reprinted by permission of New Directions Publishing Corp.

Sarmah, A. (2023) 'On Asking My Mother about Winter 1990', Poetry January 2023, Poetry Foundation.

Chapter 13

Hodgson, H. (2022) 'Mermaids on the Brain', from '163 Days', Seren.

Feaver, V. (1981) 'Coat', from 'Close Relatives', Penguin Random House.

Campbell, S. (2021) 'Longboat At Portaferry' New Hibernia Review Vol 25 issue 2. Used with permission of the author.

Old Bailey Proceedings Online (www.oldbaileyonline.org, version 9.0) February 1759. Trial of Elizabeth Jenkins, otherwise Bateman (t17590228-1). Reproduced by permission from the Old Bailey Online Project.

Reading 13.2: BBC, Small Axe: Mangrove, written by Steve McQueen and Alistair Siddons.

Reading 13.3: Jacob Ross 'Walking For My Mother', Tell No-One About This, Peepal Tree Press, 2017.

Chapter 14

Booker, M. (2017) 'Lot's Wife Speaks', from Booker, M. et al. (eds) 'Your Family, Your Body', Penguin Books.

Saul, D. (2022) 'Surrender', from 'The Room Between Us', Liverpool University Press. Reproduced with permission of the Licensor through PLSclear.

Reading 14.1: Wentworth, T. (2020) 'The Real Deal', from Fraser, M. (ed.) 'CripTales', Nick Hern Books.

Reading 14.2: Be Near Me: O'Hagan, A. (2006) Be Near Me. Faber and Faber.

Reading 14.3: The Genesis of Be Near Me: O'Hagan, A. (2007) 'In Truth – Andrew O'Hagan on the genesis of Be Near Me', The Guardian 14 July 2007. Guardian News & Media Ltd.

Chapter 15

Pajak, M., 'After Closing Time'. From 'Slide' by Mark Pajak published by Jonathan Cape. Copyright © Mark Pajak, 2022. Reprinted by permission of The Random House Group Limited.

Doshi, T. 'Everything Begins Elsewhere' (Bloodaxe Books, 2012) Reproduced with permission of Bloodaxe Books. www.bloodaxebooks.com @bloodaxebooks (twitter/facebook) #bloodaxebooks.

Reading 15.1: O'Farrell, M. (2017) 'Bloodstream: 1997', from 'I Am, I Am, I Am: Seventeen Brushes with Death', Headline Publishing Group Limited. Reproduced with permission of the Licensor through PLSclear.

Reading 15.2: Menon, C.G. (2018) 'Daylight Savings', from 'Subjunctive Moods: stories', Dahlia Publishing Ltd.

Chapter 16

Holland Rogers, B. (2009) 'What Are You Using for Bait?', from Masih, T.L. (ed.) 'The Rose Metal Press Field Guide to Writing Flash Fiction: Tips from Editors, Teachers, and Writers in the Field', Rose Metal Press.

Jones, J. (2023) 'What is Flash Fiction?' In 'Narratives from the margins: A creative and critical approach to investigating form and narrative (dis) continuity in the novella-in-flash', unpublished doctoral thesis.

Reading 16.1: McGregor, J. (2017) 'Reservoir 13', 4th Estate. Reprinted by permission of HarperCollins Publishers Ltd. © 2017 Jon McGregor.

Chapter 17

Private email correspondence 2023 between Liam Bell and Heather Richardson. Permission to use given by Liam Bell.

Baldick, C. (2008) 'theme', in The Oxford Dictionary of Literary Terms, Oxford University Press. Reproduced with permission of the Licensor through PLSclear.

Reading 17.2(c): Stansfield, K. & Oakley, C. (2022) 'Cast a Long Shadow: Welsh Women Writing Crime', Honno Press.

Every effort has been made to contact copyright holders. If any have been inadvertently overlooked the publishers will be pleased to make the necessary arrangements at the first opportunity.

Bloomsbury Publishing Plc does not have any control over, or responsibility for, any third-party websites referred to or in this book. All internet addresses given in this book were correct at the time of going to press. The authors and publisher regret any inconvenience caused if addresses have changed or sites have ceased to exist, but can accept no responsibility for any such changes.

Every effort has been made to ensure the accuracy of the short biographies of writers that accompany readings in this book. The publishers will be pleased to correct any inadvertent errors at the first opportunity so please contact The Open University at LDS-Rights@open.ac.uk or Bloomsbury at contact@bloomsbury.com.

Index

abstraction 293, 519
accents
    creating characters 112–13, 143, 145
action 519
    dramatic action 110–11, 520
    and imagery 124–6
action line 164–5, 519
adaptation 9, 183–97
    acts of creation in 188–90
    adapting the work of others 186
    adapting your own work 185
    for audio 27, 153–4, 183
    comparing script and prose versions 204–5
    and copyright 186, 187
    dramatic stories 132
    editing the text 187–90
    'faithful' and 'unfaithful' 185, 188–189
    fantasy and dystopian fiction 34–5
    and genre 27–8
    researching the visual 134–5
    for screen 183, 185, 187, 192–4
    suitability for 184–6
    third-party sources 183
    see also stage drama
Adékọluẹ́jọ, Ronke *163*
adjectives 510, 519
    in 'Lot's Wife Speaks' 297–8
Aeschylus
    Oresteia trilogy 302
Agboluaje, Oladipo 366
    The Christ of Coldharbour Lane 175, 448–9
Alderman, Naomi
    The Power 34, 42, 154, 384
Alderson, Martha 118
Alfredson, Tomas
    Tinker Tailor Soldier Spy (film) *123*, 131
allegory 34, 519
    and dystopian fiction 45
alliteration 17, *151*, 282, 519
Altman, Robert
    Short Cuts (film) 25

analogy 259, 265, 266–73, 519
    defining 265
    impact of 269–72
    the ordinary and the extraordinary 270–2
    one-word analogies 266–8
anthologies, themed 368–9
antithesis 265, 274, 278–9, 519
apostrophes
    stylising voices 23, 299–301
Aristotle
    Poetics 16
    three-act structure and the dramatic arc 164, 165, 167, 168, 171, 346, *347*, 348
Armstrong, Neil 278
Arndt, Michael 104
    Little Miss Sunshine (screenplay) 104–5, 107–8, 399–405
art, relationship of to craft 7
Arthurian legends 34, *36*, 526
assonance 282, 304, 519
Atack, Timothy X
    Forest 404 142
Atkinson, Kate
    Not the End of the World 355, 356
Attenborough, Richard
    Gandhi (film) 327
Atwood, Margaret
    The Handmaid's Tale 34
audiences
    and adaptations
        screenplays 193–4
        stage drama 191–2
    and dramatic writing
        action and images 124, 125, 126
        character attributes 102
        dramatic conventions and realism 173–5, 178
        the 'fourth wall' 173
        and thematic threads 353
audio drama 101, 124, 141–58
    adaptations for 27, 153–4, 183, 185, 187, 188, 190, 194
    characters 142–52

creating pictures with sound 142–4
creating scenes in 155
dialogue 143, 145, 146
directions in 111
formatting a script for 156–7, *157*, 176
and life writing 235
monologues 148–52, 154, 292
point of view in 147–52
settings 143
aural 141, 519
autobiographies 17, 55, 223, 519, 523
    see also life writing

backstories 105, 209, 519
    in Dawson's *Wild Boy* 312
    and flash fiction 336
ballads 519
    and narrative poems 74, 83
'Barbara Allen' (folk ballad) 74
Barnard, Clio
    The Selfish Giant (film) 173
beat sheets 169, *170–1*, *170–1*, 519
    and adaptations 186, 187
    see also story beats
Bell, Liam
    Rare Stories 356
Bell, Lindsay 153
Bennett, Alan
    The Lady in the Van 194
Zemeckis, Robert
    Beowulf (film) 34
Berger, John
    To the Wedding 212
Bergin, Tara
    'At the Lakes with Roberta' 250–1
Bevis, Kathryn
    'Delinquent' 256–7
Bible stories
    Book of Genesis and Lot's wife 294–5, 296, 298
Bigelow, Kathryn
    Zero Dark Thirty (film) 131

Index

biographies 16, 17, 55, 223, 344, 520, 523
    thematic 362
biopics 327, 520
blank verse 77, 520
Booker, Malika
    'Lot's Wife Speaks' 294–6, 297–8
Bradbury, Ray
    'The Veldt' 153
'Brokeback Mountain' (short story) 184, 195
Brook, Peter 101, 118
Bryant, Nicola *184*
Burnett, Elizabeth-Jane
    The Grassling 269–70, 273, 473
Bywaters, Frederick 326

Calder-Marshall, Anna *174*
Cameron, James
    Titanic (film) 127
Campbell, Jane
    Cat Brushing 356
Campbell, Joseph
    The Hero With a Thousand Faces 165, 166
Campbell, Siobhán
    'Fodder' 252
    Heather Richardson's interview with 365, 507–14
    'Longboat at Portaferry' 282
Campion, Jane 203
    The Power of the Dog (screenplay) 125–6, 128, 413–22
Carey, Peter
    Oscar and Lucinda 207–8, 210, 211, 212, 214, 218
Caribbean English
    in 'Lot's Wife Speaks' 297, 298
Carlisle, Stanton 184
Carter, Angela
    Wise Children 20–1
Carver, Raymond 355
    'A Small, Good Thing' 25–6
    'The Bath' 25–6
challenges, journeys involving
    in life writing 58–60, 68
challenging questions
    in life writing 226–9

Chamberlain-King, Reggie
    The Black Dreams 368, 514–15
Chaney, Lon *184*
characters
    in adaptations 185
    in audio drama 142–52
    dramatic journeys 163–7
        the dramatic arc 164, 168–72
    in dramatic stories 102–9
        conflict 103–4, 106, 107–9, 111, 114–15, 118, 185
        creating 103–7
        dialogue 111–13
        dramatic action 110–11
        idiom 112–13
        individual voices 113
        and story beats 128
        visual contrasts 126, 133
        writing character attributes 102–3
    and genre 18
    in narrative poetry 87, 89, 95
    and pace of time 316
    planning for book-length works 348
    in screenplays 102, 125–6, 127–9, 131
        visual contrasts 133
    splicing narrative strands 207–9, 211
    syntax 299
    world-building 36
Chaucer, Geoffrey
    The Canterbury Tales 61
Chaudhuri, Amit
    Afternoon Raag 342
childhood
    in life writing 64, 68, 223, 230–2, 233, 324–5, 362
chorus, speaking in 302–3
Cinderella/The Glass Slipper 185
Clavell, James
    To Sir, With Love (film) 124
cliffhangers 252, 520
climate distortion
    in dystopian fiction 43, 45
close-ups 520
Coates, Ta-Nehisi
    The Water Dancer 42, 383

Collette, Toni *108*
Collins, Wilkie
    The Woman in White 17
comic book characters in films 104
communities
    fictional 302–5
The Complete Works (mentoring scheme) 291
conflict 520
    characters and dramatic conflict 103–4, 106, 107–9, 111, 114–15, 118, 185
        initiating conflict 114–15
        interpersonal and inner conflicts 115
    dramatic conflict in poetry 244–6
content of a reading 10
Coppola, Sofia
    Marie Antoinette (film) 131
copyright 183, 186, 187, 197
couplets 81, 87, 324, 520
Cracknell, Carrie
    Persuasion (film) 173
craft, relationship of to art 7
Crichlow, Frank 274
crime fiction 344, 368
Culler, Jonathan 18
Cunningham, Michael
    The Hours 212–13, 215, 217, 327, 359, 461–4
cyclical narrative structure 327

Dabas, Parvin *133*
Daldry, Stephen
    The Hours (film) 216, *216*, 327
Dalí, Salvador
    The Persistence of Memory 322, 324
Daly, Lance
    Black '47 (film) 132
Darabont, Frank
    The Shawshank Redemption (film) 127
Davison, Peter *184*
Dawson, Jill
    Fred and Edie 326
    Wild Boy 312–14

Dayton, Jonathan
    Little Miss Sunshine (film) 104–5, 107–8, *108*, 164–5, 399–405
Dean, Graham
    Blue Mirror 2 363
Dearle, John Henry
    'Orchard' wallpaper *73*
The Deepest Blue (self-help book) 363
Defoe, Daniel
    Robinson Crusoe 20, 21
del Toro, Guillermo
    Nightmare Alley (film) 184
    Pan's Labyrinth (film) 124
Desai, Kiran *216*
    The Inheritance of Loss 214–16, 217, 218, 465
detective fiction 17, 20
Dhawan, Sabrina 133
dialect 112, 520
    stylising voices 299
dialogic 520
dialogue 25, 520
    in adaptations 187, 194
    in audio dramas 143, 145, 146, 194
    in dramatic writing 102, 110, 111–13, 124
        screenplays 125, 126
        in stage drama 173
    in narrative poems 77, 79
    and reading time 317, 318
Di'Anno, Paul *184*
Dick, Philip K.
    Do Androids Dream of Electric Sheep? 33, 34
Dickens, Charles
    A Christmas Carol 280
Dinnella, Annalisa
    The Dead Dad Show 149–50, 155, 437–41
discordant sounds 283, 520
distance
    in life writing 56–7, 68
Đỗ, Tuyền
    Summer Rolls 110, 114, 115, *117*, 405–7
Doctor Who: The Caves of Androzani 184

Doshi, Tishani
    'Memory of Wales' 324–6
    'The Comeback of Speedos' 247
Doyle, Miranda
    A Book of Untruths 362
drabbles 334
drama 8, 16, 50
    and fiction 15
dramatic action 110–11, 520
    and imagery 124–6
dramatic arc 168–72, 185, 363
    emotion line 164–5, 521
dramatic irony 243, 249–51, 520
dramatic monologues 292, 521, 525
dramatic stories 99–119, 110–11
    backstory 105
    dialogue 110, 111–13
        and imagery 124–6
    reading time 317
dramatic techniques in poetry 241–61
dramatic writing 7, 9, 95, 97–198
    adaptation 183–97
    defining 101
    dramatic journeys 163–78
        creating the world of the drama 173–5
        structure, action and emotion 164–7
    formatting scripts
        audio drama 156–7, *157*
        screenplays 176–7, *177*
        stage plays 116–18, *117*
    story and image 121–36, 121–38
        researching the visual 134–5
    three-act structure 164, 165, 167, 168, 171, 346, *347*, 348
    see also audio drama; characters; screenplays; stage drama
dramatised fiction 25–8
    adaptation 27–8
    impersonation 25
    redrafting 26–7
dribbles 334
Duffy, Carol Ann
    The Other Country 359–60

Duguay, Christian
    Screamers (film) 124
dystopian fiction 34–5, 41, 521
    building your world 48–9, 50
    defining 33
    distorting the ordinary world 43–5

Eccleshare, Thomas
    Pastoral 174, 174–5
Edison, Thomas 248
Edmundson, Helen
    stage play adaptation of *Small Island* 134, 135, 189, 453–6
Edwards, Jonathan
    'Evel Knievel Jumps over My Family' 247
Eisenstein, Sergei
    Strike (film) 126, 127
elegies 87, 255, 521
emotion line 164–5, 521
enjambment 92, 519
Enright, Anne
    Making Babies 362, 363
epic poems 16, 74, 521
epigraphs 247, 521
episodic techniques 521
    in narrative poetry 74
epistolary fiction 23, 521
Etter, Carrie
    'Divorce' 79, 80, 81, 82
    The Tethers 80
euphony 265, 282–3, 521
Evaristo, Bernardine 291
    Girl, Woman, Other 22–3, 24, 25, 212
exposition 125, 519, 521
Eynon, Rubin
    Gallos 36

family sagas 344
fantasy fiction 16, 34–5, 41, 521
    building your world 48–9, 50
    creating fictional landscapes 36–9
    defining 33
    the quest narrative 39–40
    researching imagined worlds 45–6

Faris, Valerie
  Little Miss Sunshine (film) 104–5, 107–8, *108*, 164–5, 399–405
Farley, Paul, and Griffiths, Niall
  'Netherley' 61–2, 63
Faulkner, William
  The Sound and the Fury 303
Feaver, Vicki
  'Coat' 266–7
Ferguson, Karen 203
fiction 15, 16, 25
  adapting for audio drama 154
  characters in 102–3
  dramatic adaptations of 27
  dramatic stories 101
  fictional communities 302–5
  length and characteristics of novels 344–8
  and narrative poetry 73
  planning for book-length works 348
  reading time 317
  short-form prose 333, 334–40
  splicing narrative strands 201–19
  themes 359
  time and form in prose 322–3
  world-building in 33–50
  see also flash fiction
figurative language 521
  in narrative poems 73
films
  adaptations 183, 184, 185, 187, 188, 192–4, 359
    comparing script and prose narratives 204–5
    fantasy and dystopian fiction 34–5
    splicing narrative strands 211, 216
  juxtaposed shots 207
  montage 126–7, 203
  realist 173
  time and form in 327
  see also screenplays
first-person narration 20, 20–1, 291, 292, 521
  and impersonation 25
  linking narrative strands 212

voices and voicing 292, 294–6, 298, 299, 305
  persona poems 292, 294–6, 298, 300–1, 306
  polyphonic narration 303–4
  speaking in chorus 303
  world-building in 42
five-act structure 171–2, *172*
flash fiction 333, 334, 335–7, 340, 345, 522
  planning and writing 336–7
flash non-fiction 333, 334, 335, 336–7, 522
flashbacks 127, 320, 321, 326, 522, 525
flashforwards 320–1, 324, 522
Flynn, Leontia
  'For Stuart, who Accidentally Obtained a Job in the Civil Service' 247
folk tales, adaptations of 185
food writing 21
foreshadowing 252, 320, 522
form 15, 16, 522
  and genre 16–18
  and time 322–8
Fox, Kerry 203
fractured narrative structure 327
Frame, Janet *203*, 205
  An Angel at My Table 203, 206, 457–9
    screenplay adaptation *203*, 204–5, 459–60
Frame, Polly *174*
free verse 324, 522
  in narrative poems 73, 77
freewriting 87, 522
  narrative poems 81
Frost, Robert
  '"Out, Out—"' 77–8
Furstenau, Nina Mukerjee
  Biting through the Skin 231–2, 237, 467–8
  interview with Lania Knight 233–4, 469–70

Gable, Christopher *184*
Gaiman, Neil
  Neverwhere 34, 39–41, 42, 43, 45–6, 47, 48, 154, 384–5

  Norse Mythology 37
Garcia Márquez, Gabriel 20
Gardner, John 233
Gauguin, Paul 304
genre 8, 13–30, 522
  altering 29
  as a descriptor 19–20
  and dramatic journeys 173
  and dramatic writing 124, 130, 131
    hybrid genres 130
  dramatised fiction 25–8
    adaptation 27–8
  and form 15, 16–18
  going against the grain 20–3
  and length of narrative 344–5, 347
  reading for genre 21–3
  and reading time 318
  scenes 15
  signposts 15
  trying voices from different genres 23–4
  using 18–20
Gerstler, Amy
  'What I Did With Your Ashes' 89, 91, 92
ghost stories 17
Gibson, Patrick *163*
Gothic novels 34, 522
Graeae Theatre 142
Greece, ancient 282, 294
  drama 302
  epic poetry 74
Gresham, William Lindsay 184
Griffiths, Niall, and Farley, Paul
  'Netherley' 61–2, 63
Grimm Brothers
  folk tales 185
Groarke, Vona
  Other People's Houses 355–6
Gross, Philip
  'The Wasting Game' 365
Guo, Xiaolu
  Once Upon a Time in the East 68, 393–7
Gupta, Tanika
  Sanctuary 112–13, 408–12

Index

half rhymes 73, 74, 282, 301, 522, 523
Hare, David 359
Harrison, Tony
   Furies 302
Harvey, Leah *191*
Hazanavicius, Michel
   The Artist (film) 126
Heaney, Seamus
   Beowulf 34
   'Mid-Term Break' 83–4, 86, 88, 92
heroic journeys 165–7
Hero's Journey model *166*, 165–7
Hershman, Tania
   Fuel 335
historical fiction 16, 23, 344, 522
Hodgson, Hannah
   163 Days 270
   'Mermaids on the Brain' 271
Holinshed's Chronicles 27
Homer
   Iliad 74
   Odyssey 74
Hudson, Kerry
   Lowborn 64, 67
Hughes, Frieda
   Waxworks 360
Hughes, Richard
   Danger 141
Hutcheon, Linda 153, 154
hybrid genres 130

'I wonder if ...'
   in life writing 224–5
Ibsen, Henrik 142
idiolect 299, 300, 522
idiom 24, 64, 112–13, 523
   Caribbean 296
imagery 523
   in dramatic writing 124–36
   in narrative poetry 74
imagination
   creating characters using imagination 107
   in life writing, using language to access 64–5
   and voice 298
impersonation 523
   in dramatised fiction 25

in medias res 338, 523
inciting incidents 114, 523
intended effect of a reading 10
intercutting narrative strands 203, 210, 212, 216, 218, 523
internal rhyme 523
interpersonal conflicts 115
intertextuality 213, 523
Iron Maiden *184*, 185
irony, dramatic 243, 249–51, 520

Jamie, Kathleen
   Antlers of Water 368, 369, 517
Jensen, Liz
   The Rapture 44–5
Jeunet, Jean-Pierre
   Amélie (film) 173
Johnson, Roxane Beth
   'What I Do' 89, 90, 92
Jones, Jupiter 335
Jones, Laura
   An Angel at My Table (screenplay) 204–5, 459–60
Jonson, Ben
   Bartholomew Fair 142
journeys
   in life writing 58–63, 68
      personal journeys 63
      pilgrimages 60–1
      return journeys 61–3, 68
Julian, Rupert 184

Kaan, Kamal
   Breaking Up with Bradford 143–4, 145, 146, 147–8, 155, 433–7
Kar-Wai, Wong
   In the Mood for Love (film) 132
Kay, Jackie
   'In My Country' 79–80, 80–1, 82
Keogh, Alexia 203
Kiarostami, Abbas
   Taste of Cherry (Ta'm e guilass) (film) 131–2
Kidman, Nicole *216*
Kimmerer, Robin Wall
   'The Council of Pecans' 65, 224

King, Martin Luther
   'I Have a Dream' speech 274, 278
Kingsolver, Barbara
   The Poisonwood Bible 303
Kitchen, Judith 335
Knight, Lania
   interview with Nina Mukerjee Furstenau 233–4, 469–70
Kubrick, Stanley
   Barry Lyndon (film) 188
Kureishi, Hanif
   Intimacy 210

Lahiri, Jhumpa
   'A Real Durwan' 27–8, 154, 187, 375–82
Lanchester, John
   The Debt to Pleasure 21
landscapes, creating fictional 36–9, 40–1
language
   dialect 112
   idiom 24, 64, 112–13
   in life writing, using to access memories, observations and imagination 64–6, 68
Le Guin, Ursula K. 37
   The Left Hand of Darkness 36
Lee, Andrea
   Russian Journal 48, 386–7
Lee, Ang
   Brokeback Mountain (film) 184
   Life of Pi (film) 126
Leibowitz, Judith
   on the novella 341
Leplastrier, Lucinda 208
Leroux, Gaston 185
Levy, Andrea 19
   Small Island 134, 134–5, 189, 423–31, 451–3
      stage play adaptation of 134, 135, 189, *191*, 453–6
life writing 8, 16, 334, 523
   characteristics of 345–8
   characters in 105
   comparing script and prose narratives 204–6
   construction of 55
   defining 55

Index

dramatic adaptations of 27
dramatic stories 101
inner worlds 221–39
    challenging questions 226–9
    'I wonder if...' 224–5
    metaphors for 233–4
    showing and telling 235–6
    startling moments in childhood 230–2
novella-length 341–2, 342–3
novels and equivalent-length life writing 333, 344–8
opening of 340
outer worlds 53–69, 235–6
    journeys 58–63
    proximity, distance and sensory detail 56–7
    using language to access memories, observations and imagination 64–6
    writing in the moment 67
planning for book-length works 348
reading time 317
short forms of 337–40
thematic 360–1, 362–4
linear narrative structure 326
Linton, Lynette 163
Lish, Gordon 26
Long, Rachel 252, 253–4, *253*
    'Jail Letter' 253, 254, 255, 256
lyric poems 95, 523

Mabinogion 74
McAnulty, Dara
    Diary of a Young Naturalist 56
Macfarlane, Robert
    Mountains of the Mind 62–3
McGregor, Jon
    'Charlotte' 337–8, 345, 346
    If Nobody Speaks of Remarkable Things 210
    Reservoir 13 345–6, 347, 499–505
    The Reservoir Tapes 337
McIntosh, Iain 19
Maclear, Kyo
    Birds Art Life Death 227–8
McMurtry, Larry 184
MacNeice, Louis 243

Maconie, Stuart
    'Little Boxes' 62
McQueen, Steve
    Small Axe: Mangrove 274–6, 277, 283, 474–6
magic realism 20, 523
Maiden Castle, Dorset 37
Mallory, Thomas
    La Morte D'Arthur 34
Mandela, Winnie 255
Marmion, Steve 174
Martin, Lee 36
Marvel Studios 104
Matthews, Sebastian
    'Buying Wine' 83–4, 85, 86, 87, 88
memoirs 16, 48, 55, 223, 344, 523
    see also life writing
memories, using language to access 64–5
Menon, Catherine
    'Daylight Savings' 317, 319, 320–1, 323, 338, 339, 342, 493–8
metaphors 60, 265, 267, 521, 523
    in narrative poems 86
metre in poetry 77, 524
Meyers, Bert
    'Driving Home at Night with My Children after Their Grandfather's Funeral' 247
microfiction 334
Miller, Kei
    A Light Song of Light 365
    The Same Earth 19, 19–20
mind maps 360, 524
Mitchell, David
    Cloud Atlas 22, 23–4, 25
monologues 292, 524
    and adaptations 190
    in audio drama 147–52, 154
    dramatic 292, 521, 525
    in stage drama 28
    television 292–3
montage 126–7, 524
    splicing narrative strands 203, 204, 205–6
mood 524
    in poetry 252
Moore, Julianne *216*

morality tales 34, 41, 524
Morgan, Kim 184
Morrissey, Sinéad 291
Mort, Graham 37
Mort, Helen
    A Line Above the Sky 58
motion capture 34, 524
Mueller, Lisel
    'When I Am Asked' 75–7
Murray, Dave *184*
music
    in audio drama 149, 150, 155
    and folk ballads 74

Naked Productions 142
nanofiction 334
Nair, Mira
    Monsoon Wedding (film) 133, *133*
    Salaam Bombay! (film) 124
narration
    polyphonic 303–5
    in real time 313
    see also first-person narration; third-person narration
the narrative arc 164, 168–72, 185, 524
narrative poetry 8, 71–96, 101
    action verbs in 86
    ballads 74
    conflict and tension in poems 77–81
    couplets 87
    defining 53
    drafting and revising 93–4
    encounters 79–82
    episodic techniques in 74
    inspired by another 76–7
    internal rhymes 73
    and lyric poems 95
    narrative arcs 73, 83
    origins of 74–8
    pronouns and points of view 88, 89–94
    reading and writing 75–7
    time in 83–8
narrative strands 524
    and genre 23
    see also splicing narrative strands

narrative structure
  and length of narrative 345–7
  three-act model of 164, 165, 167, 168, 171, 346, *347*, 348
  time and form 326–8
narratives 524
National Theatre, London 191, *191*, *302*
Nelson, Caleb Azumah
  Open Water 210
Nelson, Maggie
  Bluets 362–3, 364
New Zealand 37
non-linear storytelling 150, 524
Norris, Rufus 191
Norse myths 37
Nottage, Lynn
  Clyde's 163, 165
novellas 341–3, 524
  publishing 342–3
novels *see* fiction

Oakley, Caroline, and Stansfield, Katherine
  Cast a Long Shadow 368, 516–17
Oates, Joyce Carol 7, 9
observation
  creating characters using observation 107
  in life writing 64–5
Octavia Poetry Collective for Women of Colour 253
O'Farrell, Maggie
  'Bloodstream (1997)' 315, 316, 317, 322, 338, 339, 489–93
offstage action 173, 187, 195, 196, 524
O'Hagan, Andrew
  Be Near Me 299–300, 302, 485–8
Old Bailey Proceedings Online 278–9
Oldman, Gary *123*
Oliver, Mary 355
Olivier Theatre, London 191, *191*, *302*
O'Mahony, Nessa 252, 253, *253*
  'Deserted Village, Achill Island' 253, 254–5

omniscient narrators 218, 245, 524
one-word analogies 266–8
Onwuemezi, Vanessa
  'Brother' 235–6
Orozco, Sebastian *163*
Orwell, George
  Nineteen Eighty-Four 41–2, 42–3
Ossana, Diana 184
Otsuka, Julie
  The Buddha in the Attic 302–3
Oxford English Dictionary
  rare words 356
Ozeki, Ruth
  The Book of Form and Emptiness 212

Pajak, Mark
  'After Closing Time' 323–4
Paley, Nina
  Dandaka Dharma (film) 193
  Ramayana, adaptation of 193
  Sita Sings the Blues (film) *192*, 192–3
parallel narrative structure 327
parenthesis 265, 280–1, 525
parentheticals 176, 525
Parks, Suzan-Lori *366*
  365 Days/365 Plays 366–7
  Father Comes Home from the Wars 366, 367
persona 525
persona poetry 292, 294–6, 298, 300–1, 306, 521, 525
  dramatic monologues 292, 521, 525
personal essays 223, 525
personification 521
persuasive techniques 263–85
  see also analogy; rhetoric
Pfister, Manfred 110
The Phantom of the Opera, adaptations of 184, *184*, 185
Philbin, Mary *184*
phonetic spelling 299, 301
phonetics 299, 525
pilgrimages in life writing 60–1
Pinnock, Winsome
  Talking in Tongues 169–70, 443–8

Pinter, Harold
  Betrayal 326–7
Plath, Sylvia 252
plot twists 183, 252, 525, 528
  in poetry 25
podcasts *see* audio drama
Poe, Edgar Allen
  free verse 324
  'The Raven' 74
poetry 8, 16
  analogies in 266–7
  collections 359–60
  dramatic monologues 292
  dramatic techniques in 241–61
    adding further dramatic elements 258
    conflict 244–6, 258
    irony 243, 249–51, 258
    persona 243, 244
    scenes 243, 256–8
    soliloquy 243
    the swerve 252–5, 258
    titles 247–8
    trying out 247–8
  elegies 87, 255, 521
  epic poems 16, 74, 521
  and genre 19
  lyric poems 95, 523
  metre 524
  and novels, Desai's *The Inheritance of Loss* 215, 216
  persona poems 292, 294–6, 298, 300–1, 306
  sestinas 326, 526
  themes in 354, 355–6, 359–60
    poetry sequences 365
  time and form in 323–6
  voices in 291
  see also narrative poetry
point of view 525
  in audio drama 147–52
  in narrative poetry 89–94
  splicing narrative strands 218
polyphonic narration 303–4, 525
Ponnambalam, Devika
  I Am Not Your Eve 304
Porter, Edwin S.
  Life of an American Fireman (film) 207, *207*

Index

Porter, Phil
   Blink 109
Power, Ben
   Emperor and Galilean 142
Powici, Chris
   'Getting the Hang of the Wind' 56–7
premise 175, 317, 345, 525
Pritchett, V.S.
   'The Wheelbarrow' 266
pronouns
   in narrative poetry 88, 89–94
props
   and genre 15, 17–18, 19
prose
   medium-length stand-alone work 333, 341–3
   novels and equivalent-length life writing 344–8
   short-form 333, 334–40, 341
   see also fiction; life writing; novellas; short stories
protagonist 525
   in dramatic journeys 164
Proulx, Annie
   'Brokeback Mountain' 184
   'In the Pit' 273
proximity
   in life writing 56–7, 68
Pullman, Philip
   The Subtle Knife 33

radio plays *see* audio drama
radio script layout 156–7, *157*, 176
Ramayana, adaptation of 193
Ramsay, Lynne
   Ratcatcher (film) 173
Rattigan, Terence
   Separate Tables 359
Ravenhill, Mark 8
reading as a writer 10
readings 9
real time 312, 313, 314
'real time' reading or performance 525
realism 525
   and dramatic conventions 173–5
   magic realism 20, 523
   and romance 526
   recurring flashbacks 525

redrafting 29
   dramatised fiction 26–7
reflection
   and reading time 318
Reich, Steve
   Six Marimbas 149, 150, 155
Reiner, Rob
   Stand By Me (film) 127
repetition 265, 277, 278–9, 525
retrospective narrative structure 326–7
return journeys
   in life writing 61–3
rhetoric 274–83, 526
   antithesis 265, 278–9
   defining 265
   euphony 265, 282–3, 521
   parenthesis 265, 280–1
   repetition 265, 277, 278–9
rhyme 522, 526
   half rhyme 522, 523
   internal rhyme 523
   in polyphonic novels 304
Rilla, Wolf
   Village of the Damned (film) 34
Richards, Dan
   Outpost 362, 363
Richardson, Heather
   'Eastbourne' 354
   interview with Siobhán Campbell and Jane Yeh 365, 507–14
   thematic connections in life writing 360–1
Riddell, Richard *174*
Rilke, Rainer Maria 90
Rogers, Bruce Holland
   'What Are You Using for Bait?' 335–6
romance 16, 17, 20, 526
romance fiction 344, 526
Ross, Jacob
   'Walking for My Mother' 277, 282–3, 476–9
Rossetti, Christina
   'Goblin Market' 74
Rowling, J.K.
   Harry Potter and the Chamber of Secrets 46

   Harry Potter and the Half-Blood Prince 46
Royal Shakespeare Company
   Poet in Residence 295

Sant'Elia, Antonio
   La Città Nuova 38, 38–9
Sarmah, Abhijit
   'On Asking My Mother about Winter' 247
Saul, Denise
   The Room Between Us 291
   'Surrender' 291
Savage, Thomas 125
scenes 15, 526
   in dramatic writing 127–9, 131, 132–3
      audio drama 155
      dramatic conventions and realism 173–4, 175
      poetry 256–8
   in dramatised fiction 25–7
Schmidt, Victoria Lynn
   45 Master Characters 166–7
science fiction 16, 36, 344, 526
   adapting for audio 153
   films 124
Scott, Ridley
   Blade Runner (film) 34
screenplays 101, 526
   action and image 124, 125–6
   characters in 102, 125–6, 127–9
      and design 131
      Little Miss Sunshine 104–5
      visual contrasts 133
   directions in 111
   editing pictures and montage 126–7
   for feature films 16
   film genres 27, 28, 130
   formatting a script for 176–7, *177*
   The Real Deal 292–3, 481–5
   realist films 173
   scenes in 127–9
   scripts 123, 124–9
   sequences in 128–9
   settings and mood 131–3
   Small Axe: Mangrove 274–6, 277, 283, 474–6

story beats 127–9
telling stories with pictures 124–9
see also films; television dramas
script layout
   for radio 156–7, *157*, 176
   for screen 176–7, *177*
   for stage 116–18, *117*
scriptwriting 25
Sedaris, David
   'Jesus Shaves' 236, 237, 470–1
sensory details
   in life writing 56–7, 68
sensory perception 523, 526
   and monologues 293
   and showing 526
sequences 526
   visual sequences in drama 128–9
sestinas 326, 526
Sethi, Anita
   I Belong Here 60–1, 63, 230
   'A Trip to the Countryside' 230, 232
Sexton, Anne 90
Shah, Naseeruddin *133*
Shakespeare, William 27
   As You Like It 173
   Hamlet 115
   Macbeth 249
   A Midsummer Night's Dream 173
   tragedies 171
Shelley, Mary
   Frankenstein 34
Shepherd, Nan
   The Living Mountain 63, 67
short documents 169, 526
   and adaptations 186
short shorts 334
short stories 16, 333, 334, 345, 349
   adaptation of 'Brokeback Mountain' 184, 195
   characteristics of 337–40
   and novellas 342
   opening of 340
   polyphonic narration 303
   reading time 317
   splicing narrative strands 210
   themes in 355, 356
   time and form 323

short-form prose 333, 334–40, 341
showing and telling 124
   in life writing 223, 235–6
   and monologues 293
Shukla, Nikesh
   The Good Immigrant 368–9, 515–16
Siddons, Alastair
   Small Axe: Mangrove 274–6, 277, 283, 474–6
Silvera, Adam
   They Both Die at the End 210
similes 267, 521, 526
   in narrative poems 89, 92, 93
Sir Gawain and the Green Knight 37, 526
Sirett, Paul
   Bartholomew Abominations 142
   The Playwright's Manifesto 142
Skinner, Hugh *174*
Small Axe: Mangrove (screenplay) 274–6, 277, 283, 474–6
Smith, Alexander McCall 19, 20
Smith, Ali
   Hotel World 359
Smith, Stevie *244*
   'Mother, Among the Dustbins' 247
   'Not Waving But Drowning' 244–6, 248
Smith, Zadie
   On Beauty 278
social realism 19–20, 526
soliloquies 243, 527
The Sopranos 115
splicing narrative strands 201–19, 321
   challenges of story structure 218
   converging characters 207–9
   cutting quickly 204–6
   gathering strands and controlling tension 210–11
   honing character narratives 217
   intercutting 203, 210, 212, 216, 218, 523
   and intertextuality 213
   juxtaposed sections 212, 217
   montage 203, 204, 205–6
   omniscient narrators 218

   poetic cutting between strands 214–16
   stream-of-consciousness narratives 213, 215, 217
   time and length 210–11
   typographical devices 218
   using a linking narrative or trusting your readers 212–13
staccato sounds 283, 527
stage drama 16, 101
   adaptations for 27, 28, 183, 184, 185, 187, 195–6
      Levy's *Small Island* 134, 135, 189–90, 191
      venues 191–2
   and audio dramas 153
   characters in 102, 109
   dramatic action in 124
   dramatic conventions and realism 173–5
   formatting a script for 116–18, *117*
   offstage action 173, 187, 195, 196, 524
   scripts 123, 125
   stage directions 110–11
   themes in 359, 366–7
   time and form in 326–8
Stansfield, Katherine, and Oakley, Caroline
   Cast a Long Shadow 368, 516–17
stanzas 527
   in narrative poetry 74, 75–6, 79, 80, 87, 89, 92, 93, 215
   tercets 527
   time and form in poetry 324
step outlines 169, 170–1, *170–1*, 527
Stevens, Wallace 90
story 527
story beats 127–9, 527
   adaptation of texts 187, 197
      for the screen 193
      for the stage 195
   in the dramatic arc 168, 169–70
   splicing narrative strands 205–6
storyboards 169, 360, 527
Stranger Things (television) 39

Index

Strayed, Cheryl
  Wild 60, 61, 63
stream-of-consciousness narratives 213, 215, 217, 527
Streep, Meryl *216*
stylising voices 299–301
subtext 145, 527
summary 527
Sweeney, Emma Claire
  Owl Song at Dawn 301
the swerve 252–5, 258
symbolism 17
Symmons Roberts, Michael
  The Half-healed 365
  'Last words' 365
synopsis 169, 527
syntax 527
  stylising voices 298, 299, 300

Tales from the Thousand and One Nights (Arabian Nights) 34
telling 527
  see also showing and telling
Tennant, Emma
  Hotel de Dream 359
tension 527
  in narrative poetry 79, 93
tercets 326, 527
Terera, Giles *163*
Thackeray, William Makepeace
  The Luck of Barry Lyndon 188
theatre *see* stage drama
themes 351–72, 528
  defining 353–4
  developing 359–61
  discovering thematic connections 360–1
  in drama 366–7
  identifying 354
  in life writing 360–1, 362–4
  in poetry 354, 355–6, 359–60, 365
  and the reader 368–9
  in stage drama 359, 366–7
  themed anthologies 368–9
  threads and echoes 355–8
third-person narration 23–4, 528
  converging characters in 209
  linking narrative strands 212
  world-building in 42

Thompson, Edith 326
Thorpe, Adam
  Ulverton 359, 368
thrillers 17, 23, 344, 528
time jumps 312–13, 316, 528
time and timing 309–30
  acceleration 312–13, 314, 315, 316
  deceleration 314, 315, 316
  distortion of, world-building in fiction 41, 42–3
  flashbacks 127, 320, 321, 326, 522, 525
  flashforwards 320–1, 324
  and form 322–8
    in novels, feature films and stage plays 326–8
    in poetry 323–6
    in prose 322–3
  influencing reading time 317–18
  in life writing 227–8
  modulating tempo 316
  in narrative poems 83–8
  pace of 312–18
    changing the pace 318
  real time 312, 313, 314, 315, 316
  sequencing 319–21
    withholding and disclosure 319
  tight timeframes 210
  unnarrated time 316
Tolkien, J.R.R.
  The Hobbit 34, 36–7
  The Lord of the Rings 36–7
Tomalin, Claire
  Thomas Hardy: The Time-torn Man 362
Tomlinson, Barbara 233
tone 528
  in poetry 252
treatment 169, 528
Trevor, William
  The Boarding-house 359
Tsujimura, Mizuki
  Lonely Castle in the Mirror 33
Turner, J.M.W.
  Old Welsh Bridge, Shrewsbury 38, 38–9

verbs 528
  in 'Lot's Wife Speaks' 297
vernacular 528
  in audio drama 145
Verne, Jules
  Journey to the Centre of the Earth 34
visual imagery
  adapting for the screen 192–4
  in dramatic writing 124–33
Vogler, Christopher 39
  The Writer's Journey 165–6, *166*, 167
voice-over 148, 156, 190, 194
voices and voicing 287–307
  compelling voices 297–8
  distinctive voices 289
  fictional communities 302–5
  the intimacy of 'I' 291
  monologues 292
  persona and impersonation 294–8
  polyphonic narration 303–5
  speaking in chorus 302–3
  stylising 299–301
  unsung voices 296–7

Wadham, Lucy
  The Secret Life of France 227, 228
Watts, Nigel 370
ways of writing 8, 11–96
  genre 8, 13–30
  life writing 53–70
  narrative poems 71–96
  world-building in fiction 8, 33–50
Webster, David
  'Getting High in the Low Countries' 58–60, 389–92
Weir, Peter
  The Truman Show (film) 249
Wells, H.G.
  The War of the Worlds 34
Welles, Orson
  Citizen Kane (film) 327
Wentworth, Tom
  The Real Deal 292–3, 481–5
white space 338

Willis, Elizabeth
    'Tiptoe Lightning' 247
Wiman, Christian
    'Do You Remember the Rude
        Nudists?' 247
Wolff, Tobias
    'Bullet in the Brain' 209, 210
Woolf, Virginia
    A Room of One's Own 228–9
    in Cunningham's *The Hours*
        212–13, 215, 216
    Mrs Dalloway 210, 212–13, 215,
        217, 327
    To the Lighthouse 153, 280
word choices
    stylising voices 299, 300
Wordsworth, William 249, 251
    Dove Cottage *249*
workshopping 296, 528
world-building in fiction 8, 33–50,
    528
    imagined worlds from real
        foundations 48–9
    turning real worlds into
        imaginary worlds 39–42
    unsettling the reader 42–5
    using research to build worlds
        45–7
    using what you know 36–9
    see also dystopian fiction;
        fantasy fiction
Wright, Letitia *275*
writing workshops 8
Wyndham, John
    The Midwich Cuckoos 34

Yeh, Jane
    Heather Richardson's interview
        with 365, 507–14
Yorke, John
    Into the Woods 171, 172
Younge, Gary
    'Stevenage' 62